LIVERPOOL

THE OFFICIAL CENTENARY HISTORY

1892  1992

LIVER POOL

FOOTBALL CLUB

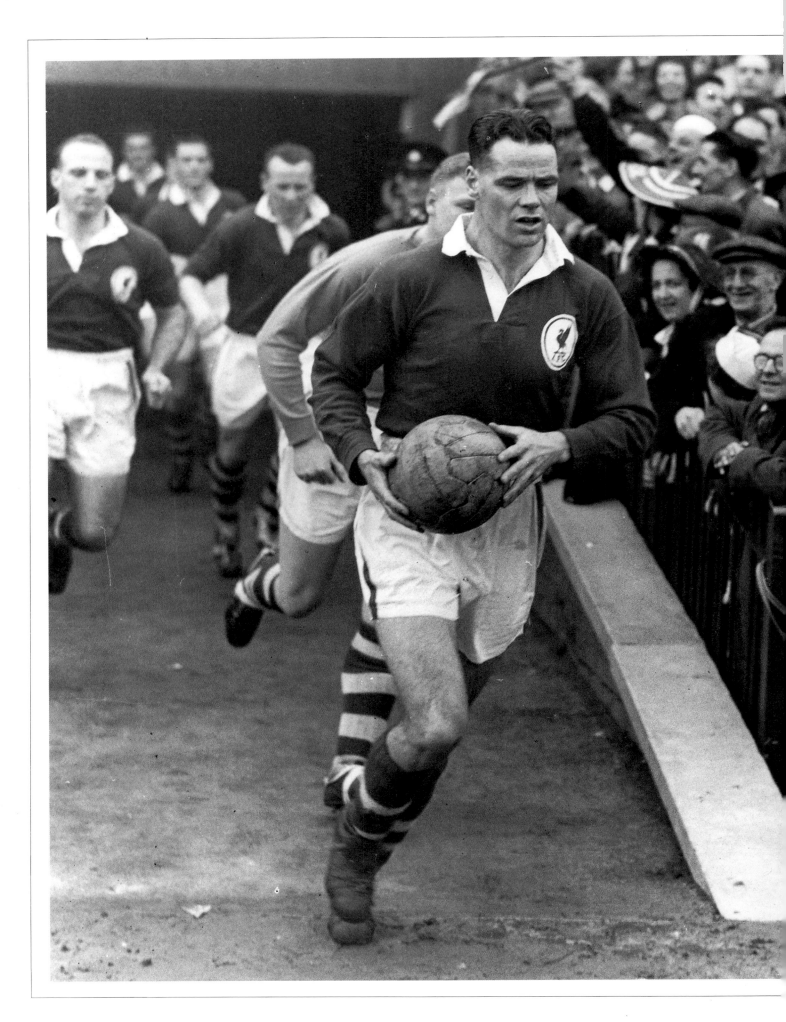

LIVERPOOL

THE OFFICIAL CENTENARY HISTORY

1892  1992

STAN LIVERSEDGE

HAMLYN

Published in 1991
by The Hamlyn Publishing Group Limited
part of Reed International Books
Michelin House, 81 Fulham Road, London
SW3 6RB

ISBN 0 600 57308 7

Produced by Mandarin Offset
Printed in China

Opposite title page: Billy Liddell takes the field, 1957–58;
title page: Bill Shankly and the 1974 Charity Shield
winners; *below:* Allerton salutes the 1978 League
Championship and European Cup 'double' winners;
right: an early taste of international soccer against
Swedish opposition on tour in the USA, *far right:* Elisha
Scott – Liverpool's goalkeeper 1912–34.

EBBETS FIELD
JUNE 18, 1948

OFFICIAL PROGRAM
TWENTY-FIVE CENTS

INTERNATIONAL SOCCER MATCH

LIVERPOOL vs. DJURGARDEN

A trio of Liverpool's famed team (from left to right)—Billy Liddell,
Jack Balmer and Bill Fagan, all top international players.

THE KICK-OFF AT 8:30 P.M.

Contents

Foreword by Bob Paisley

I haven't been around quite as long as Liverpool Football Club, but after more than 50 years at Anfield, I think I can claim to know a fair bit about the way things are run there – and, I hope, the Liverpool fans would agree that I have contributed in various ways towards the success the club has achieved through the years.

When I stepped off the train at Liverpool's Lime Street station on 8 May 1939, I never dreamed what the future would hold for me . . . certainly I never even suspected that more than half a century later I would be a director, after having served the club as player, trainer, physiotherapist, coach and manager.

It was a former Liverpool player, Andy McGuigan, who met me at the station – he was then on the scouting staff – and he took me up to Anfield, where I signed on the dotted line for a wage of £5 a week. Oh yes, I received a signing-on fee, as well . . . £10.

I didn't know it then, but the Second World War was looming, and for me the August Bank Holiday in 1941 meant a departure for Egypt, as a

soldier. We were ten weeks at sea, and my first letter from home didn't arrive until close on Christmas. It was a note from Liverpool manager George Kay, telling me to report for the first game of the season against Preston!

George had signed me, and that note had obviously been written before it was known I was going to be posted abroad. In fact, I spent four years in the desert and ended up riding on a tank through liberated Rome. Then I went back to Liverpool and football business, to enjoy a career which spanned almost 300 games.

In my time I have seen some great players come and go, served under various managers, and, eventually, I became the manager myself. In one game I was struck on the head by a fierce shot and concussed – so much so that at half-time, trainer Albert Shelley walked me up and down outside the ground to help me come to.

In the second half, back on the field, I tried to head a Billy Liddell centre – and fell unconscious for a second time. I ended up in hospital and got a telling-off from my Dad. I had to confess I didn't even remember going back on

the field, much less trying to score!

Well, players who are concussed these days are wrapped in cotton wool until they're 100 per cent again, and I've no quarrel with that. In fact, the game has evolved in so many ways . . . and, of course, so has Liverpool Football Club. I truly believe that this history of the first hundred years tells a fascinating story and I have no hesitation in commending it as a superb souvenir of the club's centenary. Indeed, I am sure that it will be a must for every Liverpool fan. And I might add that after 50-odd years at Anfield, I still regard myself among their number.

Bob Paisley.

■ Bob Paisley joined Liverpool in May 1939 and after the Second World War played nearly 300 games in midfield for the club, but that was just the start of his career at Anfield . . . .

From the Beginning to Shankly

HAT's in a name? A great deal, sometimes ... for instance, if you happen to follow Everton, instead of Liverpool. Or vice-versa. In a way, a dispute over a name is part of the story of how Liverpool Football Club came into existence a century ago.

It all began even earlier than that – in the year 1878, when St Domingo Football Club appeared on the soccer scene and became, in 1884, Everton FC. After a while, they adopted the Anfield Road ground as their own. The owner of the ground was John Houlding, an alderman and former Lord Mayor of Liverpool, who was known as 'King John of Everton'. When, after a dispute over financial matters, the disgruntled Everton faction departed for fresh pastures at Goodison, taking the name of the club with them, it left John Houlding with a ground but no team to play on it.

The now-famous 'split' occurred at a meeting in Houlding's house on 15 March 1892. W.E. Barclay, a football enthusiast friend of Houlding, suggested that while Everton were entitled to retain their name, a new club should be formed and called Liverpool Football Club. Barclay volunteered to act as Honorary Secretary, and Houlding gave his immediate support. When the Rugby Union club, which was also called Liverpool, raised an objection to the name of the soccer newcomers, the objection was met by the simple expedient of adding the word 'Association' to the Liverpool title. So honour was satisfied all round.

In the beginning, Liverpool Association Football Club kicked off playing Lancashire League football in season 1892-93, and they met opposition whose names now are buried in that dim and distant past . . . Higher Walton, West Manchester, South Shore, Heywood Central, Fairfield. But some of the names are still going strong, either in League football or as non-League outfits . . . Bury and Blackpool, for instance, and the likes of Fleetwood, Rossendale United, Nelson and – closer still to home – Bootle and Southport.

On 3 September 1892, Liverpool began by sending Higher Walton packing as they scored eight goals without reply, and when the next three matches were also won, it meant that Liverpool had scored 20 goals and conceded but one. Then a 3–0 defeat at Blackpool was followed by three more straight wins (13 goals for, one against), before Blackpool did the double with a 2–0 win.

Liverpool then won their next four matches (13 goals scored, four conceded), drew one and lost one, and won half a dozen games on the trot (scoring 19 goals and conceding four). The final game, against Southport, was drawn, so Liverpool wound up with this overall record:

P	W	D	L	F	A	W	D	L	F	A	Pts	Position
22	10	0	1	44	7	7	2	2	22	12	36	1st

It was a pretty impressive start, and the following season saw Liverpool embarking upon their first campaign in the Football League, as members of the Second Division. And at the end of the season, they were celebrating promotion to the First. The opening match of the promotion campaign saw Liverpool scoring a 2–0 away win over Middlesbrough Ironopolis, and three more victories followed. Then came a succession of wins and draws to take the club up to December.

From then on, it was one victory after another . . . 13 wins, in fact, during the final 15 fixtures, only two of those matches ending in draws. All of which meant that Liverpool were scheduled to meet Newton Heath (later to become Manchester United), who had finished bottom of the First Division, in a test match for promotion, and Liverpool won, 2–0. Their record at the end of that first season in the Second Division was just as impressive as their record had been in the Lancashire League. It read like this:

P	W	D	L	F	A	W	D	L	F	A	Pts	Position
28	14	0	0	46	6	8	6	0	31	12	50	1st

Unhappily for Liverpool, their first season in the top flight was also their last – well, for 12 months, anyway – because they finished in 16th place and dropped down to the Second Division again, after having lost a test match against Bury. However,

■ This was Liverpool's original 'Team of Macs,' as they imported footballing talent from north of the Border. Andrew Hannah was the captain who inspired Liverpool as they remained unbeaten during the promotion campaign of season 1893-4.

season 1895-96 produced an immediate revival, as Liverpool returned to the promotion trail.

They kicked off with a 3–2 win over Notts County away, claimed four more victories on the trot, and won 12, drew one and lost one of their final 14 matches, to go into the test-match arena once again. Their record read:

P	W	D	L	F	A	W	D	L	F	A	Pts	Position
30	14	1	0	65	11	8	1	6	41	21	46	1st

Their record on their home ground, even so early in the club's history, was beginning to make Liverpool seem invincible at Anfield, and when they took on Small Heath and West Bromwich Albion in the test matches for promotion, it was certainly home, sweet home. A crowd of 20,000 saw Liverpool defeat Small Heath 4–0 (they drew, no score, in the away game), and there were 20,000 at Anfield again to see Liverpool beat West Bromwich 2–0 (though Albion won the return by a similar margin). This was enough to win promotion.

League and Cup Challenge

Liverpool finished fifth and ninth in their next two seasons in the First Division, then the Championship loomed tantalisingly close in season 1898-99 as they won 19 of their 34 matches. But in the end, eight away defeats dented their title hopes, and they had to settle for being runners-up.

That was a season, also, in which the hopes of the Anfield faithful were raised when it came to the FA Cup – but, for the second time inside a few seasons, Liverpool were destined to fall at the semi-final hurdle. That had happened in season 1896-97, when – after beating Burton Swifts, West Brom and Nottingham Forest – Liverpool were knocked out by Aston Villa, who scored a 3–0 success at Bramall Lane. In season 1898-99, while striving for the Championship, Liverpool also embarked upon what turned out to be a marathon of an FA Cup campaign. The first three rounds were straightforward enough, with victories over Blackburn Rovers, Newcastle United and West Bromwich . . . then came the semi-final against Sheffield United, and that tie went to four matches before a result was achieved.

First, in a match at Nottingham, Liverpool and the Blades shared four goals . . . and then, in a replay at Bolton, they doubled their tally as each 'keeper picked the ball out of the net four times. There was a third meeting, at Fallowfield, but with the score 1–0 in Liverpool's favour this match had to be abandoned, and when the game was switched to Derby it was Sheffield United who profited, by scoring the only goal.

FA Cup glory was to elude Liverpool for more

than 60 years, but they didn't have long to wait for their first League Championship – that came at the end of season 1900-01, and it more than compensated for a knock-out in the first round of the Cup. Oddly enough, Liverpool lost to Notts County away in the League, as well as in the Cup, though they won the home encounter by the only goal.

Familiar names in the side at this time were Alex Raisbeck, Jack Cox, John Walker, Sam Raybould and Tommy Robertson. It was Robertson and Raybould who scored two of the three goals by which Liverpool beat Blackburn Rovers in the first match of the season, and Walker whose solo was the winner of the final match, at West Bromwich Albion. Raybould scored 16 goals in 31 games, Cox 10 in 32, Robertson nine in 34 and Walker seven in 29 appearances. And at the end, Liverpool's overall record read:

P	W	D	L	F	A	W	D	L	F	A	Pts	Position
34	12	2	3	36	13	7	5	5	23	22	45	1st

That Championship success was a bit of a flash in the pan, however, as Liverpool slipped to 11th, climbed to fifth, then plummeted to 17th . . . which meant relegation. Once again, though, they bounced straight back, because at the end of season 1904–05 they finished as Second Division Champions. By this time Teddy Doig was in goal, and Robert Robinson, Cox, Jack Parkinson and Arthur Goddard had joined Raisbeck and Raybould as giants in the side. Liverpool did not lose until their 14th match that term – when they went down 2–0 at Bolton on 3 December they had strung together 11 wins and drawn the other two. After losing at Bolton, beating Bristol City and losing away to Manchester United, they chalked up another unbeaten run consisting of ten victories and a draw. By the time they lost their third match of the campaign (against Burton United on 25 March), Liverpool were well and truly on their way to promotion. They had six matches to go, and they won five and drew one to wind up with this record:

P	W	D	L	F	A	W	D	L	F	A	Pts	Position
34	14	3	0	60	12	13	1	3	33	13	58	1st

Having regained First Division status, Liverpool were to retain it – and claim the Championship four times – until season 1953-54, when they suffered the indignity of finishing at the bottom of the table. But to go back to that promotion season of 1904-05 . . . it was merely the springboard for further success, because 12 months after having climbed out of the Second Division, Liverpool were lording it at the top of the First, as they took the title and almost (but not quite) got through to the final of the FA Cup.

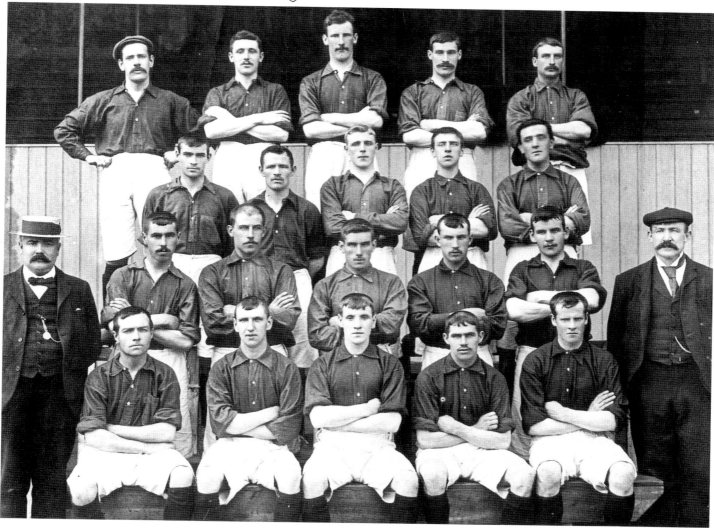

In the League, Liverpool began looking no-hopers as they lost their first three matches: 1–3, 1–3, 0–5. Then they won two, lost one, won one, lost one . . . a pattern which still didn't raise great expectations of a title chase. Then the next 11 matches produced two draws, nine victories – and Liverpool were on their way. There was a hiccup, with a defeat by Stoke City, but during the next 18 games Liverpool suffered only four defeats and claimed 11 wins – the final match being a 3–1 success over Sheffield United, as the fans celebrated the title triumph on home ground.

As for the FA Cup that season, Liverpool disposed of Leicester Fosse, Barnsley, Brentford and Southampton in turn, scoring eight goals while conceding only one; then they came up against their arch-rivals, Everton, in the semi-final, which was staged at Villa Park. There was a crowd of 37,000, and with men such as Sam Hardy, Raisbeck, Robinson, Goddard, Joe Hewitt and Parkinson – a formidable marksman – in their ranks, Liverpool were given a good chance of going all the way. It was a scoreless stalemate after the first 45 minutes, but in the second half Everton scored twice and Liverpool couldn't muster even

one counter, so they had to settle for being merely the Champions of the Football League. Their First Division record, just 12 months after having emerged from the Second, was this:

P	W	D	L	F	A	W	D	L	F	A	Pts	Position
38	14	3	2	49	15	9	2	8	30	31	51	1st

There were some undistinguished seasons for a few years, though the 1909-10 campaign ended with Liverpool claiming the runners-up spot, with 48 points; but that was the high spot of all the seasons up to the beginning of the First World War . . . apart from one, when Liverpool at last did manage to go through to the final of the FA Cup. That was in season 1913-14, when they played eight matches (including two replays) . . . although, in the end, they lost out once again.

The First FA Cup Final

In the first round Liverpool were drawn against Barnsley, at Anfield, and confidence was high; but Barnsley held the Anfield Reds to a 1–1 draw

■ This was the Liverpool look longer 100 years ago . . . and there were some notable names on the team sheet in season 1899-1900. Among them Arthur Goldie (back row, second from right), Alex Raisbeck (in the centre, third row back), Jack Cox (far left, second row back) and Tommy Robertson (centre, second row back).

THE ORIGINAL DERBY GAME

THE date of the first League game between Liverpool and Everton was 13 October 1894 – but that was not their first encounter. The original derby game was a Liverpool Senior Cup final, and it was played on the ground of the then Bootle Football Club on Saturday, 22 April 1893.

After the split between John Houlding and Everton the previous year, and the formation of Liverpool Football Club, it was not surprising that there was little love lost between the clubs, and during the initial rounds of the Liverpool Senior Cup the Liverpool Football Association was at some pains to keep the two clubs apart. However, it seemed inevitable, if ironical, that the two clubs which fought their way to the final should be Liverpool and Everton.

Liverpool beat Bootle 1–0 at Anfield in their semi-final, and at a meeting that night in the Neptune Hotel the Cup committee decided that the final should be staged at Bootle the following Saturday, with a 4pm kick-off. During the days before the match, it was rumoured that the respective clubs would field weakened teams, with Everton claiming that, since they had no fewer than 30 top-class players on their staff, they wanted to spread the chance of winning honours around.

Indeed, Everton arranged a last-minute match against a club called Renton at Goodison Park on the same afternoon (they drew 1–1), but it didn't detract from the Liverpool Senior Cup final as a drawing card.

When the teams walked out for the final at Bootle, there were 10,000 fans packing the ground, and they soon realised, as the players came out of what later became the cricket pavilion, that Everton's side consisted of a mixture of first-team and reserve-team players, while Liverpool intended to field their strongest line-up. Only four Everton men had reached double figures for League appearances that season (the maximum possible was 30),

and this is how the Blues lined up, with the tally of first-team appearances in brackets after their names:

Williams (11), A. Chadwick (3), Collins (9), Boyle (25), Holt (26), Coyle (0), Gordon (11), Murray (3), Hartley (1), McMillan (2), Elliott (captain, 2).

Liverpool, at this stage, were yet to make their bow in the Football League, so the figures in brackets after their players' names indicate the number of League games each man totalled in the following season. They lined up like this:

McOwen (22), Hannah (captain, 24), McLean (27), McCartney (19), McQue (25), McBride (25), Wyllie (0), McVean (21), Miller (0), M. McQueen (25), H. McQueen (25).

A 'Competitive' Match

Herbie Arthur, from Blackburn Rovers, had been handed the job of refereeing the match. When he blew the whistle to start the game, Miller kicked off for Liverpool, who faced the sun while Everton had to face a strong wind. From the beginning, the match was extremely competitive, to say the least, though many of the tackles went unpunished.

With the match just over half an hour old, Liverpool went ahead as Miller got possession and passed to Wyllie, whose fast, low shot beat Williams. Everton were stung by this goal, and as the tackling became fiercer, referee Arthur had a word with McQue. Half-time came with the scoreline unchanged, and the interval was extended to allow the players to recover from the effects of the heat.

On the restart, Gordon laid on an easy chance for McMillan, but he

miscued his header, then Liverpool broke away and Everton 'keeper Williams had to race out of his area to clear the danger. Time and again, the referee blew for free-kicks, and from one of them Liverpool netted again, but a goal was ruled out. The tension increased and McQue and Murray had to be separated. As the fans urged their favourites on, Everton took control and Liverpool were glad to boot the ball into touch.

In the final minutes of the match, Everton had a corner awarded, and as the ball came into the penalty area, Everton players urged referee Arthur to award a penalty, claiming that a Liverpool defender had fisted the ball away. Mr Arthur didn't see it that way, though he did consult his

■ *Above:* **Billy Dunlop . . . one of McKenna's Scottish recruits, a stalwart of the Liverpool defence from 1894 to 1909, he totalled more than 350 appearances for the club, and was capped for his country.**

linesman. He awarded a drop-ball . . . and as soon as this had been taken, the final whistle went, amid general uproar.

Everton wasted no time in protesting against the result, and complained about 'the general incompetence of the

referee'. Because of this Liverpool were not presented with the trophy after the match. Instead, the Liverpool Football Association convened a meeting at the Neptune Hotel for the following Monday to discuss the matter. Everton's appeal was dismissed, and the next day – after Liverpool's match against Preston at Anfield – the Liverpool Senior Cup was presented by Liverpool FA president Mr A.B. Hull, who offered congratulations upon Liverpool's success in having won this

■ *Below:* **Matt McQueen was a member of the original 'Team of Macs' at Liverpool. He served the club in more than one capacity, becoming the manager and also a director. As a player, he was 'Mr Versatile' – a defender, a winger, a striker . . . he even kept goal.**

Cup and the Lancashire League Cup in their first season.

John Houlding's reply was to state that he was pleased 'to welcome the piece of plate back as an old friend' . . . this was taken as a reference to the previous success of Everton, when Houlding was in charge of them. As for the Liverpool players, as well as receiving the Cup, they were presented with gold Bovril medals . . . so who said that sponsorship was a modern-day innovation?

(Billy Lacey was the Liverpool marksmen), then one goal settled the return encounter. As in the first meeting, it was Lacey who struck, but while he had given Liverpool the lead just before half-time at Anfield, he left it until the last minute of the game to snatch victory for his side in the replay.

When Gillingham tried their luck at Anfield, it seemed they, too, would salvage a replay – but nine minutes from time Lacey was on target for the third match in succession, with Ferguson adding to the tally two minutes later. So Liverpool were drawn against West Ham away from home, and in the second half a goal from Miller enabled them to take the Hammers back to Anfield, where there was never any doubt about the outcome of this third-round tie. Seven minutes gone, and Lacey was striking Liverpool's first goal; 16 minutes gone, and Miller was getting his name on the scoresheet. Just inside 35 minutes, it was Lacey again, and on the stroke of half-time Miller was banging in his second goal of the game. The

■ Donald McKinlay spent 16 seasons playing for Liverpool. A Scot, he starred in a defence which helped the club to claim the League title in successive seasons during the early 1920s when, in two campaigns, the team conceded only 67 goals.

Hammers had managed to pull one back, but when Metcalfe drilled a hole in their defence, after an hour or so, that was the end . . . Liverpool cruised into the next round, which brought a home tie against Queen's Park Rangers.

Once again, the result was seldom in doubt, as Jackie Sheldon (six minutes) and Miller (20 minutes) put Liverpool well and truly in the driving seat and on the road to the semi-final at White Hart Lane, where the opposition was provided by Aston Villa. It was a match watched by just over 27,000 people, and they saw Nicholl score a goal in each half for Liverpool. For the first time in the Anfield club's history, they were through to the final of the FA Cup. When they went to Crystal Palace for the big day on 25 April, it was Burnley whom they had to meet and (they hoped) master.

Liverpool's team that day was packed with ability and experience . . . Kenny Campbell in goal, Eph Longworth (the first Liverpool player to skipper England), Bob Pursell, Fairfoul, Ferguson, McKinlay, Sheldon, Metcalfe, Miller, Lacey and Nicholl. Burnley's team also had some big names . . . men like Halley, Boyle, Bamford, Sewell, Freeman and Mosscrop . . . and yet the 72,000 spectators wondered just what kind of fare would be served up, because both clubs were occupying a lowly position in the League. There was added interest, though, in the fact that for the first time in the history of the FA Cup, the King (George V) was gracing the final with his presence.

A contemporary report read: 'When the players settled down, Liverpool looked the better side; the combination among their forwards was at times distinctly good. The Burnley forwards were too small to trouble the Liverpool defence seriously; they forced corners, but were bundled off the ball unceremoniously whenever they tried to work into a position to shoot. When half-time came, there had not been a single example of the sustained attacks which are so often seen in League football.

'Each team kept wrecking the other's combination, and it seemed highly probable that some brilliant bit of opportunism would determine the result of a guerrilla game. Lacey and Freeman were obviously the outstanding players of genius taking part in the match and, what is more, the only men who were not afraid of taking the responsibility of an unorthodox venture . . .

'For some minutes after the resumption the game was still desultory and disjointed. Then came Burnley's well-earned goal. Ten minutes of the second half had gone when Freeman got the ball and crashed it into the net with one of the most powerful shots one could wish to see. The Liverpool 'keeper had no earthly chance of stopping this really fine shot. During the half-hour

following Burnley's goal the game certainly improved, and the spectators were treated to thrilling movements on several occasions.

'Grim earnestness and intense determination characterised the movements of both teams, but it is just possible that the one goal scored correctly reflects the respective merits of the play.'

So Burnley triumphed 1–0, and – according to the writer – the 72,000 fans 'accorded HM The King a remarkable reception' as he presented winners and runners-up with their medals.

The Reds Between the Wars

The resumption of League football after the First World War saw Liverpool bidding to make season 1919-20 one in which they became the first post-war winners of the First Division title. They managed to win 19 of their 42 games and they also drew 10, but the four defeats on home ground and the nine away meant that in the final analysis they finished in fourth place, with 48 points.

That season, also, there were hopes of another run to the final of the FA Cup, as South Shields were vanquished (after a replay) and Luton Town and Birmingham were despatched from the competition. But in the fourth round the draw paired Liverpool with Huddersfield Town – away – and that was one hurdle too many. Liverpool lost by the odd goal in three, in front of more than 44,000 people.

Season 1920-21 came along, and at the end of that term Liverpool were once again looking up at

the League champions from their position of fourth in the table, while in the FA Cup they had been knocked out by Newcastle United after having beaten Manchester United in a first-round replay. By then, the man in possession of the goalkeeper's jersey was the great Elisha Scott,

■ *Above:* **Another of yesterday's heroes, Irish international Billy Lacey, who was signed by Liverpool from their great rivals, Everton. Two players moved to Goodison Park as part of the deal – but Liverpool certainly got the better part of the bargain in February 1912.**

■ *Left:* **Liverpool have always had a reputation for producing fine goalkeepers, and one of their all-time greats, the Irish international, Elisha Scott, is pictured here in action during a game against Chelsea in January 1922.**

■ Fred 'Polly' Hopkin, one of the Liverpool stars of yesteryear, played for the club from the early 1920s to the start of the 1930s. He didn't score many goals, though he made plenty for others – in fact, when he netted for the first time it coincided with the main stand catching fire!

■ The third round of the FA Cup in season 1923-24, and as Liverpool meet Southampton at The Dell, skipper Walter Wadsworth shakes hands with his opposite number. The match ended as a 0–0 draw, and Liverpool went on to win the Anfield replay 2–0, but then were knocked out by Newcastle United.

while players such as Longworth, Lacey, McKin-lay, Sheldon and Miller had been reinforced by the likes of Tommy Bromilow, Walter Wadsworth, Dick Forshaw and Harry Chambers. And Fred 'Polly' Hopkin was about to appear on the Anfield scene and weave his magic.

The result was that Liverpool emerged from the campaign of season 1921-22 as First Division Champions – and 12 months later they were still the undisputed top-dogs of the division. As they have done so often in much more recent seasons, they proved beyond any doubt that when it comes to the season-long marathon, they had the staying power to finish with their noses in front at the end of the course.

Liverpool kicked off season 1921-22 with a trip to Sunderland, and there was a crowd of 40,000 to see the home side score a 3–0 victory. Then Liverpool beat Manchester City 3–2 and repaid Sunderland by beating them 2–1 in the Anfield return, before embarking upon a run of a dozen matches which produced 17 points from seven draws and five wins.

After beating Middlesbrough 4–0 at Anfield, Liverpool lost 3–1 away against Boro in their very next match, but after that the Anfield Reds went 15 games without one defeat (the run included ten victories). Bolton Wanderers and Arsenal temporarily halted the gallop towards the title, as they beat Liverpool in successive matches, but five more wins and one draw during the run-in were sufficient to set Liverpool up for the title. Their record for the League season read:

P	W	D	L	F	A	W	D	L	F	A	Pts	Position
42	15	4	2	43	15	7	9	5	20	21	57	1st

The euphoria of that campaign was extended into the following season when, on kick-off day, Liverpool hammered Arsenal 5–2 at Anfield, with Johnson scoring a hat-trick in front of 40,000 people. It didn't last any longer, though, because Liverpool lost their next two matches, away to Sunderland and Arsenal, each time by the only goal of the game. However, it turned out, after all, that the first match had been the true yardstick by which to measure Liverpool's potential for a repeat title performance.

A run of 13 matches in which Liverpool won 11 and drew two was the backbone of the season and they could afford five successive draws and a 1–0 home victory over Stoke City in their last six matches to retain the League Championship by a comfortable six points over Sunderland, with a record which read like this:

P	W	D	L	F	A	W	D	L	F	A	Pts	Position
42	17	3	1	50	13	9	5	7	20	18	60	1st

Needless to say, Liverpool didn't make it a hat-trick of title successes (they finished 12th the following season), and while they flattered to deceive once or twice (such as when they claimed fourth place in season 1924-25) the rest of the 1920s saw them as also-rans both in the Championship and in the FA Cup.

If the 1920s ended poorly, the 1930s proved to be worse – just about the most barren decade in the Reds' history, although they did retain their First Division status. Their best season was 1934-35, when they finished seventh in the League. Mostly they were fighting desperately against relegation. And there were few Cup

■ Christmas, 1927, is the occasion for a formal photo-session as Liverpool's players meet the Lord Mayor and the Lady Mayoress in the august setting of the Mansion House.

■ *Above:* **Down at The Valley, Liverpool take on Charlton Athletic during season 1936-37. While keeper Hobson grabs the ball on the line, Cooper and Bradshaw stand guard as Charlton inside-right Prior sizes up the situation.**

■ *Right:* **Comrades in arms . . . and the Liverpool footballers stepping out here are (from left to right) Matt Busby, Jackie Balmer, Jim Harley, Willie Fagan and Dick Kemp. It was a time when football took second place to the task of beating Germany.**

successes to compensate – the quarter-finals in 1931-32 was the best they could manage. They beat Everton at Goodison in the third round, but Chelsea knocked them out at Anfield.

When war came, Liverpool fans who thought about football at all hoped that, as after the First World War, the club's fortunes would revive on the resumption.

Champions Again

In May 1939 – three months or so before the Second World War broke out – Liverpool had finished 11th in the First Division table. In May 1947 – at the end of the first post-war season – they claimed the Championship of the Football League for the fifth time in their history.

The war, of course, took a considerable chunk out of the careers of many footballers, and those who wore Liverpool's colours were no exception; but in those early post-war years there were new names to become fixtures on the team sheet.

Welsh-international Cyril Sidlow was in goal, and there were stalwarts in Phil Taylor and Laurie Hughes, Bob Paisley, Bill Jones, Jackie Balmer, 'Nivvy' Nieuwenhuys, Ray Lambert, Billy Liddell, Cyril Done and Albert Stubbins. By the end of season 1946-47 Balmer and Stubbins had shared 48 goals, Done and Liddell had weighed in with 10 and seven respectively, and Willie Fagan also scored seven. Done got into double figures in just 17 appearances, and Fagan's goals came during 18 first-team outings. Liverpool, in fact, scored as many goals (42) away as they did at Anfield. In one sensational spell, Balmer hit hat-tricks in three successive matches and scored in seven games on the trot, while Done (twice) and Stubbins each featured as hat-trick marksmen. Those 84 goals in total more than cancelled out the 52 Liverpool conceded.

They started out by winning 1–0 and losing 1–0, then their third game had no fewer than 11 goals . . . seven to Liverpool, four to Chelsea, who battled back after being 4–0 down at half-time. Then in their next match, away to Manchester

■ The man the fans used to call the 'Flying Scot', Billy Liddell goes down the left wing and, as usual, poses problems for the opposition. Liddell's name is still revered today by those fans who saw him in action during the late 1940s and the 1950s.

■ The Second World War has just ended, and soccer returns. For Liverpool, there's the bonus of a trip to the United States aboard the luxury liner *Queen Mary*. And here are the players and officials pictured with the master of the *Queen Mary*. Not surprisingly, it was an occasion which called for an autographed photograph.

United, Liverpool failed to score even once – and conceded five goals! They then beat Grimsby Town 6–1, stuck four goals past Arsenal, Huddersfield Town and Derby County, lost 5–1 against Wolverhampton Wanderers then beat Sunderland and Aston Villa, 4–1 each time out. When Liverpool met Grimsby again, they rattled in five goals to add to the half-dozen they had scored in the first meeting . . . and, as the goals went in, so the fans flocked to the matches.

There were 49,000 for the game against Chelsea, 50,000 at the away game against Manchester United, 49,000 for Everton, 51,000 for Leeds United, 50,000 for Charlton Athletic, Stoke City and Portsmouth, 58,000 for the return with Chelsea (Liverpool lost, 3–1), 50,000 again for Sheffield United, Bolton Wanderers, Derby County and Manchester United (at Anfield), 49,000 for Blackburn Rovers, 48,000 for Arsenal and 55,000 for the final match of the season, away to Wolverhampton Wanderers . . . who a month earlier had been the red-hot favourites to walk away with the League title.

With seven matches to go, Liverpool were trailing Wolves by nine points. Then, as Bob Paisley remarked: 'We taught soccer a lesson that Liverpool have been teaching the rest ever since – you don't give up until you know you can do no more.'

Five of Liverpool's last seven games were away . . . at Villa Park, Charlton, Brentford, Highbury and Molineux. First, Liverpool kicked off by taking on Sunderland at Anfield, and more than 41,000 fans saw the men from Roker beaten by a goal from Albert Stubbins, who had previously starred for Sunderland's great North-East rivals, Newcastle United.

Aston Villa fell, 2–1, on their own ground, then a Stubbins goal beat Manchester United at Anfield. Which left Liverpool facing four away games on the trot to complete their League programme. A Stubbins hat-trick saw off Charlton Athletic, a Bob Priday goal earned a point at Brentford, and Balmer and Priday scored the goals which clinched a 2–1 win against Arsenal at Highbury. Then on the last day of May, at

Molineux, Liverpool had to win their last match to stand a chance of the title. Balmer and Stubbins hit the goals which won Liverpool the match with a final scoreline of 2–1.

So Liverpool had collected 13 out of 14 points from their last seven matches, while Wolves had picked up just one solitary point from their seven games. The men from Molineux ended up in third place, but it still wasn't quite all over for Liverpool. They had to wait and see how Stoke City had fared against Sheffield United at Bramall Lane. A win would give Stoke the Championship on goal average.

In the meantime Liverpool took on Everton in the Liverpool Senior Cup final, then the players sat back and waited at Anfield . . . to learn that Sheffield United had beaten Stoke by the odd goal in three. Liverpool knew then, for the first time, that they were League Champions, in a season when they had also gone to the semi-finals of the FA Cup, only to lose to Burnley (their conquerors in the 1914 final) in a replay at Maine Road.

Having walloped Walsall 5–2 in the third round, beaten Grimsby Town (2–0), Derby

County (1–0) and Birmingham City (4–1), they had drawn (0–0) against Burnley at Ewood Park, then lost the Maine Road return by the only goal. And, considering how many goals Liverpool had totalled in the League that term, it was remarkable that Burnley had twice prevented them from scoring in the Cup duels.

However, at the end of the day, nobody at Anfield was complaining too much – Liverpool's record in the League made certain of that. It read:

P	W	D	L	F	A	W	D	L	F	A	Pts	Position
42	13	3	5	42	24	12	4	5	42	28	57	1st

Post-War Favourites of the Kop

Mention has already been made of some of the players who figured in that Championship-winning side, and it's worth recording that Stubbins cost Liverpool a then record fee of £13,000 when they signed him from Newcastle. Jim Harley, a Scot, was a real speed merchant – he won a

■ The summer of '48, and this is Liverpool's second trip to the United States. Flying then was still very much an adventure . . . the age of high-speed jet travel had still to be ushered in.

those three hat-tricks in a row meant that Balmer had found the opposition's net ten times without one other Liverpool player managing to get a goal in between.

Cyril Done was a local-born player who had arrived at Anfield after being spotted while starring for the Bootle Boys Brigade side, and he scored on his debut in season 1939-40, then notched two hat-tricks during the Championship season of 1946-47. The first came against Huddersfield Town as Liverpool won 4–1 at Leeds Road in October (Balmer was the other marksman) and the second came against Grimsby Town as Liverpool won 5–0 at Anfield (Fagan was a two-goal man on this occasion). He later had an in-and-out spell, though he still scored goals (eight in seven successive matches during one period), and after moving to Tranmere Rovers he joined Port Vale . . . for whom he scored four times in one memorable match as Vale won 4–3. The opposition on that occasion? Liverpool!

The remaining two seasons of the 1940s were hit-and-miss affairs, so far as Liverpool were concerned, as they finished 11th and then 12th in the First Division and went out of the FA Cup in the fourth and then the fifth rounds. At the end of season 1949-50 they were in eighth place in the table and suffering the disappointment of defeat in the FA Cup final by Arsenal at Wembley. That was a game which Bob Paisley missed, after a split vote in the boardroom had given the nod to Bill Jones, and there was more than a touch of irony about the whole situation.

By season 1949-50, Bob Paisley had clocked up a century of first-team games for Liverpool, and among them were one or two memorable moments – the opening match of the League campaign, for instance, as he scored the first goal against Sunderland, whom he had supported as a youngster. In the FA Cup, Liverpool started out with a third-round tie against Blackburn Rovers at Ewood Park, and the result was a scoreless stalemate; then, when the replay took place at Anfield, Liverpool won 2–1, with goals from Payne and Fagan. Bob Paisley had missed the Ewood Park duel because of injury, but he was in the side for the replay (replacing Bill Jones, who had become a casualty himself), and Paisley stayed in the side as Liverpool accounted in turn for Exeter City, Stockport County and Blackpool, and met Everton in the semi-finals.

That match took place at Maine Road, Manchester, and it attracted a crowd of 72,000. They saw Liverpool score a 2–0 victory, thanks to goals from Paisley and Billy Liddell. The first goal came with the game coming up to the half-hour, and it was scored almost by accident. Jimmy Payne crossed the ball, Everton 'keeper George Burnett punched it clear, and it fell for Bob Paisley, who chipped it back towards the goal, where Billy

Powderhall handicap (it cost him a £10 fine for having missed training), while Phil Taylor, who became such an immaculate half-back, had joined Liverpool as a forward and, in fact, kicked off his career by scoring a goal at Derby. Taylor also had another sporting talent, because he could well have had a cricketing career at county level, with Gloucestershire.

Sidlow was originally one of the players discovered by the noted Major Frank Buckley, manager of Wolves, from whom Liverpool signed the Welsh international 'keeper after his demob from the Army and in time for him to play against Burnley in the FA Cup semi-final. Fagan, the captain, was a Scottish international who had arrived from Preston, and he possessed all the skills, as well as packing a lethal shot. Balmer had begun his footballing career as an amateur with Everton, and if he seemed to be on the frail side, he certainly packed a scoring punch.

When he struck that sensational hat-trick of hat-tricks, he became the first footballer in the League to have achieved such a feat. His goals came like this: 9 November 1946 – three goals against Portsmouth (one a penalty) at Anfield; 16 November – four goals against Derby County at the Baseball Ground; 23 November – three goals against Arsenal (one a penalty) at Anfield; and then he followed up by scoring against Blackpool, Wolves, Sunderland and Aston Villa (two goals here) in his next four outings. Remarkably, also,

Liddell was challenging Burnett and Falder, with Moore and Hedley standing on the line and alert to the danger. However, before anyone could get a touch to the ball, it dipped and fell . . . over the Everton line. So Liverpool were one up.

The ironic touch about that goal was that a week or so before the semi-final Liverpool manager George Kay had had a chat with Bob Paisley about his defensive duties, with the suggestion being made that he should not go haring off in search of a goal. So when the ball dropped just right for him, in the semi-final against Everton, his first instinct was to try a shot — then the manager's words sprang to mind, and instead of aiming to score, Paisley simply lobbed the ball upfield in the hope that one of his team-mates would knock it into the net. As it turned out, the ball found its own way there, and Bob Paisley became an instant hero with the Liverpool fans.

His omission from the final against Arsenal was

■ Phil Taylor leads out Liverpool, alongside Joe Mercer of Arsenal, for the FA Cup final of 1950.

undoubtedly one of the most bitter disappointments of his career, but he resisted the temptation to demand a transfer and, as history records, he stayed at Anfield to become arguably the most successful manager in the club's history . . . Kenny Dalglish included! In a way, though, that FA Cup final defeat of 1950 put the writing on the wall for Liverpool, as the next few seasons emphasised in the saddest of ways.

The Pre-Shankly Years

The FA Cup final of 1950 was George Kay's last match in charge at Liverpool; soon afterwards, he resigned and in March 1951 Don Welsh took over the running of team affairs. The problem, though, was that Liverpool's players were growing old together and, as the seasons came and went, this was reflected in the team's League position.

■ The reigning monarch, King George VI, shakes hands with the Anfield Reds' Scottish ace, Billy Liddell. But even he was unable to inspire his team to victory against Arsenal at Wembley.

Liverpool finished in ninth place at the end of season 1950-51, in 11th place 12 months later, and in 17th position at the end of season 1952-53.

That season, indeed, Liverpool had their work cut out to avoid taking the drop into the Second Division – they had to beat Chelsea in their final game, and (thanks to goals from Jones and Bimpson) they managed it, to the great relief of most of the 47,000 fans who had flocked anxiously to Anfield. Liverpool that season lost 15 matches on other grounds, and they also lost five and drew half a dozen of the 21 played at home.

The following season, Liverpool began badly and managed to scrape together only 16 points by the turn of the year. After kicking off with a home win over Portsmouth, a 4–4 draw against Manchester United and a 2–2 draw against Newcastle United (both at Anfield), they lost five matches in succession, and then they had mixed fortunes in their remaining games to the end of 1953. By then

they had played 25 games, winning just five and losing 14. The danger signals were indeed flashing, and the axe was wielded on some of the older players.

The last 17 matches produced a haul of just a dozen points (there were nine defeats), and though players such as Bob Paisley were recalled to the side in the later stages, the damage had been done and Liverpool wound up at the foot of the First Division, with this mediocre record of results:

P	W	D	L	F	A	W	D	L	F	A	Pts	Position
42	7	8	6	49	38	2	2	17	19	59	28	22nd

Relegation was the signal for changes, and along with Bob Paisley, Bill Jones, Eddie Spicer and Phil Taylor all hung up their playing boots, though Paisley and Taylor stayed on to become members of the backroom staff and, ultimately, both of them were to manage the club they had already

■ Liverpool have travelled the world, and they were crossing the Atlantic during Bob Paisley's days as a player, in the early 1950s. This was the scene as players and officials were reunited with their families after the tour of 1953.

served with great distinction on the playing staff.

Naturally, when season 1954-55 came around, the talk was of an immediate charge for promotion, especially after Liverpool had kicked off with a 3-2 home win over Doncaster Rovers – courtesy of a second-half hat-trick from Tony Rowley. But the next two matches were lost, the fourth one was drawn, then there were three defeats on the trot. In this way Liverpool stuttered through the season, winning, losing, drawing. At one stage, after stringing together three victories in succession, they raised brief hopes of a final charge, but they won only two of their last 11 games and, when the final placings were listed in the newspapers, they occupied 11th position in the Second Division table. As for the FA Cup, there had been no real compensation there, either – Liverpool had flattered to deceive, because after having beaten Lincoln City in a third-round replay and seen off Everton in the fourth round, they had fallen to Huddersfield Town in the fifth round – and salt had been rubbed into the wound since the 2-0 defeat was inflicted at Anfield. So once again

Liverpool's ambitions in the Cup were thwarted.

Season 1955-56 started off with a 3-1 away victory against Nottingham Forest, then it was back to the old, familiar story . . . lost, won, drawn, drawn, lost, won, lost, drawn, and so on. However, the hopes of the Liverpool fans were revived during the second half of the campaign, because their favourites managed to put together a sequence of good results – in fact, the sequence started in December as Liverpool drew against Port Vale and Burnley, then hammered Nottingham Forest 5-2 in the Anfield return (to complete a double), and beat Hull City and draw with Stoke City.

There were two defeats in succession, and that happened twice, but these reverses were cancelled out by two straight wins, then four wins on the trot, then three successive victories during the run-in for promotion. Billy Liddell, Alan Arnell, John Evans and Tony Rowley figured prominently among the Liverpool marksmen – Liddell scored 28 goals in 39 appearances, Arnell struck 13 goals in 23 games, Evans hit 13 in 31

appearances, and Rowley's contribution – half a dozen in just seven outings – included a hat-trick against Port Vale. Liddell, also, had been a hat-trick hero in the 5–2 win over Nottingham Forest. But, come the final reckoning, the goals Liverpool totalled – 52 at Anfield, 33 on other grounds – were not sufficient to clinch promotion to the First Division. Four games had been lost on home ground, and three had been drawn there; while away there had been 11 defeats and three matches drawn. So the final record looked like this:

P	W	D	L	F	A	W	D	L	F	A	Pts	Position
42	14	3	4	52	25	7	3	11	33	38	48	3rd

Liverpool decided that Don Welsh had had his chance, and they turned to Phil Taylor for the new campaign, which didn't start off on the happiest of notes as Huddersfield Town won 3–2 at Anfield. Then came a 1–1 draw away against Notts County, a 2–0 victory at Gigg Lane, Bury, a 3–3 home draw against Notts County, a 3–2 home win over Grimsby Town, and draws against West Ham United and Doncaster Rovers. So Liverpool had put together an unbeaten run of half a dozen matches before Stoke City halted them with a 2–0 success at Anfield.

Some high-scoring matches followed – a 4–3 home win over Fulham, a 4–1 defeat at Barnsley, a 4–1 home victory over Port Vale (Johnny Wheeler was a hat-trick man), a 4–0 home win over Lincoln City, and a 5–1 drubbing of Sheffield United at Anfield. And, after a defeat by Nottingham Forest, Liverpool embarked upon a run which took them through half a dozen matches with five victories and one draw. However, three defeats on the run followed, and though Liverpool lost only once in their last 13 matches, those three earlier reverses in succession (against Stoke City again, Middlesbrough and Leicester City) proved costly. As had happened 12 months previously, Liverpool had to settle for finishing as also-rans, in third place once again. Their record:

P	W	D	L	F	A	W	D	L	F	A	Pts	Position
42	16	1	4	53	26	5	10	6	29	28	53	3rd

It was evident that despite all their efforts – they had gone out in the third round of the FA Cup that term, as well – the team wasn't quite good enough to finish off the job; and season 1957-58 turned out to be another which brought disappointment. This time, Liverpool slipped to a finishing spot of fourth in the table, despite the fact that they won 17 and lost only one of their 21 home matches. Away, they lost nine games and drew seven, which meant that they had won only five matches outside Anfield.

They went to the sixth round of the FA Cup, where Blackburn Rovers ended their interest in that competition, and even though in the League they went through their last 13 games with only one defeat to eight victories, it still wasn't good enough to hoist them into a promotion-winning place. One of the most notable games that season was a match against Blackburn Rovers at Ewood Park, in which the teams shared half a dozen goals, with Billy Liddell scoring all three for Liverpool. And it was a safe bet at half-time that you would never have predicted the final scoreline, because at the end of the first 45 minutes the tally was 0–0.

Season 1958-59 saw Liverpool kicking off by again sharing six goals, this time with Grimsby Town at Anfield (Liddell scored twice), then it was a case of lose one, win one until mid-October, when Liverpool reeled off five victories in succession. Even after Ipswich Town had beaten them 2–0 at Portman Road, the signs were set fair for promotion, because Liverpool then staged another run in which they won eight matches on the trot, with Louis Bimpson, Jimmy Melia and Alan A'Court getting their names on the scoresheet regularly.

The run was ended with a 3–0 defeat at Cardiff, and Liverpool were never able to put it together again after that; so from mid-February to the end of the season they had to settle for just half a dozen victories, and a similar number of defeats, during their last 15 games. As a result, their final record for the season was dented, and so it read as follows:

P	W	D	L	F	A	W	D	L	F	A	Pts	Position
42	15	3	3	57	25	9	2	10	30	37	53	4th

Phil Taylor's reign lasted until 17 November 1959 – by which time Liverpool had played 17 matches that season and won only six. On kick-off day they had lost 3–2 at Cardiff (and two own goals from Malloy accounted for their tally). After more inconsistent results, they won on 7 November at Anfield, two goals from Dave Hickson despatching Aston Villa, but a week later, at Lincoln, goals from Hickson and Roger Hunt were not enough to prevent a 4–2 defeat. Phil Taylor, whose health was starting to give way under the strain of chasing that elusive First Division spot, was finally forced to admit defeat as he declared: 'I'm tired . . . the strain of trying to win promotion has proved too much.'

Everyone at the club was saddened by Taylor's departure, because he had always been a fine servant to Liverpool and, in addition, an excellent ambassador for the club in every way. In short, he was a gentleman and, indeed, it was completely in character that he should hand in his resignation so that someone else could have a go. That someone else, of course, turned out to be Bill Shankly . . . a man who changed the course of football history for Liverpool Football Club.

The Anfield Managers

■ **The man they called 'Honest John' . . . John McKenna, who was Liverpool's chairman during two spells in the 1900s, and who was one of the guiding lights behind the club's early years of success in the League. McKenna was indeed one of the giants in the club's formative years.**

JOHN HOULDING, the founder and first Chairman of Liverpool Football Club, was clearly a key man on the administrative scene at Anfield, and John McKenna was another major influence on Liverpool's affairs. Although never called the manager, he in fact performed most of the duties of a manager, including the signing of players. It was McKenna who took the Reds into the Football League.

McKenna was a self-made businessman who came to Liverpool from Ulster when nine years old. Patently straight, he was known as 'Honest John' McKenna. He guided Liverpool's fortunes from 1892 onwards, and later in life devoted much of his work to the Football League, although he was Liverpool's Chairman from 1909 to 1914 and from 1917 to 1919. He became Football League President from 1910 to his death in 1936 and was also a Vice-President of the Football Association.

W.E. Barclay was appointed Secretary-Manager of the club in 1892. His main tasks were administrative, but he, too, was responsible for the signing of some notable players, and was ever-ready to seek out new soccer talent as Liverpool sought to achieve a position of honour in the League – although it was reported that Barclay (who combined his footballing duties with those as headmaster of the Industrial Schools in Everton Crescent) was not in favour of Liverpool becoming members of the Football League. The story goes that Barclay learned of Liverpool's application to join the League, which had been formed in 1888, only when he received a telegram from 'Honest John' which read: 'Liverpool elected. Come to London at 3pm tomorrow to arrange fixtures.'

In 1896 another Secretary arrived at Anfield, to take over the managerial role. He was Tom Watson, whom John McKenna had persuaded to move down from the North-East, where he had been the Secretary at Sunderland – then just about the best side in the game. Tom Watson arrived at Anfield in August 1896, and succeeded Barclay as Secretary-Manager. Like McKenna and Barclay, Watson was a shrewd talent-spotter, and one of the players he signed was to become a giant both for his club and for his country. The player in question was a centre-half named Alex Raisbeck, who had originally come to the attention of John McKenna. Raisbeck played close on 350 games for Liverpool, and he served the club well for 11 seasons.

The club had only just been promoted when Watson took over as Secretary-Manager, and he soon showed that he knew the game, as he steered Liverpool into fifth place in the First Division. That was in season 1896-97, and better things were to follow, because two seasons after that

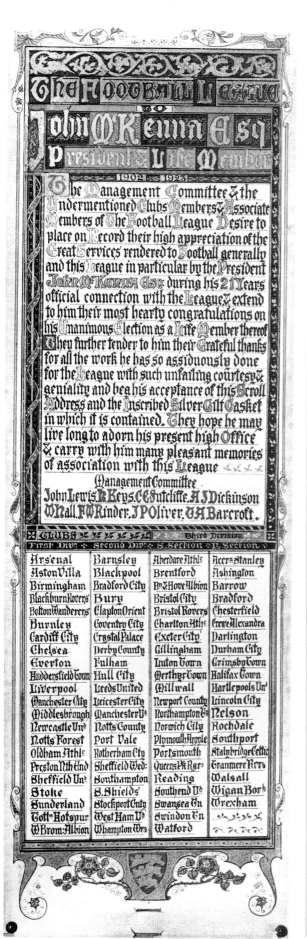

Liverpool not only went to the semi-finals of the FA Cup but improved three places to be runners-up in the League.

Came season 1900-01, and Tom Watson and his directors were indeed able to celebrate, because Liverpool, for the first time, claimed the Championship of the First Division. If the pendulum swung the other way three years later, when Liverpool slipped down to the Second Division again, Watson was the man whose guiding hand steered the club back to the top flight and enabled Liverpool to become the first team to win the Championships of the Second and First divisions in successive seasons.

Liverpool claimed the runners-up spot in season 1909-10, and it was during that campaign that they played a remarkable match against Newcastle United, running out winners by the odd goal as the final scoreline read 6–5. History has it that Tom Watson that day was somewhat apprehensive as Liverpool trailed by five goals to two and so, during the interval, he jokingly – or earnestly! – requested his opposite number not to let the Newcastle players rub salt into the wound. When the second half got under way, Watson decided against joining the onlookers and, instead, stayed in his own office. He remained there until the news was passed to

■ David Ashworth was the manager of Liverpool during the early part of the 1920s. In fact, he guided the club to the Championship of the Football League in season 1921-22, and when he left Anfield, in February 1923, they were on their way to retaining the title.

him that the scoreline now read Liverpool 5, Newcastle United 5 . . . and so Liverpool's manager emerged once again – as it turned out, he was still in time to see his players grab the goal which signalled an epic victory.

If that was one of Tom Watson's most memorable days, another was the occasion when he signed a player from Everton – Billy Lacey, an Irish international – in part exchange for two men called Gracie and Uren. While Everton's recruits each played only a handful of games for their new club, Lacey totalled more than 250 appearances during nine seasons with Liverpool.

Three more players – all goalkeepers, and great ones, at that – who arrived at Liverpool during Tom Watson's spell as manager were Teddy Doig, Elisha Scott and Sam Hardy, while winger Arthur Goddard gave Liverpool 13 seasons of service as he made more than 400 first-team appearances and scored close on a century of goals. Two other Watson-inspired signings, Jack Parkinson and Sam Raybould, were also marksmen of the highest calibre . . . between them they shared more than 250 goals.

During Tom Watson's managerial career,

Liverpool went to the final of the FA Cup for the first time, although they lost against Burnley at Crystal Palace in April 1914. Twelve months later, Watson, having served Liverpool and soccer to the very end, was being buried, with some of the men he had signed for Liverpool acting as bearers at the funeral service.

The Mystery of David Ashworth

The First World War brought a gap in football affairs, as more weighty matters occupied people's attention, but when hostilities with Germany had ceased and the great British game had got going again, a former referee called David Ashworth took over the managerial chair at Liverpool. And he had his successes, too. He didn't stay long with Liverpool, in fact, but during his tenure of office (he was with the club from 1920 to 1923) he saw the team win the League Championship for a second time. That was in season 1921-22, and the club were on their way to a second successive title when he left them in February 1923. It has never been explained satisfactorily why he left the Champions to take over Oldham, the bottom club in the division. Later still, he managed Manchester City, and resigned as the Maine Road club slid towards relegation in season 1925-26. Again there was a strange twist to the story, because after he handed in his resignation, City reached the FA Cup final.

David Ashworth's managerial career hadn't quite come to a full stop, however, because he took charge at Stockport County, and later he had a spell as a scout with Blackpool. He died in 1947, at the age of 79, by which time Liverpool were enjoying their fourth League Championship triumph. Incidentally, during Ashworth's time with the club, the team really took shape to such an extent that it was regarded as the finest to have been assembled up to that time. Some of the great names of that side were Fred 'Polly' Hopkin, Billy Lacey, Harry 'Smiler' Chambers, Tommy Bromilow, Dick Forshaw, Dick Johnson, Elisha Scott, Eph Longworth and Donald McKinlay.

The departure of David Ashworth for Oldham paved the way for the appointment as Manager of a former Liverpool player – indeed, the man in question also served the club as a director. His name was Matt McQueen, and he was one of two footballing brothers (the other was Hugh) who served Liverpool well. Matt and Hugh McQueen had arrived from Leith Athletic, a club north of the border, in 1893. The former played 87 games (and scored one goal) during his half-dozen seasons, then he qualified as a League referee.

McQueen took over the management of Liverpool in February 1923, so this meant that he was able to savour the spectacle of the club retaining

the Championship. It was to be the first and the last under McQueen's term as team boss, but before he retired in February 1928, he had earned the gratitude of the fans for signing players such as Gordon Hodgson, James Jackson, Tom Morrison and Arthur Riley.

Hodgson was a South African who became a scoring legend, as he rifled in a record number of league goals (232); Jackson, a full-back, captained the side and was known as 'Parson' (he did, in fact, enter the ministry); Morrison was a Scot who made his mark as a creative, but tough-tackling wing-half; and Riley – who, like Hodgson, hailed from South Africa – gave sterling service to the club as a goalkeeper who, during 14 seasons, totalled close on 350 first-team appearances.

Matt McQueen's career as manager contained an element of personal tragedy, because when he was on his way back from a scouting assignment he was involved in a road accident and received injuries which resulted in the amputation of a leg. Ill-health eventually brought about his retirement, though he remained a keen follower of Liverpool and was a regular visitor to Anfield – his home, indeed, was in Kemlyn Road. He died in September 1944.

The Two Georges

Following the departure of Matt McQueen in 1928, the managerial chair was occupied by George Patterson, a one-time footballer with Marine who had become Tom Watson's assistant at Liverpool in 1908. So, 20 years on, Patterson was given the title of Secretary-Manager, after having held the job of Secretary since 1915, the year Tom Watson had died. Under Patterson's management, Liverpool finished in fifth place, but hopes of the Championship were dimmed as the club after that had to settle for a mid-table spot half a dozen seasons in succession, while relegation was on the cards in season 1935-36, though at the end Liverpool survived by three points. Yet it was during Patterson's days as manager that the club unearthed more genuine talent . . . Jack Balmer (who made hat-trick history), Phil Taylor (later to become manager), Matt Busby, Tom Bradshaw and Tom Cooper.

Patterson was struck down by illness, however, and it meant that in 1936 he was forced to give up the dual role and concentrate upon the secretarial side of the game. Like Matt McQueen, he remained a regular Anfield supporter up to his death in May, 1955.

One George was followed by another. George Kay, a Mancunian, had begun his career with Bolton Wanderers and then became the first English player to captain the Irish League (he was

then playing for Distillery). Kay held another distinction, because he was the skipper of West Ham United when they were beaten by Bolton in the famous 1923 'White Horse' FA Cup final, the first at Wembley, when the crowd spilled on to the Wembley pitch and a policeman on a white horse helped to prevent a disaster.

George Kay had a five-year spell as Southampton's manager, then he moved to Liverpool in 1936. It was during his stewardship at Anfield that players like Bob Paisley, Billy Liddell and Albert Stubbins arrived to bolster the team – Stubbins had to make a choice between Liverpool and Everton, and Anfield got his vote. Under the guidance of Kay, Liverpool claimed the League Championship in season 1946-47 and they went to the final of the FA Cup in 1950, although they lost that one to Arsenal. Bob Paisley's omission from the side caused controversy, and as for George Kay, he was afflicted by ill-heath and in 1951 he retired from the managerial job at Anfield. He died in April 1965 – by which time Liverpool fans had seen two more managers (Don Welsh and Phil Taylor) come and go, while under a third (Bill Shankly) they were finally to conquer in the FA Cup.

■ George Kay was the team boss at Anfield from 1936 to 1951, during which time Liverpool claimed the League title and went to the final of the FA Cup.

Welsh and Taylor Do Their Best

■ Liverpool have a new manager, and the man in charge is former Charlton Athletic ace Don Welsh, who had guested for the Anfield club during the Second World War. Flanking him in this picture are Billy Liddell, on the left, and Phil Taylor, on the right – who later became the club's manager.

Don Welsh reigned as Anfield supremo from 1951 to 1956. He had been a favourite at Anfield when he guested for the club during the war years. He had made his name as a marksman, and was fondly remembered on the Anfield side of the city for a double hat-trick feat in a match against Southport which was played in December 1944. Liverpool rattled in a dozen goals to Southport's one, and Welsh scored three in each half of the game. His record made him appear to be an outstanding candidate to succeed George Kay. After having joined Charlton Athletic from Torquay United, he helped the London club to climb through three divisions – the Third (South) to the First (where they finished as runners-up) – in three seasons. Furthermore, he had gone to Wembley twice with Charlton for the FA Cup final (he was on the losing side in season 1945-46, and claimed a winner's medal 12 months later), and had been capped on three occasions by England. So he had an impressive pedigree both of knowledge about football and success at the highest level when Liverpool took him on.

As a captain, Don Welsh had shown that he could be an inspirational figure, and at one stage it seemed that he could be leaving Charlton to become a coach at Anfield. But though Liverpool would have been happy to take him, the London club was reluctant to let him go, so 1951 had arrived by the time that Welsh and Liverpool teamed up together. It was Don Welsh who was to bring in winger Alan A'Court and a tough-as-teak defender called Ronnie Moran, as he set about striving to assemble a side which could once more claim a place in the higher reaches of the First Division. Liverpool had not been noted as the biggest spenders in the world, but Don Welsh persuaded them to pay Wolves £12,000 for the experienced Sammy Smyth, and he added a temporary injection of hope as he hit some important goals.

Yet once again, and despite further expenditure in the transfer market (Welsh splashed more than £50,000 on reinforcements), Liverpool found themselves struggling even to remain in the First Division. In season 1951-52 they finished in 11th place; 12 months later they were 17th from the top; and at the end of season 1953-54 they were propping up the rest of the First Division clubs, and were relegated.

Their battle to regain top-flight status did not begin on an auspicious note, either, because at the end of their first season in the Second Division they could do no better than finish in a mid-table place, though by the final days of season 1955-56 they had improved to the point where they claimed third spot in the table. But that still wasn't good enough in those days to get them promotion.

Having tried, and been deemed to have failed, Don Welsh lost his job with Liverpool, and the club turned to a man who, it seemed once again, possessed impeccable references for the job – Phil Taylor, a former captain at Anfield who, during a highly successful career, had shown a polish on the field of play and the right kind of image off it to suggest that he could shoulder the burden and achieve the objective of First Division football. An England international, he had been a member of the Championship-winning side in season 1946-47; he had played in the 1950 FA Cup final; he had strung together no fewer than 345 League and Cup appearances for the club, and when – along with Bob Paisley – he had hung up his playing boots in season 1953-54, he had gone on to the coaching staff. Now, in 1956, he was being asked to begin another phase of his career at Anfield and take charge as Liverpool's manager, and he accepted the challenge.

Phil Taylor, like Don Welsh, delved into the transfer market, and he came up with a Scottish international goalkeeper, 'Big Tam' Younger, from Hibs, and an attacking midfield player from Bolton Wanderers, Johnny Wheeler. And, since Taylor himself had been a classy half-back, it was reckoned that he knew the requirements for this department well enough. It looked as if Taylor were going to get it right in his very first season, as Liverpool lost only half a dozen matches in the first half of the campaign and rounded off the year by stringing together four straight wins and a draw. They even overcame three successive defeats in the early weeks of the New Year and won seven and drew two of their last 10 matches . . . but still they were able to do no better than finish in third place again. Season 1957-58 was destined to be yet another term of disappointment, as Liverpool – finishing in fourth place, this time – knew they had missed the promotion boat by a two-point margin, and worse was to come, because next time out the team made an indifferent start which was to prove costly in the final reckoning. Even after a winning streak which saw them take maximum points from 14 out of 16 matches between mid-October and early February, the promotion jinx continued to blight Liverpool's best efforts.

While they were enjoying that sustained run of victories in the League, in fact, Liverpool suffered a severe shock to their system when they were sent spinning out of the FA Cup in their first match – little Worcester City caused the upset when they despatched the Anfield Reds from the competition with a 2-1 win.

It was a time of change on the playing side, too, as Phil Taylor did his utmost to find the right blend. Goalkeeper Younger and winger A'Court had achieved international recognition, and Ronnie Moran had been chosen to play for the Football League. Louis Bimpson and Alan Arnell became the new strike force, then dashing Dave Hickson, a hero on the Goodison Park side of the city, arrived as a £12,000 signing. But, at the same time, it seemed that Billy Liddell's days were numbered, as he lost his first-team place for the first time. And Phil Taylor himself reached the stage where he could no longer carry on.

There was general sympathy for Phil Taylor, because he had been a popular choice as manager, after his illustrious playing career at Liverpool, and he had certainly not spared himself in the effort to get the club back to the First Division. However, as is always the case in football, it soon became a matter of 'the king is dead . . . long live the king'. The only question to be answered, though, was where the next claimant to the Anfield throne was coming from . . . could Liverpool, after their previous unsuccessful attempts, at last produce a winner from the pack?

They say that cometh the hour, cometh the man; and this time Liverpool got it right all the way along the line. The hour had arrived and, with it, the man. His name was Bill Shankly.

The Coming of Bill Shankly

Bill Shankly may not have been knighted for his services to soccer, though he did receive an OBE. So far as the Liverpool faithful were concerned, he was certainly the Laird of Anfield almost from the moment he arrived. And as time went on, he became a living legend.

Born in Ayrshire, Bill Shankly first played for a local side with the romantic name of Glenbuck Cherrypickers, and in 1932 he was invited to join Carlisle United. It was the stepping stone to greatness . . . 12 months later, this wing-half who played his football with such strength and skill, not to mention 100 per cent commitment, was being signed by Preston North End, and within one season he had forced his way into the first team and was helping North End to gain promotion.

In 1937, Shankly and Preston went to Wembley to contest the final of the FA Cup with Sunderland, but at the end of the day Bill had to settle for a loser's medal. The following year, however, North End returned to the Wembley stage and a dramatic penalty goal from George

THE ANFIELD MANAGERS

Mutch brought them victory over Huddersfield Town . . . the club which, later, was to supply Bill Shankly, as a fully-fledged manager, to Liverpool.

In 1938 Shankly, capped by Scotland, played against the 'auld enemy', England, and he figured in all his country's matches the following season. Came the war, and football was relegated to the background, though games were still played as footballers 'guested' for clubs around the country, often dependent upon where they were stationed in the armed services. When the war ended, Bill Shankly resumed his soccer career and in 1949 he was appointed Manager of his first professional club, Carlisle United.

Two years later, Shankly was being asked to take charge of team affairs at Grimsby Town; then in 1954 he left Blundell Park to become the manager at Workington. From there it was on to Huddersfield Town, as Assistant Manager to fellow-Scot Andy Beattie, and when Beattie retired in November 1956, Bill stepped up to become the Leeds Road club's manager. Three

years later, he accepted his last and greatest managerial challenge when he joined Liverpool, and both he and the Anfield club never looked back. Together, indeed, they assumed the mantle of greatness.

It is worth recording that Shankly became the first manager at Anfield to have sole control over team selection. Up to his arrival, successive managers had passed on their team selection to the directors for boardroom approval. But Shankly was 'the boss' from the start.

Stories about Shankly became legion, of course, after he had been appointed Liverpool's manager on 1 December 1959 – possibly the most significant date in the club's history – and often enough they centred around his players. Like Tommy Smith, the defender who became known as the 'Anfield Iron' for his no-nonsense style of play.

Bob Paisley once said that when you saw Smithy go down, then you knew he was hurt. Bill Shankly once observed that Tommy Smith – with whom he had more than one difference of opinion

■ Two men who became legends in their own lifetimes . . . on the left, Bill Shankly, and on the right, Stanley Matthews. As players, both graced the game; and as a manager, Shankly achieved even more fame for his feats with Liverpool.

– would 'start a riot in a graveyard.' On the other hand, Shankly would never sell his players short, and he took the trouble to air his opinion, when Smith's name was being canvassed as someone who would stiffen the backbone of England's international side, that: 'Tommy Smith isn't just a hard man . . . he can play a bit of fitba', as well.'

They used to say that when Liverpool had lost, Bill Shankly would go home and give vent to his feelings by cleaning the cooker. Certainly, Liverpool built up a reputation in Shankly's day for being virtually invincible on their own ground – so much so that when the final whistle went after one match, which Liverpool had actually lost, one wag in the Press box was heard to reflect (in a fair imitation of Bill Shankly's voice) that 'the Fitba' League wull nivver accept this result!'

Bill Shankly was a Tom Finney fan. He was also a fan of the Liverpool fans and a fan of British football. While ready, willing and able to take Liverpool on a conquering trek around Europe, he never ceased to believe that 'British is best'.

Bill Shankly always stood four-square for honest endeavour throughout the 90 minutes of a match, and sent out his teams in the knowledge that they would never give him less than 100 per cent effort. Shankly himself was a man of the people, and some of those people – Liverpool fans, to be sure – found themselves the recipients of his generosity at times, when they were on the outside looking in. He was known to have slipped a match ticket into the hand of a fan who had given up all hope of getting in to see the game. He was a man who couldn't stand cheating, in any shape or form – though he would always do his damnedest to prepare his team for victory. He was a master of psychology and man-management. The notice 'This Is Anfield', which still stands above the tunnel where the players move out from the corridor on their way to the pitch, was calculated to inspire the men who wore Liverpool's colours and make the opposition feel that they hadn't really got a prayer of winning.

Behind the scenes, Liverpool's manager

■ Bill Shankly makes a point, as he takes charge at Liverpool . . . and one man still at Anfield will probably remember this occasion, because Ronnie Moran was the recipient of the advice. Ronnie stayed on to clock up close on 40 years' service, including a spell as caretaker manager himself.

demanded team effort from everyone, players and staff. When he arrived from Huddersfield, he didn't embark on wholesale changes in the backroom staff, but he did make it clear that loyalty and teamwork would be the order of the day. One thing Bill Shankly certainly wouldn't tolerate was any form of clique. And he got what he wanted – unquestioning loyalty from the men who worked alongside him.

Among them were Reuben Bennett, like Shankly, a Scot, Bob Paisley, a canny Geordie, Joe Fagan, Tom Saunders, who pioneered the job of Youth Development Officer, Ronnie Moran and Roy Evans. All these men served Liverpool well – some of them started out as players at Anfield, some of them are still there. They tell the story of Reuben Bennett, who had been a goal-keeper during his playing days. He was also a former Army physical training instructor, and in appearance almost as craggy a character as Bill Shankly himself. Reuben, so it was said, once took the longest goal kick in the history of British football . . . he kicked the ball so hard it soared out of the ground, landed on the back of a lorry – and finished up in Carlisle.

Reuben was Liverpool's trainer, and the others all had their respective jobs to do. In turn, Bob

■ Like Bill Shankly, he was a Scot and, like Bill Shankly, he served Liverpool well. His name: Reuben Bennett. He became a member of Shankly's backroom team at Anfield, after a career in the game as a goalkeeper.

Paisley was reserve team trainer, physiotherapist, coach, assistant to the manager and, ultimately, the manager. Bob proved the perfect foil to Shanks; the man who, on occasion, guided the boss in the best way to achieve a specific objective. But – make no mistake – so long as he held the title of Manager, Bill Shankly was the boss.

The Anfield bootroom became famous, too. That was where the backroom men from the visiting team could gather with their Anfield counterparts after the game and enjoy a quiet drink and a chat. And on a Sunday morning, the bootroom was the place where the inquest – if there needed to be an inquest – was held. It was the place where the staff weighed up the happen-ings of the match the previous day, the place where you could say your piece in the knowledge that it was all for the good of Liverpool Football Club.

Bill Shankly suffered the stresses a football manager must endure. One of his hardest periods was the climax to season 1972-73, when Liverpool became the first English club to carry off a European trophy and the Championship of the Football League in the same season.

The Championship was virtually won at Anfield on the Easter Monday afternoon, as Liverpool beat Leeds United. Shortly afterwards they despatched Tottenham Hotspur, holders of the UEFA Cup, from the European competition, at the semi-final stage, and they drew no-score against Leicester City in their final League game before tackling the crack West German club, Borussia Moenchengladbach, in the final of the UEFA Cup. After the title had been clinched, Shanks walked into the office of Secretary Peter Robinson. He never said a word, just dialled a number, then spoke: 'We've done it, Nessie, we've done it! There's nae-one can catch us now!' Nessie, of course, was his wife.

The two-legged tie against Borussia turned out to be a nerve-jangling affair, after Liverpool had scored a 3–0 first-leg victory at Anfield. These three goals, it appeared, had already put the tie beyond Borussia's reach . . . but when the second leg was played the West Germans, master-minded by Gunter Netzer in midfield, put a totally different complexion on matters as they surged into a 2–0 first-half lead. Suddenly, Liverpool were hanging on like grim death, as Borussia threatened to overwhelm them, but in the end they survived to win 3–2 on aggregate and take the trophy home to Merseyside.

Not surprisingly, the match had taken its toll of the Liverpool players, and while they did their best to celebrate as they got bathed and changed, it was clear that the whole thing still hadn't quite sunk in. As for Bill Shankly, he was as pale and drawn as if he had been out there battling against Borussia himself for the whole 90 minutes. It

wasn't until the team were airborne on the way home that everyone began to relax and enjoy the occasion.

Shankly Transforms the Reds

Bill Shankly's reign as the manager of Liverpool began officially on Tuesday, 1 December 1959, but Shanks had agreed to stay with Huddersfield for a further month, so he was due to arrive at Anfield in the New Year. Shanks wasn't on contract at Huddersfield, but he considered it only fair to give the Yorkshire club a chance to find a successor. He said of his appointment: 'I am pleased and proud to have been chosen as manager of a club with such great potential . . . It is my opinion that Liverpool have a crowd of followers which rank among the greatest in the game. They deserve success and I hope, in my small way, to be able to do something towards helping them to achieve it. I make no promises, except that from the moment I take over I shall put everything I have into the job.

'This appointment is a challenge to me – I rank it similar to that confronting Joe Mercer when he left Sheffield United for Aston Villa, and when Alan Brown left Burnley to go to Sunderland. These clubs, like Liverpool, are among the top-grade teams in football. When the challenge was made to me, I simply could not refuse it. There is a job to be done – perhaps a big job; but with the co-operation of the directors and staff I feel certain we shall see the task through together.

'I am not a lazy man. I like to get down to it and set the example which I will want following from the top of the club to the bottom.'

Oddly enough, Bill Shankly had seen his Huddersfield Town team beat Liverpool on the previous Saturday, and his after-match comment went like this: 'I must say that Huddersfield were a better side than Liverpool, but at least Liverpool did fight.' And he added: 'Nobody realises more than I do what a tough job getting Liverpool back into the First Division is likely to be; but I think we can do it. I have gained quite a lot of experience of Second Division football, and I know some of the difficulties.'

One of the difficulties became apparent as Shankly sat through his first match in charge of team affairs at Anfield. Liverpool were humiliated as they went down 4–0 against Cardiff City. One report said Shanks was 'a very subdued man' after seeing this debacle: 'Right from the start, Shankly was made to realise what a tremendous task lies ahead of him as this shabby Liverpool team were humbled by a Cardiff side wearing an unmistakable promotion look.'

Bill Shankly's reaction? 'Naturally, I'm disappointed,' he said, 'but it's just as well that I've seen

the team give an off-form display in my first match. I've learned quite a few things this way.' And to someone who offered condolences, the new manager answered: 'Save your sympathy . . . I can look after myself and I can look after my team. There's a job to do, but together we shall do it.'

Typically, Shanks didn't knock his players. He gave some credit to Cardiff. 'On that form they would have beaten any team in the Second Division,' he declared. 'The ball ran for them, and it made them look a very good side.'

Afterwards, so the story goes, Shankly told his

■ The man who pioneered the job of youth-development officer in football . . . Tom Saunders. This former teacher who managed schoolboy talent became an important member of the backroom staff at Anfield, not only nurturing the young footballers, but compiling dossiers on opponents.

■ Liverpool are about to make club history, as Bill Shankly leads them out to face Leeds United at Wembley in 1965, because after extra time in the FA Cup final that May afternoon, Liverpool carried home the trophy for the first time ever.

■ After the action, the words of thanks from 'the boss', and Bill Shankly offers his congratulations to skipper Ron Yeats and the Liverpool players as they celebrate success in the League Championship at the end of season 1963-64. That was indeed the start of something big . . .

directors: 'Gentlemen, I can assure you that we *will* win a match at Anfield this season . . .' In fact, Liverpool were to build a reputation for steamrollering the opposition on home ground. But in the meantime, Bill Shankly departed from the scene of disaster and went back home to Huddersfield.

The pattern was repeated several times – he would ask for a ball, and make his exit, leaving his backroom men wondering what was going on. They did find out, in due course . . . Shanks was going home to have a Sunday morning kickabout with the locals.

It took Shankly a few seasons to get it right, as Liverpool finished third, third, and then first in the Second Division. From then on, the story was one of almost continuous success. The Championship in season 1963-64, the FA Cup in season 1964-65 (Liverpool's first-ever success in that competition) and the Championship again in season 1965-66, coupled with an appearance in the final of the European Cup-Winners' Cup, after a 1965 run to the semi-finals of the European Cup.

Shankly confided that he had expected his side

of the 1960s to last longer than it did, but when he saw the signs of age creeping in, he determined to start again. Initially, he had gone 'straight down the middle', from goalkeeper Tommy Lawrence to centre-half Ron Yeats to centre-forward Ian St John; and when he started to rebuild, he signed Ray Clemence, Larry Lloyd and John Toshack, whom he called 'an essential in modern-day fitba'.

By the start of the 1970s Bill Shankly had assembled a new-look side which took Liverpool to an FA Cup final against Arsenal, and though the Gunners won that one, come 1974, Liverpool were giving Newcastle a hiding at Wembley. In between times, the team had matured sufficiently to claim the Championship and the UEFA Cup in the spring of 1973.

The FA Cup triumph over Newcastle turned out to be Shankly's swan-song, because he announced his intention to retire. The news came like a bolt from the blue, and Bob Paisley, his trusted and long-serving lieutenant, spent three weeks trying to talk Shanks out of it. But in vain. Bill stuck to his guns, and Bob got the job of following him.

■ Bill Shankly shakes hands with Kevin Keegan as the players line up for the 1974 FA Cup final. That day, Liverpool beat Newcastle United, and it turned out that the FA Cup was to be Bill Shankly's parting gift to the club he had served so well.
Above: Shankly leading the Liverpool team out at Wembley.

Later, Shanks attended a London luncheon at which Bob received the Manager-of-the-Year trophy (as Bill had done before him), and when it was time for the speech-making, the former Liverpool manager got to his feet to say a few words. Congratulating his successor, who had steered Liverpool to the European Cup – as well as the League title (and very nearly to the FA Cup, as well), Shanks looked at his audience and said, with a somewhat whimsical smile: 'Maybe you're thinking I'm a wee bit jealous . . .' Then he rasped: 'Of course I am!'

The impression was that Bill regretted having taken the decision to quit the managerial chair, and there were times when he seemed to be at a bit of a loss as to what to do afterwards, though he was consulted by various people in football who valued his knowledge and his expertise.

The Liverpool fans – with whom he had built up such a tremendous rapport (he once went and stood among them on the Kop) – will never forget the man who first gave the club a taste of greatness, and the famed Shankly Gates bear ample testimony to his achievements as Liverpool's manager.

Bob Paisley Takes Over

If ever there was a reluctant hero, that man was Bob Paisley, a Geordie who had never sought the limelight in all the time that Bill Shankly had been the Manager of Liverpool Football Club. Indeed, Paisley had been the loyal lieutenant, content to stay on the sidelines and do his own job as well as he knew how. Not that Shankly deliberately hogged the headlines or sought to keep his No. 2 out of sight . . . it was simply the way things were at Anfield.

Shankly, as the Manager, was always the man the media turned to for a quote . . . and usually he obliged; sometimes, in fact, his observations bordered on the outrageous. He seemed larger than life, even though he was no giant in physical stature, but beyond all doubt Liverpool Football Club revolved around him from the moment he walked through the door, at the end of 1959.

In consequence, when he dropped the bombshell news in 1974 that he intended to retire, after having delivered the FA Cup as his parting gift, so to speak, the world of football pondered long and hard as to where Liverpool could possibly go for a successful successor to Shanks. The man had so much charisma and such a string of triumphs to his credit that finding someone to follow in his footsteps seemed, in the eyes of most people, to be almost a pointless exercise. Bob Paisley himself tried in vain for three weeks to persuade Bill Shankly to change his mind; and others at the club did their best, behind the scenes, to prevent or, at least, postpone, the inevitable. But Shanks was adamant that he was quitting the managerial chair, and at last everyone at Anfield had to accept his verdict.

Once this had happened, no more time was wasted – Liverpool decided that they would keep the job in the family, and they announced that it would be going to Bob Paisley, with the other backroom men stepping up as well. That way, if nothing else, continuity would be preserved . . . but it still remained to be seen if Paisley would turn out to be managerial material, after having soldiered on for so long as the No. 2.

Bob Paisley had seemed to be a man who wanted to stay in the shadows. Seldom, if ever, did you see him quoted, and yet he clearly knew as much as anyone – and more than most – about the workings of the club. He never altered. For much of the time that he held the reins at Liverpool he continued to live in a modest semi-detached house on the outskirts of the city. He was never one for the bright lights and the razzmatazz, though at home he was hospitable enough and quick to offer a glass of whisky.

Paisley never really wanted the job of Manager. He would have continued to do his best for the club, no matter who had got the job. But fate decreed that he had to take up the massive challenge which had been presented by the departure of Bill Shankly – and, having been offered the job, Bob said he would do his best to make a success of it. He knew, better than anyone, just what a rapport Bill Shankly had established with the Liverpool fans, and he also knew that he would be wasting his time trying to compete in that way. Bob said, quite simply, as he took up the management: 'I hope that the team will do the talking for me.' And history records how well the team did just that.

Bob had been a player himself, and he had known the feeling of being left out of the team – notably for the FA Cup final of 1950 – so he could understand what the reaction of a player would be when he forfeited his first-team place. As a result, he started out somewhat gingerly on the managerial trail – in fact, as he admitted later: 'In my first season, I tried to please everyone . . . then I came to realise that I couldn't do this, so I concentrated on doing what I felt was right for the team and the club.'

In all the years that he has been on Merseyside, Bob Paisley has never lost that Geordie accent, and sometimes you had to listen hard to interpret just what he was trying to say. Yet through it all there shone a very real sense of humour – somewhat dry – and the man certainly knew his football from A to Z.

Paisley's First Crisis

There came a time when he lost popularity with some of his players, a time when the media men were speculating about Bob's chances of staying in the job. The loss of popularity with one or two players was easily explained – it was simply that they had been axed from the team and so they were smarting. No player likes to lose his place, and all too often when it happens, the player believes the Manager made the wrong decision. Once the player gets back into the side, the Manager isn't such a bad so-and-so, after all.

The Press speculation – not in print, but by word of mouth – came during Bob's first season as manager, when Liverpool hit a wobbly patch. They had started out with a victory over Luton Town, won five of their next half-dozen matches and, after losing 2–0 to Manchester City at Maine Road, clocked up a record 11–0 victory over Stromgodset in a European Cup-Winners Cup tie at Anfield. Then came a 3–0 home win over Stoke . . . and that was followed by the start of the wobble.

Burnley won 1–0 at Anfield, Sheffield United beat Liverpool 1–0 at Bramall Lane; then there were Liverpool victories over Stromgodset (only 1–0, this time), Carlisle United, Middlesbrough, Bristol City, Queen's Park Rangers and Leeds United. On the face of it, no problems at all. But an away goal saw Ferencvaros end Liverpool's European ambitions, and there were defeats at Ipswich and at home against Arsenal and then Middlesbrough (this last one in the League Cup).

Suddenly, all that Liverpool could aim for were the Championship and, after the turn of the year, the FA Cup. They were out of Europe, out of the League Cup, uncertain in their form . . . and due to face Everton at Goodison Park the following Saturday afternoon. And if they lost that one, hard on the heels of their defeats by the Gunners and Middlesbrough, Bob Paisley really would have had problems.

On the morning of that Goodison Park derby game, he called up Phil Neal, his first signing, and plunged him into the fray. At the end of the 90 minutes, Liverpool had emerged with a scoreless draw, and the audience of more than 56,000 went home more or less satisfied that it was a case of honours even. Meantime, the media men waited for Bob Paisley to appear – and they had to wait a considerable time. When he finally came out of the dressing-room, Bob apologised for having kept them waiting, and he explained that he hadn't done so deliberately. It was obvious that he had been well aware of the tension of the occasion, not to mention the speculation about Liverpool's form up to that point, and the after-match interview was fairly brief.

Maybe for the first time Bob Paisley had come to appreciate how moods can change as results begin to go awry, though there was no open hostility and the atmosphere was civil enough. Maybe, even, that was when Bob decided that he couldn't please everyone, after all . . . at any rate,

LIVERPOOL'S MANAGERS OF THE YEAR

THE prestigious Manager of the Year award has been up for grabs for more than 20 years, and some famous names have figured in the list of recipients – indeed two of them (Don Revie and Jack Charlton) became international team bosses. In 1972-73 Bill Shankly became the first Liverpool manager to walk up and receive the award, bringing not only the First Division Championship, but the UEFA Cup to Anfield – the first time a British club had achieved this double. Shankly was followed by Jack Charlton and Ron Saunders then, apart from a few exceptions, it was Liverpool all the way, as Bob Paisley, Joe Fagan and Kenny Dalglish claimed the managerial award one after the other.

Bob Paisley may have missed out in his first season as Liverpool's manager, but after that it was an almost annual visit to London to receive the award:

■ *Left:* It's farewell to Bill Shankly, as he bows out as the manager of Liverpool in 1974, after having steered the club to a second FA Cup success. And the fans want Shanks to know just how much they think of him.

■ *Right:* When Liverpool clinched their 18th League championship in the spring of 1990, Kenny Dalglish was rewarded yet again by being voted Manager of the Year – for the third time in five seasons. No one could have visualized that soon he would be stepping down.

1975-76 (as Bob emulated Bill Shankly be steering Liverpool to the League Championship and the UEFA Cup); 1976-77 (League title and European Cup); 1978-79 (League title); 1979-80 (League title again); 1981-82 and 1982-83 (League title and Milk Cup, each time).

Joe Fagan's first season (1983-84) brought him the Manager of the Year award for a unique feat, because under him Liverpool claimed the League Championship, the European Cup and the Milk Cup. And then it was the turn of Kenny Dalglish, promoted from player to team boss, as he led Liverpool to the classic League title/FA Cup double in season 1985-86.

In season 1987-88 it was the League title, in season 1989-90 it was the League title again – and on the first occasion, Liverpool and Kenny Dalglish went so close to achieving a second famous double. Both times, in addition to the Championship

■ *Above:* **A pause from training for a moment, and Bob Paisley has cause to ponder, as he plots the way ahead. When he took over from Bill Shankly, he said: 'I hope the team will do the talking for me' . . . and the team certainly did.**

silverware, the Manager of the Year trophy wound up on the Anfield sideboard, to make it three times overall in Kenny's five seasons in charge.

Here is the complete list of managers who have won the award since its inception in season 1968-69:

Season	Manager
1968-69	Don Revie (Leeds United)
1969-70	Don Revie (Leeds United)
1970-71	Bertie Mee (Arsenal)
1971-72	Don Revie (Leeds United)
1972-73	**Bill Shankly (Liverpool)**
1973-74	Jack Charlton (Middlesbrough)
1974-75	Ron Saunders (Aston Villa)
1975-76	**Bob Paisley (Liverpool)**
1976-77	**Bob Paisley (Liverpool)**
1977-78	Brian Clough (Nottingham Forest)
1978-79	**Bob Paisley (Liverpool)**
1979-80	**Bob Paisley (Liverpool)**
1980-81	Ron Saunders (Aston Villa)
1981-82	**Bob Paisley (Liverpool)**
1982-83	**Bob Paisley (Liverpool)**
1983-84	**Joe Fagan (Liverpool)**
1984-85	Howard Kendall (Everton)
1985-86	**Kenny Dalglish (Liverpool)**
1986-87	Howard Kendall (Everton)
1987-88	**Kenny Dalglish (Liverpool)**
1988-89	George Graham (Arsenal)
1989-90	**Kenny Dalglish (Liverpool)**
1990-91	George Graham (Arsenal)

Anfield Bosses

A complete list of Liverpool's managers shows that only 13 men have guided the Reds' fortunes in their first 100 years of football:

1892-1896	W.E. Barclay
1896-1915	Tom Watson
1920-1923	David Ashworth
1923-1928	Matt McQueen
1928-1936	George Patterson
1936-1951	George Kay
1951-1956	Don Welsh
1956-1959	Phil Taylor
1959-1974	Bill Shankly
1974-1983	Bob Paisley
1983-1985	Joe Fagan
1985-1991	Kenny Dalglish
1991-	Graeme Souness

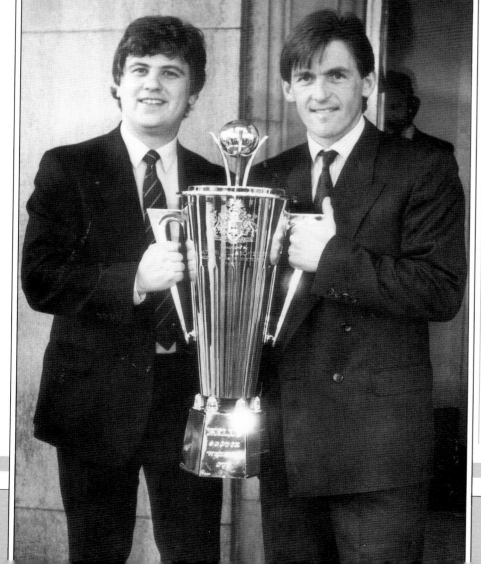

Liverpool were back on the rails, even if they could still do no better than draw their next three matches. The remainder of the season, indeed, was something of an up-and-down affair, with good victories interspersed with defeats (including an exit from the FA Cup in a fourth-round tie at Ipswich). Arsenal completed a 'double', Liverpool were hammered 4–1 by Newcastle United at St James's Park after having given Ipswich a 5–2 trouncing in the Anfield League return, and Everton maintained the status quo by holding Liverpool to a scoreless stalemate at Anfield.

At the end of the campaign, Derby County had claimed the Championship, and Liverpool had had to settle for being second best with Everton fourth. As for Bob Paisley, he had learned quite a lot from his first term in the hot seat – and he certainly made that first season's experience count!

Overall, Bob was right much more often than he was wrong, and no-one in the game knew more about soccer than he did. Yet there were occasions when he was happy to admit that he had made a miscalculation . . . and one of these concerned the emergence of Steve Heighway, whom Bill Shankly had persuaded to become a professional footballer after he had graduated with a Bachelor of Arts degree from Warwick University. Bob felt – and he wasn't the only one – that maybe Steve, for all his ability, didn't possess the attitude of a real professional, and he reckoned that he wouldn't play as many games for Liverpool as his university counterpart, Brian Hall, who possessed a Bachelor of Science degree. Steve and Brian were christened 'Big Bamber' and 'Little Bamber', respectively, after Bamber Gascoigne, of television's *University Challenge* fame.

In the end, Bob held up his hand as Steve Heighway totalled more than 400 first-team appearances, compared with some 200 that Brian Hall made. Yet both players, as Bob readily acknowledged, made their contribution to the cause of the team as Liverpool, under his management, scaled the heights in Europe, as well as on the domestic scene.

The Ultimate One-Club Man

Bob Paisley's career at Anfield spotlights the way that Liverpool keep a hold on people. There was a time, when his playing days were over, when it seemed he might well be on his way back to the North-East and turning his hand to bricklaying again. Thankfully for him and for the club, that was not to be.

Paisley arrived at Liverpool on 8 May 1939 as a player. He stayed for more than 50 years, and finished up by becoming a director of the club. In the years between his arrival and his elevation to the boardroom, he became arguably the most successful manager British football has ever known, as he steered Liverpool to success in almost every competition at home and in Europe. Only the FA Cup eluded him at home, and only the Cup-Winners' Cup failed to arrive at Anfield during Liverpool's European safari.

When Bob Paisley got off the train at Liverpool's Lime Street station that May day in 1939, he had already made his mark as a footballer with the famed North-Eastern amateur club, Bishop Auckland – indeed, Liverpool allowed Bob to play for Bishops in the Amateur Cup final, so that he could – and did – collect a winner's medal. It was a former Liverpool player, Andy McGuigan (he played in the early 1900s), who met Bob at Lime Street and whisked him off to Anfield, where for a £10 signing-on fee and a wage of a fiver a week Bob put pen to paper. Liverpool's manager at the time was George Kay, and he had already talked terms to Bob two weeks previously, when it was agreed that he could stay on to play for Bishops in the amateur final. Shades of things to come at Liverpool, because Bishops had such a fixture jam that they were required to play 13 games in 14 days!

When Bob joined Liverpool, he was in good company, because among the players at the club were Matt Busby, the noted South African Berry 'Nivvy' Nieuwenhuys, Phil Taylor (a future Liverpool manager) and Billy Liddell, who was in Bob's own age group. Bob was a mere stripling of 19 when he signed the forms that made him a Liverpool player, but because the war began a few months later he was to lose to the army a considerable number of years from his soccer career. Indeed, his first derby game against Everton came early in the war, when he was released to play in the Liverpool Senior Cup final against the Blues. Bob was stationed at a camp in Cheshire, which meant that he had to get to the game under his own steam; so he got on his bike and cycled the 30 miles to the ground. The crowd was estimated at 30,000 – double the official limit – and at the end of it all Bob Paisley pondered on whether his journey had really been necessary, because Everton won 4–2.

From the Army camp in Cheshire Bob was on the move – by boat, not bike – to Egypt, and he spent four years in the desert. When Rome was liberated by the Allies, Bob rode through the Eternal City on a tank . . . then it was back to England and playing football again, as Liverpool competed in regional matches. He became a first-team regular, seldom missing a match because of injury, and in season 1949-50 helped Liverpool make it to Wembley for the final of the FA Cup. Before that, though, he had savoured the sweet taste of success, because in season 1946-47 Bob had been a member of the team which – after a

very poor start – had stormed through to capture the League Championship. It was a season in which the club also reached the semi-finals of the FA Cup and won the Liverpool Senior Cup, the Lancashire Senior Cup and the Lancashire County Combination Championship Cup.

By the start of season 1949-50, Bob Paisley had made a century of appearances in a Liverpool jersey, and when the club reached the semi-finals, he scored one of the goals that despatched Everton from the Wembley trail. However, he also collected an injury, so he missed a League game to make sure he would be fit for the FA Cup final. It was from the evening paper that he learned he would not be playing – he wouldn't even be on the bench, because in those days there were no substitutes – and, from what he could gather, the directors who had chosen the Cup final side had been divided when it came to deciding between Bob Paisley and Bill Jones. Four wanted Paisley, but five votes went to Jones. Bob sat and watched as Jimmy Logie – the man he would have been detailed to mark – laid on a couple of goals for Reg

Lewis as Arsenal won the game and went up to collect the Cup.

There was an added touch of irony about the situation, because in League matches that season Bob had twice had the job of marking Logie, and on each occasion he and Liverpool had come off best. Bob, of course, remembers it well: 'My father was so incensed about my being left out that he wouldn't go to the game. It did cross my mind, too, that a transfer might not be a bad thing . . . but in the end I decided to stay.' And it was a good job for Liverpool that he did.

Bob saw George Kay resign as the strain of trying to steer Liverpool to major honours took its toll and Don Welsh take over team affairs. In season 1950-51 Bob Paisley was back in the side, to total 41 League appearances (more than anyone else), and the following term he gained England B recognition. But in season 1952-53 Liverpool needed to beat Chelsea in order to avoid relegation; and though the Anfield Reds won 2–0 on this occasion, the club still went down one year later.

THE **A**NFIELD **M**ANAGERS

■ One of the famed Desert Rats . . . and for Bob Paisley, it's breakfast at El Alamein on 13 July 1942. With him are his army mates, Jim Bates, Jack Bennett and Joe Beal.

■ Albert Shelley tests the fitness of Bob Paisley and Jackie Balmer, as they come back after injury in season 1946-47. They celebrated as the Anfield Reds beat Grimsby Town 6–1 away in the League and 2–0 in the FA Cup, with the title coming to Anfield at the end of the season.

■ Liverpool didn't always have their superb training headquarters at Melwood . . . once upon a time, the lads had to make do with the Anfield car park. But as Bob Paisley and company get down to it, they don't appear to be taking much harm.

■ It may look like torture, but in fact it's all part of the training routine at Liverpool. Again the players being put through their paces are Jackie Balmer and Bob Paisley. They were getting in trim for an FA Cup-tie against Grimsby Town in 1947.

Bob Paisley, Phil Taylor, Eddie Spicer and Bill Jones all pulled off their Liverpool shirts for the last time, and Bob and Phil were given jobs on the backroom side. Bob was in charge of the reserve team, and after finishing sixth and then second, the reserves made it third-time lucky as they claimed the Championship of the Central League – the first time Liverpool had managed to do this. Then came the departure of Don Welsh and the appointment of Phil Taylor as manager, but after three years Phil bowed out and Bill Shankly arrived, with the club still seeking to regain First Division status. By the time Shanks moved in at Anfield, Bob was first team trainer, and from then on he was in partnership with the new Manager . . . little dreaming that in the mid-1970s he would follow Bill as the team boss and lead Liverpool into a glorious era of yet more success.

Bob reflects: 'I would have carried on and done any job the club wanted me to do when Bill decided to call it a day, but – having accepted the job of managing the club – I decided there was only one thing to do . . . give of my best. When I looked back, I had to smile, because at the age of 14 I'd been a surface worker for a year at a colliery at Hetton-le-Hole, where I was born. Then I'd served my time as a bricklayer – and, but for Tom Williams, who was a Director, Chairman and later President, persuading me to join the backroom staff, I'd probably have gone back to bricklaying.'

Altogether, Bob Paisley played close on 300

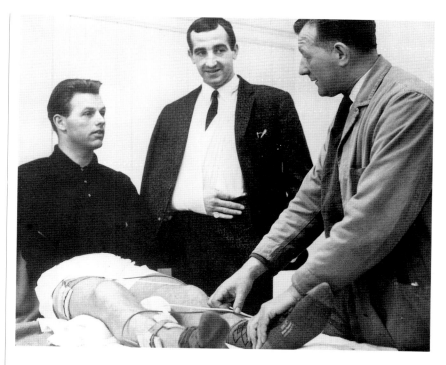

games for Liverpool, and even before he moved on to the backroom side he was preparing for a new role by learning something about the art of physiotherapy, via a correspondence course. He relates: 'I spent afternoons swotting up, and I had to thank John Moores – the man who became a power at Everton – for his help in arranging for me to visit hospitals and learn about the equipment used to treat sports injuries.'

■ The FA Cup has been won, and Wembley hero Gerry Byrne is out of action. But Gordon Milne gets treatment from Bob Paisley in the hope that he'll be fit for the European Cup semi-final against Inter-Milan.

Bob called Bill Shankly 'the most dedicated man I've ever known in football.' When he followed Shanks as Liverpool's manager, he adopted the same approach. He regarded himself as part of the furniture at Anfield, rather than the team's figurehead, but if there was one thing which gave him encouragement as he embarked upon his new job, it was the knowledge that the backroom team remained to help him along the way. And that there were no divided loyalties.

At the end of Bob's first season in charge, when Liverpool had finished as League runners-up to Derby County, Bob Paisley told the fans: 'We shall be back – and doing our best to win something again.' That was exactly what happened, because 12 months later Liverpool were bringing home the UEFA Cup, along with the League Championship Trophy. It was a performance which won for Liverpool's team boss the accolade of Manager of the Year – an award he was to claim more than once during an era of dazzling success for the club.

The European Cup at Last

Twelve months after their double achievement, Liverpool were bringing home the European Cup for the first time, to go with the Championship they had retained . . . and it was very nearly a treble, because they went to the final of the FA Cup, only to lose narrowly to Manchester United. It came as no surprise, therefore, that for the second season in succession Bob was named as Manager of the Year.

Instead of asking how Bob Paisley would make out as a manager, the question on everyone's lips now was: 'How can he and Liverpool follow that?' The answer, at the end of season 1977-78, was that Liverpool missed out on a hat-trick of League titles, missed out on the League Cup after an Old Trafford replay of the final against Nottingham Forest . . . but they retained the European Cup.

The man who scored the winning goal in the final against FC Bruges at Wembley was Kenny Dalglish – Bob Paisley's answer when Kevin Keegan departed Anfield for SV Hamburg after the 1977 European Cup final. Kenny, a £440,000 record signing from Glasgow Celtic, was himself to achieve glittering success – not only as a player but as Liverpool's team boss. That, however, was still in the future as Dalglish displayed his silky footballing skills on the Wembley turf by curling in the match-winner against Bruges.

As for Bob Paisley, he just missed out on a third Manager of the Year award (it went to Brian

■ Time for a break during the training session, and time, also, for a few words of wisdom from Bob Paisley as Liverpool's players prepare for a European game in Spain against Real Sociedad. It all turned out right, too, as Real went down against the men from Anfield.

Clough), and next season he saw Clough and Nottingham Forest knock Liverpool out of the European Cup. The first leg of the tie took place on 13 September 1978, and was Liverpool's 100th game in European competition – a game they lost, 2–0. What Bob later termed 'the saddest night of my managerial career' occurred in the return game at Anfield, when Liverpool failed to break down the Forest defence, and so they went out of the glamour competition, while Forest went on to win the trophy.

Still, that was just a hiccup along the way for Bob Paisley, the man whose endeavours not only brought Liverpool huge success, but earned him a visit to Buckingham Palace for the OBE and a trip to the television studios to be featured on the *This Is Your Life* programme.

Having gone out of the European Cup against Forest, Liverpool fought their way through to the semi-finals of the FA Cup, but they came unstuck there, as well, in a Goodison Park replay against Manchester United. Not one to shirk the issue, Liverpool's manager blamed himself for that Cup defeat, saying: 'I made a tactical switch for the replay which I later recognised had been a mistake. I switched to 4–3–3 when, game after game, we had shown that a 4–4–2 formation suited us perfectly. I should have been horse-whipped for the ridiculous decision I made.'

However, Liverpool made the rest of their rivals pay for that semi-final lapse by locking and bolting the door when it came to the League Championship. With four matches to go, there was a seven-point gap at the top, and by the time Liverpool were meeting Aston Villa on the night of Tuesday, 8 May 1979, a draw was going to see the Anfield Reds home and dry. The reserves had already won the Central League Championship – for the ninth time in 11 seasons – so the first-teamers were on their mettle when they met Villa.

Two and a half hours before kick-off time the fans were waiting in their thousands for the Anfield gates to open, and when the referee signalled the start there were more than 50,000 people inside the ground. Villa had won at Anfield the previous term, and they had beaten Liverpool at Villa Park only a few weeks earlier. But after 47 seconds Alan Kennedy struck a goal, then Kenny Dalglish made it 2–0 just before half-time, and in the second half Terry McDermott made it 3–0. It was fitting that the day was the 40th anniversary of Paisley's arrival at Anfield. No wonder the faithful were chanting his name.

Liverpool still had to play at Middlesbrough and Leeds, and they rounded off the season in style by winning both those matches to total 68

■ An occasion for celebration as the 1975 New Year's honours list reveals that one of Liverpool's players has been awarded the MBE. So Ian Callaghan, the popular recipient, was hoisted on to the shoulders of his team-mates, with the smiling approval of manager Bob Paisley.

points and overhaul the 67-point record set by Leeds themselves ten years previously. Liverpool also set a record for the fewest goals conceded (only 16) as they finished with figures which read like this:

P	W	D	L	F	A	W	D	L	F	A	Pts	Position
42	19	2	0	51	4	11	6	4	34	12	68	1st

That, it might have been thought, put Liverpool back on a pedestal and made it almost impossible to progress from there; but they simply rolled on and on . . . the Championship again in seasons 1979-80, 1981-82 and 1982-83; and to go with the title there was the League Cup in seasons 1980-81, 1981-82 and 1982-83 . . . with the European Cup thrown in, for good measure, in season 1980-81. It was indeed a golden era for the Anfield club, and Bob Paisley's astute management had enhanced and confirmed his reputation as a worthy successor to Bill Shankly.

Along the way, he had made several shrewd signings – his first, Phil Neal, followed by Joey Jones (from Wrexham) and Liverpool-born Terry McDermott (via Bury and Newcastle United), while undoubtedly his master-stroke had been the capture of Kenny Dalglish from Celtic. In addition, during the Paisley regime local lads such as Jimmy Case, Phil Thompson and David Fairclough came through the ranks. Thompson graduated not only to international status, but skippered club and country, while Fairclough gained a reputation as an exciting player who could leave his place on the bench and score goals which left the opposition battered and bemused – one notable instance was in a game which Liverpool won at Maine Road. Bob Paisley said that Fairclough – the player they began to call 'Supersub' – provided something different for the opposition to ponder when he got into the action, yet Liverpool's manager still had his reservations; in fact, on one occasion he considered taking Peter Barnes from Manchester City in an exchange deal.

Barnes never arrived at Anfield, and Fairclough subsequently made his exit, but Liverpool marched on and on to success. If Bob Paisley's first term as Manager had ended without the club seeing a trophy on the sideboard, the years that followed more than made up for that slight disappointment. By the time Bob Paisley was ready to bow out, in 1983, he and the club had seen and done just about everything. The tally under Paisley was really remarkable: the League Championship no fewer than half a dozen times, between 1974 and 1983; the European Cup on three occasions between 1977 and 1981; the League Cup three times between 1981 and 1983; and the UEFA Cup. The only trophies which hadn't decorated the Anfield sideboard were the FA Cup and the European Cup-Winners Cup – and Liverpool had missed the FA Cup only by a whisker.

By the time he retired as manager in 1983, Bob Paisley had served the club for 44 years – player, coach, trainer, physiotherapist, assistant manager and manager – and the club showed that it still valued his expertise by announcing his appointment to the board of directors. The lad from Hetton-le-Hole who had arrived at Lime Street Station in May 1939 had certainly come a long way without once leaving Liverpool.

A Treble from Fagan

Joe Fagan's tenure of office as Liverpool's Manager was comparatively brief, but between 1983 and 1985 he carved his own niche in the history of the club, because he steered Liverpool to a unique treble in his first season – one which may never be equalled (League, League Cup and European Cup). And if his period in charge of team affairs ended in tragedy, when Joe handed over the reins to Kenny Dalglish he knew that he could take his leave with no reproaches.

When Bob Paisley intimated that he intended to hand over the managerial reins, once again Liverpool had to make a major decision. In Bob, they had indeed unearthed a worthy successor to Bill Shankly . . . but after the magic of the Paisley era, who could possibly follow that? When the chips were down, Liverpool looked once more inside the club and decided to keep team affairs 'in the family'. Joe Fagan, Bob Paisley's right-hand man, was senior in years, but still youthful at heart, and he – like the rest of the backroom staff – was steeped in the Anfield tradition. He was articulate, knew what he wanted without appearing dogmatic, and had a ready smile which could smooth the way in all his dealings.

When it came to management, he showed that he could cope with the tricky business of following Bob Paisley, just as Bob had shown that he could step into Bill Shankly's shoes and find them a comfortable fit. As a player, Joe Fagan never scaled the heights – he didn't become an international, but he was what people in the game call 'a good professional', and he gave Manchester City good service. He also played for Bradford, Altrincham and Nelson – that was the start of his career on the backroom side, because he was Nelson's player-manager; then he became the trainer at Rochdale before, finally, he fetched up at Liverpool. Bill Shankly knew all about Joe Fagan, since during his days as manager at Grimsby he had tried to sign Joe from Manchester City.

When Bill Shankly stepped down, Joe moved up to become right-hand man to Bob Paisley, and

when Bob retired, Joe got the chance to show what he could do. Some people seemed surprised that he had elected to become Liverpool's manager, at an age when he might well have been thinking about putting his feet up, rather than taking on extra responsibility, but Joe gave the impression that he would have been disappointed not to have been asked to have a go.

He added three players to the squad – John Wark (from Ipswich Town), Michael Robinson (from Brighton) and Paul Walsh (from Luton

Town) – and before he had finished Liverpool had a Danish international in the shape of Jan Molby, who was signed from Ajax of Amsterdam. It was also during Joe Fagan's days as Manager that they parted with a quarter of a million pounds for a teenager called Wayne Harrison, who had shown he could find the net for Oldham Athletic.

Under Fagan, Liverpool powered their way to the League Championship for a third successive season, thus equalling the feats of Arsenal during the 1930s and Huddersfield Town during the

■ Planning for more success, Joe Fagan and his right-hand man, Ronnie Moran, fly with Liverpool for another testing match in Europe. Joe's first season as manager brought the club the League title and two cups.

1920s. Liverpool, having already beaten Everton in the 1984 final of the League Cup – Graeme Souness hit the goal which won the Maine Road replay – were left with the tantalising prospect of making it a handsome and unique treble by going to Rome and winning the European Cup.

It was a tough assignment, because Liverpool were like the early Christians going into the lions' den, since the opposition came from AS Roma and there was no doubt as to which of the teams would be feeling the more at home. But Fagan chose his team wisely, and victory seemed on when Phil Neal gave Liverpool the lead. However, Roma hit back to level the score, and it was still 1–1 when all the time had been used up . . . which meant the drama of a penalty shoot-out. Goals from Neal, Ian Rush, Souness and Alan Kennedy enabled Liverpool to claim a 4–2 victory, so the European Cup came to Anfield for the fourth time in the club's history, and the threefold triumph made Joe Fagan a hero after only 12 months in the managerial chair. Naturally, he received the Manager of the Year award.

The euphoria of that astounding success by a rookie manager, even if he were wise in years, was carried on into the following season – but not for long. With Souness bound for the crack Italian club, Sampdoria, there was a gap to be filled, and as Liverpool tried various players and ploys, so their form drifted up and down. At one stage they stood as low as 18th in the League table, but by the end of the season there was an optimistic air about Anfield again. The semi-final of the FA Cup proved to be one hurdle too many in that competition, and the League Cup had been lost months before, but the League title remained on offer for a time. However, in the final analysis it was Everton who claimed the top spot, leaving Liverpool to settle for the role of runners-up. Yet one last chance remained for glory – another tilt at the European Cup. And once again Joe Fagan steered Liverpool to the final.

As in the previous season, the opposition was provided by an Italian club – this time out, Juventus – though the final was being staged not in Rome, but in the Heysel stadium in Brussels. Even before the final it was being suggested that this would be Joe Fagan's swan-song as Liverpool's manager, and in the event this turned out to be nothing less than the truth . . . though the manner of his going was something no-one would have wished on him.

The tragedy of Heysel, with its story of disaster and death, put a blot on the actual game – in fact,

while it was decided that it should start, the result had really ceased to matter. For the record, Juventus won, by the only goal; and after such a traumatic experience Joe Fagan's reign as manager ended not with cheers, but in tears. Nothing, though, could erase what Joe had achieved in such a short period of time as Liverpool's manager. He had served the club for more than 30 years, and – like Bill Shankly and Bob Paisley before him – his name would be carved with pride as an indelible part of Liverpool's history.

King Kenny Picks Up the Reins

Twice during his career with Liverpool, Kenny Dalglish had to pick up the pieces after experiences which could only be described as traumatic. One was the Heysel stadium disaster, when Liverpool met Juventus in the 1985 European Cup final in Brussels; the other was the Hillsborough disaster, when Liverpool and Nottingham Forest faced each other for fewer than 10 minutes in that ill-starred FA Cup semi-final.

So, hand in hand with the glittering triumphs he enjoyed along the way, there have been days of stark tragedy. Yet through it all, Kenny Dalglish, the Scot who is so sparing with words, emerged as one of the major figures on the British football stage – not that he ever sought the limelight. He has been described in various terms by various people, and he would be the first to acknowledge that he was far from being everyone's favourite. He has been termed abrasive, tetchy, given to sarcasm, unyielding. He had his brushes with Pressmen – indeed, there was a period when relations became strained, to say the least, as the media men made it plain that they were less than happy with the lines of communication from Liverpool.

A team-mate some years ago described Dalglish thus: 'I don't think Kenny trusts anyone . . . not even himself.' On the other hand a member of the Anfield staff, when asked how he got on with Kenny, replied: 'Smashing . . . he gets on with his job, and he lets you get on with yours.' At the end of the day, beyond any question, he did his job as best he could, with the club's interests at heart. And his sudden decision to quit came as a bombshell to the club and the fans.

Dalglish took on the job as a challenge – although the salary must have been an inducement, he was already financially secure. There were people who expressed the view that Kenny Dalglish was so well-heeled – in an area which was suffering from high unemployment – that it was a bit of a liberty for him to have a testimonial match. On the night that Real Sociedad provided the opposition to Liverpool, more than 30,000

■ Eye-level view of the match action from the dug-out, and as the fans reflect the tension of the occasion, so do the facial expressions of Liverpool's backroom team – Kenny Dalglish, Roy Evans and Ronnie Moran, who stepped into the breach after Dalglish had dropped his resignation bombshell.

people gave their emphatic answer by turning up and ensuring that Kenny Dalglish had an emotional, yet happy farewell.

Kenny Dalglish showed that he was a very private man; he is also very much his own man, and he was determined to do things his way. Apart from his considerable record as a player and as a manager, he demanded respect from the way he went about his job, on and off the field. His behaviour after the traumatic events at Hillsborough, where 95 fans lost their lives, was impeccable. He acted with genuine concern for the bereaved, and with real dignity. His manner enhanced not only his own reputation, but reflected an excellent image for Liverpool Football Club. He did not seek to make the headlines, but he saw to it that funerals were attended by players, and he was there himself, time and again.

It was not the first time he had shown his sympathetic nature. After two policemen had been shot at a service station on the M62 motorway, near Oldham, Oldham Athletic manager Joe Royle played a leading part in arranging a Sunday afternoon charity match in aid of the dependents. Kenny Dalglish was one of those who took part in the match, as did former Liverpool team-mates such as Graeme Souness and Phil Neal. Joe Royle, an Evertonian since his earliest days – he played with distinction for the Goodison club and for England – has never been a Liverpool fan and never will be, though he recognises the Anfield club's achievements. And he certainly has a high regard for Kenny Dalglish.

One who shares it is Gordon Strachan, who went on record by expressing the part Liverpool's team boss had played in helping to extend his own career. Strachan said that during their travels together with the international team, he had taken note of the way Dalglish paid attention to

■ A Royal occasion for Kenny Dalglish and his Liverpool players, as they meet the Princess of Wales before the 1988 FA Cup final against Wimbledon. Sadly for Liverpool, their opponents scored the only goal, so the Anfield Reds had to settle for the League Championship alone.

detail – not just in playing, but in off-the-field habits. Following Dalglish's example had helped him to prolong his career and stay at the top.

Dalglish made his final First Division appearance for Liverpool in the home game against Derby County on 1 May 1990; the night that Liverpool received the League Championship trophy for the 18th time in their history. He made his farewell appearance as a player when he left the field towards the end of his testimonial match against Real Sociedad on the night of Tuesday, 14 August 1990. As one scribe recorded, shortly afterwards: 'Love him or hate him, envy him or eulogise over him, Kenny Dalglish at the Anfield end of Merseyside remains a hero.' That he does, indeed. He was 39 years of age when he bowed out as a player, and right the way through his career he had been nothing less than a team man. Despite all the goals he scored, he was never an individualist out for personal glory. It was the team that mattered – and, of course, winning.

When he went out wearing that No. 7 shirt for the last time, in front of 30,461 people at Anfield, it was to turn on a display of football which

evoked memories of his great days with the club . . . days when he had helped to make Liverpool history in matches won gloriously. As he walked off the Anfield pitch, he stripped off his shirt and handed it to 76-year-old Mrs Eileen Leffler, who was watching a match at Liverpool for the first time. It turned out that she had been a Kenny Dalglish fan way back during his days with Glasgow Celtic and, she said later: 'I used to say Kenny should come and play for Liverpool, but I never dreamed that he would. When he arrived at Anfield, it was wonderful . . . and when he handed me that red shirt I was so dumbstruck all I could say was, "Oh, thanks . . ." Now I sleep with it under my pillow!'

After the final whistle that night Dalglish returned to the challenge of trying to steer Liverpool to more major honours in the League and Cup competitions – a job he had done with such conspicuous success since he was handed the job five years previously. It was a job he continued to do in his own style – very much so – and he was not deflected from doing that job in the way he judged was best for the club.

The Dalglish Way

So far as Kenny Dalglish is concerned, football is more than a team game – it's become a squad game; and his team selections often reflected this outlook. There never was a player who enjoyed being dropped or relegated to the role of substitute, but the players at Liverpool had to accept this – very much so – while they had Kenny Dalglish as their boss. However, he had been a player himself and knew the score; and he made certain that the players were the first to know what he was intending to do. He played things very closely to his chest, whether it was team selection or managing successfully to hide injuries from the opposition. And the players, never mind the Press, had to accept it. Kenny Dalglish paid a reported £1.9 million – a British record fee at the time – for Peter Beardsley, yet Beardsley, an experienced England international, had to settle for a place on the bench at times (or even missed out altogether) as Dalglish named a squad to do a job for a particular game.

Beardsley was not the only one who suffered ... Bruce Grobbelaar dropped out through illness, and had to wait a while to get back as Mike Hooper nailed down a place during a run of 25 successive matches. Barry Venison, David Burrows (he cost £500,000), Gary Ablett, Ray Houghton (a near £1 million investment), Steve McMahon (like Beardsley, an England man), Jan Molby ... all these players discovered that you cannot take a first-team place for granted at Liverpool. Molby, indeed, summed it up in a nutshell early on in season 1990-91, after a whole season in which he had been in and out of the side (mostly as a substitute). He found himself hoping for a turn in fortune during the early weeks of the following campaign. The Danish international, who had been offered a new, four-year contract, was seeing out the 12 months left on his remaining term as he waited to see how events unfolded. He had played in the first League game, against Sheffield United at Bramall Lane (where Liverpool won 3–1), but had reverted to the bench before coming back for the testing match against Wimbledon at Plough Lane (where Liverpool won 2–1). The big Dane said: 'When I was named to play at Bramall Lane I thought I was being given an opportunity to stake a claim for a long-term place. I did well, thought I'd every chance of playing in the next match – then I was dropped, for tactical reasons. It wasn't very satisfactory; but how can you argue with a bloke who puts out winning teams every week?'

It's a question which was extremely difficult to answer, so far as the players on the outside looking in were concerned; yet apart from having shown that he was ready, willing and able to back his judgement to the tune of millions of pounds in the transfer market (Beardsley, Houghton, Burrows, Barnes, Ronnie Rosenthal, Glenn Hysen, David Speedie and Jimmy Carter cost a total in the region of £7 million), Kenny Dalglish has demonstrated that local talent was not going to be ignored. Gary Ablett made the breakthrough to first-team football. Steve Staunton is a player signed for a modest fee who has graduated to the senior squad. Week by week, almost, 'the boss' picked the team for the job, as he saw it, even if it meant switching players from bench to starting line-up, and the reverse.

Liverpool's manager also surrounded himself with ex-Liverpool players, and it says a lot for him that there was no backroom revolt when he first landed the job. People who claimed to be insiders reckoned that when Joe Fagan handed over the reins, Phil Neal or John Toshack would be the man to pick them up – and it could well be that the names of those two men figured in the calculations at boardroom level. When Kenny Dalglish got the nod, he became Liverpool's first-ever player-manager with, initially, Bob Paisley available to advise him, if required. Two men who had been at the club considerably longer than Kenny Dalglish – Ronnie Moran and Roy Evans – were asked to carry on their backroom duties under the man being promoted from the ranks of the team, and the fact that they agreed to do so must say something for the respect they had for Dalglish ... and, come to that, the respect he also had for them.

Once again, Liverpool demonstrated their belief in continuity and team effort, and the formula worked well as the honours continued to arrive at Anfield. The League Championship and the FA Cup in the same season, the League title and the FA Cup again ... all this in the first five years of the Dalglish era.

Apart from Ronnie Moran and Roy Evans, Dalglish retained the services of Tom Saunders, Liverpool's youth development officer, and as time went by he made one or two changes which saw other ex-Liverpool men augmenting the backroom staff. Phil Thompson, who had moved on briefly to Sheffield United when his playing days at Anfield came to an end, returned to take charge of the reserve team and Steve Heighway – who, like Thompson, had played alongside Dalglish at Liverpool – came back from the United States to succeed Tom Saunders as youth development officer when Tom officially retired from the job. Later, another former Liverpool player, Hugh McAuley, joined the backroom staff. When there was a change on the scouting side, with Geoff Twentyman leaving Anfield after a lengthy spell as the No. 1 talent-spotter, the job went to big Ron Yeats, once a centre-half of repute and now happy to come back into the Anfield fold as the man whose job it was to ensure that the assembly

line kept on running smoothly, so far as assessing and recruiting new players was concerned.

A Natural Talent for Football

The Kenny Dalglish story started, of course, in his native Scotland. Born in the Dalmarnock district of Glasgow, the young Dalglish first saw the light of day on 4 March 1951. It quickly became apparent that he had a natural talent for sport, because before he became a teenager he was showing promise at tennis and (as an eight-year-old) knocking a golf ball around with some proficiency. But all things considered, he was born to play football, even if he did originally have a spell as an apprentice carpenter. As a youngster he watched Glasgow Rangers and also savoured the mercurial skills of the great Denis Law; and at the age of 15, Kenny Dalglish himself had become a target for the big clubs – in fact, he was invited down to Anfield for a trial with Liverpool, and handed an invitation to pay a return visit. It was an invitation he politely, but firmly, declined. As he explained later: 'I thought I was a bit young to be leaving home.'

The day did dawn when he became, arguably, the most successful – and, for certain, one of the most popular – players ever to don a Liverpool jersey; but that was all in the future as he finally

■ Kenny Dalglish celebrates Liverpool's triumph in the first all-Merseyside FA Cup final.

settled for a soccer career with a club in his native city, not with Glasgow Rangers, but with Glasgow Celtic, whom he joined from a local amateur club, having turned his back on that joinery apprenticeship to try his luck in professional football. In those days his best pal was a youngster called Danny McGrain, and together they climbed aboard a No. 64 bus to report to Parkhead, Celtic's headquarters, in July 1967. Danny McGrain and Kenny Dalglish became two of the mainstays of a Celtic side which won trophy after trophy . . . for eight years, in fact, Dalglish was a first-team regular at Parkhead, and he skippered the side during his last couple of seasons.

Dalglish's first senior outing came during a club tour of Bermuda, and it was against a side called Somerset. By season 1975–76 he was being named Scotland's Player of the Year. By the time he was all set to head south of the border, he had claimed just about every honour going in Scottish football . . . four League Championship medals, four in the Scottish Cup and one in the League Cup.

Dalglish never claimed to be an out-and-out striker and, indeed, he displayed all the skills of a gifted craftsman who could bamboozle opposing defences with soccer science, as well as find the back of the net. Yet by the time he was leaving for Liverpool (his farewell appearance for Celtic was in a pre-season friendly at Dunfermline) he had totalled 112 League goals for Celtic and struck 185 goals in 337 games overall.

Of course, when Bob Paisley signed him for a then record fee of £440,000, Kenny Dalglish was presented with the greatest challenge of his dazzling career, because – whether you viewed him as the direct replacement or as someone whose style was somewhat different – he had to fill the boots of Kevin Keegan, a folk hero to the Anfield faithful until his departure for the Bundesliga and a new career with Sportverein Hamburg. If, after Liverpool's European Cup triumph in 1977, Keegan wanted to pit his talents against the best in Europe, and so take up a new challenge, then Dalglish was doing something similar by leaving Celtic to parade his talents on a wider stage. Irrespective of the transfer fee, or of the money he was commanding in wages, it was still a gamble for the stocky Scot, although Bob Paisley never seemed to have any doubts about the wisdom of spending such a massive sum of money.

Dalglish began to repay Paisley's faith and Liverpool's heavy investment from the first day . . . he scored on his League debut in August 1977, to earn his team a 1–1 draw against Middlesbrough, and he found the net three more times in his next three games. At one time, he had been tipped to take the same route as Keegan and sign for a crack West German club, but it was Liverpool who landed him – and how quickly they were to realise they had another gem.

■ The face was soon to become familiar at Liverpool, for this was Kenny Dalglish, pictured shortly after his £440,000 signing from Glasgow Celtic. He stayed to become a folk hero to the fans, though the manner of his departure caused shock waves in football.

If Keegan had played a notable part in Liverpool's first European Cup success, Dalglish scored the goal which enabled them to retain the trophy, as they met and mastered FC Bruges at Wembley in the spring of 1978. A through ball from Graeme Souness released Dalglish, and from the right he curled the ball over the Bruges 'keeper with clinical precision. That goal won the European Cup and instantly confirmed the status of Kenny Dalglish as a hero in the eyes of the Liverpool supporters. Keegan may not have been entirely forgotten, but he was certainly gone – and here was another idol to take his place.

A Catalogue of Success

The success story of Kenny Dalglish gathered momentum. Hat-tricks? – He struck one in a League Cup match against Wrexham at the Racecourse Ground, hit two more against Manchester City in League games; and he became the second Liverpool player in post-war years to score a century of League goals (the first had been Roger Hunt). In May, 1986, Liverpool went to Stamford Bridge in search of a victory over Chelsea which would secure for them the League title – and Dalglish it was who scored the match-winner, as Liverpool achieved an historic 'double'. By then he had become the club's first-ever player-manager, not to mention the youngest team boss in the First Division; and the end of season 1985–86 (his first in management) was climaxed not just by that golden goal at Chelsea, but by success in the first-ever FA Cup final

■ The end of the FA Cup final in 1989, and the trophy goes to Liverpool, after their victory over Everton . . . so it's the appropriate moment for Kenny Dalglish and the fans to salute each other.

between Liverpool and Everton at Wembley.

As Bill Shankly, Bob Paisley and Joe Fagan had done before him, Kenny Dalglish stepped up to receive the accolade as Manager of the Year, and it was indeed a remarkable record of success by the various team bosses at Anfield. Shankly in season 1972-73; Paisley in seasons 1975-76, 1976-77, 1978-79, 1979-80, 1981-82 and 1982-83; Fagan in season 1983-84; and Dalglish in season 1985-86. More honours were to fall into Kenny's lap, too, because he claimed the Manager of the Year award again at the end of seasons 1987-88 and 1989-90. Like Bill Shankly and Bob Paisley before him, as well, Kenny Dalglish was honoured by being invited to Buckingham Palace to receive an award for his services to football. Shanks and Paisley each collected the OBE, then for Kenny Dalglish it was an MBE to add to his list of achievements which, to put it mildly, were considerable. He had been the first player-manager to lead out an FA Cup final team at Wembley; he had become the first player to chalk up a century of goals in both the Scottish and English Leagues; he had set a record for a British player of 15 goals in the European Cup when he scored twice against BK Odense in September 1983; and the list of credits rolled on . . .

On the international scene, after having won schoolboy honours and four caps at Under-23 level, he had become the most-capped player in Scottish history. His first call-up for Scotland's senior international side came in November 1971, after just 16 League outings with Glasgow Celtic, when he went on as substitute in a match against Belgium. In November 1984, he was scoring against Spain in a game at Hampden Park, and that goal enabled him to equal Denis Law's record of 30 for his country. And, having captained his country and gone on to amass a record tally of international caps – 102 in all – Kenny Dalglish was honoured by being made a freeman of the city of Glasgow.

South of the border, he had achieved equal eminence . . . England's Footballer of the Year for season 1978-79, double Player of the Year in season 1982-83, Manager of the Year after his first season in charge and twice more after that to make it three awards in the space of five years.

By the start of season 1990-91, Kenny Dalglish was saying farewell to his audience as a player, and bowing out with a staggering record of games and goals. . .515 appearances (and 173 goals) for Liverpool; 839 appearances (and 340 goals) during his career. It would have been surprising, of course,

had his name not been linked with one or two other clubs. There was paper talk of a reunion with his former Liverpool team-mate, Graeme Souness, at Ibrox Park, with Souness taking a new role as Glasgow Rangers' supremo and Dalglish joining him as team manager. There was speculation about a return to Glasgow Celtic, as well. And there were even suggestions that when Bobby Robson stepped down as the manager of England, Kenny Dalglish would be one of the foremost names coming up for consideration. The fact of the matter, however, was that even before he made his farewell appearance in his testimonial match, Kenny Dalglish had already had his tenure of office as Liverpool's team boss extended by three years. So there was job security not only for himself, but for his club.

However, mid-way through season 1990-91 he revealed his intention to resign, and he could not be persuaded to change his mind. So Liverpool finally bowed to the inevitable and accepted that they had lost a team boss who, in no uncertain manner, had made his presence felt on the Anfield scene.

Liverpool's customary Championship challenge wobbled in the shock of Dalglish's departure, though Ronnie Moran nobly stepped into the breach as caretaker. In April 1991 it was announced that Graeme Souness, manager and part-owner of Rangers, would be returning to England to manage Liverpool. As a former Reds captain and a sharer with Dalglish of many of the triumphs of the 1970s and 1980s he was superbly qualified to lead the Reds to further glories.

■ Some of the silverware which has gone on view at the Anfield Visitor Centre . . . and the admiring glances here come from three men who contributed hugely to that display during their respective careers as team bosses for Liverpool. From left to right: Joe Fagan, Kenny Dalglish and Bob Paisley.

BILL SHANKLY's reign as manager of Liverpool lasted from 1 December 1959, to the summer of 1974. During that time he took Liverpool back into the First Division, steered them to success twice in the FA Cup (the only times they had won that coveted trophy), saw them achieve success in Europe (the UEFA Cup), and win three League titles. In the course of all this he had been rewarded by being named Manager of the Year and awarded an OBE for his services to the game.

Bob Paisley, who had served under George Kay, Don Welsh and Phil Taylor, and became Shankly's trusted lieutenant, said later: 'It took the arrival of Bill Shankly to set Liverpool's world to rights.' Paisley could look back and remember the near-misses under Don Welsh and Phil Taylor, he could recall how Liverpool almost (and that was the operative word again) achieved glory in the FA Cup as, in 1958, they had reached the sixth round of the tournament – then gone down against Blackburn Rovers at Ewood Park.

It was there that Liverpool, having despatched Southend United, Northampton Town and Scunthorpe United from the competition, looked odds-on to win by the only goal of the game (scored by Bobby Murdoch, after 19 minutes), because they were still leading when there were just eight minutes to go. But fate took a hand as Billy Liddell and Ronnie Clayton, the Rovers' star half-back, collided. At the time, it seemed that Blackburn had suffered most because Clayton split a kneecap and was switched to do a makeshift job at centre-forward. However, fortune favoured the Rovers as the ball came to him when – so the Liverpool players declared – he was standing in an offside position. Clayton tucked the ball away, the Rovers were level . . . and very soon afterwards they were leading 2–1. This time it was Ally McLeod who did the damage, and in case you are wondering, the answer is that this left-winger *did* later become Scotland's team manager as they went to the finals of the World Cup in Argentina. That day at Ewood Park, though, it was Liverpool who suffered as their Cup luck ran out.

Come season 1958-59, and Liverpool suffered an even more agonising humiliation, as they were knocked out of the FA Cup at the third round stage by a non-League outfit, Worcester City. Perhaps even then, in January 1959, the days of Phil Taylor's management were beginning to be numbered. At any rate, when he departed in the November, Bill Shankly took up the gauntlet. Bob Paisley called him: 'The most dedicated man I have ever known in football. Like George Kay, he ate, lived and breathed football – and he supplied the drive which, it seemed, had been the missing factor.'

After a 4–0 home defeat by Cardiff City, however, Shankly was left with plenty to ponder – no wonder he didn't say much when he appeared in the trainer's room under the stand afterwards. But he knew exactly which way he – and Liverpool Football Club – were going, and he communicated his sheer dedication to everyone around him. At the weekends, he was off home to Huddersfield (there to play in a Sunday match with the locals), and during the weekdays he would take part in at least four matches at Liverpool's training ground.

The Kop came to love him, the Press came to seize upon his every word and the opposition came to hate the day their fixture list read 'away to Liverpool'. Like the men who had gone before him, Bill Shankly rang the changes on the playing side as Ron Yeats, Ian St John, Gordon Milne, Willie Stevenson and Peter Thompson arrived. Yeats he introduced to the assembled Pressmen as 'a colossus', Milne was the son of a former Preston team-mate of Shankly's, Stevenson was an ex-Glasgow Rangers player who had tried his luck in Australia, and Thompson was a star with Preston who, having arrived at Anfield, was declared by his new manager to be the final piece of the jigsaw puzzle.

As for the mercurial St John, signed from Motherwell, he made an immediate impact upon the local populace, because when he made his debut for Liverpool it was in a Liverpool Senior Cup match against Everton . . . and he launched his Anfield career by hitting a hat-trick. In addition, Liverpool still had dashing Dave Hickson, Billy Liddell, Jimmy Melia, Ronnie Moran, Louis Bimpson, Alan A'Court and Johnny Wheeler . . . and coming up through the ranks they had Roger Hunt, Gerry Byrne and Ian Callaghan.

During Shankly's first half-season at Liverpool, the club called up no fewer than 26 players for first-team duty, at one time or another, although,

The Years of

Phenomenal Success

by and large, ten players could claim to be the regulars. While Doug Rudham played in 14 matches, Bert Slater wore the goalkeeper's jersey 28 times that term. John Molyneux played in 38 matches, Ronnie Moran was a 42-game ever-present – one of only two players who never missed a match – Wheeler got in 29 games, Dick White missed only one match, Melia totalled 34 appear-ance, Jimmy Harrower 26, A'Court 42, Hickson 27 (21 goals), Liddell 17 and Hunt, by now staking his claims with a vengeance, 36 games (not to mention 21 goals).

In terms of results, after that Cardiff debacle on 19 December, Liverpool won 11 and drew five of their remaining 20 matches . . . although there were some raised eyebrows as they lost 3–0 at Charlton immediately after their Anfield reverse against Cardiff. Liverpool set the record straight by beating Charlton in the Anfield return on 28 December. Ultimately they won four and drew one of their last five games of the season to finish in

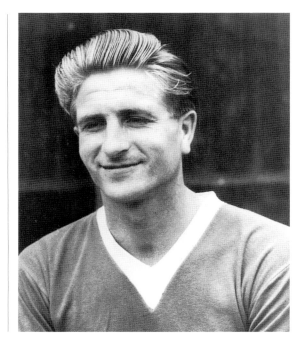

■ *Above:* **One of Liverpool's key men as Bill Shankly built a team geared to achieve success in Cup and League . . . left-back Gerry Byrne, a local lad who certainly made good. And when he finally hung up his boots Shankly, like the fans, mourned his departure.**

■ *Left:* **Dave Hickson, alias 'Dashing Dave', was one of the men who played for both Liverpool and Everton. He knew how to score goals, too.**

third place and revive hopes of promotion in 12 months' time. At the end of the season in which Bill Shankly had taken over from Phil Taylor, this was Liverpool's tally:

P	W	D	L	F	A	W	D	L	F	A	Pts	Position
42	15	3	3	59	28	5	7	9	31	38	50	3rd

The verdict, of course, was that Liverpool had done quite well – but that they would have to do better. Yet once again, although they tried as hard as they knew how, they were unable to improve upon that third place at the end of season 1960-61. Some people, indeed, looked at their record of near-misses during the Welsh-Taylor-Shankly era and began to suggest that there was a jinx on the club when it came to getting back into the First Division. Certainly few clubs could have gone as close more often, or suffered more in the process.

By season 1960-61, the changes were being rung again . . . the likes of Liddell and Arnell were preparing to bow out from the Anfield scene, while Gerry Byrne and Tommy Leishman were regulars, as was Kevin Lewis, another Shankly signing. And Ian Callaghan, who was to set a club record for appearances, added three first-team appearances to the four he had made the previous season. Liverpool kicked off the season with a 2–0 home win over Leeds United – a club they were to meet at Wembley, in Europe, and in close competition for the League Championship as the 1960s unfolded. But there followed a 4–1 defeat at Southampton and a 1–1 draw at Middlesbrough, then a 1–0 home reverse at the hands of the Saints. Shankly's boat, it seemed, was rocking. A win, a draw and two defeats still had people casting a critical eye upon the proceedings. Then Liverpool exploded into winning action.

They began with a 3–2 victory at Anfield over Scunthorpe United, carried on by beating Leyton Orient, Derby County and Lincoln City, drew with Portsmouth, beat Shankly's old club, Huddersfield Town, 4–2, then drew 1–1 with Sunderland. As if to emphasise that they were getting it right, at last, they then hit a winning streak which saw them beating Plymouth Argyle, Norwich City, Charlton Athletic, Sheffield United and Swansea Town in successive matches. Then came a 2–2 draw in the return with Leeds and a 2–1 home win over Rotherham United . . . followed by three defeats on the run. However, a 1–1 home draw against Ipswich Town steadied the boat once more, and Liverpool reeled off five wins and a draw after that, before a run-in which saw them winning, losing and drawing more or less in turn. At the end of this campaign, it was the same old story . . . third place again, as the tally read:

P	W	D	L	F	A	W	D	L	F	A	Pts	Position
42	14	5	2	49	21	7	5	9	38	37	52	3rd

So season 1961-62, it seemed, could well be crucial not only to Liverpool's continued efforts to secure a place in the First Division sun again, but to the career of Bill Shankly as their manager. Don Welsh and Phil Taylor had been and gone . . . would a similar fate await Shankly? The answer came, loud and clear, during season 1961-62, by which time Ian St John had joined the crusade, along with Ron Yeats and Gordon Milne, while Jim Furnell had taken over in goal and Ian Callaghan had staked his claims to become a regular. And youngsters like Chris Lawler, Gordon Wallace and Alf Arrowsmith were on the point of making the breakthrough. At the back, it was Bert Slater who played in the first 29 matches of the season, with Furnell coming in at the beginning of March, to total 13 appearances.

Promotion At Last

This time out, Liverpool got away to a flier . . . six straight wins, with Bristol Rovers, Sunderland, Leeds United, Sunderland again, Norwich City and Scunthorpe United all falling victims to the supercharged assault. Hunt followed up a two-goal strike against Sunderland by hitting a hat-trick in the 5–0 demolition job Liverpool did on Leeds, then he scored two more against Sunderland in the Roker Park return and two goals against Norwich, to take his tally to nine in the first five games. Liverpool scored ten goals in their first three games and didn't concede one; then they stuck four past Sunderland, and two each past Norwich and Scunthorpe to give them this scoring ratio . . . 18 goals for, three against. The seventh match was a 0–0 draw, then there were four more straight wins, with scorelines reading 2–1 (Newcastle United), 5–0 (Bury), 4–0 (Charlton Athletic) and 2–0 (the return with Newcastle). And after their first defeat of the season (2–0 at Middlesbrough), Liverpool were at it again.

It was Walsall who were made to suffer, as they went down 6–1 at Anfield, with Roger Hunt slamming home a hat-trick, and he did the trick again when Liverpool rattled in five goals without reply, against Swansea. There were one or two defeats and the odd draw, but the Liverpool bandwagon rolled on and on . . . a 5–4 win against Norwich City, another Hunt hat-trick in a 5–1 victory over Middlesbrough at Anfield, then 4–1 wins over Derby County, Preston North End and Rotherham United (St John got into the hat-trick act here).

The last eight matches of the campaign brought varied results – four victories, two draws, two defeats, with the final match of the season, at Swansea, ending in a 4–2 success for the home side. But by then, Liverpool had nothing to worry about – except, perhaps, how they would fare now

that they were going up to the First Division as Champions of the Second.

They had accomplished promotion, also, while going on a run in the FA Cup which had taken them to the fifth round of the competition, and in the process they had played five matches, because their fifth-round tie went to two replays. After beating Chelsea 4–3 and Oldham Athletic 2–1, Liverpool lost out against one of Bill Shankly's old clubs, Preston North End. It was 0–0 at Anfield, 0–0 at Preston (after extra time) and 1–0 for North End at Old Trafford.

When the final assessment was made, it was promotion which had mattered most – and Liverpool had certainly achieved this in some style. Kevin Lewis had scored 10 goals in 20 appearances, Alan A'Court had weighed in with eight and Jimmy Melia had totalled a dozen goals, while Ian St John had contributed 18 and Roger Hunt had scored the equivalent of a goal per game . . . and he had played in 41 out of the 42 matches!

Liverpool that season had called upon no more than 17 players, with Gerry Byrne, Gordon Milne, Jimmy Melia and Alan A'Court ever-presents, and Ron Yeats, Tommy Leishman and Roger Hunt all having missed just one match apiece. Ian St John had played in 40 of the games, so this meant that eight players had missed only five matches between them. As for Liverpool's

■ A youthful-looking Roger Hunt, setting out on an Anfield career which was to make him one of Liverpool's favourite sons. He hammered in a club-record number of goals and, with England, claimed a World Cup-winner's medal. The fans referred to him as 'Sir Roger', such was the esteem in which he was held.

■ Soccer may not have been the No.1 sport in America, when Liverpool were the visiting sporting celebrities in 1963, but they certainly rated some special attention – and they got it as they were invited to appear on the famous Ed Sullivan show in New York.

record in terms of victories, goals and points, this was how things stood when the final League tables were published:

P	W	D	L	F	A	W	D	L	F	A	Pts	Position
42	18	3	0	68	19	9	5	7	31	24	62	1st

An examination of those statistics reveals that Liverpool never lost at Anfield, where they amassed 68 of the 99 goals they scored overall; and they won or drew 14 of their 21 away matches. They did the double over Bristol Rovers, Sunderland, Norwich City, Newcastle United, Bury, Charlton Athletic, Preston North End and Plymouth Argyle, and they were watched regularly by crowds of more than 40,000.

So, finally, Liverpool had found a manager and a team which had been able to achieve the longed-for goal . . . First Division football would be resumed at Anfield after an interval of eight seasons. And what Bill Shankly started, men like Bob Paisley, Joe Fagan and Kenny Dalglish have carried on, because Liverpool have never slipped back to the Second Division – indeed, since they gained promotion at the end of season 1961-62, they have never finished lower than eighth in the top flight . . . and, generally, they have been either League Champions or runners-up.

The 1960s, indeed, were the start of something big, because Liverpool went from one success to another, as the League title, the FA Cup and

honours in Europe came their way. Before the dawn of 1970, in fact, they had been Champions twice, lifted the FA Cup for the first time in their history, and been to the final of a European tournament.

Season 1962-63, their first term back in the First Division, came to an end with Liverpool comfortably placed – eighth in the table – and going as far as the semi-finals of the FA Cup, although they met their match when they took on Leicester City at Hillsborough. Leicester went to Wembley because they scored the only goal of the game. But if that was a massive disappointment for the Liverpool fans, their day was about to dawn . . .

By then, the shape of the side had become very firm – Tommy Lawrence in goal, Ronnie Moran and Gerry Byrne at full-back, Ron Yeats at centre-half, Gordon Milne, Willie Stevenson, Jimmy Melia, Ian Callaghan, Ian St John, Roger Hunt and Peter Thompson, with the emerging Chris Lawler always a candidate for a place, along with Alf Arrowsmith and Phil Ferns. In addition, Liverpool had Jim Furnell as cover for Lawrence, and Gordon Wallace striving to make the breakthrough. All in all, they used no more than 17 players during season 1963-64, as they steamrollered their way to the Championship of the First Division.

Gordon Milne, Ian Callaghan and Peter Thompson were ever-presents; Roger Hunt missed only one game and Tommy Lawrence

played in 40 of the League matches, while players such as Byrne, Moran, Yeats and Stevenson played in 33 games or more. Arrowsmith made a score of appearances (and hit 15 goals), while Ferns got in 18 games. As for the goals, Hunt struck 31 in his 41 matches, to demonstrate that what he had done in the Second Division he could repeat in the First, while St John scored 21 goals in his 40 outings and Callaghan contributed eight, with Thompson finishing as a six-goal man.

Roger Hunt had already hit two dozen goals in his first season in the top flight, with St John scoring 19, and this partnership was to flourish even more as the seasons went by . . . although, as it happened, Liverpool's first marksmen of the 1963-64 campaign were Ronnie Moran and Ian Callaghan, as they beat Blackburn Rovers 2–1 at Ewood Park. Two defeats and a draw in their next three matches didn't suggest that Liverpool were the Champions-elect, and they won three and lost two of their next five games. Then they scorched through the opposition, with nine victories and only one defeat in the following ten matches, to send them shooting up the table.

The run started with a 2–1 victory over Everton in the Anfield derby game on the last Saturday in September, with Ian Callaghan the Liverpool hero as he hit both goals; it continued right the way through October and, after Leicester City had halted Liverpool by winning 1–0 at Anfield on 2 November, it was resumed and maintained until mid-December, when Arsenal managed to hold the Anfield Reds to a draw and then Blackburn Rovers inflicted a 2–1 defeat upon them at Anfield. During that extended run, Liverpool scored victories over Everton, Aston Villa, Sheffield Wednesday, West Bromwich, Ipswich Town, Bolton Wanderers, Fulham, Manchester United and Burnley, and after being halted by Arsenal and Blackburn, Liverpool defeated Blackpool, Stoke City and Chelsea in successive matches (Hunt hit four goals in the 6–1 rout of Stoke). Then came a 1–0 defeat by West Ham and a 6–1 hammering of Sheffield United (with St John a three-goal man on this occasion).

By this time, it was the beginning of February, and Liverpool had the League Championship in their sights, although they could take nothing for granted. Indeed, they lost the Goodison Park return game as Everton scored three goals to Liverpool's one and had to settle for a 2–2 draw at Villa Park . . . then they surged forward again, as they won nine and drew one of their next 11 matches. This run began with a 2–1 victory over Birmingham, a 2–2 draw against Sheffield Wednesday and a 6–0 win over Ipswich Town (who had held Liverpool to a 1–0 scoreline at half-time). The run was interrupted by Fulham, who scored the only goal of the game at Craven Cottage, then it was full steam ahead once more,

as Liverpool demolished Bolton Wanderers, Tottenham Hotspur (Hunt hit all three goals), Leicester City, Spurs again, Manchester United and Burnley . . . by which time the title was within Liverpool's grasp. Arsenal were the opposition in their next match, at Anfield, where 48,623 fans turned up in eager expectation of a Liverpool triumph. They were not to be disappointed, either, as the Anfield Reds ran riot.

Shankly's First Championship

On the afternoon of Saturday, 18 April 1964, Liverpool showed everyone in football that they could advance to the Championship in real style, and the Gunners were simply mown down as Liverpool rifled home five goals. Only seven minutes of the game had gone by when St John got his name on the scoresheet, and the cheers could have been heard way beyond Goodison Park, never mind Anfield. Seven minutes before the interval, Arrowsmith struck Liverpool's second goal, and the title was there for the taking. In the second half, Thompson, with a brace of goals after 52 and 57 minutes, had the home supporters singing and almost delirious with delight, before Hunt put the icing on the cake as he rammed home the fifth goal. There were still 30 minutes to go, but there was no way Arsenal could even dream of staging a comeback, and everyone was convinced that this was Liverpool's title triumph.

So it proved, because even though in their last three matches, they lost at Birmingham, then drew away against West Brom and lost again, at Stoke, the League Championship was secured. In the space of three seasons Liverpool had topped the Second Division and the First, and this latest success brought with it a very real bonus, because as the English League Champions they were able to embark upon the quest for the European Cup.

Liverpool's record in that Championship season, of course, was impressive – yet examination of the statistics show it was more impressive than it appeared as they had been beaten five times on their own Anfield pitch. They had won 16 matches there, and hadn't drawn once; as for their away record, that spoke for itself – not to mention the goals they had scored. Overall this was the tally for the season:

P	W	D	L	F	A	W	D	L	F	A	Pts	Position
42	16	0	5	60	18	10	5	6	32	27	57	1st

So it was into Europe and, with a bit of luck, another tilt at the title, with the FA Cup a third target at which to aim in season 1964-65. In the League, while there was no hangover, Liverpool could manage no better than a finishing place of seventh; in the European Cup, their hopes of

triumph were to be dashed on an emotional night in Milan, after they had reached the semi-final stage.

While, for a long time, there lingered that feeling of having been robbed by refereeing decisions in Europe, at the end of the season Liverpool were lifting the FA Cup for the first time in the club's history, and if the final against Leeds United was not one of the greatest ever seen at Wembley, it certainly turned out to be one of the most dramatic, when the story was ultimately told.

Liverpool's FA Cup campaign started with an away game against West Brom, and they came safely through that test as they won by the odd goal in three. Stockport County were the next in line, and when they came to Anfield it seemed a foregone conclusion that Liverpool would stroll to victory . . . but County played with the courage of their convictions, and held the Anfield Reds to a

1–1 draw. When Liverpool went to Edgeley Park for the return game, they did the business by scoring a 2–0 win, and then they went to Burnden Park and beat Bolton Wanderers 1–0. Which meant that in the sixth round they were paired with Leicester City . . . who, after the Hillsborough semi-final of 1963, had come to be regarded as something of a bogy side to Liverpool. Also Leicester had home advantage, but this time out they were held to a no-score draw, and in the Anfield return – watched by more than 53,000 fans – Roger Hunt settled matters, as he struck the match-winner with just under 20 minutes to go. That goal was the only one of the night, but Liverpool weren't worrying about it . . . they were going to Wembley . . . provided, of course, that in the semi-final they could dispose of Chelsea.

The match was staged at Villa Park (which has been a happy hunting ground for Liverpool in Cup-ties on more than one occasion), and on the day Chelsea had to concede that they were second best, although they held Liverpool during the first 45 minutes. With little more than an hour on the clock, Peter Thompson made the breakthrough, and a penalty goal from Willie Stevenson 11 minutes from time sealed the victory for the men from Anfield. They *were* on their way to Wembley, there to meet Leeds United who, to be fair, posed a very real threat. Leeds, indeed, had some star players in the side which Don Revie had assembled, and they reckoned they could win the Cup.

And Now For The Cup

On paper, the final was very evenly balanced, and so it turned out – though there was drama both before and after the big day. When Liverpool met Chelsea, Gordon Milne met his Waterloo, in the shape of a knee injury which ended his hopes of playing against Leeds; and Ian Callaghan was another casualty – in fact, as Liverpool travelled back by train Bob Paisley and Callaghan rode in the guard's van, with Paisley applying iced-water compresses to Callaghan's leg. The treatment never ceased, right up to the day of the final, and Callaghan was able to take his place in Liverpool's line-up, which read: Lawrence, Lawler, Byrne, Strong, Yeats, Stevenson, Callaghan, Hunt, St John, Smith, Thompson.

However, as the game unfolded, Gerry Byrne – who on his debut for Liverpool had put through his own goal! – received an injury which was later revealed to be a broken collar bone. That happened in the early minutes, but Byrne insisted on playing on, while Leeds never realised just how serious the injury was. Byrne, indeed, was to play a notable part in the proceedings, because apart from giving Johnny Giles a run for his money, the Liverpool full-back had a foot in the first goal.

■ Truly this was the Cup that cheers, as Liverpool skipper Ron Yeats and Gordon Milne carry the gleaming trophy round Wembley in 1965, and acknowledge the salute of their fans.

That came in extra time, after the teams had failed to score during 90 minutes. Three minutes into the first period of extra time, Liverpool broke, with Stevenson supplying a pass which Byrne, taking on the overlap, collected and steered across for Hunt to head past 'keeper Gary Sprake. It looked like Liverpool's Cup . . . until Billy Bremner struck for Leeds; but Liverpool rapped back as Ian St John directed a magnificent header into the Leeds net. That goal, after 111 minutes, was the killer, and it ensured that Liverpool had won the Cup.

The following Tuesday night Liverpool took on Inter-Milan at Anfield in the semi-final of the European Cup, and they came through the first leg 3–1 ahead, with the home supporters joyfully singing – in Scouse, not Italian – 'Go back to Italy . . .' to the tune of *Santa Lucia*. The tune was changed, after the second leg, but Liverpool always believed they should have made it to the final.

Having finished seventh in the League, gone out of the European Cup in the semi-finals, and

conquered in the FA Cup, Liverpool turned their attention the following season to the Championship and the European Cup-winners' Cup (they went out of the FA Cup in the third round), and at the end of the campaign they were installed once again as Champions, while just losing out in the European arena, as they reached the final but were beaten at Hampden Park by Borussia Dortmund.

In the Championship race, Liverpool got away to a good start by beating Leicester City, then they faltered with a home defeat against Sheffield United and a draw in the Bramall Lane return. Three straight wins after that altered the complexion of things, and after a draw and a defeat there were two more wins, including a 5–0 scoring spree against Everton, with Hunt (a hat-trick man against West Ham in an earlier match) scoring a brace of goals. Liverpool won seven and drew two matches on the trot between the end of October and mid-December, and they made it a happy New Year with a run of half a dozen victories and a draw in successive matches (Hunt

■ There's nothing the Leeds United defence can do about it, as Ian St John clinches the 1965 FA Cup final with this extra-time winner. For Liverpool, it was their very first taste of success in the competition.

struck three goals again as Sunderland went down 4–0 at Anfield). Fulham halted the victory march on February 26, but Liverpool lost only one of their last ten games after that, to regain their title crown. Their record read:

P	W	D	L	F	A	W	D	L	F	A	Pts	Position
42	17	2	2	52	15	9	7	5	27	19	61	1st

Tommy Lawrence, Gerry Byrne, Ron Yeats, Ian Callaghan and Tommy Smith were 42-game ever-presents; Willie Stevenson and Ian St John missed only one match apiece; Chris Lawler and Peter Thompson each totalled 40 appearances; Roger Hunt played 37 games and Gordon Milne 28. In all, Liverpool called upon only 14 players,

with Geoff Strong getting in 21 games, Alf Arrowsmith playing in three and Bobby Graham in one. Hunt totalled 30 goals in his 37 appearances, St John found the net ten times. And as a result of their title success, Liverpool went back into the European Cup.

Season 1966-67 turned out to be a disappointing one, though, because Liverpool were eliminated from Europe in the second round of the European Cup competition, they were knocked out of the FA Cup by Everton in the fifth round, and they finished in fifth place in the First Division. One indication of their uncertain form was the fact that they used 18 players during the course of the season, and there were a few new names among them in Ian Ross, Emlyn Hughes

■ Four men who wore Liverpool's colours savour the club's 1964 League Championship success. Bobby Graham and Gordon Wallace belong to that era, while Billy Lacey and Joe Hewitt figure in the glory days of the distant past.

(signed from Blackpool) and Davie Wilson.

At the end of season 1967-68, Liverpool had improved to finish third, but they had gone out of the European Fairs Cup in the third round and the FA Cup in a sixth-round, second replay against West Brom at Maine Road. By then, Hughes was a regular, Tony Hateley had been signed, Strong and Stevenson seemed to be on their way out as regulars, and names like Peter Wall and Doug Livermore had appeared on the first-team scene.

In season 1968-69, Liverpool were knocked out of the Fairs Cup in the first round, finished as First Division runners-up, and were beaten in a fifth round FA Cup replay by their old bogymen, Leicester City. Peter Wall was staking his claims to a regular place, with Byrne apparently bowing out; Alun Evans, the first teenager to cost £100,000 in the transfer market, had worn the No. 9 shirt many more times than Hateley, and Brian Hall, a university graduate, was striving to make the grade as a Liverpool professional. It was obvious that Liverpool's team was undergoing some surgery, though the bulk of the side retained its old, familiar look. But in season 1969-70 Liverpool went out of the Fairs Cup in the second round and out of the FA Cup in the sixth round, at Watford, while finishing fifth in the League. And they had called upon no fewer than 23 players, including new signings Larry Lloyd, Alec Lindsay and Ray Clemence. In addition, home-grown talent such as Steve Peplow, Roy Evans and John McLaughlin were being given a chance to show their paces.

Bill Shankly thought his team of the 1960s would have lasted longer than it did, but when the time came, he didn't hesitate to ring the changes, and so two dozen players featured in the line-up during season 1970-71. Ian St John – who didn't easily concede his right to be a first-team regular – said that for a time he had refused to admit his legs wouldn't take him where his brain told him he should go; and on a night flight back from a European tie, Ron Yeats, then about to bow out as a player, addressed everyone over the inter-com with these words: 'This is your ex-captain speaking . . .'

Liverpool's new-look team for the 1970s was taking shape, and the club was about to embark upon another era of greatness – one, indeed, which surpassed even that which had gone before.

A New Team For The 1970s

As Bill Shankly wrestled with the problem of assembling another successful side for the 1970s, he reluctantly began to discard some of the great names in the game . . . goalkeeper Tommy Lawrence, for example, made way for Ray

■ *Above:* **Brian Hall graduated with a B.Sc. degree from university, then graduated again, this time as a soccer professional, as he totalled more than 200 appearances in Liverpool's new-look team of the 1970s.**

■ *Left:* **Signed from Bury, Alec Lindsay totalled almost 250 appearances for Liverpool, and scored some vital goals – several from the penalty spot.**

Clemence; Ron Yeats and Ian St John made infrequent appearances, as replacements came into the side. By the end of season 1970-71 Clemence, Chris Lawler, Tommy Smith, Larry Lloyd, Emlyn Hughes, Bobby Graham, new-boy Jack Whitham, Brian Hall and another university graduate, Steve Heighway, were the names to note as Liverpool made a renewed bid for glory.

It was a season in which they knocked Everton out of the FA Cup in the semi-finals (Arsenal beating the Reds 2–1 at Wembley); a season in which they reached the semi-finals of the European Fairs Cup; a season in which they finished fifth in the First Division; a season in which they had called upon two dozen players again – including a slim Welshman by the name of John Toshack, who had cost them £110,000 from

Cardiff City after having impressed with a hat-trick display.

The year 1971 was also a year in which Liverpool snapped up a virtual unknown from Scunthorpe United for a modest £35,000. His name was Kevin Keegan, and he, Toshack and Heighway were to have a devastating impact upon the other First Division defences. Roger Hunt had gone, Ian St John and Ron Yeats were about to make their exit. Of course, they were not (and never would be) forgotten; however, the new names swiftly became Anfield heroes.

Keegan kicked off with a debut goal against Nottingham Forest, Toshack and Heighway each scored in Liverpool's second match, and all three were on the mark in the fifth game of season 1971-72. By the end of the campaign, Liverpool

■ Chris Lawler gets airborne for Liverpool. Chris, the 'quiet man' of Anfield, totalled more than 500 appearances and scored 61 goals during a career spanning 14 seasons with the club.

still had to make the breakthrough, as they finished third, but the list of players called up had been reduced to 19, and the shape of the side had become much firmer. It was Clemence, Lawler, Lindsay, Smith, Lloyd, Hughes, Keegan, Heighway, Toshack, Hall . . . and the evergreen Ian Callaghan. Peter Thompson was making way, and so were Alun Evans and Jack Whitham, while a newcomer on the fringe was local lad Phil Thompson, along with Ian Ross, Bobby Graham and Phil Boersma.

Season 1970-71 had been one of innovation and, perhaps, the success (or near-success) of the new-look Liverpool had surprised many people. Season 1971-72 was not quite as exciting, but no question about it – season 1972-73 was going to be make or break for quite a few reputations at Anfield. In the event, those reputations were made, and not broken, as Liverpool achieved a double unique to the club by carrying off their first European trophy and claiming the League Championship, as well. A fourth-round defeat by Manchester City in an FA Cup replay became something insignificant.

There was a buzz about Anfield as Liverpool won four and drew one of their opening five matches; and after a hiccup as they lost two on the trot, they marched onwards with six wins and three draws before going down 2–0 at Old Trafford. There followed three straight wins, two draws, four straight wins, one draw, then two defeats, before the team got back on the rails by losing only twice in the final 13 matches (eight of which were won).

Liverpool's new-look side had indeed come of age; no dispute about that. It had talent, it was ready to battle all the way, as was proved in the

dramatic final of the UEFA Cup against Borussia Moenchengladbach, on foreign soil. By this time, also, Liverpool had added the League Cup to the list of trophies they were seeking, and they reached the fifth round of that competition – indeed, they played no fewer than eight matches before going out against Tottenham Hotspur in a replay, having accounted for Carlisle United, West Bromwich Albion and Leeds United (all two-match affairs).

Season 1972-73 saw Liverpool call upon just 16 players, and they included the regulars of the previous term, plus new signing Peter Cormack, reserve 'keeper Frank Lane, Phil Boersma, Trevor Storton (signed from Tranmere Rovers) and Phil Thompson, who was later to captain both club and country. Lloyd, Lawler and Callaghan were

the ever-presents, Clemence, Hughes and Keegan missed only one match apiece, Heighway played 38 games, Lindsay 37, Smith 33, Cormack 30, Toshack 22, Boersma 19 and Hall 17. Toshack and Keegan each claimed 13 goals, Cormack eight, Hughes and Boersma seven apiece, Heighway half a dozen. The Liverpool tally for the season:

P	W	D	L	F	A	W	D	L	F	A	Pts	Position
42	17	3	1	45	19	8	7	6	27	23	60	1st

Not surprisingly, there was a note of genuine optimism about the prospects for season 1973-74, but when it came to the European Cup, Liverpool were down and out after the second round, and although they reached the fifth round of the

League Cup, Wembley proved a mirage as Wolves beat them 1–0 at Molineux. That left the League and the FA Cup, and though Liverpool chased as hard as they knew how, the title was to elude them, and they had to be content with second place.

FA Cup Winners Again

The FA Cup, however, turned out to be something different again – yet Wembley was not reached without its alarums and excursions. Indeed, the third round was a bit of a shocker as Doncaster Rovers, from the foot of the Fourth Division, held the Anfield Reds to a 2–2 draw on their own ground. Liverpool, though, won the

Belle Vue replay 2–0 – then found themselves being held again on home soil, as Carlisle United gained a 0–0 draw. Once more, a 2–0 scoreline saw Liverpool home and dry in the replay, then it was Ipswich Town at Anfield, and this time there was no delay – Ipswich were despatched, beaten 2–0.

Bristol City away posed a sixth-round threat, however, and it required a goal from John Toshack, shortly after half-time, to produce a Liverpool victory . . . and then the semi-final brought Liverpool up against their old Cup adversaries, Leicester City. At Old Trafford, the contest was even, and the scoreline blank; so the stage switched to Villa Park. Again there was no score when the half-time whistle blew . . . but in the second half Liverpool cut loose, and Brian

■ Liverpool-born and bred, Phil Boersma gave the Anfield club good service during seven seasons, as he totalled the best part of 100 first-team appearances.

Hall broke the deadlock one minute after the restart. Kevin Keegan pierced the Leicester defence after 62 minutes, and four minutes from time John Toshack's goal made the final scoreline read: Liverpool 3, Leicester City 1.

Newcastle United provided the opposition at Wembley, and in their team that day were two players who, eventually, were to wear the colours of Liverpool. One was a man born and bred in the North-East, Alan Kennedy; the other was a Liverpudlian, Terry McDermott, whose career had taken him from Bury to Tyneside. Neither Kennedy nor McDermott that afternoon at Wembley could do much to stop the Liverpool onslaught, and the same applied to striker Malcolm Macdonald, who failed to live up to his reputation as 'Supermac'.

Right the way through, it seemed there would be only one winner, as Newcastle failed to hit form and Liverpool rose to the occasion, with Keegan and Heighway making it a scoring double act. It

■ You're the greatest . . . and as Liverpool fans salute Bill Shankly after the Wembley triumph of 1974, he in turn acknowledges them, and the fantastic support they gave his team.

may have been 0–0 at half-time, but Liverpool soon altered that situation as Keegan clocked up his first goal of the game after 57 minutes, then Heighway rammed home the second with 15 minutes to go. Keegan rounded it off two minutes from time, to produce a 3–0 victory, and the Liverpool fans left Wembley stadium dancing a conga as they sang: 'We've all been to Wembley! We've all been to Wembley!' Indeed they had – and seen Liverpool lift the Cup.

Shankly Takes His Leave of Anfield

What the players and fans didn't know, as they celebrated success that night, was that Bill Shankly's reign had all but ended. The FA Cup was to be his parting gift as he retired from the fray, and before the start of a new season Bob Paisley had been installed in the managerial chair. He didn't make wholesale changes during his first term in office, but Ray Kennedy – Shankly's last signing (from Arsenal) – and Phil Neal (Paisley's first buy), Terry McDermott and Jimmy Case appeared on the Anfield scene, to bolster the playing squad. Kennedy and Neal each played 23 games during season 1974-75, McDermott made 14 appearances, and Case just one.

At the end of the campaign, it could be seen that Liverpool had lost out in the second round of the European Cup-winners Cup and in the fourth round of the League Cup, while in the League they had finished as runners-up. As for the FA Cup, they had fallen to Ipswich Town in round four. So it was a case of second-best all round, and hoping for better from season 1975-76. Hope

which, indeed, was amply translated into realisation.

Liverpool once again went out of the FA Cup in the fourth round, survived no further than a third-round replay in the League Cup . . . but went on and on to win the League Championship and couple with it the UEFA Cup, as they beat the Belgian club, FC Bruges. That season saw Joey Jones, signed from Wrexham, and David Fairclough, who was to become labelled as 'Supersub', made their mark – one as a no-nonsense defender, the other as a marksman whose mercurial style set people's pulses racing.

At the start of the League season, Liverpool went to Loftus Road and lost 2–0 against Queen's Park Rangers – who were to chase them all the way in the title race. There followed a 2–2 draw against West Ham at Anfield, then three wins and a draw before defeat against Ipswich Town at Portman Road. Liverpool then went 10 games without defeat (there were six victories), and after suffering a shock 3–1 defeat by Norwich at Anfield they were to win six and draw six matches, before being halted by Arsenal. Goals came from different areas of the team, but Toshack was a hat-trick man twice over – against West Ham and against Birmingham City. The Arsenal defeat was followed by a draw against Derby County and another defeat, at the hands of Middlesbrough at Anfield – but in turn after that Birmingham, Norwich, Burnley, Everton, Leicester City, Aston Villa, Stoke City, Manchester City and, finally, Wolves, were made to pay the price as Liverpool won eight of their last nine matches (the draw was at Villa Park). So the final tally read:

P	W	D	L	F	A	W	D	L	F	A	Pts	Position
42	14	5	2	41	21	9	9	3	25	10	60	1st

■ *Above:* **Steve Heighway turns away, as Newcastle United go two goals down during the FA Cup final of 1974.**

■ *Left:* **Welsh international Joey Jones, signed by Liverpool from Wrexham, and a great favourite with the Anfield faithful. He helped Liverpool to win the European Cup as he totalled almost a century of games before returning to his first club 'down the road'.**

Two trophies, including one from Europe, in Bob Paisley's second term as team boss . . . how, people asked, could Liverpool follow that? The answer came in season 1976-77, as Liverpool went full tilt for the European Cup, a League title repeat and the FA Cup, as well. In the end, they failed narrowly to achieve the treble, succeeded gloriously in claiming the European trophy and the

and Heighway in 39, Keegan in 38 and Callaghan – still going strong – in 32. The Liverpool League record:

P	W	D	L	F	A	W	D	L	F	A	Pts	Position
42	18	3	0	47	11	5	8	8	15	22	57	1st

In the FA Cup, Liverpool saw off Crystal Palace (winning the replay away), Carlisle United, Oldham Athletic, Middlesbrough and Everton (in the semi-finals – that took a Maine Road replay). And in the final Manchester United just about triumphed, 2–1, at Wembley. Liverpool then set off on their European Cup safari, and in Rome they defeated Borussia Moenchengladbach, just as they had done in the UEFA Cup final of 1972-73.

It was, perhaps, the most glorious success (or failure, depending upon which way you looked at it) that any English club had achieved, even allowing for Manchester United's European Cup conquest of the 1960s and Bill Shankly's UEFA Cup/League Championship double success a few years earlier. And, of course, as had happened 12 months previously, people reckoned that this would be an almost impossible act for Bob Paisley and Liverpool to follow. It was – and it wasn't.

Twelve months later, Liverpool were bemoaning their bad luck in a League Cup final replay against Nottingham Forest at Old Trafford, bemoaning their fate in the League, as they finished in second spot, ignoring their third-round exit from the FA Cup . . . and celebrating their retention of the European Cup after the final against FC Bruges at Wembley.

While the League Cup had finally been lost, that campaign had been remarkable for the way Liverpool had gone through nine matches while staying on the trail of the title and the European trophy. Having beaten Chelsea and Derby County, they had seen off Coventry City in a replay and given thanks to a new player on the staff for a hat-trick in the fifth round tie at Wrexham. Then they had overcome Arsenal in the semi-final legs, outplayed Nottingham Forest at Wembley, and been beaten in the Old Trafford replay by a debatable penalty goal.

That hat-trick at Wrexham was scored by a player destined to loom large in the annals of Liverpool's history, because the marksman was Kenny Dalglish – signed on the departure of Kevin Keegan for SV Hamburg. Dalglish had scored on his League debut for Liverpool, and in the next two League games, and by the end of the season he was a 20-goal man in 42 First Division matches . . . also the man whose goal had kept the European Cup at Anfield.

As the end of the 1970s approached, Liverpool's ambitions were still as great as ever, and season 1978-79 was to end on another note of triumph,

■ Skipper Emlyn Hughes and David Fairclough celebrate with the Championship trophy, and though Liverpool missed out on the FA Cup, they carried off the European Cup, to make it a double, if not a treble, in season 1976-77.

League Championship. And, as they surged towards the top of the First Division, they were never beaten on home ground.

Five wins in the first half-dozen matches set the scene, five wins and a draw in successive games during October and November maintained the pace; and from December 27 to May 16, Liverpool lost only three times in 22 outings – there were 11 victories during that spell. As for the team, it had been reinforced by former Everton striker David Johnson, signed from Ipswich Town, and overall only 17 players were called up for duty. Of these, Clemence, Neal and Hughes played in all 42 games, Ray Kennedy in 41, Jones

even if they had fallen at the first hurdle in the European Cup (to Nottingham Forest, the eventual winners), in the second round of the League Cup, and in an FA Cup semi-final replay against Manchester United at Goodison Park. Once again, they were so close to more than one trophy, but in the final analysis they were not too unhappy – because they had regained the Championship of the Football League.

A Record Championship Season

They started out like a house on fire - ten victories and one draw in successive matches, with Ipswich Town conceding three goals, Manchester City four and Tottenham Hotspur seven, as Liverpool turned on an Anfield display even now rated as one of their best ever. Spurs simply couldn't stop them, and Dalglish and Johnson shared four goals, with McDermott snapping up the seventh in superb style. Then Norwich City leaked four goals, Derby County five, and by the time that Chelsea had been beaten, Liverpool had totalled 35 goals and conceded just four in those first 11 fixtures. Inevitably, it seemed, their gallop could be stopped by only one club . . . and, sure enough, it was Everton who beat them by the only goal, at Goodison Park, in their 12th League game.

If people thought the Goodison defeat had brought the Liverpool bandwagon to a halt, they were mistaken, because Paisley's men went through their next five games unbeaten, and from Boxing Day to 17 May, through 22 matches with just one defeat, at Villa Park. For the rest, they beat Manchester United, West Brom, Birmingham, Norwich and Derby County, drew with Chelsea, Coventry City and Everton, defeated Wolves, Ipswich, Arsenal, Wolves again and Manchester United for the second time. Then, after the Villa Park reverse, Liverpool beat Bristol City, drew with Southampton and Nottingham Forest, beat Bolton, Southampton, Aston Villa, Middlesbrough and Leeds United.

Through this rich seam of victories the names of Dalglish and Johnson figured prominently, as both scored goals in almost every match. By the end of the season Dalglish, having made Keegan's No. 7 shirt his personal property, had struck 21 goals in 42 League games while Johnson had scored 16 in 30 appearances. Ray Kennedy had chipped in with ten goals, Terry McDermott and Graeme Souness with eight apiece, Jimmy Case with seven, and full-back Phil Neal with five.

As in season 1976-77, Liverpool had not been beaten in one game on their own midden, and they had lost only four matches away. In addition, they had set a defensive record by conceding only 16 goals (four of them at Anfield) in their 42 matches, and they had totalled a record number of points (68). Only 15 players had appeared in the first team, and they included a young Scot

■ Local boy makes good . . . and Jimmy Case certainly did just that when he broke through to the first team. He made more than 250 appearances, scored some vital goals, and he worked prodigiously in the cause of the team.

named Alan Hansen (34 appearances) and a local lad called Sammy Lee. Both were to make their mark in the red jersey, as time went by. But, so far as season 1978-79 went, this was how it all stacked up for Liverpool:

P	W	D	L	F	A	W	D	L	F	A	Pts	Position
42	19	2	0	51	4	11	6	4	34	12	68	1st

The last season of the decade produced yet another challenge for Bob Paisley and his players: could they carry on winning virtually one trophy every season? They went very close to claiming no fewer than three trophies during the campaign of 1979-80, because in the FA Cup they reached the

semi-finals and lost to Arsenal only after a four-match marathon, while in the League Cup they were pipped by Nottingham Forest, also at the semi-final stage. It has to be admitted that in the European Cup, Liverpool were sent packing in the first round . . . but they stayed on the trail of that trophy as they retained the Championship of the First Division.

They used 17 players that season, the regulars being augmented by Israeli international Avi Cohen, 'keeper Steve Ogrizovic (another signing), home-grown Colin Irwin, Sammy Lee and David Fairclough. By now, Steve Heighway was close to the end of what had been a long and illustrious career as a first-team regular, as he

found himself mostly on the bench and wearing the No. 12 jersey, while David Johnson had taken over at No. 9. As for Ogrizovic, he got in just one game as Clemence made 41 appearances, while Fairclough hit five goals in 14 games.

A 0–0 home draw against Bolton Wanderers wasn't what the Anfield fans had anticipated for starters, but a 3–1 victory over West Brom in the next match was much better; however, a 3–2 defeat by Southampton at The Dell was a bit of a dampener, and although Coventry City went down 4–0, Liverpool had to settle for draws against Leeds United and Norwich City before being beaten by Nottingham Forest. So the first seven games brought Liverpool only two wins.

Their next 16 matches, however, changed the whole complexion of their season, because Liverpool went through those games unbeaten as they clocked up no fewer than a dozen victories. Not until 19 January 1980 did they lose again, and that defeat came at Coventry, by the only goal. That left Liverpool with 18 games to go to the end of the campaign, and they lost only three of them . . . against Wolves (1–0), Spurs (2–0) and Middlesbrough (1–0). All three defeats came away from home.

Norwich City posed some problems at Carrow Road, as they held Liverpool to a 2–2 scoreline at half-time, but the Reds triumphed 5–3 in the end, and it was David Fairclough who emerged as a hat-trick hero, though the last two goals came from Kenny Dalglish and Jimmy Case, the first with two minutes and the second with just 60 seconds remaining.

While Liverpool were powering their way towards a title repeat, they were also battling mighty hard to get to Wembley in the two domestic Cup competitions. In the League Cup they disposed of Tranmere Rovers, Chesterfield, Exeter City and Norwich City before tackling Nottingham Forest in the semi-finals. At Nottingham, the final score was 1–0 in Forest's favour, and in the Anfield return Forest defended resolutely to defy Liverpool as the match ended all square (1–1), and Brian Clough's side went to Wembley.

In the FA Cup Liverpool hammered Grimsby Town 5–0, beat Nottingham Forest 2–0 at the City Ground, beat Bury at home and Spurs at White Hart Lane, then tried conclusions with Arsenal in the semi-finals. The game was at Hillsborough, and the scoreline finished blank. The teams met again at Villa Park, and after extra time it was still stalemate, with a 1–1 result . . . and the same thing happened again when a second replay was staged at the Midlands ground. Finally, Liverpool and Arsenal trekked to Highfield Road, Coventry, to see if they could settle this domestic dispute, and at long last there was a result, with the Gunners grabbing the only goal.

So Liverpool's visions of a double (or even a treble) had vanished but they had the satisfaction of knowing that at the end of the day they had kept the Championship trophy at Anfield. It meant that since Bob Paisley had taken over in season 1974-75 Liverpool had collected some silverware in five out of the six seasons of his stewardship – a tribute not only to Paisley's canny judgment, but to the quality of the players in his squad. The last season of the decade ended with Liverpool proudly holding on to their League title as their record read:

P	W	D	L	F	A	W	D	L	F	A	Pts	Position
42	15	6	0	46	8	10	4	7	35	22	60	1st

■ *Opposite:* **David Fairclough, the flame-haired striker the Anfield faithful joyously hailed as 'Supersub'. His goal against St Etienne in 1977 paved the way for Liverpool to go on to the final in Rome and win the European Cup for the first time.**

Triumphant Into The 1980s

A new decade, and the 1980s saw new names appearing in Liverpool's squad, as they signed Richard Money, Ian Rush and Ronnie Whelan, and groomed Howard Gayle, Kevin Sheedy and Colin Russell. Money, Gayle, Sheedy and Russell were to move on (Sheedy to become a first-teamer with Everton), while Rush and Whelan were to become key men in the first team as Liverpool went in search of more trophies. Rush, indeed, became a master-marksman, while Whelan emerged as a midfielder and eventually took on the role of captain.

Meanwhile, although nobody knew it at the time, the days of Ray Clemence as Liverpool's 'keeper were numbered, even though he played 41 games during the League campaign of season 1980-81; he was to join Tottenham Hotspur, and Liverpool were going to need another 'keeper who would be pitched straight into the firing line. That 'keeper turned out to be a Zimbabwean international named Bruce Grobbelaar, an extrovert character who, like Ray Clemence and Tommy

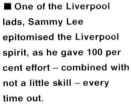

■ One of the Liverpool lads, Sammy Lee epitomised the Liverpool spirit, as he gave 100 per cent effort – combined with not a little skill – every time out.

Lawrence before him, stayed to nail down the goalkeeping spot for season after season.

By this time, Graeme Souness had become an influential figure in the Liverpool side, after his transfer from Middlesbrough during the latter part of the 1970s, and Sammy Lee was a regular, though David Fairclough was still not able to command a place week in, week out. Season 1980-81, in fact, saw Liverpool in a somewhat transitional stage again, as they called up 23 players for first-team duty – although the names, for the most part, remained the same.

Once again Liverpool were to achieve a double – this time, they collected one of the domestic cups and the European Cup for a third time – as they had to settle for a finishing place of fifth in the First Division and an FA Cup exit at the hands of Everton in a fourth-round tie at Goodison Park. In the League, Liverpool won 17 matches but lost three times at Anfield and five times away from home, so their final tally of 51 points was below the total needed to top the table.

On the European Cup front, Liverpool came up against the Spanish aces of Real Madrid in the

final, and in the Parc des Princes stadium in Paris an Alan Kennedy goal was a match-winner, just as extra time seemed certain.

Liverpool's capture of the League Cup was their first success in this domestic competition, and they had to do it the hard way, because West Ham took them to a replay at Villa Park, after seemingly having lost the Wembley final. Eyebrows were raised at the start of the League Cup campaign when Liverpool went to Bradford and were beaten 1–0 by City; but in the Anfield return there was no mistake, as Liverpool rattled in four goals without reply. Swindon Town tried their luck at Anfield, and went home feeling the draught after Liverpool had scored a nap hand of goals, then Portsmouth were beaten 4–1 at Anfield and Birmingham City fell 3–1 there. So it was Liverpool versus Manchester City in the semi-finals, with the first leg at Maine Road – where Ray Kennedy's goal, nine minutes from time, was to prove invaluable.

Liverpool hoped to build upon that 1–0 lead when City visited Anfield, but while Kenny Dalglish struck in the first half, City equalised in the second, so the Kennedy goal was the one which tipped the scales in Liverpool's favour. And so to Wembley for the meeting with West Ham. It was a final which went beyond normal time, with no goals during the first 90 minutes and no goals during the first period of extra time, either. Then Alan Kennedy struck, after 118 minutes, and at that moment you would have bet upon the League Cup going to Liverpool. But Ray Stewart was the Hammers' hero as he despatched a penalty, and the whole thing had to start all over again at Villa Park, though not until a fortnight later. And for the replay, Liverpool rang the changes... Phil Thompson in for Colin Irwin, Ian Rush in for Steve Heighway, with Jimmy Case (who had gone on at Wembley for Heighway) deputising for the absent Graeme Souness. After the 100,000 gate at Wembley, Villa Park housed a comparatively modest crowd of 36,693, but the fans who made the trip from Merseyside got their money's worth, because while West Ham beat Ray Clemence, Kenny Dalglish and Alan Hansen tipped the scales Liverpool's way with two goals in the space of four minutes. Hansen's goal was the winner, and Liverpool lifted the League Cup for the first time in their history. It went on the Anfield sideboard alongside the European Cup.

Ian Rush played only seven First Division games that season, but the following term he boosted that total to 32 – and hit the headlines as he notched 17 goals. It was a season in which Liverpool collected the First Division title yet again, a season in which they went out of the FA Cup in round five, the European Cup in round three ... and kept their grip on the League Cup (which was rechristened for the new season the

Milk Cup). Two trophies in season 1980-81, two again 12 months later.

In the Milk Cup, Exeter City sampled Liverpool's finishing power with a vengeance as the Reds rifled five goals at Anfield and six in the return (Rush scored twice in each leg); then Middlesbrough crashed 4–1 (Rush on the mark again), and Arsenal were beaten 3–0 in a replay, after extra time. Barnsley drew 0–0 at Anfield, but were shattered by a 3–1 scoreline at Oakwell, and in the two-legged semi-final Ipswich Town lost 2–0 at Portman Road (McDermott and Rush), then drew 2–2 at Anfield (Rush and Dalglish), so Liverpool cruised through on a 4–2 aggregate.

Tottenham Hotspur were waiting for them at Wembley, and at half-time Spurs were a goal to the good. It looked all over for Liverpool as only three minutes remained ... then Ronnie Whelan produced a goal to gain extra time and, after 111

■ The Liverpool fans affectionately called Alan Kennedy Barney Rubble, after the TV character. He turned out to be Liverpool's match-winner on two occasions in the final of the European Cup.

THE REDS IN THE CHARITY SHIELD

■ *Above:* **Liverpool picked up the Charity Shield in 1989 after beating Arsenal 1–0 at 'Anfield South'.**

LIVERPOOL'S prowess in the Championship, and their Cup excursions to Wembley, have made them one of the most regular contestants in the Charity Shield match which is the showgame pipe-opener to the season. In 1990, indeed, they went close to claiming the shield as their own, because they were going for a hat-trick of successes . . . but Manchester United barred the way, and a 1–1 draw meant that the shield was shared by the clubs during the following 12 months.

Liverpool have been to Wembley so often during the past 25 years that their players have come to know it by another name . . . and that is 'Anfield South'. The teams may have changed through the years, but the nickname has stuck. And there has been another feature of their regular visits to the famous stadium, because on more than one occasion in recent seasons Liverpool have had their revenge against opponents who, just a few months previously, had achieved a decisive success against the Anfield Reds.

For instance, Wimbledon were shock winners of the FA Cup final in 1988, as they scored the only goal; but, come

■ *Left:* **Steve McMahon in action for Liverpool against Manchester United in the 1990 Charity Shield match at Wembley, where the teams drew and so shared the trophy.**

four goals with Manchester United. In 1966 the Charity Shield became an all-Merseyside affair, with Liverpool beating Everton 1–0. There was a unique touch about that game, too, because apart from the Charity Shield itself, three other glittering pieces of silverware were on display . . . the FA Cup, the League Championship trophy, and the World Cup which England had just won.

In 1971 Liverpool lost 1–0 against Leicester City, in 1974 it was 1–1 against Leeds United, then in 1976 Liverpool carried off the Charity Shield with a 1–0 victory over Southampton. From then on, there was almost an annual trek to Wembley for the pre-season showgame . . . in 1977 it was Liverpool 0, Manchester United 0; in 1979 it was Liverpool 3, Arsenal 1; and in 1980 it was Liverpool 1, West Ham United 0.

There was a similar scoreline when Liverpool met Tottenham Hotspur in 1982, and Liverpool were there again in 1983, 1984 and 1986 . . . they lost 2-0 to Manchester United, 1-0 to Everton, then drew 1-1 with Everton. So, at that stage, Liverpool had played 14 times in the Charity Shield and won five and drawn five. Come 1988, and Liverpool were beating Wimbledon 2-1, while in 1989 they were meeting Arsenal and scoring a 1-0 victory. Then, in 1990, it was Wembley again, with a 1-1 draw against Manchester United.

Men on the mark for Liverpool in Charity Shield matches have been Gordon Wallace and Gerry Byrne (1964), Willie Stevenson and Ron Yeats (1965), Roger Hunt (1966), Phil Boersma (1974), John Toshack (1976), Terry McDermott (two) and Kenny Dalglish (1979), Terry McDermott (1980), Ian Rush (1982), Ian Rush again (1986), John Aldridge (two) (1988), Peter Beardsley (1989) and John Barnes (1990).

August, Liverpool were exacting retribution for that defeat as they carried off the Charity Shield. Twelve months later it was the turn of Arsenal – who had snatched the title trophy at Anfield in the May – to bow the knee as a Peter Beardsley goal ensured that the Charity Shield went to Anfield.

The origins of the Charity Shield match go back to 1908 and, as the name implies, the idea was to raise money for a good cause. At first, the match was staged between the Champions of the Football League and the Southern League, then it became Amateurs versus Professionals, and ultimately, the contestants were the League champions and the holders of the FA Cup. Liverpool's first venture into the Charity Shield arena was back in 1922, when they lost to Huddersfield Town by the only goal of the game. Since then, Liverpool have claimed the trophy on a dozen occasions.

They took part in the 1964 Charity Shield match and drew 2–2 with West Ham United, then in 1965 they shared

■ *Left:* **The Charity Shield goes to Liverpool after their 1974 duel with Leeds United at Wembley, and Emlyn Hughes and manager Bill Shankly parade the trophy for the fans.**

chalked up a score of victories, including 11 on the trot. Ian Rush hit a hat-trick against Notts County who, like Ipswich and Coventry, conceded four goals overall, while Liverpool stuck five past Manchester City at Maine Road, as if to emphasise that they were extracting revenge for their Anfield defeat.

Once again Liverpool's side had a settled look about it, with 16 players being utilised – including Mark Lawrenson and Craig Johnston, both costly imports. As for Rush, he struck 17 goals in 32 outings, McDermott collected 14 in 29 appearances, Dalglish hit 13 in his 42 games and Whelan weighed in with ten in 32 matches. So Liverpool, winners of the Milk Cup, added the League title to their list of honours with this record for the season:

P	W	D	L	F	A	W	D	L	F	A	Pts	Position
42	14	3	4	39	14	12	6	3	41	18	87	1st

Remarkably, Liverpool scored more goals away (41) than they did at Anfield (39), as they totalled 87 points in the first season that brought three points for a win. They had won almost as many matches away (12) as they had done at home (14) and conceded only 32 goals altogether while scoring 80. It all augured well for the future . . . though there was a big question mark as to what would happen when Bob Paisley eventually called it a day.

Bob Paisley's Last Season

Bob Paisley had one final fling – and season 1982-83 saw him steering Liverpool to another double of League Championship and Milk Cup, even if they missed out in the FA Cup and the European Cup. The Milk Cup trail began at Portman Road with a 2–1 win over Ipswich Town, and Liverpool won the Anfield return 2–0. Emlyn Hughes, by now the team boss at Rotherham United, took his players to Anfield for the third round, and they put up a good fight – but Liverpool scored the only goal. In the fourth round it was Liverpool 2, Norwich City 0, and in the fifth round West Ham were beaten 2–1, which meant that Liverpool had to take on Burnley in the semi-finals. At Anfield, Graeme Souness, Phil Neal (penalty) and David Hodgson (signed from Middlesbrough) gave Liverpool a 3–0 win, and at Turf Moor Burnley could score only one goal. So Liverpool went into the final against Manchester United, their conquerors in the FA Cup final in 1977 and in an FA Cup semi-final two years later.

When United took a first-half lead, the Manchester fans in the 100,000 crowd believed their team was going to chalk up a hat-trick of wins over Liverpool; but a Kennedy goal a quarter of an hour from the end ensured that the match went

■ Signed from Middlesbrough, Craig Johnston made a very real contribution to Liverpool's success during the 1980s – notably when he got his name on the FA Cup final scoresheet as Liverpool did the double in season 1985-86.

minutes of play, he struck again to put Liverpool in the driving seat. Eight minutes later Rush found the net, and Liverpool were on course for a 3–1 win and the trophy again.

Far from relaxing, however, they had to turn their attention to the League campaign once more, because the title was still in their sights. Liverpool had not started too well, and when Manchester United won 2–1 at Anfield in late October the title seemed to be a little bit distant . . . but Liverpool recovered to win at Sunderland, beat Everton at Anfield and draw with West Brom at The Hawthorns. Then it was lose, win, lose again until Manchester City beat Liverpool 3–1 at Anfield on Boxing Day, but from then on only Swansea and Brighton were to emerge victorious from contests with Liverpool, who sailed through their remaining 25 matches and, in the process,

into extra time . . . and who should pop up with the winner but Ronnie Whelan, the man who had done so much damage against Spurs the previous year. Eight minutes into the first spell of extra time he found the net, and Manchester United – the club he had supported as a youngster – were beaten.

In the League, Liverpool began with seven games without defeat, then they lost 1–0 at Ipswich and 3–1 at West Ham; they also drew 0–0 at home against Manchester United and 1–1 at Stoke. So by the end of their 11th game they had not exactly pulled up any trees. However, they went on a run which saw them winning 19 and drawing five of their next 25 matches, the sole defeat coming at Carrow Road, where Norwich City scored the only goal. That run included some staggering results: 5–0 against Everton (with four goals for Rush), 4–0 against Coventry City in the next match (a Rush hat-trick), 4–2 against Aston Villa, 5–2 against Manchester City (a Dalglish hat-trick), 5–1 against Notts County (three more for Rush), 5–1 against Stoke and 4–0 in the return against Manchester City.

There was another twist to the story of Liverpool's surge to the title, because in fact when the heat was off they lost five and drew one of their last half-dozen matches . . . yet at the end of the season

they were still well and truly on top, with a total of 82 points and a record overall which read like this:

P	W	D	L	F	A	W	D	L	F	A	Pts	Position
42	16	4	1	55	16	8	6	7	32	21	82	1st

Rush had hit two dozen goals in 34 League games, Dalglish 18 in 42, with Souness having scored nine, Neal eight and Johnston seven. For Bob Paisley it was truly the right note on which to signal his departure as Liverpool's Manager, and when he did bow out, his record suggested that he had outdone Bill Shankly, with six League titles, three European Cup successes, one UEFA Cup and three League/Milk Cup wins on the trot. The only trophies he had not managed to collect were the FA Cup and the European Cup-winners Cup – and who was carping about that?

For Liverpool and their fans, the most important question was who – if anyone – could fill Bob Paisley's shoes and, in the short term, the answer turned out to be his No. 2, Joe Fagan. He was steeped in Liverpool history and tradition, but that didn't necessarily mean he would be a success. Joe's reign may have been brief, but while he was in charge of team affairs he certainly made his presence felt because, yet again, Liverpool kept on collecting the trophies.

■ Danger for Manchester United, as Kenny Dalglish tries to get the better of Kevin Moran at Wembley. Liverpool beat United 2–1 in the 1983 Milk Cup Final, which meant they retained the trophy for the second year in succession.

Joe Fagan's Great Start

For starters, Liverpool wound up season 1983-84 by gaining Joe the League Championship, the European Cup and the League/Milk Cup . . . a fantastic finish to his first season as Manager and a unique collection for the Anfield trophy room. It mattered not that Liverpool had lost to Brighton in the fourth round of the FA Cup. And they could almost have gone to Wembley twice over in the other domestic Cup competition, because they played no fewer than 13 games in winning the trophy.

Brentford were beaten 4–1 away, 4–0 at home; Fulham drew 1–1 at Craven Cottage and 1–1 at Anfield (after extra time), then went out to a Graeme Souness goal in extra time of the Griffin Park second replay; Birmingham went to Anfield on the strength of a 1–1 home draw and were beaten 3–0; Sheffield Wednesday's 2–2 draw at Hillsborough was the forerunner to a 3–0 defeat at Anfield; and Walsall drew their semi-final first leg at Anfield before going down 2–0 in the return.

There was a 100,000 crowd at Wembley on 25 March 1984, and the stadium was a sea of red and blue as the Liverpool and Everton supporters gathered for this first all-Merseyside final. But while both teams did their utmost to obtain a result, the 90 minutes came and went without a goal, and the same thing happened in the 30 minutes of extra time. So it meant a replay at Maine Road the following mid-week, and Liverpool had the same team on duty . . . Grobbelaar, Neal, Kennedy, Lawrenson, Whelan, Hansen, Dalglish, Lee, Rush, Johnston, Souness. The game drew more than 52,000 fans, and this time

■ *Opposite above:* **John Wark's career at Liverpool was relatively brief, but he certainly made his mark. He was a hat-trick man in the League, the European Cup and the FA Cup – all in the same season.**

■ *Opposite below:* **Steve Nicol . . . signed as 'a player for the future', but he quickly made the breakthrough to first-team football, and has now totalled more than 300 appearances in a Liverpool jersey.**

■ *Right:* **Michael Robinson distinguished himself by scoring all the Liverpool goals as they beat West Ham United 3–1 at Upton Park in season 1983-84.**

they were to see a decisive strike. It came from Graeme Souness, who drilled a hole through the Everton defence, and that goal in the 22nd minute ensured not only that the trophy remained on Merseyside, but that it stayed at the Anfield end of the city.

In the European Cup Liverpool got through to the final, where they met AS Roma in their own Olympic stadium, and after a 1–1 draw the Anfield Reds came through the penalty shoot-out as winners. As for the Championship, that story was one of almost uninterrupted success, because Liverpool lost only two games at Anfield and four on tour, while winning 22 overall, to total 80 points and finish first.

Seven games went by before they were beaten, by Manchester United and Sunderland in successive matches; then Liverpool won six and drew two of their next eight matches. Against West Ham, Michael Robinson (signed from Brighton) had hit all three of Liverpool's goals as they won 3–1; against Luton Town, Ian Rush struck five in the 6–0 victory. And while Liverpool slumped to a 4–0 defeat at Coventry, they bounced back with a five-match unbeaten run and, after losing 1–0 against Wolves at Anfield, lost only two of their remaining 19 games.

They started with a Rush hat-trick against Aston Villa, reeled off a 6–0 triumph over West Ham, and repaid Coventry by beating them 5–0 at Anfield, with Rush scoring four of the goals, including a rare one from the penalty spot. The Liverpool record for the season was impressive. It read like this:

P	W	D	L	F	A	W	D	L	F	A	Pts	Position
42	14	5	2	50	12	8	9	4	23	20	80	1st

Fifteen players were called up, with five of them – Grobbelaar, Alan Kennedy, Lawrenson (a £900,000 capture from Brighton), Hansen and Lee – ever-presents through the League campaign, while Neal missed just one match, as did Rush. Once again the squad had been reinforced, because apart from Lawrenson and Robinson, Liverpool had signed John Wark from Ipswich Town, and Steve Nicol had broken through to the senior side. Liverpool certainly relied upon goals from Rush that season, though – he scored 32 in his 41 matches, and the next-best marksmen were Kenny Dalglish and Graeme Souness (seven goals apiece).

When Liverpool kicked off on 25 August 1984, no-one realised that in a few months' time they would be involved in a tragedy which had tremendous repercussions for English football. It was a tragedy witnessed by millions via television, and it ended Liverpool's 21-year campaign in European football. What should have been a glorious finale for Joe Fagan ended on a note of

■ Paul Walsh was signed
by Liverpool from Luton
Town, and he scored some
vital goals during his time
at Anfield – notably on one
occasion when he was a
hat-trick marksman.

sorrow as he wound up his brief career in management.

As usual, Liverpool started out with the intention of winning every one of the honours going, and in the League they were always in contention for the Championship. They surrendered their hold on the Milk Cup as they went out against Tottenham Hotspur in the third round, and their visions of a run to Wembley in the FA Cup were dashed after they had reached the semi-final stage, because after drawing 2–2 against Manchester United at Goodison Park in the first encounter, Liverpool were beaten 2–1 in the replay at Maine Road.

In the League, they won two and drew two of their first four matches, lost at Highbury, drew three and lost three, then won four and drew one. Chelsea halted that run, then Liverpool lost only

the title, and the Reds made do with second place.

Once again, Ian Rush had been on target – 14 goals in 28 games – while John Wark had finished as the leading scorer, with 18 goals in his 40 outings. Another recruit, Paul Walsh, totalled eight goals in 26 appearances, and other new names on the team sheet at various times were Gary Gillespie, Jim Beglin and Kevin MacDonald. Liverpool called upon 18 players during the season.

Heysel and the Era of Dalglish

Six days after their final League match, Liverpool met Juventus in the final of the European Cup. The venue was the Heysel stadium in Brussels, and the horror scenes there were to be flashed

one of their next 11 games (seven of which were won). That took them to mid-March, when a home defeat by Tottenham Hotspur and another by Manchester United, after victory over West Bromwich Albion, jolted Liverpool's title ambitions. There were then 11 matches to go, and Liverpool set about the task with renewed determination . . . so much so that they won eight games and drew two . . . but they lost their final match, against Everton at Goodison Park. Everton took

around the world, as fans became involved in feuding and lives were lost.

The game eventually did get under way, after much heart-searching as to whether the final should be abandoned altogether, and the record books show that one goal in favour of Juventus settled the issue. It was an evening of terror and tragedy which was to culminate in a ban on English clubs which lasted five years . . . and even then, Liverpool had to wait another year to gain

admission back into the European arena.

In the meantime, though, Kenny Dalglish was given the daunting task of taking over from Joe Fagan at a time when the club was still reeling from the blows of the Heysel stadium disaster. In his first programme notes of the season, Liverpool's new team boss reflected on the recent events and offered the opinion that the players had – to some extent, at least – managed to get things out of their system as they went through their pre-season games.

Typically, Kenny Dalglish made no extravagant promises, except that he and the men on the backroom side – who had stayed loyal to the cause – would do their utmost to bring success to the club. And, of course, it remained to be seen how the men who had been his equals as team-mates would react to his being 'the boss'. As events

at Anfield, and he played in the final match of the campaign, as Liverpool won 1–0 at Stamford Bridge. The goal that beat Chelsea was the goal that clinched the League Championship . . . and, fittingly, it was scored by Dalglish. It was one of three he struck in the League – his first came after only 20 seconds of the Goodison Park derby game against Everton (Liverpool won 3–2), and his second was towards the end of the season, as Liverpool won 2–1 at West Bromwich.

During the season, Liverpool slammed four goals against Spurs, West Brom and Queen's Park Rangers, hit five against Coventry City, Birmingham City and Ipswich Town, and hit hapless Oxford United for six. Coventry were the victims of a Ronnie Whelan hat-trick, Birmingham suffered as Gary Gillespie collected three goals. And the name of Danish international Jan Molby was

■ One of the Liverpool Scots . . . Gary Gillespie, whose luck wasn't always of the best. He was taken ill on the eve of one Cup final, and missed other big games through injury, but he still proved that he could help the team to win major honours.

turned out, the Dalglish era was to become one of sustained success – by the end of his first season he was being named Manager of the Year as his team achieved an historic 'double' of League Championship and FA Cup, with a Wembley victory over Everton the grand finale.

Kenny Dalglish was still registered as a player, and he made 17 League appearances, plus four as substitute, during season 1985-86. He played in the opening game, as Liverpool beat Arsenal 2–0

to the fore, because he showed that he could hit the target, too – notably from the penalty spot. He scored twice from penalties against Spurs, was spot-on against Chelsea, West Ham, Oxford United and Birmingham, and finished up with a tally of 14 goals in 39 games. Ian Rush was the top scorer, with 22 goals in 40 appearances and Paul Walsh weighed in with 11 in a score of matches, while Ronnie Whelan also reached double figures. A former Everton player, Steve McMahon, who

had become the first Dalglish signing, played in 23 games and scored half a dozen goals after his arrival from Aston Villa. And Liverpool's overall record in the League read like this:

P	W	D	L	F	A	W	D	L	F	A	Pts	Position
42	16	4	1	58	14	10	6	5	31	23	88	1st

In the League/Milk Cup, Liverpool were bang on course for Wembley until they met Queen's Park Rangers in the semi-finals. When they returned home trailing by a single goal after the first leg, they were everyone's favourites to reach the final. But Rangers rode their luck at Anfield and held on for a 2–2 draw, so they finished up going to Wembley.

At the after-match Press conference, Dalglish – clearly disappointed – took nothing away from Rangers. Liverpool had held their fate in their own hands . . . and they had let success slip from their grasp. But by the time that second leg of the semi-final was played, in early March, Liverpool were on their way to Wembley in the FA Cup, although it took them into extra time, as it were,

because they needed a couple of replays along the road. On a bitterly cold January day, with snow swirling all around Anfield, Liverpool met Norwich City in the third round and despatched them clinically, with a 5–0 victory; and towards the end of the month they were brushing aside the opposition from Chelsea, as they went to Stamford Bridge and won 2–1. But the fifth round posed some problems for Liverpool, and so did round six.

On 15 February 1986, Liverpool travelled to York City's Bootham Crescent ground and found themselves trailing to a Gary Ford goal, with an hour of the game gone. Four minutes later came the chance of a reprieve, as Liverpool were awarded a penalty; and up stepped Jan Molby to beat 'keeper Andy Leaning and ensure an Anfield replay. As it had been at York, so it was at Anfield, because the score stood at 1–1 after 90 minutes – though, in extra time, Liverpool ran out 3–1 winners. The men whose goals took them into the sixth round: Kenny Dalglish, John Wark and Jan Molby.

It was First Division Watford who barred

■ The Littlewoods Cup final of 1987 saw Ian Rush scoring for Liverpool, but Arsenal countered with two goals, to claim the trophy. This shot shows Jan Molby doing his best to create danger for his team.

Liverpool's route to the semi-finals, and the tie was at Anfield; but Watford gave such a good account of themselves that they earned a scoreless draw and, therefore, a replay at Vicarage Road – where a stunning free-kick goal from John Barnes put them ahead. However, in the dying minutes Liverpool were awarded a spot-kick, and once again it proved to be a life-saver as Jan Molby scored to stretch the match into extra time. And then Ian Rush struck to snatch a winner.

All-Merseyside FA Cup Final

In the semi-finals it was Liverpool v Southampton, Everton v Sheffield Wednesday, so an historic, all-Merseyside FA Cup final was on the cards. That was how it turned out, too, as Everton knocked out Wednesday at Villa Park and Liverpool disposed of the Saints at White Hart Lane . . . though both matches went to extra time. While Graeme Sharp hit the decisive goal for Everton, Ian Rush was Liverpool's two-goal hero as the Wembley final became a reality.

The match between Liverpool and Everton produced real drama, and the story of this is told elsewhere. It is sufficient to say here that Liverpool won the battle by three goals to one, to complete the traditional League-FA Cup 'double' and earn Kenny Dalglish the Manager of the Year accolade he so richly deserved. But, of course, once the summer had been and almost gone, Liverpool had to set out along the trail again and show that they could still deliver the goods. Season 1986-87 presented much more than a token challenge.

It was, as Kenny Dalglish observed at the halfway mark, a bit like the curate's egg – good in parts. 'We haven't picked up as many points as I would have liked, and I have to admit that in some respects this is our fault. Yet we have hung on and remain among the top group of clubs, and we can claim that we remain in contention for all the trophies which are going. So we live in hopes that fortune will favour us, somewhere along the line.'

Fortune didn't favour Liverpool in the League, the FA Cup or the League Cup, now called the Littlewoods Cup, because they had to settle for finishing second to Everton in the First Division, while in the FA Cup they were knocked out in the third round by Luton Town – although it took three matches to do it. There were two no-score draws, then Luton won at the third time of asking, with a 3–0 victory on their artificial surface at Kenilworth Road. As for the Littlewoods Cup, Liverpool safely negotiated the hurdles presented by Fulham, Leicester City, Coventry City, Everton and Southampton, to reach the final . . . though, once again, they had a tricky tie or two. Their first engagement, though, brought them a resounding, 10–0 record victory in the first leg against Fulham, with Steve McMahon hitting four goals – and when Liverpool beat Leicester City 4–1 McMahon was a hat-trick hero.

A 0–0 draw against Coventry City meant a replay, and this time it was Jan Molby who scored three goals, then Ian Rush despatched Everton, while Southampton lost their second-leg semi-final 3–0. Which brought Liverpool up against Arsenal at Wembley; and there, the myth that Liverpool never lost when Rush found the net was finally laid to rest, because although Rush did the business, Arsenal scored twice to carry off the Cup.

There was one small consolation for Liverpool: they won the Screen Sport Super Cup, a trophy which was not exactly ranking high on the honours list. Yet to win it they had to dispose of Everton – and they did this with brisk efficiency. The first leg of the final put Liverpool firmly in control, as they won 3–1 with goals from Ian Rush (2) and Steve McMahon; and when the second leg was played, Rush hit a hat-trick as Liverpool scored a 4–1 success to make it 7–2 on aggregate.

For Rush, season 1986-87 was his swan song as a Liverpool player, because he was on his way to Juventus for a record-breaking fee of £3.2 million. He had been Liverpool's leading scorer in the League for five seasons out of six, had topped the century mark for goals in the First Division and scored more than 200 altogether for Liverpool in 331 appearances . . . and on the eve of his departure he scored the winner against Watford on his Anfield farewell, then was on the mark as Liverpool drew 3–3 with Chelsea at Stamford Bridge, in their final League match. That goal took his tally in the League to 30 and his total for the season to 40, so he had certainly kept his early season promise to the fans . . . that he intended to score as many goals as possible before moving on.

Among his tally was a hat-trick against Leicester City at Anfield – the 11th hat-trick of his career – and the winner against Arsenal in a vital match at Highbury, while the first of two goals he struck against Queen's Park Rangers was the 200th of his Liverpool career. When he scored against Arsenal in the Littlewoods Cup final, it seemed he could be the match-winner again, but when the Gunners rapped back with two goals to claim the trophy, Liverpool's defeat ended a run of 144 games in which Rush had never been on the losing side after scoring. Ian was philosophical about it all. 'If that record of mine was going to be broken, there's no better place than Wembley for it,' he said.

When he scored twice against Everton in his final derby game appearance (or so it seemed, at the time), the goals took him level with the legendary Dixie Dean, who had scored 19 goals in derby games. And when Rush took the field for his Anfield farewell, Liverpool made him captain

against Watford. So he maintained his record of being the only ever-present during the season.

So season 1986-87 ended on a highly emotional note for the Welsh international, and for the Liverpool fans, even if they hadn't seen their favourites carry all before them. Second in the League, runners-up in the Littlewoods Cup, winners of the Screen Sport Super Cup . . . the fans just hoped that there were greater glories in store for season 1987-88. They were not disappointed.

Beardsley and Barnes Arrive

The title chase wasn't quite a one-horse race, but Liverpool finished comfortably ahead of the field; and as they surged towards the Championship they set new standards, while the fans found an instant new hero as the successor to Ian Rush. His name was John Aldridge, and he was a Scouser born and bred, although he was signed from Oxford United. Also signed for the new season were two England international forwards: Peter Beardsley (for £1.9 million from Newcastle United) and John Barnes (for £900,000 from Watford).

There was one major disappointment – that Liverpool didn't achieve a League-FA Cup 'double' for the second time in their history; but although they went all the way to Wembley, Wimbledon were the unlikely winners of the FA Cup final. So Liverpool had to be satisfied with the League trophy – and with an FA Charity Shield victory over Wimbledon when the teams met again at Wembley in August 1988.

The departure of Rush inevitably brought speculation as to how Liverpool would fare without his marksmanship. John Aldridge had shown he could score goals in three divisions of the League, but had to prove that he could deliver them consistently at the highest level. His Oxford team-mates gave him a vote of confidence when they declared that if Liverpool gave him a decent run in their side, he would total 30 goals in a season – and he missed out by just one goal, because he struck 26 in the League and three in the Cup competitions.

Aldridge was on the mark in his first half-dozen appearances, and after missing out in one match he more than made up for this by knocking in a hat-trick against Derby County. There were more golden goals to come, too. Aldridge found the net in each of his next three outings, went four games without scoring, then rattled in half a dozen goals in the next nine matches and celebrated New Year's Day by scoring against Coventry City. Aldridge had scored Liverpool's first League goal of the season, against Arsenal, and he was on the scoresheet again when the Gunners visited Anfield in January. There were goals against Watford,

Wimbledon and Nottingham Forest . . . who also felt the impact of the Aldridge shooting boots as he struck twice when Liverpool and Forest met in the semi-finals of the FA Cup. He hit his 11th penalty goal of the season to beat Forest 'keeper Steve Sutton for his first goal, and hammered a stunning volley for his second.

Aldridge was Liverpool's first and last League marksman of the campaign, and the leading scorer in all competitions. He was one of two hat-trick marksmen, because Steve Nicol blitzed Newcastle United as Liverpool produced a dazzling display at St James's Park. As for John Barnes, who had regained his England place, he collected the Player of the Year award after his fellow-professionals had cast their votes, then he was named Footballer of the Year by the nation's sportswriters. Meanwhile, Kenny Dalglish went to London to pick up the Manager of the Year trophy for the second time in three seasons.

The Fair Play Trophy

Along the way to Wembley and the League Championship, Liverpool drew more than three-quarters of a million fans to matches at Anfield – and that was just in the League. It gave them an average home gate of 39,657. As well as the League title they collected the Fair Play trophy presented by the Professional Footballers Association, whose chief executive, Gordon Taylor, said: 'I'm delighted that Liverpool were the inaugural recipients of the trophy . . . they've shown they can be not only the most successful team, but have the best disciplinary record. This proves the point that you don't need to go beyond the laws of the game to be successful. The finest testimony to the health of the League as it celebrated 100 years of football was the level of performances we saw from Liverpool throughout the season. Every game was a Cup-tie for them, because every other team wanted to knock them off their perch. Yet Liverpool continued to do their utmost to set the best standards, both from a footballing point of view, and when it comes to behaviour.'

The one area where Liverpool felt they had let themselves and their fans down was in the FA Cup, because when they went to Wembley they were red-hot favourites to add that famous old trophy to their list of honours. Before the final on 14 May they had played their outstanding four League games, and drawn against Chelsea, Southampton and Luton Town, while hitting five goals past Sheffield Wednesday. The final, it seemed, would be the icing on the cake.

In the third round, Liverpool had taken Stoke City back to Anfield and won the replay; then they had gone to Villa Park and scored twice, to reach the fifth round. This meant a trip across the

park to Goodison, for an encounter with Everton (who had knocked Liverpool out of the Little-woods Cup) . . . and a goal from Ray Houghton turned out to be the match-winner. Once again, it was an away-day for the Anfield Reds, but they made short work of Manchester City, scoring four goals without reply in the game at Maine Road. Then came the semi-final against Nottingham Forest at Hillsborough, and a brace of goals from John Aldridge saw Liverpool through to Wembley.

The final, however, became a story of might-have-beens, as Liverpool tried to impose them-selves upon Wimbledon, but found they were being harried every step of the way by opponents who were certainly not prepared either to change their style or concede that they were inferior in any way. It looked as if the Dons were going to be beaten when Peter Beardsley shrugged off two challenges, regained his balance, then beat the advancing Dave Beasant . . . but referee Brian Hill had blown for a foul for Liverpool, so the goal was ruled out.

Minutes later, Wimbledon won a free-kick and as the ball came curling over Lawrie Sanchez rose above the defence to glance home a header. It was still 0–1 at half-time, with Liverpool reflecting not

only upon the disallowed goal but upon a penalty they felt they should have had after Aldridge was fouled. In the second half, however, Aldridge was downed again, and this time referee Hill awarded a spot-kick. Aldridge stepped up and drove the ball firmly to Beasant's left – but the 'keeper threw himself across the goal and prevented the ball from going into the net.

On two other occasions Beasant saved his side, tipping one effort away and then saving feet first. And so the under-dogs triumphed and Liverpool were denied the 'double'. But that could not detract from what had gone before.

Liverpool dominated the League season, even though Queen's Park Rangers were top of the table after four games. They had ten points to Liverpool's six – but the Anfielders had played only two matches. Rangers were still top towards the end of September, with Chelsea, Nottingham Forest and Tottenham Hotspur all ahead of Liverpool, but by the end of October the table read Arsenal, Rangers, Liverpool – and on 1 November 1987, Liverpool leap-frogged the London clubs to take pole position. Liverpool beat Rangers 4–0, inflicted a defeat on rivals Everton and, when they met Sheffield Wednesday, they were bidding to extend an unbeaten League run

■ Liverpool went to Wembley in 1988, and Wimbledon sprang a shock, 1–0 victory. Here Peter Beardsley does his best to break down the Dons' defence, but they were to hang on to their slender lead.

to 19 matches, which would equal the club's best start in the First Division – a record which had been set in 1949. A Gary Gillespie goal was enough to beat Wednesday, and Liverpool marched on. A new record of 20 games unbeaten was achieved when Liverpool won 3–0 at Oxford, and by then the bookmakers were taking bets not on who would win the Championship, but on who would finish second to Liverpool.

On 28 December 1987 Liverpool beat Newcastle United 4–0 at Anfield to complete a double, and as they stretched their unbeaten run to 21 matches they also became the first club in the division to pass the 50-goal mark for the season. But skipper Alan Hansen still cautioned: 'We haven't won anything yet!' And Kenny Dalglish was saying: 'We haven't listened to the bookmakers so far, and we're not going to listen to them now.' But if Liverpool weren't saying much, other people were. One of their ex-players, 'keeper Steve Ogrizovic, reckoned: 'They'll walk away with the title', after he had conceded four goals as Coventry City fell on New Year's Day, and the Sky Blues' manager, John Sillett, said: 'I tipped Liverpool to win the title after they had beaten us in the second game of the season, and I'm on to a good thing. We went the way other teams have gone . . .'

Liverpool topped the First Division table through December, January, February, March and April, and after a devastating display when they beat Nottingham Forest 5–0 one of football's all-time greats, Tom Finney, was moved to say: 'This was the finest exhibition by any team in all my time of playing and watching the game.'

Liverpool, in fact, clinched the Championship on Saturday, 23 April 1988 – St George's Day – when they beat Tottenham Hotspur by the only goal of the game at Anfield. The match-winner was Peter Beardsley, and Liverpool still had four games to go. Spurs manager Terry Venables declared afterwards: 'Our passing and movement were so good on the day that I believe we would have scored goals against any other defence in the League.' That was meant as a compliment to the opposition, of course – and while it was a minor point, it was also a fact that Liverpool had become the first club to claim the League title before the playing of the Littlewoods Cup final.

A Record Run

One of the features of the season was the manner in which Liverpool equalled the record of 29 matches without defeat from the beginning of the season – a record set by Leeds United in 1973-74, when they kicked off with a 3–1 home win over Everton on 25 August 1973 and did not lose again until they went to Stoke City's Victoria Ground

on 23 February 1974. That Leeds run had beaten the previous best post-war record of 19 games without defeat – a record set in 1949 by Liverpool.

In season 1987-88, Liverpool went through their 29-match unbeaten run as they started with a 2–1 victory at Highbury on 15 August 1987, and finished with a 1–1 draw against Derby County at the Baseball Ground. Along the way they clocked up 22 victories, including doubles against Oxford United, Newcastle United, Coventry City, Arsenal, Charlton Athletic, Watford, Portsmouth and Queen's Park Rangers. West Ham were the most successful against Liverpool, because they drew both their League games.

When the Anfield club failed to extend that run to 30 matches it was, perhaps, predictable and inevitable that the team to beat them came from the same city . . . yes, Everton inflicted their first defeat upon Liverpool when, at Goodison Park on 20 March 1988, they ended that tremendous run. Remarkably, Everton had also won a Littlewoods Cup-tie at Anfield, which made them the only club to have beaten Liverpool through 37 matches in the various competitions. Liverpool had also set a club record of ten clean sheets in successive matches, with Bruce Grobbelaar in goal for six and Mike Hooper for the other four games. Overall, Liverpool kept 18 clean sheets in their unbeaten League run, failed to score only four times in 37 matches. And when they clinched the Championship, they equalled Everton's record of 90 points – but they did it in 40 games, compared with Everton's 42 in season 1984-85.

The final League table of season 1987-88 showed that Liverpool, as Champions, boasted a record like this:

P	W	D	L	F	A	W	D	L	F	A	Pts	Position
40	15	5	0	49	9	11	7	2	38	15	90	1st

Season 1988-89 was memorable for a variety of reasons, not least because Liverpool, for the second time in recent years, were caught up in the trauma of a stadium-crowd disaster. They were also to be denied the 'double' of League title and FA Cup for the second season in succession, and this in the most dramatic of circumstances, as Arsenal snatched the Championship at Anfield with almost the last kick of the final match.

It was Liverpool versus Arsenal in the Littlewoods Cup, too, and the Gunners offered stern resistance before being despatched after a second replay. Then another London club, West Ham – who were struggling to survive in the First Division – administered a 4–1 hiding to Liverpool in the next round.

Liverpool now had Ian Rush back again, as well as John Aldridge, John Barnes and Peter Beardsley, and all were to play their part in the bid to win the League title and the FA Cup. Right

at the start, though, it was Rush who had to settle for a seat on the bench as Aldridge wore the No. 8 jersey – and, in the opening game against Charlton Athletic at Selhurst Park, Aldo fired a three-goal broadside, as if to emphasise that he wasn't going to surrender his place without a battle.

As the season went by, it was Aldridge or Rush, or Aldridge *and* Rush as striking partners, with Beardsley and Barnes as regulars. The final tally showed that Aldridge played 35 League games and scored 21 goals, with six goals in half a dozen FA Cup matches, while Rush scored seven League goals in two dozen appearances, plus three goals in two FA Cup outings. Beardsley totalled 37 League games (ten goals) and five FA Cup appearances (two goals), Barnes 33 League games (eight goals) and six FA Cup appearances (three goals).

In the title race, Everton led the way after the opening two matches, but while they had won both, the same applied to Southampton, Liverpool and Norwich City. After six games it was Millwall, Norwich, Liverpool, Southampton, Manchester United and Arsenal, and after ten games Norwich were top, Arsenal second and Liverpool fourth, behind Millwall. Norwich, in fact, led the field by six points. Towards the end of November it was still Norwich, Arsenal, Millwall and Liverpool, while on the last day of 1988 the Gunners led the way, with 37 points from 18 games, while Norwich also had 37, but from 19 matches. Then came Millwall, Everton and Liverpool, with the Anfield Reds nine points adrift. Come the end of January, and it was Arsenal, Norwich, Coventry City and Liverpool, in that order, and by the end of February the Gunners still led the field. By then, Liverpool were down in eighth position. The Gunners had 54 points, Liverpool 36, but Arsenal had played three matches more – and towards the end of March Liverpool had narrowed the gap to 11 points, while still having three games in hand. On Saturday, 1 April, indeed, Arsenal were at the top still . . . but Liverpool had climbed into second spot, just two points adrift . . . then, one week later, the Gunners had a three-point advantage, but Liverpool had a game in hand.

On Tuesday, 11 April it was neck and neck at the top – Arsenal led the way on goal difference, because both clubs had 63 points from 32 matches. But by Saturday, 29 April it was Arsenal on 66 points from 33 games, Liverpool on 63 from 32 matches. Arsenal won again, to go six points clear (Liverpool than had two games in hand), and by Saturday, 13 May the picture had changed again. Arsenal still held the lead, with 72 points from 36 matches, but Liverpool were only two points behind, and they had a game in hand. On 16 May Liverpool hit the top, with 73 points from 36 games, but 24 hours later the Gunners had leap-

frogged back into the leadership, level on points but having played a match more.

In the later stages of this neck-and-neck race, Liverpool had to contend with what became known as the Hillsborough tragedy . . . an FA Cup semi-final in mid-April which was abandoned after only six minutes because a crowd disaster exacted a grim toll of 95 lives. Liverpool, in fact, did not play football from the day of the disaster, Saturday, 15 April until they met Everton in League action on 3 May. In the interim, there were discussions as to whether or not Liverpool should carry on in the FA Cup or voluntarily surrender a place at Wembley to Nottingham Forest.

Instead of kicking a football around, team-manager Kenny Dalglish and his players were donning dark suits and attending one funeral after another, while the wives played their part by

■ Not only did they look alike, but they both proved to be expert marksmen for Liverpool. Yes, John Aldridge and Ian Rush hit the target regularly before 'Aldo' moved on to Real Sociedad, in Spain.

and Nottingham city councils each donated £25,000 and there were similar gestures from Manchester United, Everton, Tranmere Rovers – and the fans of these clubs all banded together to try to help the injured and the bereaved.

Non-Leaguers Runcorn donated £1,000 gate receipts, and the crowd of 700 boosted that total by another £400, while the Rugby League clubs at Wigan and St Helens each contributed £1,000. And so the helping hands linked together in the effort to make

THE HILLSBOROUGH

IF EVER a city became united, it was the city of Liverpool during the dark days after what became known throughout football as the Hillsborough disaster. It happened on the afternoon of Saturday, 15 April 1989, when Liverpool and Nottingham Forest met in the semi-final of the FA Cup at Sheffield and, in a matter of minutes, football became forgotten and abandoned as the full horror of the events on the terraces began to unfold.

The match itself lasted no more than half a dozen minutes; then it became apparent that tragedy had struck . . . and, in the final analysis, the death toll mounted as the disaster claimed no fewer than 95 lives. For once, it seemed, football fans forgot their rivalry as they banded together to offer practical help. In a matter of days, contributions towards the disaster appeal fund topped the £1 million mark.

The Government contributed £500,000, there was a donation of £100,000 from Liverpool Football Club and another £100,000 came from Ford, of Halewood, Liverpool, while Sheffield

■ The scene at Hillsborough on the day of the crowd disaster when Liverpool met Nottingham Forest in the FA Cup semi-final.

the loss more bearable.

There was help from abroad, too. Bayern Munich and Napoli, who met in the semi-finals of the UEFA Cup, each pledged donations of £17,000, while Borussia Dortmund offered the gate receipts from an exhibition match

mourned in Liverpool. The San Siro is a stadium where many fans from Merseyside have watched big games, and the original plan before the AC Milan-Real Madrid match was for a minute's silence . . . but then the strains of 'You'll Never Walk Alone' rose all

Liverpool colours on the blue railings of the Hillsborough ground . . . and before they had finished, football fans from near and far had made the Anfield pitch a mass of flowers, while the famous Shankly Gates were festooned with scarves and other

DISASTER

against Moscow Dynamo. And at home, major stores acted as collecting points for donations, while major banks such as Barclays and the National Westminster each pledged £25,000 – as did Manchester Airport.

John Broughton, a 14-year-old from Rochdale, had made his first parachute jump just before the Hillsborough disaster, and he decided to donate the money he had raised towards the fund. There was help from the world of pop music, too, with Liverpudlian Gerry Marsden (of Gerry and the Pacemakers fame) doing a remake of his hit record, 'Ferry 'cross the Mersey'.

The appeal which had been launched by Sheffield Lord Mayor, Phyllis Smith, received donations and pledges from all over – fans of Nottingham Forest, for instance, packed £100 into a jam-jar and donated the money, while at the awards dinner held by the Professional Footballers Association the sum of £12,000 was raised, and the crowd at the Watford-Walsall game weighed in with another £7,000.

The Football League pledged a quarter of a million pounds, thus matching the amount donated by the Football Association, and in the San Siro stadium in Italy, where AC Milan and Real Madrid were due to play their European Cup semi-final, there was a double tribute to those being

around that famous stadium, and as the fans of both teams sang the 'Anfield anthem' they raised red scarves in tribute.

The Hillsborough disaster brought two former Liverpool players, John Toshack and Craig Johnston, back from Spain and Australia, while the players and wives at the Anfield club offered solace to those who had been bereaved. Within a matter of days after Hillsborough, it was estimated that a quarter of a million people had visited Liverpool's ground to pay their homage to the dead. One of the most moving messages was placed with flowers in the Kop goalmouth at Anfield . . . it came from a 17-year-old, Lee Connolly, of Norris Green, who had tried in vain to save the life of a little boy at Hillsborough. The message said simply: 'To all my friends, but especially to the little boy I tried to help. Sorry . . . Lee.'

And people from Sheffield paid their tributes. One note which came with a bunch of flowers read: 'To all families in Liverpool, from a family in Sheffield.'

There was a 17-year-old Liverpool supporter, Wayne Adams, who lived in Sheffield, and he draped a bedsheet in

■ After the tragedy of Hillsborough, Anfield became the focal point for hundreds of thousands of people who felt that they had to make the pilgrimage and pay their respects to those who had lost their lives.

football favours. Liverpool and Everton scarves hung from those gates, side by side, as the fans united in tribute.

In spite of the horrendous loss of life, there were some heartwarming stories, as well. One of the most remarkable

dramas unfolded in the presence of Liverpool team-manager Kenny Dalglish at the Royal Hallamshire hospital in Sheffield. Just before the Liverpool team arrived to visit the injured, 20-year-old Sean Luckett, from Claverdon, Warwick, had been deeply unconscious – in fact, doctors believed it would be days before he came round. But as Kenny Dalglish went to Sean's bedside, the young man awoke and, with just the trace of a smile, he murmured: 'Kenny Dalglish . . .' Dr David Edbrooke, a consultant anaesthetist, admitted: 'I've never known anything like it . . . it brought tears to my eyes.'

Kenny's former club, Glasgow Celtic, met Liverpool at Parkhead in a charity match to raise funds for the Hillsborough disaster appeal, and that example triggered off a similar game thousands of miles away . . . in Riyadh, Saudi Arabia, where a charity match was arranged between English and Scottish expatriates. Through the generosity of these people, and local Saudi-Arabians, £5,000 was raised on the night, and the cheque was presented to Liverpool's chairman, to be handed on to the fund. Dave Warrington, who was the manager of a superstore branch close to Hillsborough, recalled how on the day of the tragedy Liverpool fans used the store's facilities to phone home and reassure their families as to their safety. Later, Dave wrote to the *Anfield Review*: 'A few people have returned to Sheffield, to remember . . . and some have nipped in to say "Thanks", while we also received Christmas cards from the same kind of people. I was at Hillsborough for the game against Liverpool in November (six months after the tragedy), and I saw the emotion of only a few thousand, as the rest of them were unable to get tickets. April 15 is coming round again soon, and I'm sure it will be another very emotional day.

'As a fanatical *football* fan, I say to Liverpool fans that while Sheffield may not now be a happy place for many of you, you do have a lot of friends here. I live about five miles from Hillsborough,

and while many of you will return to Sheffield in April, I would be more than willing to help anyone who wishes to visit any other time. My local knowledge could prove useful, so please feel free to write to me.' And Dave enclosed his address.

The return to Hillsborough in the November was, of course, a solemn and sad occasion. When Liverpool had gone there to play Forest the previous April, the Leppings Lane terraces were packed to overflowing . . . this time, they were deserted save for tributes which had been laid reverently on the terrace steps. Alan Hansen and Chris Turner, the two club captains, also paid their personal respects, and the respects of the clubs and players, by laying wreaths before the game kicked off, and everyone certainly responded to the appeal which had been made by Kenny Dalglish.

He had asked for the fans to ensure that the occasion was graced with dignity, and the supporters of both sides responded to the call. The police had requested Liverpool fans not to travel, unless they had tickets and, for the most part, that plea was heeded. There were still 4,500 Liverpool supporters (all had tickets) at the match, and they played their part in the proceedings.

With ten minutes to go to the

scheduled kick-off, it was estimated that around 2,000 Liverpool supporters were still en route to Hillsborough, because of traffic jams up to eight miles long on the M1. So the kick-off time was put back 15 minutes, by which time almost everyone was safely inside

the ground. And when a minute's silence was observed, the 32,000 fans who had come both to watch the match and to pay their respects were so quiet that you could have heard a pin drop.

For most of the supporters who had travelled from Liverpool, it was their first sight of Hillsborough since the disaster, and many of them had returned bearing flowers, which were placed inside the ground. Afterwards Chief Superintendent John Nesbit, who was in charge of the police operation that night, paid the Liverpool fans a sincere and moving tribute as he said: 'They were a credit to their city and to football generally. The game has been the winner tonight. I think all of us involved feel better, now that this occasion has taken place.'

One year on from the Hillsborough tragedy, on Easter Sunday, the exact anniversary day, there was a memorial service at Anfield for the victims, with the unveiling of an 'eternal flame' outside the ground. The flame, encased in protective glass, is close to the

Shankly Gates and, fittingly, the ceremony was carried out by Bill's widow, Nessie. Before the unveiling and dedication of the memorial, there was a service on the Anfield pitch and it was attended by many thousands of people . . . almost as many as Anfield would house for a capacity crowd when a game was being played.

The service was beamed live by television around the country, and it was a most moving occasion. Families

of the Hillsborough victims gathered round the 'eternal flame', and the light shone on the names, carved in granite, of the 95 people who lost their lives in British football's greatest crowd tragedy. Those names are now indelibly linked with the history of Liverpool Football Club.

giving comfort to the bereaved. In the end, it was decided that the team should fulfil its FA Cup commitments. That first Everton match, which was in effect a dress rehearsal for another FA Cup-final meeting between Merseyside's Big Two, ended in a scoreless draw, and the next item on the agenda for Liverpool was their delayed Cup semi-final against Nottingham Forest.

Not surprisingly, the venue this time wasn't Hillsborough; instead, it was Old Trafford, and – as had happened the previous season – it was John Aldridge who made Forest wish he had never gone back to Merseyside, because he rattled in two goals as Liverpool won the contest 3–1 to clinch a

on home ground with Arsenal on the night of Friday, 26 May. As the teams kicked off at Anfield, the issue was clear-cut: Arsenal, lagging by three points, needed to win by two clear goals if they were to capture the Championship. And manager George Graham declared his belief that they could do it.

By the end of the first 45 minutes, millions of television viewers were ready to put their money on Liverpool taking the title, as well as the Cup, because there was no score at Anfield, and the Gunners now needed to get two goals in 45 minutes *and* prevent Liverpool from scoring. Soon after the restart, the picture changed, to give

■ The goal that won the League championship for Arsenal at Anfield on 26 May 1989. Michael Thomas is the Gunners' marksman, and as Liverpool lose 2–0, the title trophy goes down the motorway to London.

Wembley meeting with Everton. Liverpool also beat Forest in the League immediately afterwards, then defeated Wimbledon and Queen's Park Rangers before tackling Everton at Wembley, where there was more drama before the men from Anfield emerged victorious.

Robbed In The Last Minutes

Having won the FA Cup (and that story is told elsewhere), Liverpool met West Ham at Anfield and slammed them 5–1, to set up a title clincher

Arsenal renewed hope, because Alan Smith broke the deadlock. Liverpool appealed against the award of a goal, the referee consulted a linesman – then signalled that the goal must stand. And that decision really set the game alight.

The Gunners held that slender lead until the dying seconds of the match, as Liverpool repulsed their raids. It seemed certain that they would keep Arsenal out, but George Graham's men braced themselves for one last effort – and, suddenly, there was danger as Michael Thomas burst through into the 18-yard box. He beat Bruce Grobbelaar to snatch that precious second goal

which carried with it the all-important prize.

When the final whistle went, the home fans and the Liverpool players seemed stunned – some of the players were on the ground, drained of energy and seemingly shellshocked by what had happened. The Arsenal contingent, of course, hailed the near-miracle their heroes had achieved. And Liverpool had to swallow the bitter pill of seeing their rivals presented with the Championship trophy on the Anfield turf. It was indeed an extraordinary ending to a traumatic season as the 1980s drew to a close.

The Reds Power Into The 1990s

The start of a new decade brought Liverpool their 18th League title, although again there was disappointment at their failure to achieve the 'double'. After Wimbledon had claimed the FA Cup in 1988 and Arsenal had snatched the title in 1989, to leave Liverpool with 'only' one of the two great prizes, so in 1990 Liverpool had to settle for regaining the Championship, after having got almost to the gates of Wembley.

When the 1989-90 campaign opened, there was no doubting Liverpool's priority . . . Steve McMahon summed up the feelings of all the players when he declared that they were determined to win back the Championship trophy. By then they had signed Sweden's World Cup captain, Glenn Hysen, and they had Alan Hansen back after an absence of nearly a season.

The Reds still had both John Aldridge and Ian Rush competing for the role of main striker. Aldridge was to find himself substitute for the first five games of the season . . . and his first appearance, on 12 September in that fifth match, was also his farewell. Liverpool played host to promoted Crystal Palace, and by the end of 90 minutes the visitors were just glad to hear the final whistle, because not only had they failed to score – they had conceded nine goals, with substitute Aldridge tucking away a spot-kick with his first touch. At the final whistle, Aldridge threw his boots and jersey to the Kop, and hours later he was a Real Sociedad player. His Liverpool career had been relatively brief, but in 104 appearances he had totalled 64 goals, and that spot-kick against Palace was his 50th in the League for Liverpool.

With Aldridge gone, Rush, Beardsley and Barnes kept the goals flowing, and the last two proved that they were equal to the task of following Aldridge as spot-kick experts. At the end of the season a £1 million newcomer, Israeli international Ronny Rosenthal, made an instant impact by scoring seven goals in eight appearances, including a hat-trick against Charlton Athletic at Selhurst Park.

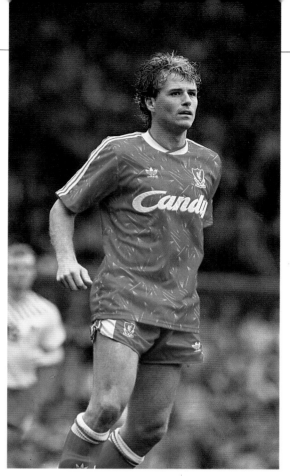

■ *Left:* Glenn Hysen, Sweden's World Cup skipper and a player who, like Ronnie Whelan, wore the captain's armband at Liverpool. He slotted into the side straight away and, again like Whelan, Manchester United's loss was Liverpool's gain, because Hysen had seemed set to sign for United.

■ *Below:* Action-man Ronny Rosenthal, who arrived at Liverpool on loan from Standard Liege, and was signed by the Anfield club in a package deal estimated to have totalled £1 million.

■ One of the young players who rapidly developed into an international, Steve Staunton went to the finals of the World Cup with the Republic of Ireland team in 1990.

By Sunday, 8 April, only Aston Villa had a chance of catching Liverpool in the League, while the Reds had a date with Crystal Palace in the semi-final of the FA Cup at Villa Park. This was Liverpool's fifth semi-final in six seasons, and when Ian Rush gave them the lead, only the Palace diehards would have dared to bet money on their side staging a comeback. However, fate took a hand in the first half when Rush had to go off injured, and Gary Gillespie, too, was unable to resume after half-time. The game got under way again in sensational style, with Mark Bright's fierce volley spinning off Steve McMahon's head for an equaliser. Suddenly, Palace began to present problems from set-pieces such as corners and free-kicks, and with little more than 20 minutes to go they conjured up another goal as Bright nodded the ball down and Gary O'Reilly hit his first goal of the season. The drama was far from over, though, because inside the last 10 minutes Liverpool were given the chance to haul themselves back into the game and

drive on to secure another visit to Wembley.

First, they gained a free-kick, and when substitute Barry Venison drove the ball in low, from the right, Steve McMahon rifled a rising shot past 'keeper Nigel Martyn from the edge of the 18-yard box. Sixty seconds later, and Liverpool fans were leaping with delight as Steve Staunton went down inside the penalty area and John Barnes stepped up to slot the spot-kick home. It was his 21st goal of the season and, it appeared, the goal that had booked Liverpool's place in the final. Yet still the drama wasn't over . . .

Another free-kick for Palace, and as the ball rebounded from Geoff Thomas's header, Andy Gray was on the spot to head an equaliser . . . and with only seconds to go, Andy Thorn saw another header rap back off the Liverpool bar. So the semi-final went into extra time, and when Alan Pardew headed a corner into the net Liverpool, who had hit 14 goals past Palace during the season, found there was no way back. The post-match verdict of manager Kenny Dalglish

summed up Liverpool feelings: 'We hung ourselves today.'

Liverpool shrugged off that semi-final disappointment and soon clinched the League title with two games still to go. The decider took place at Anfield, just as it had done when Arsenal were the visitors 12 months previously . . . but this time, with Queen's Park Rangers as opponents, Liverpool ensured a 2–1 victory and the title with goals from Ian Rush and John Barnes (penalty).

The following Tuesday night at Anfield, when Derby County were beaten 1–0, the Championship trophy was duly presented to the victors. It was an emotional occasion, because Kenny Dalglish had come from the bench to play a part in the proceedings. It was to be the final First Division appearance of Dalglish, although he postponed his official retirement as a player until the night of his testimonial match at Anfield.

The last match of the campaign, at Coventry, was not important, but Liverpool went out as they always do – with the idea of winning the match – and they blasted six goals. John Barnes took his tally for the season to 28 with a hat-trick. For the second time since his arrival at Anfield he was hailed as the Footballer of the Year, while Kenny Dalglish claimed the Manager of the Year award for the third time in five seasons.

Along the way, Liverpool achieved the double

over Everton, with Ian Rush overtaking Dixie Dean's record for goals in derby games. Liverpool also gained revenge for the previous season by beating Arsenal at Anfield, and they defeated Manchester United at Old Trafford, which banished a jinx, since United had a fine record of results against the Anfield Reds during the previous decade.

Overall, John Barnes with 28 had pipped Ian Rush with 26 by two goals for the honour of being leading marksman. Peter Beardsley had contributed 16, while Ronny Rosenthal had certainly made a hit with the fans after his seven-goal stint. The final League table of the season read like this:

P	W	D	L	F	A	W	D	L	F	A	Pts	Position
38	13	5	1	38	15	10	5	4	40	22	79	1st

And so as Champions again to season 1990-91, which proved to be traumatic as the Reds sensationally lost a.manager and won their place back in Europe. To begin with Liverpool's rivals began spending ever more money in the bid to topple the country's most successful club. Arsenal, for instance, invested more than £3 million in three players; Chelsea poured £2.8 million into the transfer market as they made two signings; promoted Leeds United splashed out £2 million on two new recruits; Everton paid £1 million for a

■ Another season is over, and another title success comes Liverpool's way, as season 1989-90 ends on a high note. Celebrating are Ronny Rosenthal (seven goals in eight League games), Ian Rush, Ronnie Whelan, Alan Hansen and John Barnes.

■ *Right:* **Kenny Dalglish acknowledges the cheers of the fans at his testimonial game at the start of the 1990-91 season, in a match against the Spanish club Real Sociedad which brought John Aldridge back to Anfield.**

■ *Opposite above:* **Peter Beardsley exhibiting his characteristic close control of the ball in the 3–1 away defeat of Tottenham in November. Later in the season he was often to find himself consigned to the substitute's bench, much to the mystification of his many admirers in the game.**

■ *Opposite below:* **John Barnes takes on the United defence in Liverpool's four-nil drubbing of their Manchester rivals at Anfield in September.**

player; and Manchester United topped up their £12 million squad by spending threequarters of a million on yet another signing.

Yes, they all knew Liverpool remained the team they must beat – and as the season unfolded, Liverpool emphasised this by reeling off victories in their first eight League games, to make their best-ever start to a season and to set a new mark of 12 consecutive League wins (having finished with four straight wins the previous term). Their results included a 4–0 success against Manchester United (Peter Beardsley was a hat-trick marksman) and a Goodison Park victory over Everton, while in the League Cup (now carrying the name of a new sponsor – Rumbelows) Ian Rush hit the 15th hat-trick of his career against Crewe Alexandra.

As the season progressed, though, the Liverpool gallop was slowed and they went out of the domestic cup competitions, while Arsenal forged ahead in the title chase. More than that, however,

Liverpool lost manager Kenny Dalglish in sensational fashion, right in the middle of an FA Cup duel with Everton. After a 0–0 draw in the fifth-round tie at Anfield (which followed a 3–1 League win by Liverpool in the home leg of the derby game), the Reds went to Goodison and took the lead four times . . . yet still finished up at 4–4 and facing a second replay. That match was played on the night of 20 February 1991, and the next day Kenny Dalglish dropped the bombshell – he wanted to quit.

Liverpool were top of the First Division, facing a second replay with Everton . . . and their manager was adamant that the pressures had caught up with him and that he must make his exit. So Liverpool had to accept the inevitable and look for a new team boss. In the meantime, long-serving Ronnie Moran took charge.

There were mixed results during the following weeks – a League defeat at Luton, exit from the

FA Cup to Everton, a home defeat by Arsenal, a 3–0 win at Maine Road, a 2–1 home victory over Sunderland and a 7–1 success at Derby . . . followed by a home defeat from Queen's Park Rangers, a 1–0 reverse at Southampton, a 1–1 home draw with Coventry City and a 5–4 success at Leeds.

By then, names had been bandied about for the managerial job – John Toshack, Graeme Souness and, of course, Ronnie Moran, who had been officially declared in charge until the end of the season. 'Tosh' ruled himself out of the reckoning as he reaffirmed his loyalty to Real Sociedad, and Graeme Souness seemingly remained determined to stick with Glasgow Rangers – then, overnight, the story broke that Liverpool had persuaded their former midfield star to say 'Yes', though he would not be leaving Ibrox until the summer.

Within hours, however, there were dramatic developments, as Rangers and their manager parted company and Souness drove down to take charge of team affairs at Liverpool. At the hurriedly called Press conference, he declared his determination to give the new job his best shot – and that included trying to regain the leadership of the First Division and prevent Arsenal from snatching the title.

By that stage, it was mid-April and Liverpool had just five games to go. They still trailed the Gunners, but after Arsenal had lost an FA Cup semi-final against Tottenham Hotspur (and thus

their chance of the double), Liverpool's hopes rose as the Gunners were held to a draw at Highbury by Manchester City, who had hit back after going two goals down.

The new manager refused to admit the Anfield Reds were out of the title chase and tackled the remainder of the season with the determination with which he used to tackle opposing forwards. Souness, of course, had once been a charismatic

midfielder with the Anfield club, and his return – amid a storm of controversy in Glasgow – was hailed with delight by Liverpool supporters, who knew from experience that he was a winner.

The Souness career had begun when he moved from Scotland to Tottenham Hotspur as a youngster, travelled on to Middlesbrough and Ayresome Park, and fetched up at Anfield in January 1978, when Liverpool paid what was then a club record fee of £352,000 for him. As Souness orchestrated the midfield moves, so Liverpool savoured success . . . in his six years at Anfield, the club won the League title five times (including a hat-trick from 1982 to 1984), the European Cup three times, and the League/Milk Cup four times (in successive seasons).

Souness it was whose pass created the opportunity for Kenny Dalglish to score the goal which kept the European Cup at Anfield in 1978; Souness himself scored the goal which beat Everton in the Milk Cup-final replay of 1984 . . . and his was one of the penalty goals which ensured European Cup final success that same year, as

■ **Barnes scores for Liverpool in the dramatic 4–4 draw with Everton in the first replay of their fifth round FA Cup tie. Four times the Reds took the lead in the match, and four times they were pegged back by their Merseyside rivals, going on to lose the second replay 1–0 at Goodison Park.**

Liverpool and AS Roma wound up with a spot-kick shoot-out.

Souness skippered Liverpool for three seasons, before moving on to the Italian club Sampdoria in 1984 – Liverpool made a £300,000 profit on their original investment – and after two years in Italy he returned to Scotland, this time to become player-manager of Glasgow Rangers. In May 1989, he signed a five-year contract, and the following November he was being made manager-director; indeed, it was believed he had a substantial shareholding in the Ibrox club and that the bonds were so strong he would be there for life.

However, when the news was leaked that he was destined for Anfield, Rangers declared that he could leave at once, and in a matter of hours he had left one Press conference in Glasgow, to appear at another in Anfield.

So, after 352 appearances (and 56 goals) as a Liverpool player, he was back in the limelight as he made his lounge-suited entrance as a manager. Once again, Liverpool had staged a coup and got their man.

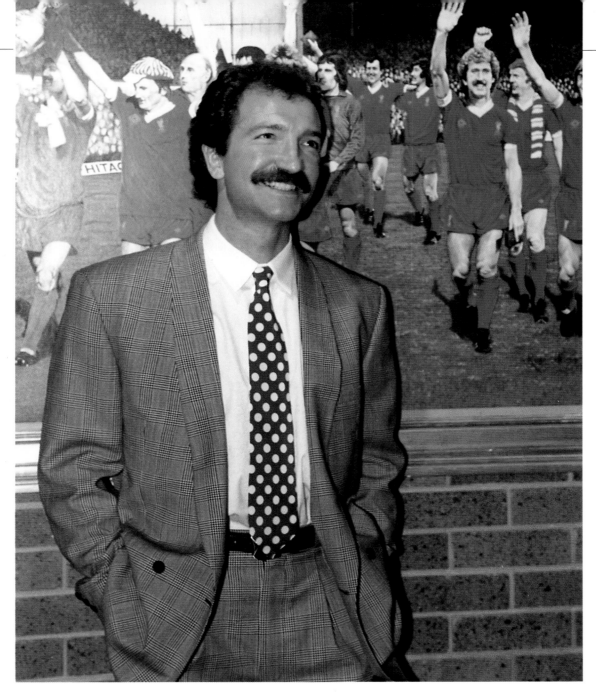

In the same week as Souness' appointment was announced, UEFA confirmed that the Reds would be admitted back into Europe in 1991-92. A defeat of third-placed title chasers Crystal Palace soon assured Liverpool of first or second spot in the Championship, so as they went into those last three crucial games they were not only playing for the title, but to decide which European competition they would be playing in the following season: the prestigious European Cup or a more muted re-entry in the UEFA Cup.

In the event, Liverpool lost away against Chelsea and Nottingham Forest, while Arsenal drew at Sunderland, so – with two games still to go – the Gunners were crowned champions and Liverpool, finishing second, qualified for the UEFA Cup in their centenary season. They did so with this declaration of intent from Graeme Souness ringing in his players' ears: 'I know the burden I must carry – to be compared with all my predecessors in the Liverpool manager's chair. I accepted that when I took the job on. My target for next season? . . . To maintain the high standards Liverpool have set over the years, to get hold of some players and go on to win the First Division.'

After a home victory against Spurs in the last match of the season, Liverpool took a jet plane to Singapore where, somewhat ironically, they met the new League champions in a challenge match. It was, as shrewd observers sagely noted, a sign of the way things were going to shape up once again, as Liverpool and Arsenal – not to mention Everton, Manchester United and others – braced themselves for a renewed battle for supremacy at the start of the Anfield club's second century. Liverpool's mission was to reassert themselves as the undisputed champions of British football.

Chairmen and Backroom Staff

■ One of Liverpool's longest-serving directors, Mr Sidney Reakes, who was the club's chairman when the FA Cup came to Anfield for the first time, in 1965

JOHN HOULDING was the first Chairman of Liverpool Football Club, and his reign lasted from 1892 to 1904, during which time the club emerged from the Lancashire League and the Second Division to win the Championship of the Football League. Long before Houlding finally bowed out, the name of John McKenna became ever more prominent in club affairs.

McKenna – he became known as 'Honest John' – was an Ulsterman, and he had arrived on Merseyside as a mere nine-year-old, starting off as an errand-boy and graduating to the status of prominent businessman. He was duly elected to the Liverpool committee.

McKenna was a man of many parts and he played various roles at the club, including two spells as Chairman (from 1909 to 1914 and from 1917 to 1919). Alongside John Houlding, McKenna was instrumental in seeing to it that Liverpool graduated from the Lancashire League to the Second Division of the Football League, and he deserved credit for his astute signings – he was responsible to a large degree for the recruit-

ment of more than a dozen footballers from Scotland.

One of the players whom he was responsible for signing, centre-forward George Allan, became the first footballer at the club to win a Scotland cap; and McKenna also had a big say in the arrival of the great Alex Raisbeck, who starred equally for Liverpool and for Scotland. 'Honest John' certainly earned his title, too, because he was a man who, according to someone who knew him well, 'fought straight' and 'never shirked an issue.' Indeed, as his influence in football widened, and he assumed Presidential offices in both the Football League and the Football Association, he built himself a reputation for considering how the poorer clubs could benefit from the way football was run, as he used his influence to ensure that power was wielded wisely.

In between John Houlding and John McKenna, Liverpool had Edwin Berry as Chairman – he had been a player and treasurer at Everton before the split in 1892 – and after McKenna, there was John Astbury, then W.R. Williams and R.L. Martindale, followed by T. Crompton and W.H. Cartwright. The Martindale and Cartwright families, in fact, have played notable parts in club affairs at Liverpool, and three other names worthy of mention are William Harrop, W.H. 'Billy' McConnell and Thomas Valentine Williams.

William Harrop, like John McKenna, had two terms as Chairman, and he became the first Liverpool director since McKenna to be elected to the League's management committee. 'Billy' McConnell, chairman from 1944 to 1947, played a major role in the signing of centre-forward Albert Stubbins from Newcastle United (in the face of stiff competition from Everton). Stubbins helped Liverpool win the League Championship in season 1946-47, and though McConnell had to miss the run-in to the title because of illness, he was able to receive the trophy when the presentation ceremony took place at the next annual meeting of the League.

T.V. Williams, as he was always referred to, was Liverpool's Chairman from 1956 to 1964, so he saw the club's rise from the Second Division to the First, and was able to savour the Championship and FA Cup triumphs of the mid-1960s. No question about it . . . he played one of the most influential roles of any Chairman in the club's affairs. At one time, indeed, he was often to be seen at other grounds around the country, as he carried out scouting missions, and after having joined the board in 1948 and served as Chairman for eight successive seasons he was elected Liverpool's first Life President.

One of the club's present directors, Sidney Reakes, was Chairman when Liverpool carried off the FA Cup for the first time in the club's history,

in 1965, while Eric Roberts, who was in the chair during the late 1960s and early 1970s, saw Liverpool claiming their first European trophy, the UEFA Cup. That was in season 1972-73 – the season Liverpool also won the League Championship – and, as the record shows, it was indeed the start of an altogether magnificent and sustained period of success for Liverpool Football Club.

The man who followed Eric Roberts as Liverpool's chairman was John W. Smith – now Sir John, after his knighthood for services to sport – and under his guidance the club went on to achieve even greater glory than ever before, as one manager after another – Bill Shankly, Bob Paisley, Joe Fagan and Kenny Dalglish – produced teams which won silverware at home and (in the case of the first three) abroad. Undoubtedly Sir John Smith has been a Liverpool man through and through, for more than 60 years. When he stepped down from the chair at the start of the 1990s, he was 69 years old . . . and he had been a Liverpool supporter since he saw his first match as a four-year-old. He once described his love affair with Liverpool Football Club: 'For me, Liverpool has become almost a religion.'

The man who was Liverpool's chairman from

■ Thomas Valentine Williams was a director, chairman and then the club's first life president. T.V. played a major role in the progress of Liverpool Football Club, not least when it came to scouting for new talent on the football pitch.

■ EE-aye-addio, we've won the Cup! Celebrating Liverpool's 1974 success at Wembley are Steve Heighway, the then club chairman, John W. Smith, and Kevin Keegan, who had scored two of the goals, with Heighway notching the other.

1973 to 1990 admits to having played truant from school on more than one occasion, in order to see his soccer idols in action on the playing field at Anfield. His father was a shareholder of the club, and he himself can recall when the gates used to be opened about quarter of an hour from the end of a match. 'That's when the youngsters would get in free, and my father used to remark that the "shareholders" were arriving, when he saw the influx of schoolboys.' He added: 'I didn't even begin to suspect, then, that one day I would become the Chairman of such a famous club.'

John Smith's favourite player in the early days was the great Irish international goalkeeper, Elisha Scott. 'The finest 'keeper I ever saw – and we've had some good ones,' he said. 'I remember one occasion when Liverpool were playing Everton and they had Dixie Dean at centre-forward . . . that day, Scott took a real tumble, because when Dean scored a goal he bundled both Scott and the ball into the net. The goalkeeper wasn't given the kind of protection that he gets today, of course.'

One of Scott's team-mates was 'Parson' Jackson, a full-back who saved his pay so that it could be used to contribute towards his studies for the ministry. John Smith recalls how Scott had what he terms 'a rich command of choice words . . . and "Parson" Jackson used to remonstrate with him, but to no avail.'

The former Liverpool chairman can remember when, at one time, it appeared to be Everton and Manchester City who reigned supreme at their respective ends of the East Lancashire road; then Manchester United emerged from the doldrums and, after an indifferent spell during the 1920s and 1930s, Liverpool became giants on Merseyside. As for the players, in addition to giants such as Elisha Scott and 'Parson' Jackson, Liverpool had stars like Fred Hopkin, Harry Chambers, Arthur Riley, Gordon Hodgson, Berry Nieuwenhuys and Bob Priday. Hopkin – known to the fans as 'Polly' – was a winger who had a reputation for making goals, rather than scoring them. In fact, the fans never expected to see him get his name on the scoresheet. 'But one day,' John Smith recalls, '"Polly" Hopkin did score a goal – and, suddenly, as the crowd roared its delight, you realised that the old Kemlyn Road stand was on fire! I don't know exactly how that happened, but I do remember the fire engine arriving . . .'

It was 'Polly' Hopkin who used to supply the ammunition for 'Smiler' Chambers to fire past opposing goalkeepers; then eventually, as always, time took its toll and players such as Hopkin, Chambers and Scott bowed out. But John Smith stayed to enjoy the football served up by players such as 'Nivvy' Nieuwenhuys who, like Arthur Riley, Gordon Hodgson and Bob Priday, came from South Africa. John Smith recalled: 'We used to have very close commercial ties with South

Africa, and with the football authorities over there, and when the South Africans sent over a touring side in 1924 that set the ball rolling. Hodgson and Riley were both members of that side – Hodgson became a fast bowler with Lancashire, as well as a famous footballer with Liverpool (in fact, he scored 240 goals for the club, overall). He went on to Leeds United and Aston Villa, and then became the manager of Port Vale.'

On the subject of goals, the former chairman can remember one outstanding derby game in which Liverpool defeated Everton 7–4. 'That, for me, was one of the finest derby games ever . . . it was the day Harold "Boy" Barton scored a hat-trick from the wing.' That match was played in February 1933, and there have been other great scoring performances since that day, of course. Yes, the Anfield faithful have seen many more heroes, as has John Smith. He believes that Anfield has an atmosphere all of its own – something special. 'It has always been a ground with a family atmosphere, because the spectators

have been close to the pitch and they have been able to feel more involved with the game and the players than at many other grounds. This close-ness has given our supporters the feeling that they are part and parcel of the club . . . as, indeed, is the case.'

John Smith has always been a great believer in teamwork, too, and was instrumental in the decision to appoint Bob Paisley as manager in succession to Bill Shankly. 'Other clubs have had problems galore, when it came to appointing managers . . . we decided that the thing to do was to keep it in the family, and so we handed Bob Paisley the job. We didn't bring in one man from outside – we promoted Joe Fagan, Ronnie Moran and Roy Evans, and so we maintained the family feeling and the continuity. Right through the years, our club has had players who have stayed to serve in other capacities, once their playing days were over.' That, indeed, was what John Smith was ready to do himself, once he had decided to make way for a new Chairman, because he declared his willingness to carry on as a director

■ **Gordon Hodgson (left) . . . one of several South Africans that Liverpool brought over to play top class football.**

THIS IS ANFIELD

ANFIELD is a football stadium which has become famous around the world. It was opened on 28 September 1884, when Everton were playing on the ground. The first match was against Earlestown. When the Liverpool club came into being, after the split of 1892, the annual rent charged was just £100. John Houlding, the owner, who was elected chairman, donated £500, saying the money could be repaid, interest-free, though he would not press for it. He had previously paid almost £6,000 for the Anfield ground during the days when it was used by Everton . . . one wonders what he would have thought about the kind of money that self-same ground, with all its facilities, would bring today.

The first competitive matches Liverpool played were in the Lancashire League, with the opening game taking place on 3 September 1892, against Higher Walton. By half-time Liverpool had scored a nap hand of goals, and at the end of 90 minutes they had run out 8–0 winners. The team sheet read like this: Ross, Hannah, McLean, Pearson, McQue, McBride, Wyllie, Smith, McVean, Cameron, Kelvin. And that gave a fair indication of the number of Scots in the ranks. The marksmen that day were Smith (2), McQue (2), Cameron (2), McBride and McVean. And the gate?

■ *Above:* **The sign which is calculated to inspire Liverpool and give the opposition the jitters, as they go out to do battle.** *Below:* **The tender for building a grandstand in 1886.**

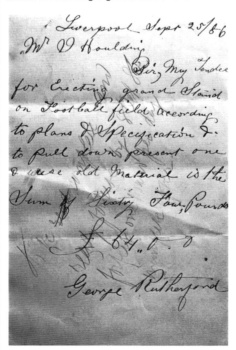

That numbered just 200 . . .

The first Football League game was played on 9 September 1893, and a crowd of around 5,000 saw Liverpool beat Lincoln City 4–0. These days, even with its reduced capacity, Anfield regularly caters for crowds of around 38,000, and the playing area is one of the finest in the country. Facilities for

television are regarded as ideal, the dressing-room area and the administrative quarters compare with the best anywhere, there are lounges and an executive suite, there are guided tours of the visitor centre and ground, there is a 24-hour service for ticket inquiries, and the club shop caters for just about every requirement of the Liverpool fans.

The attendance figures these days may not be as high as in years gone by, as Liverpool – like other clubs – have considered the safety of spectators as being paramount, but through the years there have indeed been some fantastic gates at Anfield. Even before the First World War, gates of 40,000 were common, and in season 1971-72, for the first (but certainly not the last) time, more than a million spectators attended for League matches alone.

The Anfield ground record was set on 2 February 1952, when Liverpool met Wolves in the fourth round of the FA Cup, and the tie was watched by 61,905 people. They saw Liverpool score twice in the first four minutes, though by the end the margin was narrow enough: 2–1.

The Famous Kop

The Kop at Anfield is arguably the most famous section of any football ground throughout Europe. It derives

its name from the battle during the Boer War in South Africa where, on 23 January 1900, the British captured a hill called Spion Kop as part of the plan to relieve Ladysmith. The following day the commanding officer was killed, and the British retreated. When the Boers renewed their attack the following day and regained the hill, they discovered that it had been defended by 300 British soldiers . . . and every single one of them was dead.

Liverpool's Kop was first created in 1906 as a mound of cinders, rubble and earth, and it was later covered with concrete. It was rebuilt in 1928 – 425 feet by 131 feet, 80 feet high at the tallest point, and capable of accommodating 24,000 people under the cantilever roof which, at that time, was the largest single-span structure in English football.

If the steps had been laid end to end, they would have stretched the length of Liverpool docks. With certain modifications, the Kop remained a unique setting for the most passionate and vocally humorous set of football supporters . . . and, indeed, more than one youngster who stood on the Kop went on to play for Liverpool Football Cub. The new Kop was opened officially at the first home game of season 1928-29, and the joyous fans saw Liverpool beat Bury 3–2.

■ *Right:* **Liverpool's public relations officer, Christine Moss, stands by the Shankly Corner, one of the Anfield Visitors' Centre's most notable features.**

■ *Below:* **One of the most stirring sights in football . . . the Kop in full cry at Anfield. The fans who stand on the Kop give their massed support to Liverpool with genuine humour.**

■ The famous bootroom at Anfield, where after the game there was hospitality for the opposition's backroom team. The bootroom was also the place where the Liverpool backroom boys discussed the events of the game . . . and planned how to win the next one.

and to continue to give the club his support in any way he was asked.

Today, Anfield is a soccer stadium to compare with the best in British football, but Liverpool's former Chairman can also remember when the players used to walk to the ground after having got changed elsewhere. That was back in the very early days, the days of John Houlding, who was a brewer with premises in Breck Road. Among the public houses which he owned was the Sandon, only a few hundred yards from the ground at Anfield. There was a time, indeed, when players used to change at the Sandon and then walk across to the Kop. And there was a Houlding Street close to the ground.

While Thomas Valentine Williams played a major role in securing the services of Bill Shankly as manager, John Smith believes the act which T.V. would have rated as possibly his greatest achievement was the building of Liverpool's impressive training headquarters. These are situated at Melwood, and the training complex came into being after T.V. Williams had been instrumental in purchasing nine or 10 acres of land.

T.V. used to recall an occasion in season 1905-06, when Liverpool won the First Division Championship, and – having scored eight goals for his school team in the morning – he sat on a bench at the corner of Anfield Road and Kemlyn Road, while the Press sent details of the match back to their offices by carrier pigeon. That was the day when the Kop – no more than a third of its present

size – started to sing the songs which were to make that section of supporters famous throughout football.

One of the heroes of John Smith's early days as a supporter was Tommy Bromilow, and he adopted a fashion which some other players have followed, down the years. 'Tommy Bromilow was the first footballer I ever saw who played with his shirt outside his shorts,' says Sir John. During his 17-year spell as Chairman, he saw Liverpool collect more than a score of major trophies – a staggering haul, by any standards. After the title and the UEFA Cup in 1973, there was the FA Cup, which Liverpool won in 1974 for a second time while Bill Shankly was manager. Then came the League Championship and the UEFA Cup at the end of season 1975-76, and more honours followed, thick and fast. In 1977 there was the League Championship again, coupled with – for the first time in the club's history – the European Cup; and 12 months later the European trophy remained on the Anfield sideboard. In 1979 and 1980 Liverpool were the undisputed League Champions, in 1981 they carried off the European Cup for the third time and the League Cup for the first time.

In 1982 and 1983 there were other doubles – the Championship to go with the League Cup, on each occasion – while in 1984 Liverpool went one better by adding the European Cup to the League title and the League Cup which, by then, was known as the Milk Cup. After a 12-month gap, Liverpool achieved the great traditional 'double' – again, unique for the club – as they claimed the

League Championship and swept Everton aside in the first FA Cup final Merseyside derby game. In 1988 it was the Championship on its own, in 1989 the FA Cup, and in 1990 the Championship yet again, for the 18th time in Liverpool's history.

When Sir John stepped down at the start of the 1990s, he handed over the Chairmanship to Noel White, an FA councillor who was 10 years younger and who had been co-opted on to the Liverpool board in 1986 after having impressed by his work as the Merseyside and Cheshire FA representative. His beginnings in football were relatively modest – in 1961 he had started out as the Vice-Chairman of his home-town club, non-Leaguers Altrincham, whose Chairman then was Peter Swales (later to become the Chairman of Manchester City).

White and Swales were business partners, as well as partners in the Altrincham soccer venture, and they saw the club prosper and gain a considerable reputation as FA Cup giant-killers, not to mention prospective candidates for a place in the Football League. After six years, Noel White took over as Chairman, and he stayed with Altrincham – the Robins, as they are known – for 19 years. Then he joined the board at Liverpool.

Peter Swales recalls how he and Noel White played football together in their firm's team in the Manchester Wednesday League – in those days, they were teenagers working for a firm of accountants. 'Noel was a centre-half, and a good footballer – he was on Chester's books as an amateur and could have turned professional with them. He made our firm's team virtually unbeatable. He has a love for the game, and he's also a good judge of a footballer.'

Noel White is also one of the quiet men of football, preferring to maintain a low profile and content to let people like the manager get on with the job of ensuring that the club remains successful.

Of his own role as Chairman, he said simply: 'I know it's a cliché, but it's a hard act to follow Sir John, and it's nice to know he will still be here to provide experience in any decision-making. It's an immense challenge for me, but one I'm looking forward to.' And, of course, Liverpool Football Club, as ever, has continued to prosper.

This, perhaps, is an appropriate place to mention other people on the backroom side of the game at Anfield . . . men such as Peter Robinson and Ronnie Moran, who between them have served the club for close on 70 years. Peter Robinson had done the rounds of the smaller clubs before he arrived at Anfield in June, 1965 . . . he had worked in the office at places like Crewe and Stockport, graduated to Secretary, then moved on to Scunthorpe and Brighton before fetching up at Liverpool. His administrative ability was clearly recognised at each and every one of the

■ *Above:* **Liverpool chairman Mr Noel White gained a great deal of experience during his days on the board at non-League Altrincham, and he succeeded Sir John W. Smith at Anfield in 1990.**

■ *Left:* **Peter Robinson – the chief executive of Liverpool Football Club, and one of the most experienced and most respected administrators in football. He has served the Anfield club for more than 25 years.**

clubs he served, but during his time with Liverpool he has truly emerged as one of the most respected and influential administrators in the game. Now he is Liverpool's Chief Executive, and his advice is sought by many folk at other clubs – at home and abroad.

Ronnie Moran? Like Bob Paisley, Joe Fagan, Roy Evans, Phil Thompson, Ron Yeats and Steve Heighway, he became what Bob Paisley used to call 'part of the furniture' at Anfield. Ronnie, a product of Crosby schoolboys, joined Liverpool as a youngster back in 1952, so he has now clocked up practically 40 years' service (his playing career alone spanned 13 seasons). Remarkably, it was the local postman who started the ball rolling, so

far as Ronnie was concerned, because he it was who first suggested to T.V. Williams that this young footballer was worth some attention. Liverpool didn't ignore the tip, and Ronnie Moran became a professional footballer. He was a rugged full-back who became a fixture during the late 1950s and the early 1960s, and he was one of the hardest dead-ball kickers the club has ever had. Not surprising, then, that he became an expert in the art of scoring from the penalty spot. During five seasons, from 1955-56, he missed only half a dozen of the 210 League matches Liverpool played, and in season 1963-64 he was rewarded with a League Championship medal. By the end of his playing career, Ronnie had totalled close on

■ **The boys from the backroom. The expressions on the faces of Bob Paisley, Joe Fagan and Ronnie Moran reflect the importance of the occasion – it's a European Cup semi-final against FC Zurich. Happily, the end result was right, so far as Liverpool were concerned.**

■ *Far right:* **He was a tough-as-teak defender, and one of the hardest dead-ball kickers in the game. This was Ronnie Moran the player . . . and he retained that will-to-win attitude after he had become a backroom man at Anfield. Now he's served the club close on 40 years, taking on the manager's job mid-season in 1990-91.**

400 appearances for his one and only club, and in his first season as reserve team trainer (1972-73) he steered his charges to the Championship of what was then the Central League.

When Kenny Dalglish stunned soccer by leaving Liverpool, Ronnie Moran stepped into the breach and took over the duties of management until Graeme Souness arrived, doing his utmost for the club which has virtually been his life.

It is, perhaps, worth noting that Ronnie Moran's attitude is typical of that adopted by the club as a whole: no-one dwells on what's gone before, everyone has to keep his mind on the job in hand. Maybe that sums up the secret of Liverpool's astounding run of success. You're not encouraged to relax on cloud nine after a major success, and you're certainly not encouraged to think overmuch about the games you've lost – except to learn the lessons from them.

Ronnie Moran was once asked about his League debut for Liverpool. Normally, that's an occasion no player forgets, because it marks a red-letter day in his career. Ronnie in fact made his debut in a red jersey against Derby County at the Baseball Ground in November 1952. When reminded that Liverpool had lost by the odd goal in five, his reaction was short, and very much to the point. 'Oh, I never remember things like that,' he said. He meant it – and that's the Liverpool attitude.

CHAIRMEN
AND
BACKROOM
STAFF

The Merseyside Derby

DERBY-GAME days are days to remember or forget . . . depending upon the performance or the result your side has achieved. Ian St John scored a hat-trick in a Liverpool Senior Cup final against Everton on his debut. Ian Rush has certainly enjoyed his successes against the men from Goodison Park.

One member of Liverpool's backroom staff today, Steve Heighway, still recalls a derby game in season 1970-71, when he was a new boy. The game took place at Anfield, and on the morning of the match Heighway was afflicted with a searing migraine and looked like missing out. But after spending some time lying down in a darkened hotel room he reported fit to play . . . only to see Everton forge a two-goal lead. But Liverpool drew level (Steve scored one of the goals), and Chris Lawler cracked in a late match-winner. Steve said afterwards: 'That was the first time I really came to appreciate what winning a derby game meant, both to the players and to the fans.'

Alan Hansen went on record as saying that he didn't really enjoy playing in derby games . . . but that didn't stop him from overtaking Ian Callaghan and clocking up a new record for appearances in matches against Everton. As for Steve McMahon, he can proudly claim to be the only Scouser who has captained both Liverpool and Everton, and to be the only Scouser also who has collected League Championship and FA Cup winner's medals in the same season.

Derby games are always momentous occasions, and Liverpool have met Everton close on 150 times in League games alone; there have also been four historic meetings in Cup final matches – two of them in the FA Cup final at Wembley. First,

though, there was the final of the Milk Cup, which went to a Maine Road replay that was won by Liverpool; then came the first-ever Liverpool-Everton meeting in the final of the FA Cup, and the Anfield club came out on top once more. The next Cup final was the two-legged tie in the Screen Sport Super Cup, which resulted in another trophy going to Anfield, then Liverpool and Everton did battle at Wembley once more, with the FA Cup at stake . . . and Liverpool won yet again.

The first League game between Liverpool and Everton took place on 13 October 1894, and it was staged at Goodison Park, where a crowd of 44,000 had gathered for this auspicious occasion. It goes without saying that subsequent derby games have always attracted big crowds, no matter how the respective clubs have been faring. And the one sure thing about a derby game is that the outcome can never be taken for granted!

Derby Games between Liverpool and Everton always feature as the 'Match of the Day' so far as Merseyside is concerned, and there have been some high-scoring duels . . . for instance, in seasons 1922-23 and 1925-26, when Liverpool won 5–1 each time at Anfield. In the first game Harry Chambers hit three goals, and in the second Dick Forshaw scored a hat-trick.

In season 1932-33, it was Liverpool 7, Everton 4, as the men from Anfield extracted revenge for a 3–1 defeat earlier in the campaign at Goodison Park. The return match took place on 11 February 1933, and at half-time Liverpool were ahead by the odd goal in five. The Anfield heroes that day were 'Boy' Barton (a hat-trick), Hanson, Morrison, Taylor and Roberts. And the match was watched by 50,000 people.

Season 1935-36 saw Liverpool registering another significant victory . . . 6–0 on home ground. Four goals from Fred Howe (15, 42, 86 and 89 minutes) and two from Gordon Hodgson (28 and 35 minutes) did the damage. In contrast the Goodison game ended goalless.

In seasons 1947-48 and 1971-72, Liverpool scored four goals each time without reply. In 1948, after having won the Goodison duel 3–0, the Anfield Reds had Albert Stubbins, Billy Liddell, Ken Brierley and Jackie Balmer to thank for their 4–0 win. Balmer and Stubbins had been on the mark in the first game, and in the second encounter Stubbins opened the scoring after 14 minutes, while the other three goals came in the space of four minutes late in the second half . . . Liddell (80), Brierley (81) and Balmer (83).

There was a 5–0 home win for the Anfield Reds in season 1965-66, while Goodison Park was the scene of a 4–2 victory for Liverpool in season 1907-08, and in season 1982-83 the scoreline read Everton 0, Liverpool 5. Almost inevitably, Ian Rush was a scorer – indeed, he stuck four of the

goals, with Mark Lawrenson getting the other.

In the FA Cup, season 1954-55 produced a 4–0 fourth-round victory for Liverpool at Goodison Park (the goals came from Liddell, A'Court and two from Evans), and in the final of the Screen Sport Super Cup Ian Rush scored twice in the first leg at Anfield and followed up with a hat-trick in the Goodison Park return.

Here's a question for you to answer . . . can you name the occasion when 98,000 fans saw a derby game in this country? The answer, of course, is at Wembley in 1986, when Liverpool defeated Everton. There were also 82,800 at Wembley for the 1989 FA Cup final between the two clubs, while in the earlier years there was a Goodison Park derby game which attracted an audience of 90,000 fans. There were 50,000 of them packed into Everton's ground, where the match was played, and another 40,000 people watched the game live at Anfield, via closed-circuit television. It has to be recorded that this was one Cup duel Everton won (by the only goal).

For a long time it was that former Everton hero, the legendary William Ralph 'Dixie' Dean, who held sway as the leading marksman in derby games, with 19 goals to his credit; but in recent seasons Ian Rush has struck time and again, to eclipse the Dean record and take his tally well past the 20 mark by the start of the 1990s. It seemed that if 'Rushy' couldn't find the net against Manchester United in 21 attempts to do so, he simply couldn't miss beating his Welsh international team-mate, Neville Southall, at least once when Liverpool and Everton were duelling. Rush, in fact, struck twice against Everton during season 1989-90 to take his derby game goal tally to an astonishing 23 in two dozen appearances, and

in the remarkable 4–4 draw in a fifth-round FA Cup replay at Goodison in season 1990-91 Rush took his haul to a couple of dozen goals.

As with many of the big city clubs which are great rivals, as well as close neighbours, Liverpool and Everton have had players who have worn the colours of both. Back in 1897 Fred Geary was transferred from Everton to Liverpool, and just before the First World War, Liverpool signed an Irish international named Billy Lacey (they undoubtedly got the better of the bargain in this exchange deal). Lacey, capped ten times while with Everton, collected 13 more Irish caps while he was at Anfield. Another old-timer who wore the colours of both clubs was Andrew Hannah.

In between the two world wars, Liverpool signed Tommy Johnson and sold Dick Forshaw, and in more recent times Tony McNamara and Dave Hickson both left Goodison Park for Anfield, while Jimmy Payne, Johnny Morrissey, Alan Harper and Kevin Sheedy all made the journey in the opposite direction. More recently still, of course, Steve McMahon – who had started out as a ball-boy at Goodison and became a first-teamer there – arrived at Liverpool via Aston Villa, while a former reserve centre-half at Anfield, Dave Watson, moved from Norwich City to Goodison Park. And striker David Johnson, who kicked off with Everton, became a Liverpool player after service with Ipswich Town.

Incidentally, it's worth remembering that between them Liverpool and Everton have

■ David Johnson – one of the men who played for both Liverpool and Everton – seen here going for goal during the 1977 FA Cup Final against Manchester United.

exerted what could be termed a Merseyside monopoly of the game's major domestic honours during the past decade or so – in fact, when it comes to the League Championship, the title (with just three notable exceptions) has finished up at either Anfield or Goodison Park. Manchester has scarcely had a look in, while London has been given tantalising glimpses of the title. The exceptions were Aston Villa, who claimed the Championship in season 1980-81, and Arsenal, who did the trick with virtually the last kick at Anfield in 1988-89, and won again in 1990-91.

Milk Cup Final, 1984

Liverpool 0 Everton 0 (Wembley, 25 March)

REPLAY

Liverpool 1 Everton 0 (Maine Road, 28 March)

For the first time, Liverpool and Everton met in a Cup final at Wembley when, in the spring of 1984, they came up against each other in the Milk Cup.

Liverpool were the holders – indeed, they were going for a hat-trick of successes which would see the trophy become theirs for keeps . . . and it was Everton who barred their way.

At Wembley, in fact, it was generally agreed that Liverpool did not produce their best form and that they might have been a shade fortunate to have kept the old enemy at bay – although Alan Kennedy had a 'winner' disallowed, and Everton 'keeper Neville Southall emerged as man of the match after an electrifying save during extra time as Ian Rush sent in a rocket-like volley from the edge of the box.

Liverpool manager Joe Fagan admitted he was thankful for the draw, though; Everton manager Howard Kendall believed that Liverpool had been 'subdued by the quality of the Everton performance'; and Liverpool skipper Graeme Souness reckoned: 'We were lucky Everton didn't score in the opening 45 minutes . . . but I was surprised they were still there at the finish.'

Then it was on to Maine Road for the replay – a replay which was decided by a Souness goal, as he

drilled the ball through the Everton defence to leave Southall diving in vain to his left.

FA Cup Final 1986

Liverpool 3 Everton 1 (Wembley, 10 May)

When Liverpool and Everton went to Wembley to contest the final of the FA Cup, it revived memories of the 1984 Milk Cup final, which ended in a draw and a 1–0 replay victory for Liverpool at Maine Road. As for the 1986 FA Cup final, that was another dream come true . . . although someone, eventually, would wind up as the losers.

There were 98,000 fans inside Wembley stadium, thousands more – unable to get tickets – who waited outside, their ears glued to transistor radios as the drama unfolded. Liverpool player-manager Kenny Dalglish made history by leading out his team, but for defender Gary Gillespie, there was a cruel stroke of luck. Only hours before the final, he had been struck down by a stomach virus; so Mark Lawrenson took over the No. 2 jersey, playing alongside Alan Hansen at the heart of the defence.

Liverpool were the first to show signs of settling, but Everton eventually began to gain their rhythm and, inside the first half-hour, the Blues struck the first blow. Peter Reid's piercing, lofted midfield pass dropped just right for the spring-heeled Gary Lineker, who sped past Alan Hansen, then drove in a shot which Bruce Grobbelaar could only parry. Lineker followed up to drive the ball back, and while Grobbelaar got a second touch, he couldn't prevent the ball from crossing the line. Then it was half-time, with the score still 1–0 to Everton.

As the second half got under way, Everton tried to exert the kind of pressure which would bring another goal and kill off Liverpool, and twice fortune favoured Bruce Grobbelaar. There was danger when Kevin Sheedy – himself a former Liverpool player – drove a shot across the face of goal; then a goal-bound header from Graeme Sharp was tipped over by the 'keeper in brilliant fashion. That save, indeed, turned out to be a

■ At the Maine Road replay of the Milk Cup final in 1984, Graeme Souness emerges as Liverpool's hero, as he drills a shot through the Everton defence. It's the match-winner, so the trophy stays on the Anfield sideboard.

crucial one, because it came after Liverpool had drawn level.

Their equaliser came when Danish international Jan Molby intercepted a clearance and delivered a through pass which caught the Everton defence flat-footed. But not Ian Rush . . . he was pouncing, to take the ball in his stride and, as 'keeper Bobby Mimms came out in a desperate attempt to block, Rush just took the ball round him and glanced an angled shot into the net. That goal set Liverpool pulses racing.

After Grobbelaar's super-save, Liverpool simply became stronger and stronger, and it was Molby again who set up a goal when he squared the ball. It evaded bodies and legs until Craig Johnston got his foot to the ball, and he had the composure to stick away a close-range shot.

Everton sent on Adrian Heath, in the hope that 'Inchy' could pull something out of the bag as he

had done on previous occasions; but when a goal came, once again it was for Liverpool. This time the ball moved sweetly from Rush to Molby and on to Ronnie Whelan, who delivered a pass of precision back to the Welsh international. And in a split-second Rush had driven the ball past Mimms and into the far corner. So ended the 1986 FA Cup final, which meant that Liverpool had achieved the legendary 'double', as they had already claimed the League title.

FA Cup Final 1989

Liverpool 3 Everton 2 (Wembley, 20 May)

This was the third time that Liverpool and Everton had met in a Wembley Cup final – the third time in six years – and Everton fans hoped that it would be 'third time lucky' for their team. Once more, however, their hopes were dashed, come the final whistle.

The final kicked off in sizzling style, went into the last minute of normal time with an explosive equaliser, and finished as a stunner in extra time. Team boss Kenny Dalglish kept faith with John Aldridge (a two-goal hero in the semi-final), so Ian Rush, who had turned up trumps with a brace of goals in 1986, had to settle for a seat on the bench. Wembley was indeed a cauldron of sound . . . and heat, because the temperature soared to 90 degrees, so the players had to try to strike a balance between conserving energy while giving 100 per cent effort. Four minutes into the match Liverpool fans were roaring with delight as Steve

■ **Action from the FA Cup final of 1986, when Liverpool achieved an historic double as they beat Everton at Wembley and claimed the League Championship, as well.** *Above:* **Ian Rush hammers in his second goal.** *Right:* **Gary Stevens and Jan Molby during the Wembley duel.**

Nicol produced a telling pass to start an attack, Steve McMahon helped the ball on to Aldridge, whose first-time shot had Neville Southall well and truly beaten.

By half-time, Liverpool should have had one or two more goals, because they had certainly been in the driving seat; yet as the minutes ticked away, only that one goal separated the sides. Liverpool sent on Ian Rush, and the arrival of Stuart McCall gave Everton an injection of fresh blood, but with mere seconds to the final whistle, it seemed McCall and the Blues were fighting a lost cause. However, as Everton tried one last time, it was McCall who, in a goalmouth scramble, forced the ball over the line and rescued his side, to take Liverpool into extra time.

Liverpool took off Steve Staunton and sent on Barry Venison; and they switched Steve Nicol from right-back to left-back. It was Nicol who went upfield and paved the way for another Liverpool strike, as Rush collected the ball, turned on a sixpence, and crashed a power-drive into the top corner of the net. It seemed that he would be the match-winner. But once again Everton produced an ace from up their sleeve, and once again the ace was named McCall. As Everton attacked, Alan Hansen headed the ball out of defence, and it fell for McCall, who was about 25 yards from goal. But when he fired the ball back, it fairly flew past Bruce Grobbelaar, so Everton were level and they still had everything to play for.

At that stage, people were starting to think about a replay on 8 June . . . then Rush took a hand in the proceedings once more. The ball came

across, and he got a touch to it with his head. Rush was at full stretch, but that glancing header was sufficient to curl the ball beyond Southall's reach. This time, there was no way back for Everton – and Rush himself had overtaken the derby game record of the legendary Dixie Dean, by having scored a total of 21 goals, to Dean's tally of 19. Rush had also become the first footballer to have scored two goals twice in Wembley FA Cup finals – and, remarkably, it was also the first time that two substitutes (Rush and McCall) had scored in an FA Cup final.

■ **It's the Liverpool–Everton FA Cup final at Wembley in 1989, and once again Everton suffer from the attentions of Ian Rush.** *Below:* **he tucks away a scoring chance to help set up victory for Liverpool.** *Above:* **Scoring his second goal of the game.**

LIVERPOOL V EVERTON RESULTS

LIVERPOOL have enjoyed far greater success in derby games at Anfield during the last 20 years than they did in the first two decades of their duels. From season 1894-95 to season 1919-20 (ignoring the First World War years) Liverpool won only three of the Anfield encounters with their old rivals; in contrast, the 20 years from season 1971-72 to 1990-91 yielded them 11 victories on home ground and only two defeats (they lost ten times at Anfield between season 1899-1900 and season 1914-15). At Goodison Park Liverpool won seven times from season 1894-95 to season 1919-20, while during the most recent couple of decades they scored nine victories. Opposite is the complete list of Liverpool–Everton League results (the Liverpool score is given first, both home and away:

The FA Cup

Here is a complete list of results between Liverpool and Everton in the FA Cup (home team first):

First Round 1901-02
Liverpool 2   Everton 2
Everton 0   Liverpool 2

First Round 1904-05
Liverpool 1   Everton 1
Everton 2   Liverpool 1

Semi-final 1905-06
Everton 2   Liverpool 0   (*Villa Park*)

Second Round 1910-11
Everton 2   Liverpool 1

Third Round 1931-32
Everton 1   Liverpool 2

Semi-final 1949-50
Liverpool 2   Everton 0   (*Maine Road*)

Fourth Round 1954-55
Everton 0   Liverpool 4

Fifth Round 1966-67
Everton 1   Liverpool 0

Semi-final 1970-71
Liverpool 2   Everton 1   (*Old Trafford*)

Semi-final 1976-77
Liverpool 2   Everton 2   (*Maine Road*)
Liverpool 3   Everton 0   (*Maine Road*)

Fourth Round 1980-81
Everton 2   Liverpool 1

Final 1985-86
Liverpool 3   Everton 1   (*Wembley*)

Fifth Round 1987-88
Everton 0   Liverpool 1

Final 1988-89
Liverpool 3   Everton 2   (*Wembley*)

Fifth Round 1990-91
Liverpool 0   Everton 0
Everton 4   Liverpool 4
Everton 1   Liverpool 0

Season	Home	Away	Season	Home	Away	Season	Home	Away	Season	Home	Away
1894-95	2–2	0–3	1914-15	0–5	3–1	1937-38	1–2	3–1	1973-74	0–0	1–0
1896-97	0–0	1–2	1919-20	3–1	0–0	1938-39	0–3	1–2	1974-75	0–0	0–0
1897-98	3–1	0–3	1920-21	1–0	3–0	1946-47	0–0	0–1	1975-76	1–0	0–0
1898-99	2–0	2–1	1921-22	1–1	1–1	1947-48	4–0	3–0	1976-77	3–1	0–0
1899-1900	1–2	1–3	1922-23	5–1	1–0	1948-49	0–0	1–1	1977-78	0–0	1–0
1900-01	1–2	1–1	1923-24	1–2	0–1	1949-50	3–1	0–0	1978-79	1–1	0–1
1901-02	2–2	0–4	1924-25	3–1	1–0	1950-51	0–2	3–1	1979-80	2–2	2–1
1902-03	0–0	1–3	1925-26	5–1	3–3	1962-63	0–0	2–2	1980-81	1–0	2–2
1903-04	2–2	2–5	1926-27	1–0	0–1	1963-64	2–1	1–3	1981-82	3–1	3–1
1905-06	1–1	2–4	1927-28	3–3	1–1	1964-65	0–4	1–2	1982-83	0–0	5–0
1906-07	1–2	0–0	1928-29	1–2	0–1	1965-66	5–0	0–0	1983-84	3–0	1–1
1907-08	0–0	4–2	1929-30	0–3	3–3	1966-67	0–0	1–3	1984-85	0–1	0–1
1908-09	0–1	0–5	1931-32	1–3	1–2	1967-68	1–0	0–1	1985-86	0–2	3–2
1909-10	0–1	3–2	1932-33	7–4	1–3	1968-69	1–1	0–0	1986-87	3–1	0–0
1910-11	0–2	1–0	1933-34	3–2	0–0	1969-70	0–2	3–0	1987-88	2–0	0–1
1911-12	1–3	1–2	1934-35	2–1	0–1	1970-71	3–2	0–0	1988-89	1–1	0–0
1912-13	0–2	2–0	1935-36	6–0	0–0	1971-72	4–0	0–1	1989-90	2–1	3–1
1913-14	1–2	2–1	1936-37	3–2	0–2	1972-73	1–0	2–0	1990-91	3–1	3–2

■ *Left:* **One of the all-time great derby-game occasions . . . the FA Cup replay in 1991 when Liverpool and Everton shared eight goals. And this was one of the brace scored by Peter Beardsley.**

The League Cup

Liverpool and Everton have met once in the League Cup (then called the Milk Cup):

Final 1983-84

Liverpool 0 Everton 0 (*Wembley*)
Liverpool 1 Everton 0 (*Maine Road*)

The Charity Shield

Liverpool and Everton have met three times in the Charity Shield:

1966-67

Everton 0 Liverpool 1 (*Goodison Park*)

1984-85

Everton 1 Liverpool 0 (*Wembley*)

1986-87 (shared)

Liverpool 1 Everton 1 (*Wembley*)

The Screen Sport Super Cup

Liverpool and Everton met in the two-leg final (home and away):

1986-87

Liverpool 3 Everton 1
Everton 1 Liverpool 4

■ **Mark Lawrenson in action during the 1984 Milk Cup final. An outstanding, all-round footballer who could switch with equal facility from defence to midfield, it was a cruel blow to club and player when injury forced him to bow out of top-class football.**

IVERPOOL have had so many players through the 100 years of their history who could truly be termed great that it is difficult to know where to begin . . . and so easy to omit someone who deserves to be included. So if in this chapter there are any favourite players omitted, it could be purely by accident, through pressure of space, or that we all have our ideas of what constitutes greatness in a footballer.

The chapter starts with the section on goal-keepers – and Liverpool have had their fair share of top-line 'keepers. When it comes to the men who play in defence there have been more than a few, too, who could operate at full-back, in the middle of the back-four line, or (just as effect-ively) in midfield. So the allocation of players to the section on defenders and the section on mid-fielders that follows is somewhat

Golden Greats

arbitrary. Again, the wingers in some cases could play wide as mid-fielders, while some strikers could be termed inside-forwards and in at least one instance (Billy Liddell) you could say that here was a player who was a one-man forward line, since he could operate down the flank or go straight through the middle.

All in all, this chapter illustrates just how well Liverpool have been served by players in every position, down the years . . . and today's crop is no exception. Indeed, it is truly remarkable when you consider that only three goalkeepers (Tommy Lawrence, Ray Clemence and, now, Bruce Grob-belaar) have collectively spanned three decades and, in the process, given precious few others more than a brief glimpse of the first-team peg in the Anfield dressing-room. Lawrence was Liverpool's 'keeper of the 1960s, Clemence the 'keeper of the 1970s and Grobbelaar has been the 'keeper through the 1980s and into the 1990s.

Another astonishing feature of the Liverpool scene is the fact that the club has had a clutch of players who have clocked up 600 games or more, or 100 goals or more . . . Ian Callaghan, Ray Clemence, Emlyn Hughes, Phil Neal, Tommy Smith, Kenny Dalglish and Alan Hansen come into the former category, while not so long ago Liverpool could boast five players who, between them, had totalled more than 1,000 goals. Into the 100-goal category came Ian Rush, Kenny Dalg-

lish, John Aldridge, Peter Beardsley and John Barnes – and all were at Anfield at the same time. It seems doubtful that any other club in British football could ever have had five such men on their books, all at the same time.

GOALKEEPERS

No wonder Liverpool decided to make their telegraphic address 'Goalkeeper' because, down the years, they have had some of the finest and most famous last lines of defence in the business. Indeed, people who have supported the club for more than half a century have to think long and hard before they can come up with the name of the goalkeeper they consider the best of the lot.

There was Harry Storer at the start; there was Teddy Doig; there was the great Elisha Scott, who nailed down the job for many seasons; there was Sam Hardy; there was the South African, Arthur Riley; there was Kenny Campbell; there was Doug Rudham (another Springbok); there was Welsh international Cyril Sidlow; there were Scottish internationals Tommy Younger and Tommy Lawrence; there was the England ace, Ray Clemence; and now there is the Zimbabwean international, Bruce Grobbelaar.

Harry Storer's Anfield career spanned five seasons. He made his bow on New Year's Day, 1896, totalled more than 120 appearances, and won a Second Division Championship medal in season 1895-96, while the following term, when Liverpool finished fifth in the First Division, Storer and his defenders conceded only ten goals at Anfield and 28 in their away matches – a total which, in fact, equalled the feat of Aston Villa, who carried off the Championship. Some of the goals came in high-scoring games, too – a 4–3 defeat at Sunderland, a 3–3 home draw against Villa, a 3–2 defeat at Derby, a 4–1 defeat at Burnley . . . and a 6-1 hiding at Stoke. So 17 of the 28 goals conceded away came in just four matches.

In season 1898-99 Liverpool chased Villa home all the way, to wind up in second place, and that term the Anfield Reds claimed the best defensive record in the top flight – 23 goals conceded away, only ten on their own ground. The turn of the year was a landmark in Storer's career, because after having kicked off with Liverpool on New Year's Day, he bowed out on Christmas Day, 1899.

If the name of Storer has a familiar ring about it for present-day followers of football, that is

because he came from a sporting family. He himself played cricket for Derbyshire, his brother (William) also played cricket for the county, and for England, and his son, Harry, played cricket for Derbyshire, football for Derby County and England, and later managed Coventry City, Birmingham City and Derby County. From all of this, it might be gathered that the Storers originally came from the Derby area, and that is the case. Indeed, before he joined Liverpool Harry Storer had played for Derby Midland, then Loughborough Town and Woolwich Arsenal.

Chesterfield, of course, is also in Derbyshire, and when you think of the town famous for its crooked church spire you think also of goalkeepers from Chesterfield who became famous in League football. The first name that probably springs to mind is that of Gordon Banks of Leicester and Stoke, who helped England win the World Cup. But Banks wasn't the first top-class goalkeeper to come from Chesterfield . . . many years before his arrival on the big-time soccer scene there was a

fellow called Sam Hardy, who joined Liverpool in 1905. In his first season with the club he claimed a Championship medal. Hardy cost Liverpool what would now be the laughable fee of £500, and during the course of seven seasons he totalled the best part of 250 games.

Sam Hardy

They say that all goalkeepers let soft ones in, at some time or another, but it's those who let in the fewest soft ones who are the best. Hardy was not cast in the mould of spectacular 'keepers, but he was certainly consistent when it came to stopping the ball going into the net; and his goalkeeping prowess led to his being capped 21 times by England. When he left Liverpool for Aston Villa in 1912 it was to achieve the further distinction of collecting two FA Cup medals, and he also played for another Midlands club, Nottingham Forest – indeed, he didn't hang up his boots and take off

■ Sam Hardy, who joined Liverpool in 1905 – just in time to win a League Championship medal – cost the club £500. He totalled the best part of 250 appearances in the course of seven seasons, and won 21 England caps.

those goalkeeping gloves until he was 41 years of age.

The 'keeper who had to make way for Hardy at Anfield was Teddy Doig, a three-club man who served Blackburn Rovers and Sunderland, as well as Liverpool – indeed, he spent 14 years with the North-East club and was one of a trio of players (McCombie and Watson were the others) capped by Scotland against England in 1903. Doig joined Liverpool the following year, and became a regular in the side which gained promotion: in fact, during his first season Liverpool conceded no more than 25 goals as they headed the Second Division.

Hardy took over when Doig retired in 1908, and he maintained the Anfield goalkeeping tradition. He won 14 of his caps while in the service of Liverpool and, long after he had vacated his position between the posts, he retained one ambition – that was 'to see Liverpool win the Cup'. Hardy lived long enough to see the Anfield club do just that (in 1965) and, having done so, he died a few months afterwards, at the age of 79.

Elisha Scott

If Hardy became a regular for England, another Liverpool goalkeeper, Elisha Scott (whose brother, Billy . . . whisper it . . . played for Everton), became a legendary figure with both club and country – meaning Liverpool and Ireland. Scott played for his country on 31 occasions, and between 1912 and 1934 he set a club record of more than 425 League appearances (later overtaken by players such as Billy Liddell, Ian Callaghan, Emlyn Hughes, Ray Clemence, Phil Neal and Alan Hansen). Scott's brother, who figured in Everton's 1906 FA Cup-winning side, was also a goalkeeping international, but it was Elisha whom people remembered most.

Having started his career in his native Ulster, where he played for the Belfast Boys Brigade team, he joined the Irish League club, Linfield, though they then allowed him to go to a junior club. Linfield's loss was Liverpool's gain, and the Anfield club could have sold Scott on at least a couple of occasions. He was no giant, for sure – he stood no more than 5ft 9½in (1.77m) tall – but his agility was such that the fans used to call him 'The Cat', and he had just about the safest pair of hands in the business. When Liverpool captured the Championship of the First Division in two successive seasons during the early 1920s, Scott played in 81 of the 84 matches and conceded only 63 goals . . . shades of Liverpool defensive feats in later years.

Scott won 27 of his caps during his Anfield career, which spanned not only 18 playing seasons, but a world war. That interruption cost him many more outings for Liverpool, and surely

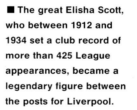

■ The great Elisha Scott, who between 1912 and 1934 set a club record of more than 425 League appearances, became a legendary figure between the posts for Liverpool.

more caps, as well; but as it was, he was still playing for his country when he was almost 42 years of age, and when he finally moved on it was to return to Ireland as player-manager of Belfast Celtic. His Anfield farewell turned out to be an emotional occasion, and there were tears in the eyes of fans who had idolised one of football's all-time goalkeeping greats.

A contemporary of Scott was Kenny Campbell, who was one of seven Scottish players in Liverpool's 1914 FA Cup final side which lost to Burnley. Campbell had arrived from Cambuslang in 1911, and he stayed for ten years at Anfield, though the war, and the emergence of Scott, restricted him to fewer than 150 games. It was during his spell at Anfield that Campbell won the first three of his eight caps and, remarkably, although he made way for Scott, when Ireland and Scotland came up against each other in 1922, the pair were in opposition as the last line of defence for their respective countries. Campbell travelled on from Anfield, back to Scotland to Partick Thistle, then back into English football with Stoke City and Leicester City before finally making Merseyside his home once more, as he had a spell playing for New Brighton. Kenny Campbell remained a Liverpool man at heart, and – like Sam Hardy – he lived to see the club win the FA Cup.

In years gone by there was a South African contingent at Anfield, and two of these players – Arthur Riley and Doug Rudham – kept goal for the club. Rudham, indeed, could claim the distinction of having been the last amateur to play for Liverpool, because in season 1954-55 he made 25 appearances in League and Cup games before signing the forms which made him a professional. But long before that, Arthur Riley had been Liverpool's last line of defence.

He had played with the great Gordon Hodgson in the South African touring side of 1924, and while at the outset he was in the shadow of Elisha Scott, when the Irishman stepped down Riley really came into his own, because in an Anfield career spanning 14 seasons he totalled more than 330 appearances. Later still, he worked on the Anfield ground staff, and as someone who had been a top-class 'keeper, he was able to pass on valuable tips about the job to players such as Cyril Sidlow, who himself won international honours with Wales.

Sidlow, who had begun his career with Wolverhampton Wanderers, was a £4,000 investment by Liverpool when he left Molineux in February 1946, and that made him a record-priced goalkeeper for the club. Capped by Wales at junior and amateur level while playing for Colwyn Bay, he won seven senior international caps during his time with Liverpool, and there was one notable occasion when he starred against his old club,

■ Arthur Riley in action, as Liverpool's last line of defence. His Anfield career spanned 14 seasons and he played more than 330 games – then he worked on the ground staff and passed on tips about goalkeeping to players who followed in his footsteps.

■ Scottish international Tommy Younger joined the Anfield club from Hibernian. 'Big Tam' proudly claimed that he never played second-team football during his three seasons with Liverpool, and he missed only four senior matches.

Wolves, in an end-of-season match which Liverpool won 2–1 on their way to the League Championship in season 1946-47. Sidlow, who totalled more than 160 games for the Reds, was in the FA Cup final side beaten by Arsenal in 1950.

During the mid-1950s Liverpool went prospecting north of the border for a goalkeeper, and they came back with an amiable giant of a fellow called Tommy Younger. 'Big Tam', ever-ready to smile, had won two Scottish League medals with one of the Edinburgh clubs, Hibernian, and when he signed for Liverpool in June 1956, Hibs pocketed a £9,000 fee. Capped eight times by Scotland already, Younger was honoured on 16 other occasions during his career with Liverpool, and he played in the finals of the 1958 World Cup. He had no more than three seasons at Anfield, but he played more than 125 games, missing only four senior matches, and proudly claimed that he never played second-team football while at Liverpool. Then he returned to Scotland to become player-manager of Falkirk (another 'keeper, Bert Slater, arrived at Anfield as part of the deal). 'Big

Tam' also had spells with Stoke City and Leeds United, went back to Scotland to rejoin his first club, Hibs – this time as a director – and became President of the Scottish Football Association (an office he still held at the time of his death).

Tommy Lawrence

Moving closer to the present, we come to another Scot named Tommy – although this time, the accent had a distinctly Lancashire flavour about it. Tommy Lawrence arrived at Anfield shortly after Tommy Younger – he signed professional in 1957 – and he had to play the waiting game before he broke through to the senior side. However, when Tommy Lawrence did get his big chance, he seized it with both hands, and while it sometimes seemed that he was under-rated by critics who weren't regulars at Anfield, he certainly proved his worth to Liverpool.

Tommy was a down-to-earth character who did his job in a workmanlike, rather than a showy,

fashion, and after having made his debut in season 1962-63 he proved impossible to shift for the best part of seven campaigns, as he became an ever-present virtually season by season. He it was who kept Ray Clemence waiting in the wings for some two and a half years, and his remarkable consistency meant that Tommy Lawrence missed no more than a handful of matches in eight seasons overall. Medals came his way in the League Championship (twice) and the FA Cup, and in season 1968-69 he figured in a Liverpool defence which set a record by conceding only 24 goals throughout the entire 42-game season. It was a record which Ray Clemence and his team-mates were later to beat, but that in no way detracts from the feat of Lawrence and company.

Bill Shankly certainly admired the man people called the 'sweeper-keeper' . . . Lawrence utilised his anticipation as Liverpool's last line of defence to such an extent that he reckoned there were times when he played virtually as an extra back. Capped three times by Scotland (and rated unlucky not to have won more international honours), he totalled close on 400 appearances for the Anfield club before moving on to Tranmere Rovers. It was significant that in season 1970-71 Tommy Lawrence made only one appearance in Liverpool's first team . . . significant, because at that time Bill Shankly was giving the entire side a new look – and in goal the figure of Ray Clemence was coming more and more to the fore. The previous term, Clemence had managed 14 League games . . . season 1970-71 saw him playing in 41 League matches, and during the next 10 terms he was (like Lawrence before him) virtually an ever-present. By the time he left Liverpool for Tottenham Hotspur he had totalled more than 650 games, and he went on to top the 1,000 mark during his career.

Ray Clemence

Clemence turned out to be one of the bargain buys of all time, because he was signed from Scunthorpe United in 1967 for a modest fee, reported to be £20,000. Capped by England at Under-23 level, he made his first senior international appearance in a World Cup qualifying game against Wales at Cardiff in November 1972, and that made him the club's first England international goalkeeper since Sam Hardy, more than 60 years previously.

On 14 October 1978, the Anfield faithful reserved a special cheer for Ray Clemence, because when Liverpool played Derby County he was making his 500th appearance in goal for the club, and playing the 550th game of his career. This was the man who, in his school days, had been told to 'go in goal, or don't play at all' when a

■ *Above:* **Ron Yeats watches, as 'keeper Tommy Lawrence – another of the stalwarts in Liverpool's team of the 1960s – makes certain that a header from Manchester City's Colin Bell doesn't sneak inside the post.**

■ *Left:* **Ray Clemence had to play the waiting game for more than two years, but when he finally took over from Tommy Lawrence he became a fixture in goal for Liverpool. By the time he moved to Tottenham Hotspur he had totalled more than 650 appearances for the Anfield club.**

cup final was being staged – by October 1978, he had played in almost 150 Cup-ties at home and in Europe. By September, 1979, Ray Clemence had kept more than 300 clean sheets, and by March 1981 he was looking forward to taking his total of career appearances to 700, while he had collected more than 50 England caps. At that stage, his medal haul was five in the League Championship, two in the European Cup, two in the UEFA Cup, and one in the FA Cup. And it had all started when he played his first game in goal (previously he had been a centre-half) for Skegness Youth Club.

Records? In season 1978-79, Ray had beaten Bob Wilson's Arsenal record of 25 clean sheets in First Division matches and in a career spanning Scunthorpe United, Liverpool and England he had prevented the opposition from scoring in 304 of his 630 games . . . more than any other goalkeeper in history. In season 1978-79, also, he had conceded only 16 League goals, thus shattering the previous record of 21 for a 42-match League programme. And only four of those 16 goals had been scored at Anfield. Yet another record went when Ray totalled 325 consecutive matches and in December 1980 he clocked up his 500th appearance in the Football League, as Liverpool met Manchester United at Old Trafford on Boxing Day. Once again, he kept a clean sheet . . . in contrast to his fourth outing with Scunthorpe, when he let in seven goals at Grimsby. Ray recalled that while only one of those goals was really his fault, he was worried that, at the age of 18, his career as a 'keeper could be finished!

Ray Clemence and Peter Shilton were rivals for the England jersey over the years, with Ray having the edge for quite a while. And while Shilton himself has paid tribute to Clemence on more than one occasion, a former Everton manager also summed up what Ray meant to Liverpool: 'I rate him the best in the business. It's difficult to measure his value to Liverpool, but I rate him their top player – yes, even higher than Kenny Dalglish. Clemence is basically an individual performer – he plays behind a solid defence, but whenever called on he makes breathtaking saves. In one-versus-one situations, "Clem" is brilliant. He's so quick off his line he often beats opposition strikers to through balls. His timing of runs and his bravery when diving into a forest of flying boots make him a great 'keeper. Over a season, I believe Ray is worth 12 points to Liverpool. It must be sickening for opponents to see him making save after save when he should be picking the ball out of the net.' The man who said that about Ray Clemence was Gordon Lee, whose career in management took him from Blackburn Rovers to Newcastle United and on to Goodison Park. And Lee had his own method of assessing

players . . . to get a closer look at 'keepers in the thick of the action, he made a point of standing on the terraces behind the goal to weigh up the 'keeper's positioning and awareness.

The day came when 'Clem' decided that he had spent long enough at Anfield, and he opted for a transfer to Tottenham Hotspur. It was a day when everyone wondered just how Liverpool would be able to replace the man who had been such a rock-solid last line of defence through a dozen campaigns and more than 650 matches. In a way, it was a similar sort of situation which the club had faced when Kevin Keegan departed for SV Hamburg; then, Liverpool had come up with Kenny Dalglish, and now they proved that there was life after Ray Clemence by coming up with an extrovert goalkeeper called Bruce Grobbelaar.

Bruce Grobbelaar

It took a fair period of patient stalking before Liverpool finally landed Bruce, because there was the little matter of a work permit, for one thing, and interest had been shown by various other clubs as Bruce did a stint with Crewe Alexandra in this country. Born in Durban, he had shown all-round excellence as a sportsman . . . he was good at basketball, baseball, cricket and rugby union, and was an expert swimmer. As a youngster he had one sporting hero above all others – Babe Ruth, the American baseball star – and Bruce himself might have achieved fame as a top pitcher had he taken up the offer of a scholarship to play baseball in the United States. He was then 19, so the world was his oyster; yet, having played soccer from the age of seven, and competitive matches by the time he was 13 or 14, he stuck with football.

Behind Grobbelaar was a spell of Army service – at 17, he was in the Rhodesian Army and fighting guerrillas – and ahead of him was a career in top-class soccer. It seemed he had indeed been born to become a goalkeeper, because both his parents kept goal (his mother was a hockey player), and at the age of 18 he was playing for Rhodesia. Bruce travelled on . . . to play for Vancouver Whitecaps, in the North American Soccer League, and briefly for Crewe Alexandra, in the English League – where he added to the fans' enjoyment of the game by electing to take a penalty in one match . . . and scoring from the spot.

Tony Waddington, who managed Bruce during his spell with Crewe, had no doubts about his ability to get to the very top in English soccer. 'He has the strength of Peter Shilton and the suppleness of Gordon Banks' was the Waddington verdict; and clubs such as Manchester United, Nottingham Forest, Derby County, West Bromwich Albion and Bournemouth all weighed up the

prospects of signing Bruce. But it was Liverpool who kept on the trail, after he had rejoined the Whitecaps, and the game of patience paid off when Bob Paisley flew out to the west coast of Canada and clinched the transfer.

So Bruce arrived at Anfield, and it was expected that he would have to wait for his chance. But in no time at all, he had been pitched in at the deep end, as Ray Clemence departed for Spurs. It was a big test of temperament and ability for the new boy, but after making his League debut against Wolves at Molineux in August 1981, he went on to justify the £250,000 Liverpool had paid for him by turning in the kind of displays which made him an ever-present through his first five seasons at Anfield. And he remained Liverpool's first-choice 'keeper through the remainder of the 1980s, though he did have a spell out of action through illness.

Not surprisingly, for such a colourful character, Bruce has had to contend with criticism, as well as praise, but through a decade he has provided the best possible answer by holding down a very demanding job with a club which will accept nothing less than the best. Ray Clemence termed Bruce Grobbelaar 'one of the top 'keepers – he's been tremendously consistent since I left . . .' and Neville Southall (rated by some as the world's No. 1) voted Bruce one of the top three goalkeepers in Britain, while former team-mate Graeme Souness rated him simply as the best.

Like Ray Clemence before him, Bruce goes out with the intention of winding up as the 'keeper who has kept the greatest number of clean sheets in a season, and by the start of the 1990s he had managed to prevent the opposition from scoring on more than 200 occasions during a career which had seen him top the 500 mark for appearances with Liverpool. One of his saves – against Everton in an FA Cup final – was said to have been the turning point of the match, and he came out on top in the 1984 European Cup final against AS Roma, when there was a penalty shoot-out to decide the destination of the trophy.

When it comes to medals, Bruce has collected his fair share . . . six in the Championship, plus medals in the European Cup, the FA Cup and the Milk Cup. He was a member of the side which did the League/FA Cup 'double' during the mid-1980s, and at the start of the 1990s Liverpool were underlining their confidence in him as they offered him a new deal at a time when he still had a year to run on his current contract. If there was one major disappointment for Bruce Grobbelaar, it lay in the fact that, despite his having a British passport, he was denied the chance to stake his claims to international recognition with England, though he was chosen for the Football League side which played in Belfast against the Irish League (whose centenary it was) in

November 1990. In the meantime, he carried on helping Liverpool as they made their bid to retain the Championship of the Football League.

As a footnote, let us not forget one goalkeeper whose claim to fame lay in his name, his nationality and the circumstances of his debut for Liverpool. The 'keeper in question was called Bill McOwen, and despite the fact that his name had a tartan ring about it, he was the only English member in a team of Liverpool Scots. What's more, that was the team which kicked off in the club's first-ever League game, at the start of season 1893-94.

■ Bruce Grobbelaar was pitched in at the deep end when Ray Clemence joined Spurs, but Bruce stayed the course to clock up more than 500 first-team appearances for Liverpool, as he fended off all challenges for the 'keeper's jersey.

DEFENDERS

You could have picked four teams, from the list of players who have served Liverpool so well as defenders, and still have had a few left over for a

fifth eleven; not only that, but some of these players could operate just as effectively in other roles. The one thing that they had in common, other than their undoubted ability, was that they possessed hearts of oak.

In the days when Liverpool's team had a distinctly tartan flavour about it, there were stalwarts such as Andrew Hannah, Joe McQue, Archie Goldie, Billy Dunlop and, of course, the great Alex Raisbeck. All were Scots, and all arrived at Anfield during the 1890s – Hannah and McQue kicked off in Liverpool's first League season (1893-94), Dunlop played from 1894 to 1909, Goldie from 1895 to 1900, and Raisbeck from 1898 to 1909.

Hannah's term at Liverpool was the briefest of the lot, because he was there only two seasons, after having been signed from a club north of the border named Renton. He had played in three Scottish Cup finals, been capped for Scotland in 1888 – the year the Football League was founded – and helped Everton to win the First Division Championship. That was in between two spells with Renton. Hannah was appointed captain of Liverpool, and he led them to promotion in his first campaign, when they went through the season without defeat.

McQue enjoyed the distinction of being a centre-half who scored for Liverpool in their first-ever League game and in their final League match of that inaugural season (1893-94), and the man who joined the club from Celtic totalled more than a century of first-team appearances in just five seasons. He proved to be an inspirational player, too, when Liverpool beat West Brom in an Anfield test match and thus gained promotion in season 1895-96.

As for Dunlop, he certainly earned his corn through 15 seasons at Anfield, and in the eyes of many folk his one cap for Scotland was scant reward for his ability. While it took Dunlop three seasons to become an established first-teamer, once he had nailed down a place he became a fixture; and he was an absentee only twice as

■ **Eph Longworth leads out the team. He became the first Liverpool player to captain England, and was a key man for his club in the Championship seasons of 1921-22 and 1922-23.**

Liverpool stormed to their first-ever League Championship, while he also played a key role as they won promotion, then the Championship, in successive campaigns. Dunlop's record was on a par with players of much more recent years, because he totalled more than 350 appearances for the club . . . and, bear in mind, the early seasons consisted of 30 League matches, before increasing to 34 and, in the early 1900s, to 38. Archie Goldie, too, was seldom absent during his five seasons with Liverpool, and he totalled 150 appearances after his transfer from Clyde.

Alex Raisbeck

So to Alex Raisbeck, who gave Liverpool sterling service through 11 seasons as he totalled close on 350 appearances and, indeed, demonstrated that he could play in a variety of positions, from outside-right to half-back, where he showed that he could tackle like a terrier, win the ball in the

air, and outpace opponents. In six of his 11 seasons he played 30 League games or more, and he was a human dynamo. He won two Championship medals and a Second Division medal, but his greatest disappointment came when he passed up the chance of a Scottish cap to help his club in the bid to achieve a League-Cup 'double'. Liverpool missed out on both, but Raisbeck did have the consolation of winning eight international caps. Signed from Stoke City, he returned to Scotland when he joined Partick Thistle in 1909. Later still, he returned to the Merseyside area and did some scouting for the club he had served with such distinction.

The 1900s also saw the emergence of players like Alfred West, Robert Crawford, Donald McKinlay, Ephraim Longworth and Bob Pursell. West, Crawford, Pursell and Longworth played at full-back, McKinlay at full-back, centre-half and in attack. So McKinlay could be termed an all-rounder. As for West, he was another tough-tackling player, and he joined Liverpool from Barnsley in 1903, totalling close on 150 appearances during seven seasons, and winning a Championship medal before travelling on to Reading.

Eph Longworth

Crawford and Longworth played alongside each other – Crawford, indeed, was the man who replaced West after joining Liverpool in 1909, and while injury restricted his appearances, he totalled more than 100 during his seven seasons at Anfield . . . meantime, Longworth (who served the club from season 1910-11 to season 1927-28) played close on 350 League games and more than a score of Cup-ties . . . though by the end of his career with Liverpool he had still failed to score a goal.

Eph Longworth was born near Bolton, but played for Leyton in the Southern League for a spell. The first Liverpool player to captain England (in the second of five games he played for his country), he had already enjoyed success in his first international, as England came back from 4–2 down to beat Scotland 5–4 at Hillsborough. The old-timers who watched Longworth in action might well have seen some resemblance to another right-back, Chris Lawler, in more modern times, because both players demonstrated class as they played cultured football. As was the case with Lawler in later years, so Longworth played a key role in Liverpool's Championship successes of seasons 1921-22 and 1922-23.

Like Longworth, Bob Pursell was in the 1914 FA Cup final side which lost to Burnley. He had joined Liverpool in 1911 from the famed Scottish amateur club, Queen's Park, and he stayed at Anfield for five seasons, finishing just one game

LIVERPOOL'S
BARGAIN BUYS

WHILE Liverpool have splashed millions of pounds on individual players such as Ian Rush and Peter Beardsley, there is no denying that through their history they have come up with players who have turned out to be bargain buys – indeed, it should be remembered that Rush himself, while having cost more than £2 million on his return from Juventus, was originally a £300,000 investment when he left Chester for Anfield, and Juventus paid Liverpool more than £3 million for his services. Beardsley, too, whose transfer fee stood at a then British record of £1.9 million, would be worth even more, should Liverpool ever agree to sell him.

As for John Barnes, he was a £900,000 signing from Watford, and he turned out to be a snip, even at that price, because at any given time Liverpool could easily have cashed in and collected more than four times the fee they had paid for him. It should not be forgotten, either, that their record of home-produced players stands up to scrutiny, and that the vast majority of the club's signings have paid their way.

Three outstanding examples in modern times are Kevin Keegan, Ray Clemence and Phil Neal, and Kenny Dalglish, at £440,000, can surely be added to the list. Keegan cost around £35,000 when – like Clemence – he was signed from Scunthorpe, and he went to West Germany for something in the region of half a million pounds. Clemence was a mere £20,000 acquisition, and after 14 years at Anfield (and more than 650 appearances) he was still rated good enough by Spurs for them to pay £300,000.

Neal was Bob Paisley's first signing – about £65,000 worth of footballing talent from Northampton Town – and while he did not bring the Anfield club a big transfer fee when he became the team boss at Bolton, he repaid the money Liverpool had laid out for him many times over. The same can be said

■ *Left:* **Kevin Keegan ponders his future as he perches on a dustbin outside the club's temporary offices at Anfield, in the spring of 1971.** *Right:* **Ray Clemence switches from soccer to a part-time job as deck-chair attendant in the close season of 1967.**

about Alan Hansen, a £100,000 recruit from Scotland who totalled well over 600 games for Liverpool.

The Anfield club believes in getting full value for money, and it has always been cost-conscious; yet it may come as a surprise to modern-day fans when they learn that before May 1961, Liverpool had never paid more than £15,000 for a player. It was in that month Liverpool really splashed out by paying Motherwell £35,000 for Ian St John. In the club's earliest years, the top-priced signing was Jimmy Ross, who cost just £75 when he arrived from Preston North End in 1894. Not until 1929 did Liverpool figure as buyers who made headlines news when they paid Ayr £5,000-plus for centre-forward Jimmy Smith, to equal the existing record; and the following year, Bury's finances were boosted by £9,000 as they sold Tom Bradshaw to Liverpool – that, in fact, was the third-highest fee any club had paid.

It also remained a Liverpool record until 1946, when Albert Stubbins arrived from Newcastle United as a £13,000 investment – Liverpool's first five-figure fee; then in June 1960, the club paid Sheffield United £15,000 for Kevin Lewis and, after paying Preston North End a similar sum for Gordon Milne, Liverpool landed Ian St John.

Of course, transfer fees escalated, and Liverpool made Alun Evans the first £100,000 teenager when he moved to Anfield from Wolves . . . since when fees have gone up and up again. Yet through all the years, Liverpool have managed to get top-class value for the money they have spent – most signings have come off, and those that didn't brought Liverpool decent fees as they were allowed to move on.

It should be said, also, that two of the outstanding signings of all time concerned players who didn't even cost a transfer fee . . . Steve Heighway, who arrived from non-Leaguers Skelmersdale United as a raw recruit,

fresh from University with a Bachelor of Arts degree, and Billy Liddell, the lad from Lochgelly Violet. Heighway, with his high-stepping stride and uncomplicated approach as he ran at defenders, stayed for 11 seasons and totalled more than 460 first-team appearances, scoring 76 goals. Liddell, who combined professional football with a job in an accountant's office, was (and still is) an unassuming person as he went about his work . . . but he was idolised by the Liverpool fans and feared by opposing defences. His 229 goals in 537 appearances testify to his shooting power.

■ Alun Evans became the first teenager to be transferred for £100,000 when Bill Shankly took him from Wolves to Liverpool.

short of a century in the League. Donald McKinlay – like Pursell, he was a Scot – spent 16 seasons playing for Liverpool, and he totalled close on 450 appearances for the club. He arrived in season 1909-10, and moved to Prescot Cables at the end of season 1928-29. McKinlay was certainly a 'Liverpool-type player', because he could do a job in several positions, and his attacking ability brought him more than 30 goals. Like Raisbeck, he could get in a telling tackle, and he could get forward in the manner of more modern players such as Graeme Souness and Terry McDermott. Overall, he was virtually the complete footballer. McKinlay starred in the Scott-Lucas-McKinlay defence which helped Liverpool claim the Championship in successive seasons during the early 1920s when, in the two campaigns, the team conceded only 67 goals. He captained the club in both their title-winning seasons, and was capped

by Scotland against Wales and Ireland in 1922.

Another player whose career spanned a considerable number of years around that time was Walter Wadsworth – he was a Bootle lad who arrived on the eve of the First World War and, but for that interruption, he would surely have totalled many more than the 240 games he played for Liverpool. As with McKinlay, so with Wadsworth . . . he could defend when necessary, tackle hard and win the ball . . . but he could also go marauding in the opposition's half of the field.

There was a time when Ephraim Longworth kept Tommy Lucas out of the Liverpool team, yet Lucas contrived to become one of four international full-backs who were on the club's books at the same time – they were Lucas and Longworth (England), McKinlay (Scotland) and Parry (Wales). Lucas, like McKinlay, was a versatile player, and his ability to operate in

several positions contributed towards his 340-odd League appearances between 1919 and 1933.

That was also the era (give or take a year or two) of James 'Parson' Jackson, Tom 'Tiny' Bradshaw, Tom Bush and Jim Harley, the Powderhall sprinter. Jackson, signed from Aberdeen, was at Anfield from season 1925-26 to season 1932-33, and his 224 appearances testify to his ability. He also had a spell as Liverpool's captain. He was indeed a man of many parts, because he had worked in a shipyard and an office, and he finished up entering the ministry, as has been related elsewhere. Hence the nickname of 'Parson'. While on Liverpool's books he played in both full-back positions, at centre-half, wing-half and inside-forward (though he scored only two goals), and was rated unlucky to have got no further than a representative game for the Football League when it came to international recognition (he was born in Newcastle, though his parents were Scottish). 'Parson' Jackson was ordained in the church in 1933, and in 1947 he was officiating at the funeral of a one-time Liverpool chairman, Billy McConnell.

From 1930 to 1938 'Tiny' Bradshaw graced the Anfield stage, and in 1928 he figured in the Scotland side which became known as the 'Wembley wizards'. He cost Liverpool £8,000 when he was signed from Bury, in what was then the fourth-highest transfer fee in football. When he left Anfield for Third Lanark in 1938 he had totalled almost 300 first-team appearances during his nine seasons – though, in fact, the vast majority of those games were played in seven campaigns.

One player who finished up by joining the office staff at Anfield was Tom Bush. He kicked off in season 1933-34, and was just getting into his stride when the war broke out. So when he hung up his boots in season 1946-47, he could look back on just 72 appearances in his career. Yet, like others before him, he gave the club fine service as he adapted to various roles . . . centre-half, wing-half and full-back.

During the same period Liverpool had Jim Harley and Tom Cooper – the former a Scot, the latter from Fenton in the Potteries. Harley, as befitted a Powderhall sprinter, was a full-back whose pace gave him a head start, and he joined Liverpool in 1935. Once again, here was a case of a career being interrupted by the war (though Harley was capped twice in wartime internationals), and so, when injury finally forced the Scot to hang up his boots, he had totalled fewer than 150 games in his seven playing seasons at Anfield.

Cooper managed more than 150 outings in his five seasons, after previously playing for Port Vale and Derby County (with whom he totalled more than 250 games). He was capped 15 times while with Derby, and skippered his country, as well,

and after joining Liverpool in 1934 he became the club's captain. Sadly, he died in an accident towards the end of 1940, while serving in the Army.

The mid-1940s saw the emergence of two players who both gained international honours . . . Laurie Hughes and Ray Lambert. Hughes played for England, Lambert for Wales, and the pair of them gave Liverpool excellent service, too. They were, of course, contemporaries of Bob Paisley.

Hughes started out as an amateur with Tranmere Rovers, then in 1943 he signed for Liverpool, his first and only club as a professional. Through a dozen post-war seasons he totalled more than 300 appearances at club level, was capped by England but had the embarrassing experience of figuring in the World Cup side which was beaten by the no-hopers of the United States at Belo Horizonte in 1950. With Liverpool, he did claim a Championship medal at the end of season 1946-47, though again there was the disappointment of defeat in the 1950 FA Cup final.

Ray Lambert

Lambert, too, was a member of the side which got to Wembley, and he was in the Championship-winning outfit. A former Welsh schoolboy international at centre-half, he became a Liverpool professional in July 1939 – but, because war broke out in the September, he did not make his senior debut until season 1946-47. So he lost six years of his career. By the time he became a regular with Liverpool, he had switched with genuine success from centre-half to full-back, and he became noted for his great positional sense and his cool play when under pressure. Once again, shades of Eph Longworth in earlier years and Chris Lawler later.

Ray Lambert totalled close on 350 appearances for Liverpool, and during the 1950s as he and Laurie Hughes, along with Bob Paisley and Phil Taylor, bowed out, four other players began to make their presence felt at Anfield. They were Ronnie Moran, John Molyneux, Gerry Byrne and Geoff Twentyman. Ronnie Moran's career has already been outlined – it spanned 13 seasons and close on 400 games – and the story of Byrne's heroics in the 1965 FA Cup final has also been dealt with elsewhere. He was on the playing staff for a dozen seasons and played more than 300 games, as well as gaining England recognition.

Molyneux, signed from Chester in 1955 for only £3,500, became Ronnie Moran's full-back partner and played close on 250 times for Liverpool; then, having made way for Byrne, he returned to the club from which Liverpool had signed him. In seven seasons at Anfield he had certainly proved to be one of the club's all-time

■ *Right:* **Tommy Smith, the player they called 'The Anfield Iron', skippered Liverpool, and totalled more than 600 appearances. He also won England honours. He crowned his Anfield career with a goal in the 1977 final of the European Cup.**

■ *Below:* **Ron Yeats led Liverpool to some of their greatest triumphs during the 1960s – the League title, the FA Cup and the title again, in successive seasons. No wonder Bill Shankly termed him 'the colossus'.**

bargain buys. Geoff Twentyman also had seven seasons with Liverpool, after his transfer from Carlisle United, and between seasons 1953-54 and 1959-60 he totalled the best part of 200 games. He played at centre-half and wing-half, captained the team for a spell, joined Ballymena United as player-manager, rejoined Carlisle and, ultimately, returned to Liverpool for a lengthy period as the club's chief scout.

Liverpool were now approaching the Shankly era; the era which saw players like Tommy Smith and Chris Lawler blossom as first-team regulars. Both were Liverpool lads, with rich red blood running through their veins. Smith, who became known as 'the Anfield Iron', could play more than one role, and the same applied to Lawler, a cultured footballer who never seemed to be under pressure.

Lawler played close on 550 games and scored 61 goals – not one from the penalty spot – while Smith topped the 630 mark for appearances and scored close on 50 goals. And as players like Smith and Lawler made their mark, so did a giant Scot called Ron Yeats, whom Shankly signed from Dundee United. Not only did he block the route to goal; he led Liverpool to glory in the FA Cup and the League, and very nearly in two European competitions. In fact, he was the first Liverpool skipper to walk up the steps to the royal box at Wembley to collect the FA Cup.

Ron played 450 games for the club, and apart from turning in some sterling displays at centre-half, he had a few outings at full-back. This one-time slaughterman certainly slaughtered opposing attacks season after season; he may not have been the fastest thing on two legs, but he proved to be a granite-like bulwark at the heart of Liverpool's defence. Today, he's Liverpool's chief scout and, as such, playing another – and equally important – role in the Anfield scheme of things.

Yeats was the player who took over from where Dick White, another centre-half, had left off, because White – signed from Scunthorpe United in the mid-1950s – switched to right-back to accommodate Yeats, and so he, too, claimed a Second Division Championship medal in the spring of 1962. However, that was his swan song, because after more than 200 appearances for Liverpool, he moved to Doncaster in the summer of 1962. Meanwhile, as the team of the 1960s flourished and then began to grow older, Bill Shankly delved into the transfer market yet again.

Emlyn Hughes

Shankly came up with some new names to bolster his squad, and prominent among them were Emlyn Hughes, Alec Lindsay and Larry Lloyd, who were all to play alongisde the likes of Yeats, St John, Hall, Heighway and company – for a spell, at any rate. Barrow-born, and proud of it, Emlyn had barely got his soccer career going at Blackpool before Bill Shankly was splashing out £65,000 to take him to Anfield. His ebullient enthusiasm was always infectious; and his ability became apparent more and more as he showed that he could play in a variety of roles – back-four line, midfield, full-back. Not to mention the fact that as time went by, he scored some crucial goals for Liverpool. And he went on to captain his country, as well as his club.

'Crazy Horse', as the fans liked to call him, was capped on 62 occasions (59 times while with Liverpool), and at club level he won medals in just about every competition – indeed, he led Liverpool to their first European Cup success in 1977. Overall, he played more than 650 games for the Anfield club, then went to Wolves and later became player-manager at Rotherham. And, of course, he carved out another career as a television personality.

Alec Lindsay had played more than 100 games for his home-town club, Bury, when Bill Shankly snapped him up for Liverpool during the late 1960s, and this left-back with the educated left foot became a first-team regular through five seasons and totalled almost 250 appearances before his Anfield career drew to a close, mid-way through the 1970s. He featured in Liverpool's

double-winning side of season 1972-73 (League title, UEFA Cup), and in 1974 collected an FA Cup medal. It was when Bob Paisley signed Phil Neal from Northampton Town that Lindsay's first-team future began to look uncertain, and eventually he was transferred to Stoke City.

Larry Lloyd was the player who, as a strapping 20-year-old centre-half, arrived at Liverpool a few weeks after Alec Lindsay, and he proved himself

to be a worthy successor to Ron Yeats. A £50,000 signing, Lloyd had played fewer than 50 games for Bristol Rovers (he was a Bristol lad) when Bill Shankly took him to Anfield. Standing 6ft 2in (1.88m) tall, Lloyd was the winner nine times out of ten in aerial duels, and he swiftly proved that he could cope with the demands of First Division football. He was an ever-present as Liverpool took the title and the UEFA Cup in season 1972-73,

■ An all-action shot of an all-action player, Emlyn Hughes, who led Liverpool to glory and who also captained England. Through more than 650 games he gave Liverpool total commitment – and scored close on 50 goals.

and he achieved more success after leaving Anfield, because he moved on from Coventry City to Nottingham Forest, with whom he won medals in the League and the European Cup. He also added to the three England caps he had collected while he was at Anfield.

Lloyd left Liverpool in 1974, and once again there were new names to conjure with on the Anfield team sheet. Phil Neal became arguably Bob Paisley's best buy (up to Kenny Dalglish) when he arrived from Northampton Town for around £60,000 in 1974; Joey Jones was recruited from Wrexham in 1975; Alan Hansen was signed from Partick Thistle in 1977; while Alan Kennedy was bought from Newcastle United in 1978. In addition, there was a player on the staff – by the name of Phil Thompson – who cost nothing . . . and this youngster who used to stand on the Kop became the captain of club and country.

■ Phil Neal, Bob Paisley's first signing, was thrown in at the deep end, for a Goodison Park derby game against Everton, and went on to become a fixture in the side, with more than 600 appearances to his credit.

Phil Neal

Neal could play either full-back position, in midfield or even up front, and as well as becoming a fixture in the Liverpool team he became an England regular as he won more than 50 caps. In his first season with Liverpool, Phil clocked up 23 League appearances, and in each of the following five seasons he finished as an ever-present in League games to make it a total of 233 consecutive First Division appearances. By March 1982, he was credited with more than 325 consecutive matches and was aiming for his 50th game in European competition, as well as the 630th game of his career.

There was a time when he suffered a depressed cheek-bone injury one Saturday, had an operation 48 hours later and – against doctor's orders – played again the following Saturday. Once, he broke a toe during a match against Arsenal, so for some days he walked around with one foot bare and, on match day, he wore odd boots . . . one size $6\frac{1}{2}$, the other two sizes bigger. With the help of pain-killers he got through the game.

On another occasion Neal went down with food poisoning before a League match against Sunderland, yet he still managed to line up for the kick-off. By the start of season 1984-85 he had totalled 400 League games alone for Liverpool, and the player who had kicked off with Northampton as a 16-year-old was heading for a career total of 800 appearances.

Phil Neal had passed the 700 mark in April 1983, he had won 53 caps by April 1984, and with the departure of Graeme Souness for Italy he had become Liverpool's captain . . . and equalled Phil Thompson's all-time record (as it was then) by claiming a seventh League Championship medal. Neal had also played in four European Cup and four League Cup-winning sides, as well as the UEFA Cup-winning side of the 1975-76 season and, as he looked back on his Liverpool career, he reflected: 'I remember my first day at Anfield, and I was getting changed, next to Ian Callaghan. It came home to me just what a model professional he was, and I determined to follow his example.' By the time he became Bolton Wanderers' team boss in December 1985, Phil Neal had played more than 630 games for Liverpool and scored 60 goals for the club – a record of which he could justly be proud.

By comparison with Neal, the career of Joey Jones was brief at Liverpool – three seasons – yet he, too, collected medals as he totalled just under 100 games for the Anfield club. Joey was a crowd favourite, a full-back who gave it everything he'd got, whether it was with Liverpool or playing for Wales, and when he moved on it was to return to Wrexham, the club from which he had joined Liverpool. Which brings us to another left-back

who became a favourite of the fans . . . Alan Kennedy, who had played for Newcastle United against Liverpool in the 1974 FA Cup final. The Anfield faithful christened Kennedy 'Barney', after the character in *The Flintstones* TV show, and he it was who took over from Joey Jones. 'Barney' scored two European Cup-winning goals, totalled nearly 350 first-team games for Liverpool, and crowned his club career by winning two England caps. He left for Sunderland in 1985 with a pocketful of medals from every competition Liverpool had won during his eight seasons at Anfield.

Phil Thompson's career has been referred to elsewhere . . . it spanned a dozen seasons, from 1971-72 to 1982-83, and encompassed more than 450 appearances. Capped 42 times, he led his country into action, as well as his club, and there was always rich red blood running through his veins. The emergence of Alan Hansen and Mark Lawrenson meant that Phil was running out of time, but though he was eventually transferred to Sheffield United (towards the end of season 1984-85) it seemed almost inevitable that one day he would return to his first love. And he duly became a coach at Anfield.

Alan Hansen

As for Alan Hansen, his career was one of the most remarkable ever, judged even by Liverpool standards. This classy defender, who cost a mere £100,000 when he was signed from Partick Thistle in the spring of 1977, overtook most records at the club, including the Championship-medal haul, because he collected his eighth as Liverpool did the title trick yet again in season 1989-90. And all this after having missed out for practically an entire season and always playing with the fear that his career could end through injury. This fear became reality late in the 1990-91 season, when he had to give up.

Nicknamed 'Jocky' by the fans, Hansen could have become a sporting celebrity in another field, because as a youngster he represented Scotland at golf, squash and volleyball. At 16 he was playing off a golf handicap of 2, and the 'Golden Bear', Jack Nicklaus, was one of his sporting heroes (along with Denis Law and Pelé). He worked for ten weeks in an insurance office, then became a part-timer with Partick and, after having started out as a winger and played in half a dozen positions altogether, he settled for centre-back.

Capped by Scotland at Under-21 level, he followed elder brother John into the Under-23 side, and eventually, he was to win 26 caps at senior level . . . though many people believed he should have had 100. While he was at Partick, there was talk of a transfer to Bolton or Newcastle, but he fetched up at Anfield in May 1977, and he

was playing in the European Cup final 12 months later. His cool, classy style endeared him to the fans and frustrated opposing forwards. He led Liverpool to the 'double' of League title and FA Cup in season 1985-86, then staged an astonishing comeback after injury to claim more medals.

By the start of the 1990s Alan Hansen had picked up 17 medals in major competitions – eight in the League (to become joint record-holder with Phil Neal), four in the League Cup, three in the European Cup and two in the FA Cup. Apart from having led Liverpool to the 'double', he figured in the side which conceded only 16 League goals in season 1978-79, and in the treble-winning team of season 1983-84 (Championship, European Cup, League Cup). He also set a record for derby game appearances when he overtook Ian Callaghan's 31-match tally and, at the start of the new decade, was Liverpool's longest-serving player, with more than 600 appearances for the

■ Alan Hansen captained Liverpool to the double in season 1985-86. He won many honours, including Scotland caps, but towards the end of season 1990-91 he had to quit playing through injury. He had totalled more than 720 games – 620 of them for Liverpool – by then.

club and a career total exceeding 700. It all seemed a far cry from the day in August 1980, when he had what he termed a 'nightmare' match at Leicester as Liverpool lost 2–0 and he vowed he would never play as badly again. The fans would say that in the remainder of his career you could count the number of bad games 'Jocky' Hansen played on the fingers of one hand.

The same could probably be said about a player who was often referred to as the finest all-rounder in football – Mark Lawrenson. He was said to have cost Liverpool £900,000 when he was signed from Brighton in August 1981, though it was also reported that he did, in fact, become Liverpool's first £1 million recruit. Be that as it may, Lawrenson, like Hansen, simply oozed class, and he helped Liverpool to win Championships and Cups. He was a regular for the Republic of Ireland, and during his five-year stay at Anfield he played close on 300 games. Sadly, however, in the end injury took its toll and his top-class playing days became numbered, as he moved into management.

Along with Alan Hansen, two other Scots have certainly made their mark during the 1980s and the early 1990s at Liverpool. One is Gary Gillespie, the other Steve Nicol. Both have been capped by their country, and but for injury each man would surely have played more often in the dark-blue jersey, for they certainly come up for automatic consideration every time the Scots have a big game. Of the two, Gillespie, signed from Coventry City, has probably been the unluckier, because it took him some time to break into the side and then he had to miss one or two showgames (notably an FA Cup final) through illness or injury. Yet since he put together a sequence of appearances in season 1990-91, Gillespie has emphasised his value to the side, especially in the absence of Hansen.

By the end of 1990, Gillespie had taken his appearance tally for Liverpool to 200 and his career total past the 420 mark, and he had distinguished himself also by figuring on the club's list of hat-trick marksmen. As for Nicol, he had shown he could play in either full-back position, wide on the left or right side of midfield or, in emergency, at the heart of the defence. And the £300,000 transfer fee paid when he arrived from Ayr United during the early 1980s had long since seemed a snip. Nicol, indeed, had played more than 300 games for Liverpool and 400 in his career by the beginning of 1991, and he looked set to play a great many more for both club and country. Like Gillespie, also, he had on occasion been a hat-trick hero.

Liverpool have never been content to rest on their laurels, though, and the quest for players to bolster the squad never ceases . . . hence the signing of Sweden's World Cup captain, Glenn Hysen, Barry Venison, David Burrows, David Speedie and Jimmy Carter, while, at the same time, players such as Gary Ablett and Steve Staunton were challenging for places. The talent search has taken Liverpool further afield several times – Israeli stars Avi Cohen and Ronny Rosenthal were signed, as was Danish international Jan Molby, while Craig Johnston arrived from Australia, via Middlesbrough.

MIDFIELDERS

In the beginning (before the term midfield had even been thought of) Liverpool settled for a Scottish clan in the middle of the park at Anfield, including John McCartney and John Walker, while there were also Charlie Wilson and Maurice Parry (the last-named from Wales).

McCartney, one of the 'old originals', played for Liverpool from season 1893-94 to season 1897-98, and totalled close on 150 games; Walker had already won international honours when he arrived in 1897, and he played more than 130 games for Liverpool in five seasons. Wilson hailed from Stockport, and while his career spanned eight seasons yet saw him playing just 90 matches, he stayed to serve the club for more than 30 years on the backroom side – indeed, perhaps his major claim to fame was that he was the trainer when Liverpool won the League title in successive seasons during the early 1920s. Parry arrived at Liverpool as a centre-half, but switched to wing-half with outstanding success, and in nine seasons from 1900 he totalled more than 220 appearances, as well as winning 16 caps with Wales. First and Second Division Championship medals came his way, and he was a firm favourite with the fans.

Three Scots already mentioned elsewhere are Matt McQueen (who was a player, manager and director), Malcolm McVean (he scored Liverpool's first goal in League football, against Middlesbrough Ironopolis on 2 September 1893), and Jimmy Ross (40 goals in 85 games), and there were others who followed them across the Border. One was Jock McNab, another Ronald Orr; and there was also Tom Morrison, while from Manchester City Liverpool recruited a name still familiar to football fans . . . Matt Busby.

Busby arrived at Anfield around the same time as George Kay became manager, and he recalled: 'Liverpool were really struggling then, and in danger of being relegated to the Second Division. George Kay worked like a trojan to put things right. It was at a time when men who had been great players were coming towards the close of illustrious careers . . . I remember Tommy Cooper and Ernie Blenkinsop, who had been regarded as the best full-back pairing in the country, left-half Jimmy McDougall, centre-half 'Tiny' Bradshaw

and the South African contingent of 'Nivvy' Nieuwenhuys, Arthur Riley, Dirk Kemp and Lance Carr.

'I formed a close friendship with Riley and Kemp, and though both eventually returned to South Africa we kept in touch. I also grew to admire George Kay for the resolute way he set about transforming Liverpool – but for the war, I feel the club would have been among the major honours in the 1940s. He did have the satisfaction of seeing his team win the League title and play in the 1950 FA Cup final, and although the war took a chunk out of my career, the years I spent at Anfield were among the happiest of my time in football.'

Sir Matt, as he became, added: 'I remember Bob Paisley's arrival, and the signing of Billy Liddell – I played a part in that. I still kept in touch with my old team-mate, Alex Herd, and we golfed together in Scotland during the close season. One day he went missing, and I learned he had taken Hamilton Academicals manager Willie McAndrew to watch a lad called Liddell playing for Lochgelly Violet. Billy was only 15 then, and his folks wanted to be sure he had a future in football before they gave permission for him to join a club. When Alex told me what had happened, I phoned George Kay and suggested he might succeed where Hamilton had failed. And Liverpool landed Billy Liddell.'

Sir Matt also recalled: 'Liverpool have always been a good club and deserving of success – they treated their staff with real consideration. I remember them re-signing Jimmy McDougall on top wages, though he was out of the first team, and the following year he was retained, though he wasn't playing at all. When he decided to quit, Liverpool paid him a second benefit.'

Matt Busby's own career at Anfield lasted from season 1935-36 to season 1939-40, during which time he played 125 games for Liverpool. After war service he had the chance to stay at Anfield on the backroom side, but his ambitions lay in management, and so he became the team boss of Manchester United, at a time when it was, as Winston Churchill once observed, a case of 'blood, toil, sweat and tears'. Liverpool's loss was United's gain, because Matt Busby steered the Old Trafford club to greatness, just as Bill Shankly pioneered the way for Liverpool's all-conquering era.

The 1930s saw the departure of players like Tommy Bromilow and the emergence of Phil Taylor and Willie Fagan. Bromilow, whose career had begun in season 1919-20 and spanned more than 370 appearances, was another of the Liverpool lads who, with his football boots tucked under one arm, presented himself at Anfield with the simple request: 'I'd like you to give me a trial.' It was a trial he passed with flying colours.

■ Left: Tommy Bromilow, with club mascot. This Liverpool-born player turned up at Anfield with his boots tucked under one arm and asked for a trial. He got one, and made good – his career lasted from 1919 to the start of the 1930s, and spanned more than 370 games.

■ Below: Two men who were team-mates of Bob Paisley . . . on the left, Eddie Spicer, on the right, Willie Fagan. Like Bill Shankly, Fagan had played for Preston, while Spicer was a local lad.

As for Taylor and Fagan, they were followed by the likes of Bill Jones, Bob Paisley, Eddie Spicer and Jimmy Payne – Taylor joined Liverpool in season 1935-36, stayed until the mid-1950s, and became the club's manager after having totalled close on 350 appearances and having also been capped by England. And he was still around at the start of the 1990s, when he and Billy Liddell were

there to recall old times with Bob Paisley as the new Bob Paisley Suite was officially opened at Anfield. Bill Jones, incidentally, played exactly the same number of games for Liverpool (278) as Bob Paisley.

Like Bill Shankly, Willie Fagan had played for Preston before he signed on at Anfield for season 1937-38 and, again like Shankly, he was capped by Scotland. He had nine seasons with Liverpool, played in almost 200 games, and was a member of the Championship-winning side in season 1946-47. Ironically, he had wound up with a loser's medal after the 1937 FA Cup final between Preston and Sunderland, and he was at Anfield when Preston lifted the trophy in 1938 . . . then, in 1950, Fagan again missed out, as Liverpool lost to Arsenal at Wembley. In 1952 he left Liverpool to become player-manager of Weymouth, and later he became a prison officer.

The 1950s brought a new crop of players, among them Roy Saunders (the father of Welsh international Dean Saunders), Jimmy Harrower, Johnny Wheeler, Tommy Leishman and Brian Jackson, and then came Gordon Milne, Geoff Strong and Willie Stevenson, to reinforce the side Bill Shankly had assembled for an assault not only upon the Second Division Championship, but upon the First Division title, the FA Cup and European trophies. Saunders, Harrower,

■ Gordon Milne goes for goal. He was one of the players Bill Shankly bought from his old club, Preston North End, and Milne repaid that faith by totalling close on 300 games and helping Liverpool to win promotion and two League Championships.

Wheeler, Leishman and Jackson between them played almost 700 games for Liverpool, while Milne made more than 270 first-team appearances and Stevenson and Strong totalled close on 250 and almost 200 games, respectively. All three played their parts in the glorious years of success under Shankly during the 1960s.

It was in this era, also, that yet another of the Liverpool lads, Jimmy Melia (later to take Brighton to the final of the FA Cup), came to the fore as he totalled almost 300 games for the Anfield club and scored close on 80 goals. Melia was an inside-forward who could scheme scoring openings and find the net himself and, like Lawler, Smith, Byrne and Callaghan, he didn't cost Liverpool a penny.

Then came yet another new-look team, and the names the fans chanted were different again. Peter Cormack was signed from Nottingham Forest for more than £100,000 in the summer of 1972, and in four seasons he played in more than 160 games and claimed medals in the Championship and UEFA Cup (his first season) and the FA Cup (1974). He had already been capped by Scotland during his days with Forest and Hibs, but his Anfield career went by without any more honours at international level.

It was at the start of the 1970s that the name of Phil Thompson – yet another of the Liverpool lads

■ Ray Kennedy arrived at Anfield as a striker and became a key man in midfield. Arsenal had achieved the double during his time at Highbury, but more honours were to come Ray's way as he found his niche at Liverpool.

– began to appear on the team sheet, and the gangling lad who used to stand on the Kop captained both club and country, before he had finished. He also became a joint record holder when it came to League championship medals, and during his dozen seasons as a Liverpool player Phil totalled more than 460 appearances. He moved to Sheffield United for a brief spell, but returned to Anfield to become a coach.

Ray Kennedy

The arrival of Ray Kennedy gave soccer's wheel of fortune yet another spin, because he had been a member of Arsenal's double-winning side in season 1970-71, and he was Bill Shankly's final signing for Liverpool, in July 1974. He arrived with a reputation as a striker, but achieved his real success when he moved to the left side of midfield, and he still scored 72 goals as he totalled close on 400 appearances for Liverpool. He also finished up with a medal collection to match the best – six European medals (including three European Cups), five Championship medals (one with Arsenal) and an FA Cup-winner's medal (again with Arsenal) – while his 17 England caps emphasised his all-round quality. He cost Liverpool just under £200,000, and when he left them for Swansea he was still valued at £160,000 . . . after having given Liverpool eight great seasons.

Two home-grown players came into their own during the 1970s . . . Jimmy Case and Sammy Lee. The former packed a kick like a mule, but he developed from a front-line player into a midfield man, while the latter also became a key player in

■ Terry McDermott – yet another of the Liverpool lads. However, he arrived at Anfield via a roundabout route, as his career took him first to Bury and then to Newcastle United. He was in the Newcastle side which lost the 1974 FA Cup final, but savoured success in his years with Liverpool.

the midfield department. Case had played for South Liverpool before signing on at Anfield for season 1974-75, and Lee became a Liverpool apprentice in the spring of 1976. Once again, the honours came thick and fast – Case scored in the 1977 FA Cup final, which was lost, but he was able to celebrate European Cup triumphs as well as Championship successes, and he had already savoured victory in the UEFA Cup. Altogether, he figured in four title-winning sides and three European Cup teams, while Lee – capped 14 times by England – enjoyed the club's great moments of the 1980s. Case totalled more than 250 appearances before he left for Brighton, Lee close on 300 before he moved on.

Two more players enjoyed even more success during the 1970s and 1980s – if that were possible – and each contributed to the Liverpool cause in his own, inimitable style. The players were Terry McDermott and Graeme Souness: one a Scouser born and bred, the other a Scot from Edinburgh. McDermott arrived at Anfield via Bury and Newcastle (he had played against Liverpool in the 1974 FA Cup final), and he became a specialist in the art of ghosting through defences and sticking the ball away as the opposition stood bewildered. 'Terry Mac', as the fans called him, had played close on 100 games for Bury in the four seasons since he signed apprentice forms for them, and Newcastle snapped him up in 1973. In November 1974, however, he was on his way home to Liverpool, and by the time he was returning to Newcastle once more (September 1982) he had played more than two dozen times for England and scored 75 goals in more than 300 appearances for Liverpool. At Newcastle, he teamed up once more with Kevin Keegan, and helped the Magpies regain First Division status. Later, he had a spell playing in Cyprus.

Graeme Souness

Graeme Souness, too, arrived at Liverpool via a roundabout route, because he had stopped off at Spurs on his way to Middlesbrough, and when he left Ayresome Park in January 1978, he cost a £350,000 fee. For their money, Liverpool got a player who, as time went by, demonstrated that he could win the ball, pass it with accuracy and vision, and score goals. He could also lead the side by example. It was Souness who laid on the chance for Kenny Dalglish to score the 1978 European Cup final winner against FC Bruges, Souness whose goal won the 1984 Milk Cup final replay against Everton, and Souness who was one of the penalty marksmen in the 1984 European Cup final shoot-out against AS Roma.

Souness played his football with the air of a Franz Beckenbauer, as if he knew his undoubted quality, and wasn't afraid to let other people see it. He was as keen a competitor as you could meet, neither asked for nor gave any quarter; and his all-round ability led to him collecting more than 50 Scotland caps, as well as his medals with Liverpool. He was at Anfield from 1978 to 1984, brought Liverpool almost twice as much as they had paid for him, when he moved into Italian football with Sampdoria . . . and Liverpool could also reflect that, since he had played some 350 games for them, the money they had paid to Middlesbrough made him a bargain buy.

Around the time that Souness was preparing to make his exit, Liverpool signed another midfield player, John Wark, from Ipswich Town, and while he stayed for only three seasons, he finished one of them as the club's leading League marksman (18 goals) and overall averaged a goal almost every other game. Alongside Wark, there was another player whose career was blossoming . . .

■ Signed from Middlesbrough, Graeme Souness became Liverpool's captain and a key man in midfield, as he orchestrated attacking moves and showed he could score goals himself – notably a hat-trick against CSKA Sofia in the European Cup.

■ Ronnie Whelan followed Alan Hansen as Liverpool's captain. He was a Wembley match-winner for the club, and Manchester United's loss was certainly Liverpool's gain, as they signed the player who had been tipped to go to Old Trafford.

Irishman Ronnie Whelan, who had looked a certainty to finish up at Manchester United, but who in the end put pen to paper for Liverpool.

Whelan graduated with honours both at club and international level, as befitted the son of a Republic of Ireland international. His talent for scoring vital goals has been mentioned elsewhere, and since he made his bow in Liverpool's first team, during season 1980-81 (he made it a scoring debut), he has become an automatic choice – which just about says it all. Like Graeme Souness before him, Ronnie Whelan has strength, skill and vision.

Steve McMahon

The same can be said about the player who became the first signing of manager Kenny Dalglish . . . Steve McMahon, a Scouser who (like

Terry McDermott) travelled on before he arrived back on Merseyside. Once a ball-boy at Everton, then a first-team regular there, he moved to Aston Villa in preference to joining Liverpool. When he was offered the chance once more, he didn't hesitate: 'You don't mess around, the second time,' was how he put it. And he signed on the dotted line.

Since he returned to Merseyside, Steve McMahon has become recognised as another of the players whose names go down on the Anfield team sheet straight away, week in and week out, and that recognition extended to the international scene, as well, because he figured in England's 1990 World Cup team and in their subsequent European Championship squad. Rarely indeed have Ronnie Whelan and Steve McMahon missed the action because of injury, and as a result Whelan has clocked up around 450 games for Liverpool and some 500 in his career (heading for a century of goals), while McMahon is well on the way to a career total of 500 games (more than 70 goals) and is heading for the 300 mark when it comes to appearances for Liverpool.

WINGERS

Liverpool have had almost a score of top-class wingers, going back to the earliest days of Jack Cox and Tommy Robertson, who both played for the club before 1900. Cox spent a dozen seasons at Anfield after having been transferred from Blackpool, his home-town club, and he could find the net often enough, as his 80 goals in 360 appearances testified. In season 1900-01 he was the second-highest scorer, with ten goals, and he got into double figures in successive campaigns (1903-04, when he was leading League marksman, and 1904-05). So he played a key part in Liverpool's Championship success of season 1900-01 and in their promotion season of 1904-05, and while he was regarded as a right-winger at club level, he showed he could switch effectively to the left when he was called up by England.

As for Robertson, a left-winger who had been with Motherwell and Hearts, he scored on his debut for both Liverpool and Scotland, and in season 1898-99 he was the club's joint top scorer,

with ten goals. Like Cox, he claimed a Championship medal, though he left Anfield for Hearts in 1902, but while with Liverpool he and Cox figured in a remarkable scoring feat against Manchester City in season 1900-01. Both players actually got the ball into the City net in the same minute – the fifth – and Robertson was a marksman again just before half-time.

Arthur Goddard was another winger who gave Liverpool sterling service during the early 1900s and, indeed, right up to the First World War. He arrived at Anfield in time to make 11 appearances during season 1901-02, and during the following nine campaigns he was virtually an ever-present. By the end of season 1913-14 he had taken his tally of appearances for the club beyond the 400 mark, and – like Jack Cox – had totalled 80 goals. First and Second Division Championship medals came Goddard's way before he moved on to Cardiff City in 1914. It was towards the end of the Goddard era that Liverpool signed Billy Lacey from Everton, in an exchange deal involving two players, while they also had Jackie Sheldon on their books around the same period.

The First World War interrupted Sheldon's career – he kicked off with Liverpool in season 1913-14, after having been in the shadow of the legendary Billy Meredith at Manchester United, and his Anfield career came to a close in season 1920-21. But he played close on 150 games. As for Lacey, this Irish international joined Liverpool in season 1911-12 and stayed until season 1923-24, by which time he had totalled more than 250 appearances, although he couldn't be called a prolific marksman, since he managed no more than 29 goals. He did hit a purple patch during season 1913-14, though, when he found the net five times in just eight Cup games. Capped 23 times, he left Liverpool for New Brighton.

Fred 'Polly' Hopkin arrived on the Anfield scene during the early 1920s, and he stayed around for a decade. Like Sheldon, he was recruited from Manchester United, and he became a firm favourite with the Anfield brigade. He was the man who provided so much ammunition for hot-shot Harry Chambers. Hopkin himself was never expected by the fans to score, and his record of only 11 goals in more than 350 games for Liverpool explains why.

The late 1920s to the mid-1930s produced three more names for the Liverpool fans to conjure with . . . Dick Edmed, Gordon Gunson and Harold 'Boy' Barton. Edmed was at Anfield only five seasons – from 1926 to 1931 – but he totalled 46 goals in 170 appearances, and after he had moved on to Bolton he figured as a marksman in a remarkable 8–1 win for Wanderers against . . . Liverpool. Gunson, meanwhile, played from season 1929-30 to season 1932-33, and he managed to total 26 goals in his 87 outings. Of those goals, 17

came in season 1931-32 when he featured as the club's second-highest scorer. Harold Barton's 29 goals in 106 appearances included all four in an FA Cup match against Chesterfield and a hat-trick in a famous 7–4 success against Everton. Barton arrived at Anfield in season 1929-30, and he departed in season 1933-34. But he is still remembered with affection by the old-timers – especially those who witnessed that hat-trick against the club from across the park.

The 1930s also saw another winger who played a starring role for the club. His name was Alf Hanson, and he hailed from Bootle. His Anfield career lasted from season 1932-33 to season 1937-38 and, while he totalled more than 50 goals himself in 177 appearances, he also acted as a provider of chances for that even more consistent marksman, Gordon Hodgson – who, indeed, benefitted, as well, from the service laid on by the likes of Barton and Gunson.

During the 1930s, of course, Liverpool fans revelled in the scoring feats of Hodgson, and they enjoyed almost as much the contribution of his fellow-Springbok, Berry 'Nivvy' Nieuwenhuys, who spent nine playing seasons at Anfield (from 1933 to 1939 and then, after the war, from 1945 to 1947). Speed and a powerful shot were 'Nivvy's'

■ Berry 'Nivvy' Nieuwenhuys, one of the South African contingent who fetched up at Anfield. He stayed for nine seasons and played more than 250 games as a left-winger who packed a powerful shot.

stock in trade, and he could operate on either wing. During the war he served in the Royal Air Force, and after taking his tally of appearances to 260 (and scoring 79 goals overall), he left his one and only English League club to return to South Africa in 1949.

Billy Liddell

Liverpool fans did not realise at the time they were bidding farewell to 'Nivvy' Nieuwenhuys that they were about to witness the arrival of another winger who was to make an even greater impact. His name: William Beveridge Liddell. He was a Scot who was modest in demeanour, had an equable temperament, no matter how fierce the action, and could be relied upon to give a good account of himself every time out. In short, he became one of football's all-time greats – not just for Liverpool, but for the game itself.

The game may have changed dramatically since Billy Liddell's hey-day, but no-one who saw him in action would dispute that he would still command a regular first-team place in modern-day football. They called him the Flying Scot, they called his club 'Liddellpool'; and here was a forward who could play with equal effect in any of the front-line positions, though it was as a marauding left-winger that he most often figured as a destroyer of defences, as he cut inside the full-back and unleashed a piledriver of a shot.

Billy joined Liverpool at the age of 16, recovered from a leg injury which, it seemed, might finish his career almost before it had begun, and

made his mark after having served during the war as a navigator in the Royal Air Force. He did not make his League debut, therefore, until season 1946-47, by which time he was 24 years old, but he went on to total close on 500 League games between 1946 and 1960, with more than 40 FA Cup-ties in succession, for good measure. His League record remained intact until it was overtaken by Ian Callaghan (the youngster who replaced him in a game against Bristol Rovers), and he was the club's leading marksman in eight seasons. Billy Liddell played with dash and determination, yet he was scrupulously fair. His ability to play in any forward position demonstrated his exceptional versatility, and he gained representative honours on 30 occasions – indeed, he scored on his debut for Scotland. That was in a wartime match against England in 1942, when Billy was still in his teens.

One of the most famous incidents during Billy's career with Liverpool occurred during a fifth-round FA Cup replay against Manchester City, who were 2–1 ahead with mere seconds to go. Then Liddell raced on to the ball on the half-way line, sprinted down the wing and cut inside to send a fierce drive past City's 'keeper, Bert Trautmann . . . only to realise, moments later, that the referee had just blown for time. On 21 September 1960, Trautmann was in goal again, this time for an international side which provided the opposition to Liverpool in Billy Liddell's testimonial match . . . and it speaks volumes for the affection in which the Liverpool Scot was held when you read that 38,750 fans turned up to pay their tribute to one of Anfield's most respected figures.

■ The great Billy Liddell in typical shooting action. He scored more than 200 goals for his one and only club, and won the respect of all his opponents.

From the 1950s to the 1960s Liverpool unearthed two more wingers who were to win acclaim and international honours. Both were local lads, as well – Alan A'Court, from Rainhill, whose Anfield career began in season 1952-53 and lasted until season 1964-65; and Ian Callaghan, who kicked off in season 1959-60 and was still ready to give 100 per cent commitment to Liverpool's cause close on 20 years later, after having overhauled some records and set new ones in other respects.

A'Court knew the lean years, when the Anfield Reds were in the Second Division, but he also experienced the joy of helping them to regain top-flight status; and as he progressed at club level, so he became an England international, making his debut for his country against Northern Ireland in 1957 at Wembley. His team lost, by the odd goal in five, but he got his name on the scoresheet, and he went to the World Cup finals in Sweden in 1958, playing against Brazil, Russia and Austria. By the time he left Liverpool for Tranmere Rovers, in 1964, he had scored more than 60 goals and totalled close on 400 games for the club.

Ian Callaghan

Ian Callaghan, meantime, arrived with four League appearances during season 1959-60, and by the time he was moving on, almost 20 years later, he had carved out two careers with Liverpool. His career has been mentioned elsewhere, but his contribution to the cause of Liverpool can never be over-estimated, as he went into the record books for the most appearances in all competitions – 850 between 1960 and 1978 – and in League games (640). He first made club history when he overtook Billy Liddell's record of 532 appearances in competitive matches, and he played a leading role in the success achieved by the club, not to mention being rewarded also by selection for his country.

After only six weeks as a professional, Cally made his debut in April 1960. He was just 17, and replaced his idol, Billy Liddell. When, in March 1973, he played against Everton at Goodison Park, he set a record of 20 appearances in League derby games, overtaking the totals of Elisha Scott (Liverpool) and Ted Sagar (Everton). After having started out as a winger, Cally became a key player on the right side of midfield, and it was all the more to his credit that he came back after an injury which, in the view of some people, had looked likely to put paid to his career. Finally, having bid Liverpool farewell . . . and his testimonial was indeed an emotional occasion . . . Ian Callaghan took his boots to Swansea, there to team up with John Toshack as the Swans made their promotion push.

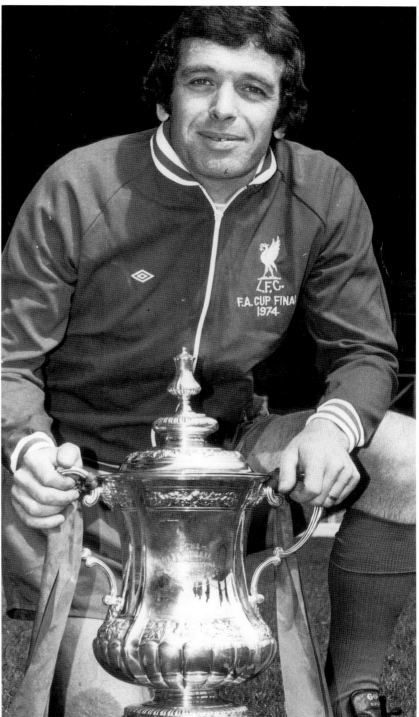

Cally had cost Liverpool just a £10 signing-on fee, and he left them on a free transfer. His England Under-23 honours were followed by full caps, he was voted Footballer of the Year, and collected three Championship medals, two in the FA Cup, one in the UEFA Cup and, finally, one in the European Cup. At the age of 35 he won an England recall, and even after having helped Swansea claim promotion he was playing with the old enthusiasm, first in Ireland and then in Norway. He was, like Billy Liddell, a player who commanded the respect of all who came into

■ **Ian Callaghan holds the FA Cup. 'Cally' set appearance records for Liverpool during the course of what amounted to two careers, as he bridged the gap between the team of the 1960s and the team of the 1970s.**

contact with him, both on the field and off it. And you can't give a footballer, or indeed any man, higher praise than that.

Peter Thompson

Another player who won respect and admiration through the golden years of the Shankly reign was Peter Thompson, the winger Shanks signed from Preston for less than £40,000 and who, according to Liverpool's manager, was 'the final piece of the jigsaw puzzle.' Like Thompson, Shankly had played for Preston, and he had drooled over the skills of Tom Finney at Deepdale . . . so, when Peter Thompson began to weave his wing magic for North End, Bill Shankly knew what was what. It didn't take him long to decide that Peter was the man to complete his team building at Liverpool.

In his first season at Anfield (1963-64) Thompson was an ever-present, and he missed very few matches during the next eight campaigns, as the team went for major honours at home and abroad. This former schoolboy international could dazzle full-backs as he sped down the wing

■ Winger Peter Thompson was signed by Bill Shankly from his old club, Preston North End. Shankly rated Thompson 'the final piece of the jigsaw', as he assembled a side equipped to win major honours.

to deliver pinpoint crosses. He followed up four England Under-23 caps during his first term at Anfield by claiming 16 senior international caps, and his haul of medals at club level was equally impressive – two Championship medals, one in the FA Cup. When he left Liverpool for Bolton Wanderers in the early 1970s he had played more than 400 games for the Anfield club and scored 54 goals. And by then Liverpool had found his successor in the shape of a virtual unknown called Steve Heighway, who, with another university graduate (Brian Hall), was to give the fans their moneysworth all right.

Steve Heighway

Bob Paisley always claimed his sons, Robert and Graham, 'discovered' Steve for Liverpool, because they were the ones who first brought him to Bob's attention. He took their advice and went to watch Steve, who ran the South Liverpool defence ragged that day. Bob told coach Tony Waiters: 'This is the best amateur footballer I've seen.' And Tony was just as impressed.

Steve had that wide-eyed look of a soccer

innocent about him during his first season as a professional. It seemed that he couldn't really believe it was all happening to him . . . but it did, and very swiftly. Though he did learn one salutory lesson at the outset, from one of Liverpool's battle-hardened players. It happened when Steve was named in the party to travel to Burnley for the opening game of the season. The night before the match, as was the usual custom, Liverpool's players stayed at an hotel, and – again as usual – the players doubled up, two to a room. But since Steve was No. 13, it meant that he had a room to himself, so around nine o'clock he went up to watch television. Then he rang room service, and when the waiter appeared he ordered a soft drink and some chicken sandwiches . . . but before he could start to enjoy this supper snack, Peter Thompson was at the door and asking: 'Did you order these?'

When Steve nodded, Peter offered him some advice . . . because the rest of the players, sitting downstairs in the lounge, had seen the waiter go past bearing the tray, and skipper Tommy Smith had his curiosity aroused. It was Peter Thompson who followed the waiter, and when Steve asked Peter what it was all about, he was told: 'We all usually assemble downstairs for tea and toast about quarter to ten.' Then he added: 'Now you've ordered the sandwiches, you'd better eat them. I'll explain what happened.' What had happened, of course, was that Steve Heighway simply didn't realise the routine that was followed; but while nothing more was said at the time, he made sure that he never made a similar mistake again. As time went by, he did begin to wonder if he would ever settle into the routine of professional football, because he certainly found it a great deal different to life as an amateur player and, as he admitted, there were occasions when he felt tempted to chuck it up.

'You have to grow another skin,' was how he put it, when he talked about his experiences during his early days, and there were occasions when his head dropped as the going got rough. Yet he survived, and more than that – in the end he flourished. Some of the Anfield regulars may have viewed him with a modicum of suspicion at the beginning, as they saw this late starter – he had turned 20 when he signed for Liverpool – striving to adapt to a new way of life, but long before he had finished he had become accepted for what he was . . . an extremely talented footballer who was a

■ Steve Heighway, a high-stepping winger who gave the Anfield Reds tremendous service after his move into full-time professional football. A university man, he made the grade in professional football, too, as he totalled more than 450 games for Liverpool.

valued member of the team. And opposing sides paid him a great deal of attention in their efforts to prevent him from setting up scoring chances for Kevin Keegan and John Toshack. Not that Steve was a slow-coach when it came to getting his name on the scoresheet – he could get goals, as well as make chances for others. His style was different from that of the industrious Brian Hall, but both players gave Liverpool excellent service throughout the 1970s, as Bill Shankly assembled another fine side which was a compelling mixture of the old and the new.

Brian Hall totalled more than 200 first-team appearances between 1968 and 1976 and, like Steve, he won Championship and UEFA Cup medals in season 1972-73, while also playing in both FA Cup finals (1971 and 1974). Steve scored in each of those finals, laid on scoring chances

twice in the 1977 European Cup triumph in Rome, and his tally of 76 goals in more than 450 first-team appearances speaks for itself, as does the fact that he became a regular with the Republic of Ireland. He made his Liverpool debut in season 1970-71, and his final games were played in season 1980-81 . . . then, at the start of the 1990s, he was back at Anfield in a new role, as Liverpool's Youth Development Officer.

John Barnes

This brings us up to the present and sets the scene for the arrival of another winger who, like Steve Heighway, Peter Thompson, Ian Callaghan and Billy Liddell, became a firm favourite with the Anfield faithful. His name, of course, is John Barnes . . . and (it seems astonishing, in retrospect) he had never even considered professional football as a career until three months before he signed on the dotted line for Watford. 'I spent the first 13 years of my life in Jamaica, and when I came to England I thought I would only be here for four years,' he said.

John was born in Kingston, and he arrived in England when his father, a colonel in the Jamaican army, was posted for a four-year stint as military attaché. John Barnes had already acquired a taste for football, back in the sunshine of Jamaica, because he used to enjoy watching the likes of Beckenbauer and Overath on television, while the one and only Pelé was his boyhood idol. 'I thought he was the best player in the world – I used to watch him on video, and I saw him playing for New York Cosmos in 1976, and though he'd lost a yard or two of pace by then, you could tell what a great player he'd been.'

Three years after his arrival in England, John himself was playing soccer for a club called Sudbury Court, in the Middlesex League. He was spotted by Watford, and on 13 July 1981, he signed the forms which made him a professional. He was just 17. He kicked off by playing on the left-hand side of midfield, and after three reserve-team outings he broke through to the senior side, as a left-winger. His debut was against Oldham Athletic, early in September 1981, when he went on as substitute in a Second Division match, and he swiftly emerged as an eye-catching talent who could leave opponents trailing, then either tee up scoring chances for team-mates or stick the ball into the net himself.

Usually, the number on his back was 11, but as well as playing at outside-left he showed that he could operate equally effectively through the middle and, at 5ft 11in (1.80m) and weighing in at around 12st 5lb (78kg), he's not so easily knocked off the ball. By season 1985-86 John had clocked up his 200th appearance for Watford, and

■ John Barnes turned out to be a bargain buy from Watford, at £900,000. After his arrival at Liverpool, he claimed the Footballer-of-the-Year award twice in three seasons.

by the time he left the Vicarage Road club he had played something like 300 games, while heading also for a century of goals – in fact, for six seasons in succession he got into double figures as a marksman, and that made him the only player in Watford's history to have achieved such a feat.

Even before he joined Liverpool, the Anfield club had a taste of his ability, for during an FA Cup replay he rifled home a free-kick to give Watford the lead, though at the end of the day it was Liverpool who were marching on to Wembley. With Watford, though, John Barnes had played in an FA Cup final and achieved promotion to the First Division. There were greater honours in store, of course, including getting into World Cup action for England – he first went on for a quarter of an hour against Argentina in Mexico – and people still talk about the stunning goal he scored against Brazil in the Maracana stadium in Rio de Janeiro as England recorded their first-ever victory in Brazil. There was a touch of irony, though, about season 1982-83, because when Watford were going for the Championship, it was Liverpool who pipped them.

John said of his decision to sign for Liverpool: 'I thought I would find it easy to settle in, and that's how it's turned out.' So much so that he was twice voted Footballer of the Year in his first three seasons, while he won FA Cup and Championship medals, and took his tally of England appearances past the half-century mark. By the start of the 1990s, he had also taken his total of goals to 150 and totalled more than 450 games in his career.

Barnes' first hat-trick for Liverpool came in a 6–1 demolition job on Coventry City in the final League game of season 1989-90, by which time the Anfield Reds had already claimed the Championship, and he was being hailed by team-mates and opponents alike. Peter Beardsley, for instance, termed him 'the best player in the country'; Alan Hanson said of him: 'John has strength, pace, ability, limitless stamina, discipline – he's the complete player'; while Brian Clough delivered this verdict: 'He's become the outstanding player in our League'. And John Barnes himself? 'I'm a lot better player since I came to Liverpool. I'm a naturally laid-back person, but I love winning – and I hurt inside when we lose.' Like Liverpool, he's been a winner almost all of the way.

STRIKERS

The list of players who have scored goals for Liverpool runs into hundreds and, when you start to whittle it down, eventually you still have three dozen or more who could be counted as marksmen. Some of these players flitted relatively briefly across the Anfield scene, of course, and some of them were not regarded as out-and-out strikers. In modern times, Liverpool fans have seen the likes of Alun Evans, David Fairclough, Paul Walsh and David Johnson become scoring heroes during their Liverpool careers, and before them there were players such as Tony Hateley, John Evans and Bobby Graham, while earlier still Liverpool had Dave Wright, Sam English, Fred Pagnam and Tom Miller, and back in the dim and distant past there were Jimmy Ross and Andy McGuigan.

Having given players such as these a mention – and they were no slouches when it came to finding the net – there remain almost a score of names still to conjure with, although one (Billy Liddell) has been featured elsewhere. As for the rest, where do you start? – In alphabetical order, you can reel off the names of John Aldridge, George Allan, Jackie Balmer, Peter Beardsley, Louis Bimpson, Harry Bradshaw, Harry Chambers, Kenny Dalglish, Cyril Done, Dick Forshaw, Joe Hewitt, Gordon Hodgson, Roger Hunt, Dick Johnson, Kevin Keegan, Jimmy Melia, Jack Parkinson, Sam Raybould, Robert Robinson, Ian Rush, Ian St John, Albert Stubbins and John Toshack.

Once again, not all these players might be regarded as truly great marksmen, but they certainly all made their mark at Liverpool. And four of them played for the club around the turn of the century . . . they were George Allan, Harry Bradshaw, Jack Parkinson and Sam Raybould. Allan arrived at Anfield in 1895, Bradshaw was at Anfield from 1893 to 1898, Parkinson was there from 1899 to 1914, and Raybould's career extended from 1899 to 1907. Allan played in the Liverpool attack which plundered 106 goals in only 30 League matches to win promotion to the First Division in 1896, and when he was chosen to lead the Scotland attack (he came from Leith) against England in 1897 he became Liverpool's first Scottish international. There was one famous story about Allan and Sheffield United's giant of a goalkeeper, Billy Foulke, who weighed in at 19 stone . . . Foulke reckoned that he had been fouled by Allan – and without more ado he picked up the centre-forward by his ankles and dumped him on his head in the muddy goal area!

Allan had a spell with Glasgow Celtic, then he played for Liverpool a second time, helping the club to finish as runners-up in the First Division in season 1898-99 and to reach the semi-finals of the FA Cup when the Anfield Reds met Sheffield United in a tie which went to four games. Tragically, George Allan died of consumption when he was still only 24.

Harry Bradshaw, signed from Northwich Victoria, had the distinction not only of scoring on his debut, but of clinching promotion for Liverpool in a test match against Newton Heath (later Manchester United), and he claimed two Second Division Championship medals and won one

England cap before moving south to sign for Tottenham Hotspur.

Jack Parkinson, Bootle-born, shrugged off frequent injuries to score more than 120 League goals and total more than 220 appearances through a dozen seasons with his one and only club. He arrived as an amateur in 1899 and eventually joined Sam Raybould and Robert Robinson in a front-line partnership which produced more than 20 goals apiece for all three of them as Liverpool claimed the Championship of the Second Division. In season 1909-10, he hit 30 out of the team's 78 goals in only 31 games, helping Liverpool to finish as First Division runners-up and, in the process, collecting two England caps. He and Roger Hunt (41 goals in season 1961-62) became the only Liverpool players to top the Football League scoring list until John Aldridge and Ian Rush came along.

Sam Raybould

Sam Raybould, too, distinguished himself when, in season 1902-03, he struck 31 goals in his 33 League games, and during his career with Liverpool he averaged a goal at least every other game, totalling 127 goals in 224 appearances. Raybould's 31-goal record stood for close on 30 years – it was broken by Gordon Hodgson – and his scoring feats enabled Liverpool to claim two Championships, as well as head the Second Division. His Anfield career came to a close when he joined Sunderland, in 1907.

Two more marksmen emerged during the early 1900s . . . Robert Robinson (1903-1912) and Joe Hewitt (1903-10). While Raybould moved on to Sunderland, Robinson left the North-East club to try his luck with Liverpool, and he ended his first season at Anfield as the top scorer, with 23 goals . . . including all four in one match against Leicester City. He won First and Second Division Championship medals, and if his total haul of 65 goals in 271 appearances doesn't seem to indicate a great marksman, it should be remembered that he switched to the half-back line during his last three seasons at Anfield.

Joe Hewitt was around for a long, long time, because although his playing career spanned no more than seven seasons, he gave the club 60 years of his life, as he did other jobs after he had hung up his boots. Like Robinson, he arrived from Sunderland, and twice he proved to be a major factor with his contribution to the team's tally of goals – notably in the Championship season of 1905-06, when he hit 23 out of the 79 goals scored overall.

After the Hewitt era, Liverpool looked to three more players to carry on the good work . . . Harry Chambers, Dick Forshaw and Dick Johnson.

Chambers played at Anfield from 1919 to 1928, Forshaw from 1919 to 1927, and Johnson from 1919 to 1925. Harry 'Smiler' Chambers certainly benefitted from the service of Fred 'Polly' Hopkin, and he totalled more than 150 goals in 338 matches, which gave him an average of a goal virtually every other game. Chambers' left foot was deadly, and in the two successive Championship seasons of 1921-22 and 1922-23 he hammered in 41 goals. His scoring prowess won him England recognition, and he was capped eight times. Eventually he joined West Brom', and – like Stanley Matthews – he carried on playing until he was in his 50s, though in Chambers' case he ended his career in non-League football.

Dick Forshaw was another goal-every-other-game striker – he hit 124 goals in 287 appearances, and he was an ever-present in the title-winning sides of the early 1920s. As for Dick Johnson, he struck 27 goals in 63 matches during seasons 1920-21 and 1922-23, after having missed the whole of season 1921-22 through injury.

Gordon Hodgson

Gordon Hodgson's career at Liverpool spanned 11 seasons during which he was an outstanding and consistent success as a marksman – indeed, he set a record when he struck 36 goals in season 1930-31. His 232 League goals were also a club record – one which stood until the arrival of Roger Hunt on the Anfield scene. Hodgson, a member of the South African touring side, stayed on to become not only a star soccer performer with Liverpool, but a county cricketer with Lancashire, and his hat-trick feats for the Anfield club emphasise what a deadly marksman he was. In that season of 1930-31, he helped himself to hat-tricks against Chelsea, Sheffield United and Blackpool, and went one better as he scored four times against Sheffield Wednesday as Liverpool won 5–3 at Hillsborough. Hodgson's total of 240 goals in 378 games for Liverpool illustrated his remarkable talent for piercing opposing defences season after season – only in his first term and his last term (when each time he played relatively few matches) did he fail to reach double figures.

As Hodgson came towards the end of his career at Anfield, another marksman began to make an impact . . . Jackie Balmer, whose hat-trick feats have also been recorded elsewhere. His three consecutive hat-tricks in the Championship season of 1946-47 set a League record, and Everton must certainly have rued the day they lost him, because he had started out as an amateur with the Goodison club before switching to Anfield in season 1935-36. When Balmer took his leave of Liverpool in 1951, he had totalled 111 goals in 313 appearances and, in fact, was just one goal short of

having scored a century in the League alone. Had the Second World War not interrupted his career, the tally would surely have been much greater.

Like Balmer, Cyril Done was a local lad who made good, and his career also was interrupted by the war years – indeed, he played just one League game (and scored) in season 1939-40, then he had to wait until season 1946-47 for his next League outing. Overall, he totalled 109 appearances up to 1952, and he hit 37 goals. Done claimed a Championship medal in season 1946-47 . . . and so did another striker who became a tremendous favourite with the Anfield supporters . . . Albert Stubbins, a genial Geordie who had become a legend in his own lifetime at Newcastle United.

Albert Stubbins

Albert was another of Liverpool's hat-trick heroes, and while he didn't hit three goals in a particular game back in 1952, the near-49,000 crowd rose to him as he stuck two goals inside ten minutes past the 'keeper of his former club, Newcastle, with Liverpool running out 3–0 winners after the 90 minutes were up.

Albert recalled vividly just how he came to sign for Liverpool. 'I was sitting in a news theatre and

■ *Left:* **Jackie Balmer . . . his three hat-tricks in a row became a part of the Liverpool legend. And he had started out as an amateur footballer with the club 'across the park'.**

■ *Below:* **Albert Stubbins, one of the crowd's favourites of the post-war years, carried on scoring goals for Liverpool, just as he had done for Newcastle United. Everton wanted Stubbins, too – but the flip of a coin meant that Liverpool won the chase for his signature.**

LIVERPOOL have had some outstanding marksmen. In modern times there have been no finer exponents in the art of scoring goals than Ian Rush and Kenny Dalglish. Both of these men figures on the list of those who have scored 100 goals or more for the Anfield club – Rush, indeed, is now threatening to overtake the record holder, Roger Hunt, as a Liverpool marksman.

Hunt struck 285 goals in 489 appearances, and he has offered the opinion that before Rush has finished, he will emerge as the new record-holder. At the start of the 1990s Rush had already taken his tally of goals for Liverpool past the 250 mark, to overhaul Gordon Hodgson's total of 240 goals in close on 380 games.

The legendary Billy Liddell scored more than 225 goals in almost 550 matches, and another Scot, Ian St John, hit 118 goals in something over 420 appearances. Much further back in time, Sam Raybould totalled 127 goals in 224 games, Jack Parkinson hit 128 goals in 222 matches, and Harry 'Smiler' Chambers hit 151 goals in 338

■ Roger Hunt, Liverpool's master-marksman, goes in search of yet another goal, with Ian St John in close support.

appearances) and David Johnson (204 appearances, while Dick Forshaw was a 124-goal marksman in almost 290 appearances and Jackie Balmer rattled in 111 goals in 313 outings.

Keevin Keegan hit the century mark in just over 320 appearances, and his fellow-striker, John Toshack, collected 95 goals in just under 250 appearances. Albert Stubbins collected more than 80 goals in 180 matches, and further back in time Jack Cox and Arthur Goddard each totalled 80 goals also – Cox in 360 outings, Goddard in 415 games. 'Nivvy' Nieuwenhuys scored 79 goals in

LIVERPOOL'S

260 matches, Jimmy Melia (287 games) each collected 78 goals, while Steve Heighway struck 76 in his 467 matches.

Terry McDermott (322 games) was a 75-goal man, Ray Kennedy (384 games) hit 72 goals, and Ronnie Whelan has also reached the 70-goal

League Marksmen Season by Season

Second Division
1893-94	Jimmy Stott (14 goals)

First Division
1894-95	Harry Bradshaw (17 goals)

Second Division
1895-96	George Allan (25 goals)

First Division
1896-97	George Allan (17 goals)
1897-98	Frank Becton (11 goals)
1898-99	Hugh Morgan (10 goals)
	Tommy Robertson (10 goals)
1899-1900	John Walker (10 goals)
1900-01	Sam Raybould (16 goals)
1901-02	Sam Raybould (16 goals)
1902-03	Sam Raybould (31 goals)
1903-04	Jack Cox (10 goals)

Second Division
1904-05	Robert Robinson (23 goals)

First Division
1905-06	Joe Hewitt (23 goals)

milestone during his career at Anfield. By the middle of season 1990-91, John Barnes had reached the 70-goal mark, and other players whose scoring ability took them into the 60s were Robert Robinson, Alan A'Court, Ian Callaghan and two full-backs, Phil Neal and Chris Lawler.

■ *Left:* **Signed from Chester in 1980, Ian Rush has set many goalscoring records during his spell at Anfield.** *Right:* **Kevin Keegan and his striking partner, John Toshack, savour another triumph in Europe.**

LEADING MARKSMEN

1906-07	Sam Raybould (15 goals)	1938-39	Berry Nieuwenhuys (14 goals)	1964-65	Roger Hunt (25 goals)
1907-08	Joe Hewitt (21 goals)		Phil Taylor (14 goals)	1965-66	Roger Hunt (30 goals)
1908-09	Ronald Orr (20 goals)		Willie Fagan (14 goals)	1966-67	Roger Hunt (14 goals)
1909-10	Jack Parkinson (30 goals)	1946-47	Jackie Balmer (24 goals)	1967-68	Roger Hunt (25 goals)
1910-11	Jack Parkinson (19 goals)		Albert Stubbins (24 goals)	1968-69	Roger Hunt (13 goals)
1911-12	Jack Parkinson (12 goals)	1947-48	Albert Stubbins (24 goals)	1969-70	Bobby Graham (13 goals)
1912-13	Arthur Metcalfe (15 goals)	1948-49	Jackie Balmer (14 goals)	1970-71	Alun Evans (10 goals)
1913-14	Tom Miller (16 goals)	1949-50	Billy Liddell (18 goals)	1971-72	John Toshack (13 goals)
1914-15	Fred Pagnam (24 goals)	1950-51	Billy Liddell (15 goals)	1972-73	John Toshack (13 goals)
1919-20	Harry Chambers (15 goals)	1951-52	Billy Liddell (19 goals)		Kevin Keegan (13 goals)
1920-21	Harry Chambers (22 goals)	1952-53	Billy Liddell (13 goals)	1973-74	Kevin Keegan (12 goals)
1921-22	Harry Chambers (19 goals)	1953-54	Sammy Smyth (13 goals)	1974-75	John Toshack (12 goals)
1922-23	Harry Chambers (22 goals)		Louis Bimpson (13 goals)	1975-76	John Toshack (16 goals)
1923-24	Jimmy Walsh (16 goals)			1976-77	Kevin Keegan (12 goals)
1924-25	Dick Forshaw (19 goals)	**Second Division**		1977-78	Kenny Dalglish (20 goals)
1925-26	Dick Forshaw (27 goals)	1954-55	Billy Liddell (30 goals)	1978-79	Kenny Dalglish (21 goals)
1926-27	Harry Chambers (17 goals)	1955-56	Billy Liddell (28 goals)	1979-80	David Johnson (21 goals)
1927-28	Gordon Hodgson (23 goals)	1956-57	Billy Liddell (21 goals)	1980-81	Terry McDermott (13 goals)
1928-29	Gordon Hodgson (30 goals)	1957-58	Billy Liddell (22 goals)	1981-82	Ian Rush (17 goals)
1929-30	Jimmy Smith (23 goals)	1958-59	Jimmy Melia (21 goals)	1982-83	Ian Rush (24 goals)
1930-31	Gordon Hodgson (36 goals)	1959-60	Dave Hickson (21 goals)	1983-84	Ian Rush (32 goals)
1931-32	Gordon Hodgson (26 goals)		Roger Hunt (21 goals)	1984-85	John Wark (18 goals)
1932-33	Gordon Hodgson (24 goals)	1960-61	Kevin Lewis (19 goals)	1985-86	Ian Rush (22 goals)
1933-34	Gordon Hodgson (23 goals)	1961-62	Roger Hunt (41 goals)	1986-87	Ian Rush (30 goals)
1934-35	Gordon Hodgson (27 goals)			1987-88	John Aldridge (26 goals)
1935-36	Fred Howe (17 goals)	**First Division**		1988-89	John Aldridge (21 goals)
1936-37	Fred Howe (16 goals)	1962-63	Roger Hunt (24 goals)	1989-90	John Barnes (22 goals)
1937-38	Alf Hanson (14 goals)	1963-64	Roger Hunt (31 goals)	1990-91	Ian Rush (26 goals)

saw a message flashed on the screen saying that if I was in the audience I should report immediately to St James's Park. I got there to find Liverpool chairman Bill McConnell and manager George Kay were wanting to sign me . . . and so was Everton manager Theo Kelly. Newcastle chairman Stan Seymour asked me: "Which of the two do you want to talk to first?" I told him: "Spin a coin" . . . and it came down heads for Liverpool.

'So I talked to their representatives, and agreed to sign. Then I saw Theo Kelly, who took my decision very well when I told him I had already agreed to Liverpool's terms. He shook my hand and wished me all the best.' Liverpool were said to have paid a record £13,000 fee for Albert . . . Everton, it was said, were prepared to go as high as £20,000. Be that as it may, Liverpool found they had landed a bargain, as Albert made his debut at Bolton and scored in a 3–1 victory.

He had arrived with a reputation for being able to find the net – 265 goals in 199 games for Newcastle – and he immediately confirmed that reputation as he helped Liverpool win the League title in season 1946-47. His contribution was 24 goals. He also struck 26 goals during his second season at Anfield. And during his half-dozen campaigns with Liverpool, he figured in some remarkable scoring feats – like the winner he got against Wolves at Molineux when they needed a point for a chance of the title, and nothing less than victory would do for the Anfield Reds. Albert recalled exactly what happened, that fateful day: 'Before the game, I told winger Bob Priday that if he got the ball anywhere near the half-way line, all he needed to do was to hit it high past centre-half Stan Cullis and between the full-backs. I'd try to do the rest . . .'

It happened just as Albert had asked, and as Priday lofted the ball forward the Liverpool striker was already on his way, outspeeding Cullis and the Wolves full-backs and getting first to the ball. Then, as 'keeper Bert Williams came out, Stubbins slotted the ball past him to clinch a 2–1 win which brought Liverpool the Championship.

There was another astonishing goal from Albert Stubbins during a sixth-round FA Cup-tie against Birmingham City at Anfield . . . one that became known for ever as 'the goal in the snow'. Billy Liddell took a free-kick and sent the ball skimming about two feet high across the pitch – and there was Stubbins, flinging himself full length and ramming the ball into the net. And 51,000 fans acclaimed that goal, which was one of three Albert scored in Liverpool's 4–1 win.

In 159 League appearances for Liverpool, Albert hit 77 goals, and 48 of them came in his first two seasons. While he eventually got his wish to return to his native Tyneside, he never lost his popularity with the fans who enjoyed watching him during his days at Anfield. Later on in life, he

retained a keen interest in the game, as he became a freelance journalist and broadcaster back on his home territory.

Albert bowed out at Liverpool during the early part of the 1950s, and three other players began to hit the headlines . . . Louis Bimpson, Jimmy Melia and Roger Hunt. Bimpson played exactly 100 games for Liverpool, and his 40 goals were a very good return, especially considering that he cost nothing in the transfer market, since he joined the club from local non-Leaguers Burscough. Big Louis didn't command a regular first-team place, but in typical Liverpool fashion he gave it everything he'd got.

Jimmy Melia is referred to elsewhere as one of the Liverpool lads, and he was on the Anfield ground staff by the time he was 15, with his senior career extending from 1955 to 1964. Like others before him, Jimmy scored on his Liverpool debut, and in season 1958-59 he was the club's leading League marksman, with 21 goals. He was also an ever-present in the promotion season of 1961-62 . . . which brings us neatly to Roger Hunt, the player whom the fans were to idolise and refer to as 'Sir Roger'.

Roger Hunt

Like Melia, Roger Hunt hit the target on his League debut, and he carried on scoring goals right the way through his 11-season career at Anfield. He, too, had cost Liverpool nothing, and he set one record after another: most goals (245 in 401 League games), most FA Cup goals (18), most goals in European games (17), most goals in a season (41 in season 1961-62), and most caps (34). And while he was indeed a willing workhorse, both in the cause of club and country, those who questioned his right to be an England regular were reminded that during his time as an international he was on the losing side only twice . . . and, of course, in 1966 he claimed a World Cup winner's medal. As a matter of interest, also, he scored on his full England debut.

At club level he scored Liverpool's first goal when the FA Cup went to Anfield for the first time, in 1965, and he certainly played a notable part in Liverpool's Championship successes (First Division, seasons 1963-64 and 1965-66, Second Division, season 1961-62). He had joined the club as a 21-year-old in 1959 and, despite being on the receiving end of some rough treatment from defenders, he had his name taken only twice during his career of almost 500 appearances. Before he finally moved on, to play for Bolton Wanderers for a spell, Roger had a testimonial match at Anfield, and such was the esteem and affection in which he was held that 56,000 people defied a downpour to turn up and pay their

■ Ian St John won the hearts of the Anfield faithful by his skill and 100 per cent endeavour. His was the goal that took the FA Cup to Liverpool for the first time ever, in 1965, and he gave the club sterling service.

tribute to a player they had hero-worshipped for so long.

Alongside 'Gentleman Roger', of course, there was Ian St John, a fiery, combative forward who neither gave nor asked for quarter – yet he relied upon his footballing skill, as well as his competitive approach, to get the goals he sought. And when the need arose, he showed that he could do a good job as a schemer, too. His was the goal that ensured Liverpool's victory in the 1965 FA Cup final, and he amply repaid the club record transfer fee of £35,000 which Liverpool had paid to Motherwell at the end of season 1960-61. Naturally, the wits on the Kop soon dubbed Ian 'The Saint' – but, like Roger Hunt, he was so often the villain of the piece, so far as opposing defences were concerned, and his scoring record of 95 goals

in 336 League appearances gives ample proof of the power that lay in his stocky frame. Yet the St John-Hunt partnership might easily never have got off the ground, so to speak.

Roger started out playing as an amateur for a club called Stockton Heath and, as he admitted, when he had completed his National Service it seemed more than likely that he would go into the family haulage business. But Liverpool spotted him, and when they stepped in to offer him the chance of a career in the professional game, they gave Roger Hunt a new – and unique – identity. There will be plenty of Anfield regulars who can testify to having seen a Roger Hunt 'special'. One was a right-footer which he hammered home in the Anfield leg of the 1965 European Cup semi-final against Inter-Milan; another was the left-

■ Kevin Keegan – one of Liverpool's all-time bargain buys. Keegan was snapped up from Scunthorpe after a scouting mission from Anfield had decided swiftly that here was a player who would make it to the top. He went all the way as he wound up European Footballer of the Year.

foot volley which he smashed past Gordon Banks (then playing for Leicester City) in a Cup replay; yet another was his record-breaking goal against Chelsea at Stamford Bridge; and still another was the fifth goal Liverpool rattled in against Arsenal in 1964, as they chalked up another League Championship success.

Roger was always a front-line man, whereas St John eventually showed that he could play deeper and spray the passes around. Between them, they totalled more than 900 appearances for Liverpool and scored more than 400 goals . . . what, you

might ask, would any manager give to have such a pair in his team today?

Kevin Keegan

The era of Hunt and St John was drawing to a close when a young, unknown footballer was attempting to carve out a career as a professional with Scunthorpe United. His name, of course, was Kevin Keegan. To be fair, more than one club had noted his displays for the Fourth Division club

at that time, was striving to get back after a cartilage operation.

Cally, indeed, appeared to be on his way out of top-class football, because he was struggling to regain form, as well as fitness, yet in the end both he and Keegan played in the same side . . . the one which, six years later, captured the European Cup in Rome. But all that was in the future when Liverpool splashed a £35,000 fee on the lad from Scunthorpe. He was pictured sitting on a dustbin the day he arrived at Anfield, but he went on to scale the heights in soccer.

He joined Liverpool on the eve of the 1971 FA Cup final (which they lost to Arsenal), and was making an impact only a few months later, as Cally bedded down in a midfield berth and Keegan slotted into a front-line role. Steve Heighway once told me: 'I just don't know where Kevin gets his energy from . . . he's got such tremendous stamina that he can cover every blade of grass on the park, and still seem fresh at the end of the match. The same in training – then he'll be off to attend to some business matters or visit his folks. I know I couldn't get through such a workload.'

At Scunthorpe, Kevin had played in a right-sided midfield role (and, according to Bob Paisley, he detested it), but the Liverpool contingent noted that he always seemed to be veering to his left. So, though Liverpool had pencilled in a right-sided role, in place of Ian Callaghan, in the end the two players found their own niche, with Keegan building up a formidable striking part-nership with John Toshack, the Welshman Shanks had signed from Cardiff City for £110,000.

In his opening season, Keegan was capped by England at Under-23 level, and on the summer tour of Russia, Poland and East Germany in 1972 he was a huge success. By the November, he was winning his first senior cap (against Wales in a World Cup qualifying game at Ninian Park), and by the end of season 1972-73 he had won League Championship and UEFA Cup medals with Liverpool. In the spring of 1974 he was scoring twice as Liverpool beat Newcastle United 3–0 in the FA Cup final, and in season 1975-76 he was playing a key role in the club's second UEFA Cup triumph, as he scored an equaliser which enabled Liverpool to beat FC Bruges 4–3 on aggregate.

Alongside him Toshack used his height and his head to win the aerial duels (though Keegan could outjump defenders, too), and in his 245 games for Liverpool the Welsh international struck 95 goals, so he maintained the same kind of ratio as his partner. It was a double act.

Toshack collected an FA Cup-winner's medal in 1974, after having played a key role in the UEFA Cup success of season 1972-73, while during his career at Anfield, Kevin played in three Championship-winning sides, added a European

but, as usual, the big question was whether or not he could perform on a higher stage. Bill Shankly sent Bob Paisley and Joe Fagan to Scunthorpe one night, after having been told by his fellow-Scot, Andy Beattie, that Keegan would make the grade.

Keegan was skippering Scunthorpe, and after having watched him for no more than 20 minutes Bob Paisley and his partner were ready to head for home. When Shanks asked the question, Bob had the answer: 'Take him.' The reasoning, as Bob told me later, was that Kevin Keegan, most likely, could be the replacement for Ian Callaghan who,

Cup medal to his haul, and became an England regular – indeed, he captained his country and was capped 63 times. He wound up with 100 goals to his credit at Liverpool, and had totalled more than 300 games. All this in the space of half a dozen seasons . . . and then he went to Germany and twice became the European Footballer of the Year, in 1978 and 1979. By this time the Anfield faithful were declaring, if not in so many words: 'The king is dead . . . long live the king.' For Kenny Dalglish had appeared in their midst.

Bob Paisley said that he went for Kenny not just because Kevin had left Liverpool, but because the Celtic forward looked to him to be so much what Bob called 'a Liverpool-type player'. Bob said: 'I was impressed by his attitude to the game. He did the simple things, and he was so consistent.' Steve Heighway once defined what he had learned about being a 'Liverpool-type player'. Steve said: 'People talk about the magical secret of this club, but the truth is that they keep everything simple – you're simply told to pass it to the nearest red shirt.'

Kenny Dalglish

There's more to Liverpool's game than that, of course, and they have refined the style which Bill Shankly first used with such conspicuous success; but Kenneth Mathieson Dalglish, without a shadow of a doubt, showed over and over again during his time at Anfield that he was the 'Liverpool type' – both as a player and, later, as the club's manager. At £440,000, he turned out to

be a snip. His career has been examined in detail elsewhere, but it's worth recalling here just what Bob Paisley thought about the way he played his football. Bob gave Kevin Keegan the edge in speed and, perhaps, physical strength, but where Kenny scored was in speed of thought. Bob recalled a game at West Brom when Kenny nipped in to score, and he made the point which the Scot emphasised time and time again . . . his finishing was clinical.

Bob summed up: 'Kenny doesn't waste time trying to get the ball when he knows it just isn't on – he's looking to see where it will go next, and he's moving away to meet it. Take the goal that won the European Cup final against Bruges in 1978. Credit goes to Graeme Souness for his perception in putting the pass through – but Kenny was waiting, and ready to react when the ball came.'

Kenny Dalglish played for Liverpool from the start of season 1977-78 to the end of season 1989-90, although his appearances in the first team became less and less frequent as the 1980s drew to a close. Now and again, also, he played in a reserve-team game, and no matter what the occasion, he demonstrated every time out that he was a team man, in every sense of the word. An ever-present five times during his first six seasons, he was a model of consistency in his approach to the game, and he has carried this attitude into his career in management.

Kenny said that he didn't regard himself as an out-and-out striker whose sole job it was to score goals, and that is absolutely true, because he made so many goals for the likes of Ian Rush; yet that staggering record of 839 appearances with Liver-

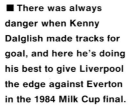

■ There was always danger when Kenny Dalglish made tracks for goal, and here he's doing his best to give Liverpool the edge against Everton in the 1984 Milk Cup final.

pool and Glasgow Celtic, plus his 340 goals, serves to emphasise what a truly great player he was.

Ian Rush

Another man who in recent years has worn Liverpool's colours with equal distinction comes into the category which labels him one of the all-time greats . . . Ian Rush. Standing a shade under 6ft (1.83m) tall, Rushy has what Shakespeare called that 'lean and hungry look', and this is not surprising – for two reasons. First, Ian has never lost his appetite for scoring goals, and secondly, when he was only six year old, he contracted meningitis and, as he spent three weeks in an oxygen tent, the weight rolled off him. 'I never seemed to put it back on,' he said.

Born in Flint, just across the border from England, he used to go with his pals to watch Everton, though the first League match he saw was Spurs versus Liverpool, at White Hart Lane. He had trials with Wrexham and Chester, and was also a target for Burnley after having made his name as a schoolboy marksman – as an 11-year-old, he hit 72 goals to help Deeside Primary Schools win all their 33 matches. Eventually, he opted to sign for Chester, and he signed off with a flourish on 12 April 1980, because his last two goals for the club effectively ended Colchester United's promotion bid. So he joined Liverpool, as a £300,000 fee changed hands. Not that he hit the headlines straight away . . . indeed, for a brief spell he began to wonder if he had a future at Anfield. Bob Paisley suggested that the best way to find out was to score goals. And Rushy took him at his word.

When he left Chester, his manager at the time, Alan Oakes, forecast: 'Ian can go all the way to the top.' He wasn't a bad judge, because Rush became rated the deadliest marksman of the 1980s, as he finished top League scorer for Liverpool in five seasons out of six and became a target for Juventus. In his final derby game against Everton he scored twice, to equal Dixie Dean's haul of 19 derby game goals, and on his return from Italy he resumed scoring against the Blues . . . two goals in an FA Cup final, two more at Goodison, to take his tally to 23 in 24 games.

Rushy's haul of hat-tricks began when he struck three goals for the Welsh schoolboy side against the Republic of Ireland in 1978, and he also hit a hat-trick for Juventus against Pescara in season 1987-88. In the First Division he scored his first hat-trick during season 1981-82 (against Notts County), and he hit four goals against Everton, and three against Coventry City and Notts County again the following season. Next time out, it was five against Luton Town, four against Coventry and three against Aston Villa – then

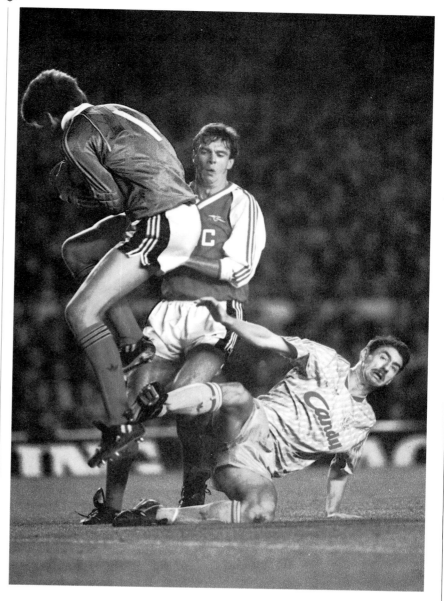

came a hat-trick against Leicester City in season 1986-87.

For good measure, he struck three goals in an FA Cup-tie against Barnsley (1984-85) and Swansea City (1989-90), while in the European Cup Benfica felt the impact of a Rush hat-trick in season 1984-85. In the Screen Sport Super Cup final against Everton (1986-87) he hit three goals, while another Cup hat-trick came in season 1990-91, this time in the Rumbelows (League) Cup return against Crewe Alexandra, to take his overall tally of hat-tricks to 15.

As records have fallen to Ian Rush, so he has shown that you can come back to a club and achieve success again the second time around. There were those who doubted if the Ian Rush who returned to Liverpool from Juventus would ever be the Ian Rush of old, especially since he had to overcome illness and injury during the settling-in period, and there was also the competition from John Aldridge to contend with – they played

■ Ian Rush, the striker who set scoring records and transfer records as he starred for Liverpool, moved to Juventus, then returned to Anfield to demonstrate that he had lost none of his killer instinct.

alongside each other and they played instead of each other – yet, at the end of the day, Rushy took it all in his stride and demonstrated in the best possible way that he was back to his best.

John Aldridge

■ **Liverpool-born and bred, John Aldridge declared it to be a dream come true when he joined the club he had supported as a lad. He showed that he could rifle goals, too, in the top flight – 64 in 104 appearances for the Anfield Reds.**

Aldo, meanwhile, did an Ian Rush as he bowed out at Anfield . . . while Ian had scored the winner against Watford on his farewell appearance before joining Juventus, John went on as a substitute in the early-season League match against Crystal Palace and immediately scored from the penalty spot. That was an emotional night, too, because Liverpool set a record by beating Palace 9–0 and Aldo shed a tear or two as he peeled off his jersey, took off his boots, and threw them into the Kop for some lucky fans to keep as souvenirs.

John Aldridge did a remarkable job for Liverpool during his brief stay, because when this Scouser arrived from Oxford United, it might have been, as he said at the time, 'a dream come true' . . . but it was also the greatest challenge of his footballing career. Aldo had scored goals down the divisions, but now he was being asked to fill the boots of Ian Rush and do the job at the very highest level. It says much for the perspicacity of Kenny Dalglish in signing him, and the ability of Aldridge as a marksman, that the striker succeeded from the day he donned a Liverpool jersey. His former team-mates at Oxford had backed him to finish up as a 30-goal marksman, if he were given a long run in the Liverpool side, and he went very close to that figure. He became a consistent scorer – so much so that Rush was scarcely missed . . . and there's no greater tribute than that.

Once Rush had returned, of course, he had to accommodated in the side, and the day arrived when John Aldridge recognised he must be the one to move on. He had spent the first four games of season 1989-90 on the bench, and he was sitting it out in the fifth match until he got the call to go on and score that penalty against Crystal Palace. The following day he signed for Real Sociedad and carried on scoring goals in Spain . . . having totalled 64 goals in his 104 appearances for Liverpool and 241 goals in 452 games during his career.

John Aldridge had taken Liverpool to the final of the FA Cup and finished as their leading League scorer in successive seasons, with 26 and 21 goals, so he had done all that could have been asked of him; and he had never become too big for his boots during his time at Anfield – indeed, considering the job he was asked to do, he turned out to be a success all the way. Not that he was out on his own, because Kenny Dalglish had also made two other signings – John Barnes and Peter Beardsley. And they, too, had become key men for Liverpool.

Peter Beardsley

The story of John Barnes has been told in the section devoted to wingers; as for Peter Beardsley, he has made his own impact at Anfield, after having (like Bruce Grobbelaar) travelled a roundabout route to get there. Indeed, when he walked off the pitch at Anfield on a winter's day in January 1987, he didn't realise that a few months hence he would be back and wearing Liverpool's colours. That day, he had been playing for Newcastle United, and even though the Magpies had lost, Beardsley had won the admiration of the home fans. At the end of the match, he went over to acknowledge the salute of the Newcastle supporters and, as he made his way towards the

tunnel, the Liverpool fans gave him an ovation and he responded to them. It was all unrehearsed of course, but speculation was fuelled that Beardsley would become a Liverpool player. 'It's amazing how stories like this originate, but there was nothing to it at the time,' he said later.

When a move from Newcastle was mooted, clubs like Manchester United and Tottenham Hotspur were also linked with his name. Peter said: 'At the end of the day, Liverpool were the only club actually to put their money down.' And that money amounted to a British record fee of £1.9 million. Manchester United, among others, must have pondered on the might-have-beens, because at one time they could have had him for much, much less.

Born in Long Benton, a suburb of Newcastle, Peter harboured ambitions about playing for Newcastle, and they did indeed offer him a contract; but he was attracted to Carlisle United by former Magpies skipper Bobby Moncur, then the Cumbrian club's manager, because, as he said: 'I felt I would have a better chance of breaking through to regular first-team football. In fact, I played only two reserve-team games for Carlisle before I was making my debut in the senior side, at the age of 18, and I went on to become a regular before crossing the Atlantic to join Vancouver Whitecaps.'

Peter gives top marks to John Pickering, who coached him at Carlisle: 'He used to come back to the ground every afternoon and work on me to improve my game. He gave up a lot of his own time to try to make me a better player, and I owe him a great deal.' Later, Peter Beardsley was to play alongside Kevin Keegan at Newcastle, as the two of them, with Chris Waddle, helped the Magpies regain First Division status. 'Kevin was very unselfish – he took a lot of the knocks for me,' he says.

Before those exciting days with Newcastle, and while Peter was plying his trade with the Whitecaps in Vancouver, he had a brief spell with Manchester United, who wanted to weigh up whether or not to sign him. They didn't – he never even played one League game for them – though Peter said later: 'Nothing really went wrong . . . Norman Whiteside was given his chance, and he took it so well he went on to play in the World Cup at the end of that season. I was probably just unlucky; after three months I knew it wasn't going to be. But I wasn't too disappointed, because I knew the Whitecaps were always ready to have me back.'

It wasn't for long, though . . . Newcastle stepped in to sign him, then along came Liverpool, and Kenny Dalglish became the eighth team boss for whom Peter had played. Not content with becoming an Anfield crowd favourite, Peter Beardsley graduated as a fully-fledged England inter-

national, and while there have been times when he has found himself on the Reds' bench (in company with one or two other big names) he has shown that he possesses the kind of individual talent which produces some magical moments and some notable goals. When left out, he has always insisted that he is first and foremost a team man, and this, of course, makes him what Bob Paisley calls 'a Liverpool-type player'.

By the end of season 1990-91 Peter Beardsley had topped the century mark for League games with Liverpool and had taken his career total of appearances past 450, while he had scored well over 50 goals for the Anfield club and totalled more than 150 overall. Like Kenny Dalglish and John Barnes, he may not be regarded as an out-and-out striker, because he possesses considerable skills in other directions as well, but like Dalglish and Barnes, Beardsley must certainly go down as one of the Liverpool players who has truly made his mark.

■ Peter Beardsley cost Liverpool a British-record fee of £1.9 million . . . and his goal against Tottenham Hotspur clinched the League Championship for the Anfield club in season 1987-88.

LIVERPOOL's first goal in European competition was scored by Gordon Wallace, on 17 August 1964, and their last goal was scored by Mark Lawrenson on 24 April 1985. In the years between, Liverpool had maintained English football's longest-running European show by competing against the Continentals during 22 consecutive years . . . years which were suddenly and sorrowfully brought to an end by the Heysel stadium disaster in Brussels.

Altogether Liverpool played 140 matches against clubs from France, the Netherlands, Belgium, Spain, Portugal, Yugoslavia, Norway, Denmark, Iceland, Finland, East and West

Since that day, more than quarter of a century ago, the stories have multiplied and, in some instances, become embellished in the telling. But what can never be embellished is the manner in which Liverpool took on the best that Europe had to offer, as well as clubs from the Irish League, the League of Ireland, Scotand and England. More often than not, the men from Anfield triumphed.

That first test was the forerunner of many more – and sterner – outings. Liverpool went to Iceland beset by injury problems, because Alf Arrowsmith and Ian St John were absentees through injury; but their replacements, Gordon Wallace and Phil Chisnall, did their stuff as Reykjavik went down 5–0, thanks to a brace of goals from Roger Hunt, two more from Wallace, and one from Chisnall. Wallace got his name on the scoresheet after only

European Nights

Germany, Italy, Hungary, Rumania, Sweden, Switzerland, Luxembourg, Greece, Poland, Turkey, Bulgaria, Austria and the Soviet Union. They competed in the European Cup, the European Cup-Winners' Cup, the old Inter-Cities Fairs Cup and the UEFA Cup. Four times they won the European Cup, twice they captured the UEFA Cup, and they reached the final of the European Cup-Winners' Cup, a record of which Liverpool can indeed be proud.

European Cup 1964-65

The journey started when Liverpool, as the English League champions, entered the European Cup in season 1964-65 and found themselves paired with the part-timers of Reykjavik, from Iceland. The first leg of the tie was on foreign soil, and to this day those who travelled with Liverpool fondly recall the story of Bill Shankly and the man at the gate. On the outward leg of the trip there was a stop at Prestwick, so Liverpool took in the delights of a holiday camp at Ayr, before embarking on their flight to Iceland. The team coach halted outside the camp gates, and Shanks walked to the front of the vehicle to hail the gateman. 'We're Liverpool – on our way to Iceland!' he informed that worthy . . . and back came the riposte: 'Och, well then, ye've taken the wrong road!'

three minutes, and he was on the mark again on the hour; Hunt scored one minute after half-time, Chisnall after 57 minutes, and Hunt again two minutes from time.

The first team that Liverpool fielded in European competition read like this: Lawrence, Byrne, Moran, Milne, Yeats, Stevenson, Callaghan, Hunt, Chisnall, Wallace, Thompson. For the return game, St John, Bobby Graham and Alan A'Court came in to replace Wallace, Chisnall and Thompson, and the result was a 6–1 victory at Anfield, with St John a two-goal man, and the other goals coming from Hunt, Graham, Gerry Byrne and Willie Stevenson.

After Reykjavik, it was Anderlecht, the crack Belgian club – and if Liverpool needed any warning in advance of their task it was given when no fewer than seven of the players from the Brussels club were called up to play for their country a month before the first leg of the European tie. Not only that; against England at Wembley, Belgium were rated unfortunate to have to settle for a 2–2 draw. But when Anderlecht went to Anfield, Bill Shankly indulged in one of his famous brain-washing speeches, as he told his players not to concern them selves about the opposition. 'They're rub bish', was how he described them. Remarkably, Liverpool – while not quite taking Shanks at his word – gave Anderlecht a going-over, and goals from St John, Hunt and Ron Yeats gave them thecushion of a

3–0 lead for the return . . . with Shankly completely reversing his pre-match view when he greeted his players as they walked off the Anfield pitch. There and then, he made his men feel ten feet tall as he announced: 'You've just beaten one of the best teams in Europe!'

Anderlecht couldn't really hope to overturn that 3–0 deficit on their own ground, and when it came to the crunch, it was Liverpool who held all the aces. They kept the Belgians out for the first 45 minutes, did the same for the next 44 minutes . . . then struck in the dying seconds, as Roger Hunt plundered a match-winner via a post. Liverpool had indeed served notice that they were in Europe to stay.

Yet their next assignment was even tougher than the one they had just completed with such

# of Glory

conspicuous success, because after Anderlecht they were paired with the equally famous West German club, FC Cologne. And their quarter-final tie turned into a three-match marathon which, ultimately, was decided only on the flip of a disc. It was the first experience Liverpool had of this way of deciding a European tie . . . but it was by no means their last.

The first leg of the quarter-final took place in Cologne, and there were 40,000 fans there for the occasion – including some vociferous Liverpudlians. At the end of the game Liverpool were on their way home quietly satisfied that they had prevented Cologne from scoring, even if they hadn't got a goal themselves. At the end of the second leg, however, it was the West Germans who had cause to smile, for they, too, had emerged unscathed, with a scoreless draw.

The sequel was a third meeting, this time at a neutral venue; and it meant that Liverpool and their opponents had to travel to Rotterdam for the tie-breaker. This time Cologne got their name on the scoresheet in the first half – but so did Liverpool . . . twice. However, Cologne equalised in the second half, so the match went into extra time. And after the 30-minute period was up, it was still a 2–2 stalemate. The outcome now depended upon the flip of a disc, and when it was spun into the air it fell down in the mud – and stuck on its edge. The disc was flipped up once more, and this time when it came down it registered in favour of Liverpool. So they were two matches away from the final. But in the semi-finals they had to tangle with the giants of Inter-Milan.

That European tie wasn't the only semi-final which occupied the attention of Liverpool; they

had to meet and beat Chelsea in the FA Cup if they were to travel on to Wembley. And at Villa Park, on the Saturday after their triumph over Cologne, they achieved their objective as they did the business against the Londoners, then went to the final and – after extra time – emerged triumphant again with a 2–1 victory over Leeds United. Liverpool went to Wembley as the reigning League champions, and they came away carrying the FA Cup for the first time in the club's history. Three nights later, they were back in business, trying conclusions with Inter-Milan at Anfield. And there were few brave enough to predict the outcome of this particular battle. For one thing, Liverpool had Gerry Byrne missing after he had fractured a collarbone in the Wembley game; for another, there was the question of whether or not that final against Leeds had taken its toll of Liverpool.

On the night, though, the Anfield Reds showed the world that they were made of extremely stern stuff. . . so much so that they over-ran the Italians. Ronnie Moran was in for Byrne, and if Gordon

■ Airborne action as Liverpool do battle in the European Cup with Inter-Milan, and there's no quarter asked or given as Ian St John and his opponent battle for the ball.

Milne remained a casualty Ian Callaghan had recovered from his Wembley injury to take his place in a line-up which read like this: Lawrence, Lawler, Moran, Strong, Yeats, Stevenson, Callaghan, Hunt, St John, Smith, Thompson. The crowd of more than 54,000 was in a fever of anticipation – part expectation of great deeds from Liverpool, part anxiety that it might all go wrong on the night. The home fans needn't have worried – Liverpool set about Inter with gusto. The Italians, managed by the famous Helenio Herrera, had stars such as Luis Suarez and Joaquin Peiro, from Spain, and they had home-produced idols like Giacinto Facchetti, Mario Corso and Sandro Mazzola; but on the night, they were overshadowed by the men in red.

The gates had been locked more than an hour before kick-off time, and the spectacle of the FA Cup being paraded around the Anfield ground set the adrenalin flowing as Byrne and Milne showed off the gleaming trophy to the fans. It all helped to build up an atmosphere which turned the stadium into a buzzing cauldron of excitement. But still no-one knew how Liverpool would fare. Liverpool, in fact, took fewer than five minutes to stoke up the game to boiling point, because they struck with a goal. Strong got the ball to Callaghan on the right, and after he had sprinted forward and released a cross, Hunt collected the ball and volleyed it past 'keeper Sarti. First blood to Liverpool . . . but only minutes later Mazzola had made the scoreline 1–1.

Liverpool, however, were far from finished, and they forged ahead once more with the game just 34 minutes old. This time they were awarded a free-kick and they sold Inter's defenders a real dummy, as Ian Callaghan made as if to shoot, then he leaped over the ball and carried on while Willie Stevenson simply passed the ball to Roger Hunt, who side-footed it to Callaghan . . . who stuck it past Sarti to make the scoreline Liverpool 2, Inter-Milan 1. They put the ball into the net a third time just before the interval, when Chris Lawler rattled in a shot from 15 yards or so, but Austrian referee Karl Kainer disallowed the goal for offside. Liverpool's players didn't agree with that verdict, but neither did they let it affect their game, and they drove forward once more in the second half, and scored a third goal with 15 minutes left just as Inter were beginning to have visions of a 2–1 result. A shot from Hunt came back off the 'keeper, and St John was on the spot to send the rebound into the net. So Liverpool took with them a two-goal cushion for the return in the San Siro stadium.

Ask anyone who has witnessed a European tie in that ground, and they will tell you that the atmosphere can be unnerving, to say the least. As at Anfield, so in San Siro . . . there is a crescendo of sound; and the Italian fans are just as passionate as their Liverpool counterparts. In fact, the home fans made their presence felt in no uncertain manner even before the game had started in Milan. But it was when the match was over that Liverpool felt they had been the victims of some dubious refereeing decisions, and years after that semi-final they were still declaring their belief that they should have gone through to the final. In the event, they were beaten 3–0 on the night and thus they lost the tie 4–3 on aggregate.

The referee was a Spaniard, Senor Ortiz de Mendibil, and Liverpool's players laid the blame at his door for what they regarded as several bad decisions. First, Inter were awarded a free-kick which, according to the Liverpool manager and his men, was signalled as being indirect; yet when Corso took the kick and sent the ball swerving past Tommy Lawrence, a goal was awarded. So now it was Liverpool 3, Inter-Milan 2 overall.

If Liverpool protested about that refereeing verdict, they were even stronger in their indignation when Peiro kicked the ball out of Lawrence's hands, then stuck it into the net. The referee once again came down on the side of the Italians, though, as he saw nothing wrong, and that meant the scoreline stood at three-all. The tie then was certainly tilting the Italians' way, and it swung completely in their favour when left-back Facchetti finished off a fine passing move involving Corso and Suarez. At the end of the night it was Inter-Milan 4, Liverpool 3 on aggregate, and the Italians went on to retain the trophy they had won the previous year.

Had Liverpool's luck not been out, they might well have become the first British club to carry off the European Cup; as it was, that honour fell to Glasgow Celtic in 1967, with Manchester United the first English club to do the trick when they succeeded in 1968. By which time Liverpool had also been to the final of the European Cup-Winners' Cup and lost out to a team from the West German Bundesliga.

European Cup-Winners' Cup 1965–66

Their 1965 FA Cup triumph meant that Liverpool competed in the European Cup-Winners' Cup competition when season 1965-66 came around, and they had to negotiate a tricky tie in a preliminary round, because they were up against yet another big Italian name, Juventus, the pride of Turin. Liverpool lost the away leg by the only goal, but came back strongly to win the Anfield return 2–0, thanks to goals from Chris Lawler and Geoff Strong. So they went into the first round and drew opposition from Belgium – not Anderlecht again, but Standard Liege.

Lawler, who certainly made his mark as a

defender able to score goals, put the ball into Standard's net twice in the first leg at Anfield, and another goal from Peter Thompson gave Liverpool a 3–1 advantage for the return. They were to make no mistake, either, when the second leg was played. Goals from Roger Hunt and Ian St John enabled Liverpool to overturn a half-time deficit, and they ran out 2–1 winners on the night and 5–2 victors overall, to find that in the next round they would have to break new territory, because a trip to Hungary was involved. So for their quarter-final tie they had to penetrate the Iron Curtain and try their luck against the famous Army club, Honved, in Budapest.

English fans knew the name of Honved because the mighty Ferenc Puskas had played for this noted club and, of course, the magical Magyars of some years previously had humbled England 6–3 at Wembley. So Honved were not rated as easy meat, even for the redoubtable Bill Shankly and his men. Yet the trip to Budapest turned out to be a satisfactory one, because Liverpool held Honved to a scoreless draw. All they had to do now was finish off the job in front of their own fans at Anfield – and there was a crowd of more than 54,000 to see if this could be done on the night of 8 March 1966. Liverpool duly delivered, with goals from Chris Lawler and Ian St John, to set themselves up for a semi-final meeting which was culled right out of the fiction books. Because Glasgow Celtic would provide the opposition.

The first leg was scheduled for Parkhead, and even before a ball had been kicked people were labelling this match the Championship of Britain. At the end of the night at Parkhead, Celtic had inched their way into a 1–0 lead, thanks to a goal from Bobby Lennox, who beat the conditions – a swirling wind and a bone-hard pitch – as well as 'keeper Tommy Lawrence. The crowd of 80,000 came, saw – and left for home wondering if that slender lead would be sufficient.

Liverpool had had one notable absentee at Parkhead – the injured Roger Hunt – and he was to miss the return game at Anfield, as well. But Geoff Strong was in, replacing Phil Chisnall (Hunt's stand-in at Parkhead), and the other first-team regulars were there to line up in front of 54,000 fans at Anfield, where Celtic had their own massed ranks of support. It was Tommy Smith, now rapidly being regarded as an integral part of this great Liverpool side, who put his team on course for victory as he made the overall score 1–1, and it was Strong who dealt the killer blow to Celtic's hopes of survival.

Strong, indeed, proved that he could live up to his name, because he was injured and hobbling when he scored the vital goal in the second half. Despite the fact that he really had only one good leg, he made light of the injury as he rose to meet a cross from Callaghan, and he steered a header past 'keeper Ronnie Simpson. So Liverpool were through to the final, and inside the next couple of weeks they had beaten Chelsea to clinch the League title. It meant that in three seasons they

■ Liverpool's first appearance in a European final – it was against Borussia Dortmund at Hampden Park, Glasgow, in the Cup-Winners' Cup, in 1966. Here Roger Hunt goes close. He did get his name on the scoresheet, but Borussia won, 2–1.

had won the League, then the FA Cup, then the League again – and, all the time, they were going for a trophy in Europe, as well.

In the 1966 final of the European Cup-Winners' Cup at Hampden Park, it was Borussia Dortmund who barred the way. They had knocked out another English club, West Ham United, in their semi-final, and they were a tough proposition for Liverpool. Yet Bill Shankly's team looked capable of beating the Germans – until Siggi Held put Borussia in the lead, after 'keeper Hans Tilkowski had made some great saves.

Roger Hunt stabbed the ball home to renew Liverpool hopes of success, but though the game went into extra time it was Borussia who managed to produce a winner. Lothar Emmerich, who had laid on the first goal for Held, combined with his team-mate in a passing move which culminated with Libuda curling the ball in towards goal. Ron Yeats went up and attempted to clear, but though he made the interception he could do no more than help the ball home.

European Cup 1966-67

So it was another night of heartbreak for Liverpool, and they had to be content with the knowledge that the following term they would be going for the European Cup again. Season 1966-67, however, was destined to end on a dismal note so far as European ambitions were concerned, because after pitting their wits – and succeeding – against a Rumanian club in far-flung Ploesti, Liverpool bowed out when they met their masters in Holland.

Petrolul Ploesti played their football in the heartland of the Rumanian oilfields, and though Liverpool scored a 2–0 success in the first leg at Anfield, the Rumanians repaid that scoreline with interest when Bill Shankly took his team on the long trek across Europe. At the end of the game in Ploesti, the aggregate scoreline was 3–3, which meant another journey, this time to a neutral ground. The venue was Brussels.

In the play-off on Belgian soil, Liverpool finally came through to win 2–0, thanks to goals from St John and Thompson, so the stage was set for a tilt against opposition from Holland in the shape of Ajax Amsterdam. The first leg was scheduled for Holland early in December, and the ground was blanketed in fog. As for Liverpool, they found themselves chasing shadows as Ajax – who had an up-and-coming forward named Johan Cruyff in their side – put five goals past Tommy Lawrence. It was 4–0 to the Dutch team at half-time, and not until the last minute of the match did Liverpool manage to get their name on the scoresheet. Their goal came from Chris Lawler, but it was scarcely enough to give Shanks and his men much hope of

reversing the tide when the Anfield return got under way. Bill Shankly was defiant in his words, rather than optimistic, but Ajax took no notice, in any event.

There was a gate of close on 54,000 at Anfield, and many of the fans had gone because they wanted to see just how good these Dutchmen were, to have plastered Liverpool with a nap hand of goals. There were few who would have backed Shankly's side to score five without reply, in the return; and as it turned out, Liverpool fell a long way short of that figure. It was 0–0 at half-time – Peter Thompson had hit the woodwork early on – but in the second half there were four goals . . . and two of them came from Ajax. Cruyff, who had scored one of his side's goals in Amsterdam, hit the two at Anfield, with Roger Hunt also a two-goal man for Liverpool, so the final and aggregate tally was seven goals to Ajax, three to Liverpool. Once again, they were out of the European Cup. Happily for them, though, they finished high enough in the First Division to keep on qualifying for European competition.

European Fairs Cup 1967-68

Season 1967-68 saw Liverpool competing in the Fairs Cup, and after knocking out the Swedish club, Malmo, they ran riot against a West German side, Munich 1860, as they hammered eight goals without reply at Anfield. But when they came up against Ferencvaros, from Hungary, they suffered a 1–0 defeat both at home and away. The Hungarians, in fact, were one of only a handful of clubs ever to win a European match on the Anfield turf.

European Fairs Cup 1968–69 and 1969–70

In season 1968-69, Liverpool did not get as far even as the third round; they fell to Athletic Bilbao in round one – beaten 2–1 away, winners 2–1 at home and vanquished by the spin of a disc after the aggregate draw. They fared little better, either, the following season, because while they clocked up a record, 10–0 scoreline against the League of Ireland club Dundalk at Anfield (and won the return game 4–0), they went out against opposition from Portugal in the second round.

The game against Dundalk at Anfield was remarkable for the fact that there wasn't a hat-trick man among those ten goals, which were spread around seven players, while the second-round match against Vitoria Setubal, from Portugal, was remarkable for the way it see-sawed and left many Liverpool fans believing their team had squeezed through at the last gasp.

When the first leg took place in Setubal, Liverpool lost 1–0, so it meant that they needed to win the Anfield game 2–0 . . . and at half-time, they were trailing by yet another goal. So they had it all to do, after the restart. On the hour a penalty goal from Tommy Smith gave Liverpool renewed hope, and when Alun Evans scored with two minutes to go and – on the stroke of time – Roger Hunt conjured up a third goal, the home fans believed their team had gained a reprieve, even though Setubal had also got a second-half goal to make the final scoreline 3–3 on aggregate.

Many supporters stayed in their places, in the expectation of extra time; then came the announcement over the public-address system . . . the Portuguese were through on the ruling that in the event of a tie, away goals counted double. So another European night ended on a note of deep disappointment. But there was always next season . . . and when it came, Liverpool promised to go all the way in the Fairs Cup as they surmounted one hurdle after another.

European Fairs Cup 1970-71

There were not too many smiling faces when they were drawn against Ferencvaros in the first round – the memory of what had happened three seasons earlier was still fresh in people's minds. But this time out Liverpool had home advantage first, and a first-half goal from Bobby Graham gave them a slim lead for the return. In Hungary it was 0–0 at half-time, 1–1 at the final whistle (Emlyn Hughes was the Liverpool marksman), so it all came right on the night.

There was more uncharted territory for Liverpool when the draw for round two took them to meet Dinamo Bucharest, in Rumania, but after a first-leg, 3–0 victory at Anfield they achieved a 1–1 draw away and so they came up against Scottish opposition in Hibernian. At Easter Road, Liverpool had John Toshack to thank for his match-winner, and at Anfield Steve Heighway and Phil Boersma completed the job as they gave Liverpool an aggregate 3–0 win.

However, the next item on the agenda was a name which tended to make people purse their lips and ponder upon Liverpool's chances, because in the quarter-finals they had been paired with the West German giants, Bayern Munich. The brightest of Bayern's stars was 'Der Kaiser', the elegant Franz Beckenbauer, and he alone was reckoned to be worth the price of admission. Yet when Liverpool flexed their muscles against Bayern at Anfield, it was the West Germans who were found wanting . . . the hero of the night was a fair-haired young striker who had become the first £100,000 teenager when Liverpool signed him from Wolves. Alun Evans was his name, although his mop of hair had one wag calling him 'rag doll' – but he certainly ran the Bayern defence ragged as he struck three goals past their 'keeper. So Liverpool went to Germany feeling full of confidence, and their confidence was not misplaced, either, because an Ian Ross goal ensured a 1–1 draw and a 4–1 victory overall. Which was the signal for someone to say: 'Bring on Leeds . . .' And that was exactly what happened.

The draw for the semi-finals paired Liverpool with Don Revie's side and, as had happened when Celtic had been in opposition, the stage was set for a real cliffhanger, with the first leg scheduled for Anfield. The crowd of more than 52,000 waited for a goal, but by half-time one hadn't materialised; then, Leeds took the lead with a fine goal from Billy Bremner, and despite throwing everything at them, Liverpool couldn't unlock their defence. So at the end it was Liverpool 0, Leeds United 1. There was a gate of 40,000 at Elland Road, to see if Liverpool could retrieve the situation, and certainly Bill Shankly's men gave it their best shot. This time, Leeds couldn't find a way through the Liverpool defence – but Liverpool couldn't make the breakthrough, either. So the game ended 0–0 and Leeds went through to the final, there to beat Juventus.

European Cup-Winners' Cup 1971-72

It seemed as if Liverpool were never going to claim a European trophy, although they went into the European Cup-Winners' Cup once more in season 1971-72, despite having lost the FA Cup final against Arsenal (who were in the European Cup, since they had done the 'double'). And when Liverpool were paired with the unrated Swiss club, Servette Geneva, it seemed that they had an easy touch, for starters.

Servette, however, scored a 2–1 victory on their own ground, and in the end Liverpool were glad to win 2–0 at Anfield and scrape through on a 3–2 aggregate. Bayern Munich loomed large in their sights again when the second-round draw was made, but this time there was to be no Anfield hat-trick from Evans . . . he played in the first leg at home, but Bayern kept Liverpool out and the match finished scoreless. Evans did find the net in the return game, but Bayern hit three goals, so once more Liverpool made their exit.

UEFA Cup 1972-73

By season 1972-73, the Fairs Cup had become the UEFA Cup competition and, indeed, the trophy was held by an English club, Tottenham Hotspur. And Liverpool, after having suffered at the hands

of one German club, Bayern Munich, the previous season, had to take on another, Eintracht Frankfurt, at the start of their UEFA Cup campaign. Eintracht's name reminded everyone that they had been beaten finalists in one of the great European Cup jousts – a game of ten goals at Glasgow's Hampden Park. That was in the days when Real Madrid were all-conquering, and they beat Eintracht – who played well – 7–3 in that final. Now they were coming to Anfield in the UEFA Cup, and everyone was anxious to see what kind of team they had these days.

After little more than ten minutes, Kevin Keegan had breached their defence, and an Emlyn Hughes goal 15 minutes from time gave Liverpool a 2–0 cushion for the return. That finished without another goal having been scored,

were paired with the holders, Tottenham Hotspur.

The first leg took place at Anfield, and Liverpool were in little doubt that they needed to do the business on home ground, if they wanted to reach the final. Spurs boss Bill Nicholson, never one for shouting the odds, smiled slowly and said little after Alec Lindsay had given Liverpool a 1–0 lead for the return at White Hart Lane. Bill Shankly wasn't talking overmuch, either . . . Nicholson, Shanks and everyone else knew that this tie really was balanced on a razor's edge.

There were almost 47,000 people at Tottenham, and when half-time came without a goal, Liverpool were half-way there. But in the second half there were three goals – two of them to Spurs, one for Liverpool from Steve Heighway. When

■ **Liverpool are on their way to glory in the UEFA Cup in season 1972–73, and among the teams they conquered were AEK Athens. Phil Boersma tucks away a cross from Steve Heighway – in fact, Boersma was on the mark in both games, as Liverpool beat AEK home and away.**

so it was on to the next round, and a first-time meeting with a club from Greece, AEK Athens. At Anfield, Liverpool struck three times and didn't concede one goal; in Athens, they added three more goals while conceding only one. Suddenly, people began to wonder if this might just be their season to conquer in Europe.

First, Liverpool had to meet and master opposition from the other side of the Iron Curtain – Dynamo Berlin, who had an impressive record, especially on home soil. Liverpool emerged unscathed from the trip to Berlin, and at Anfield they scored a 3–1 win, to go through to the quarter-finals . . . only to find that, once more, they had to travel to East Germany. This time, the opposition came from Dynamo Dresden, who were rated even more highly than their Berlin counterparts.

The first meeting took place at Anfield, and Brian Hall and Phil Boersma ensured that Liverpool travelled to East Germany with a two-goal lead. They returned home boosted by a 1–0 victory, thanks to Kevin Keegan, and the knowledge that they were through to the semi-finals . . . which meant, when the draw was made, that they

the final whistle blew, the brace of goals scored by Martin Peters mattered little – Liverpool had done a Vitoria Setubal, by going through on the ruling that away goals counted double. They were through to their second European final.

As in 1966, so in 1973 . . . the other finalists came from West Germany. In 1966 it was Borussia Dortmund; in 1973, it was Borussia Moenchengladbach, managed by that shrewdest of coaches, Hennes Weisweiler. His team were known as The Colts, because of their dashing style of play. By the time that they met Borussia, Liverpool had clinched the Championship of the Football League, so a unique double was in prospect – if they could beat Borussia.

The first leg of the UEFA Cup final was scheduled for Anfield on the night of Wednesday, 9 May 1973; and it lasted less than half an hour. As the rain swept down, so the pitch became increasingly waterlogged, and after 27 minutes the Austrian referee, Erich Linemayr, decided that enough was enough. The teams and the match officials retreated to the dressing-rooms, and the game was declared to be over – for that night, at any rate. It would take place 24 hours later . . . weather permitting.

On the Thursday night, Bill Shankly sprang a surprise by omitting the diminutive Brian Hall and calling on the aerial power of John Toshack; he thus swapped a wide man for a centre-forward. And the ploy worked. Inside the first 35 minutes Toshack had laid on a couple of goals for Kevin Keegan, and the home fans in the 41,000 crowd were buzzing with happy excitement, not to

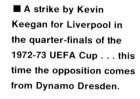

■ A strike by Kevin Keegan for Liverpool in the quarter-finals of the 1972-73 UEFA Cup . . . this time the opposition comes from Dynamo Dresden.

■ Kevin Keegan scores his second goal against Borussia Moenchengladbach in the first leg of the UEFA Cup final in 1973. Liverpool won 3–0, but they had to hang on before they claimed the trophy after the return game in Germany.

mention anticipation that the second half would see the pattern repeated. Liverpool did score again, through centre-half Larry Lloyd, and that was it – a 3–0 result which gave them a comfortable lead for the second leg of the final. Liverpool took with them the UEFA Cup, knowing that they would either be bringing it back to Merseyside in the early hours of the morning, or – if things went woefully wrong – leaving it in Germany. And as the second leg progressed, it became crystal-clear that it was going to be touch and go.

At that stage, the people watching the game were giving more than a little thought to a couple of incidents which had taken place during the first leg . . . when Kevin Keegan had a spot-kick pushed round a post, and when Ray Clemence had brilliantly saved a Jupp Heynckes penalty, to protect his team. It could so easily have been Liverpool 4, Borussia 1 . . . and the way things went in the return game, Borussia looked as if they might yet steal Liverpool's thunder. They were master-minded by their midfield maestro, Gunter Netzer, who created problems aplenty as he sprayed the passes around. This time, Heynckes was on the mark . . . twice, so that cut the lead down to 3–2 overall, and at half-time the Liverpool fans were biting their nails with anxiety. They feared the worst when play was resumed.

Naturally, Bill Shankly saw no reason to voice any doubts he might have had – he told his players they could still go out and snatch victory. And when the game got under way again, after an initial opening spell of pressure it seemed that Borussia might just have taken too much out of themselves with their herculean efforts of the first half. The longer the game went, the stronger Liverpool seemed to become, and as the closing minutes loomed, it was Borussia who began to look desperate. Not surprisingly, though, the final whistle came as a relief to the men from Anfield, and in the Liverpool dressing-room afterwards there were some strained and pale-looking faces – including that of Bill Shankly. It didn't really seem to sink in that the UEFA Cup had been won – not until the team reached the airport and boarded the plane for home.

As Liverpool flew back through the night skies over Europe, with the glittering trophy safely aboard, the atmosphere began to change. People were talking happily – perhaps a little faster than usual – and the laughter came quickly. Then, as if on cue, people began to go forward, one by one, to the microphone normally used by the stewardess for making announcements. And, one by one, players went up and 'did a turn' – a song, a funny story, it didn't matter what.

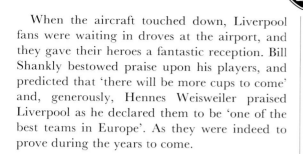

When the aircraft touched down, Liverpool fans were waiting in droves at the airport, and they gave their heroes a fantastic reception. Bill Shankly bestowed praise upon his players, and predicted that 'there will be more cups to come' and, generously, Hennes Weisweiler praised Liverpool as he declared them to be 'one of the best teams in Europe'. As they were indeed to prove during the years to come.

European Cup 1973-74

Liverpool's next assignment was another crack at the European Cup, but after the euphoria of their UEFA Cup success, there was a feeling of let-down in season 1973-74, because – after having knocked out the Luxembourg side, Jeunesse d'Esch – Liverpool fell in the second round to Red Star Belgrade, who were managed by that old stager Miljan Miljanic. Like Ferencvaros, Red Star won home and away, to put the skids under Liverpool.

European Cup-Winners' Cup 1974-75

In the summer of 1974, Bill Shankly bowed out, after having steered his club to another FA Cup success, so Bob Paisley took up the challenge, and in Europe Liverpool entered the European Cup-Winners' Cup once more . . . only to fall to Ferencvaros after having hammered Norwegian-club Stromgodset 11–0 at Anfield, where nine players got their names on the scoresheet. That scoreline remains a record for Liverpool in European competition . . . ironically, as people expected another onslaught of goals in the return, the Norwegians restricted Liverpool to 1–0. Against Ferencvaros it was 1–1 at Anfield, 0–0 in Hungary; so the away-goal rule spelled defeat for Liverpool.

UEFA Cup 1975-76

Season 1975-76 brought glory, glory all the way though, as Liverpool competed in – and, for the second time, won – the UEFA Cup. The 12-match marathon began with a tie against Hibernian, who had fallen to Liverpool in their 1970 Fairs Cup contest, and this time the Easter Road club scored the only goal on their own ground. The Anfield return, though, was a personal triumph for John Toshack, because he hammered in a hat-trick, and indeed could truthfully be said to be the man who turned the tide Liverpool's way, because with a final scoreline of 3–1 the tie went to the Anfield club on a 3–2 aggregate.

There was new opposition in the shape of a Spanish club called Real Sociedad, when Liverpool learned their fate in the draw for the next round, and this meant a trip to sunny San Sebastian late in October. Liverpool emerged from this match with a 3–1 lead, so they could feel comfortable about the Anfield return . . . but, just to emphasise their superiority, they reeled off half a dozen goals there without reply. That match took place on 4 November 1975, and 22 days later Liverpool were taking their chances for the first time in far-away Poland.

They were certainly entering the unknown, as they tried to build up a dossier on their opponents, whose very name – Slask Wroclaw (say it Vrosh-lav) – was far from easy to pronounce. And the conditions, too, were vastly different from those Liverpool had enjoyed in Spain, because the temperature in Poland was well below freezing point, as the coaches carrying the team, club officials and Pressmen negotiated the icy roads from the airport to the hotel. When Liverpool went for a training session, the ground was covered in frozen snow, and when the match kicked off – early in the afternoon – the media men had to settle for accommodation in a kind of Portakabin with a concrete floor . . . and more than one Pressman fortified himself with tots of neat whisky to try to keep out the bitter cold.

Down on the pitch, the Slask Wroclaw players were slithering about as they tried to keep their feet on the hard-packed snow – it was almost like an ice rink – but Liverpool found the going easier than their opponents, because they were better equipped, thanks to the foresight of the men responsible for the players' kit. They had taken some special boots with them to cover for just such an eventuality, and those boots enabled Liverpool's players to go about their business in a reasonably sure-footed manner – so much so, that by the end of 90 minutes the men from Merseyside had forged a 2–1 lead.

There was no time to linger, though – the airport was closing down at 7pm because of the weather, and Liverpool's party had to get there very quickly. The coach trip took on the appearance of a death-defying ride at times, as the drivers tried to beat the clock, and the plane was boarded with literally only minutes to spare. The plane crew had already gone ahead and prepared everything for take-off, and as Liverpool flew back across Polish territory and dinner was served, the atmosphere was relaxed, as if everyone realised this had been a good job well done.

The Anfield leg of the tie turned out to be somewhat more than a formality, because it was a case of one man taking the honours. Against Hibs, John Toshack had been the three-goal marksman . . . against Slask Wroclaw, it was Jimmy Case who struck three times, to register his first goals in

Europe and make the tally 3–0 on the night and 5–1 on aggregate. So Liverpool cruised through to the quarter-finals and, with a break from December to March, they could turn their attention back to the League and the FA Cup.

Come March, and the draw paired Liverpool – not for the first time – with the East German club Dynamo Dresden, with the first leg away. The result after 90 minutes was 0–0, thanks to a penalty save by Ray Clemence, who tipped the spot-kick from Peter Kotte round a post, and when the second leg took place at Anfield, Liverpool established their mastery with goals from Jimmy Case and Kevin Keegan which brought them a 2–1 win. That victory took them into the semi-finals, and a confrontation with one of Spain's top clubs, Barcelona.

It was also the occasion for a reunion with two old adversaries, because Johan Cruyff was now plying his trade with Barcelona, and they were under the management of Hennes Weisweiler, previously at Borussia Moenchengladbach. So there was added spice to the pairing of these two great clubs. Barcelona also had another Dutch ace, Johan Neeskens, in their ranks, but on the night it wasn't Cruyff and Neeskens who ran the show . . . that honour fell to the Toshack-Keegan combination.

Well before the end of the first half, Liverpool had silenced the home fans by taking the lead, as a long kick from Ray Clemence was collected by Keegan. He wasted no time in helping the ball on its way, with Toshack the recipient of the pass, and the lanky Welshman beat 'keeper Mora, to edge Liverpool in front. Before the match had

ended, the home supporters were giving vent to their displeasure by throwing cushions down on to the pitch.

When Barcelona visited Anfield, however, they soon showed that they were not simply going to roll over and die – in fact, they put up such a spirited performance that in the end Liverpool were happy to settle for a goal from Phil Thompson and a 1–1 result on the night which secured an aggregate 2–1 victory over the Spanish club. So, for the second time in four seasons, Liverpool had reached the final of the UEFA Cup competition . . . and, for the second time, also, they were about to win it.

The last hurdle was presented by FC Bruges, from Belgium, and the first leg of the final was scheduled for Anfield, where there was a crowd which fell only 19 short of the 50,000 mark. The fans certainly got their moneysworth as Bruges and Liverpool became locked together in a cliffhanger of a match. Anfield, indeed, was no place for those who suffered from heart trouble, because Bruges didn't sit back and invite Liverpool to come at them. Instead, they embarked upon an attacking policy which, by half-time, had paid handsome dividends, because when the whistle went for the interval Liverpool were walking off with that stunned sensation, as they trailed by two goals, scored by Raoul Lambert and Julien Cools.

The half-time gossip, of course, was how on earth Liverpool could stage a comeback from this seeming disaster, especially as 90 of the remaining 135 minutes had to be endured on the ground of the Belgian club. In short, people felt that

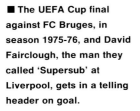

■ The UEFA Cup final against FC Bruges, in season 1975-76, and David Fairclough, the man they called 'Supersub' at Liverpool, gets in a telling header on goal.

Liverpool needed to do what they had to do during the remaining 45 minutes at Anfield, or resign themselves to losing the final. When the teams emerged for the second half, Liverpool had rung the changes, with Jimmy Case replacing John Toshack; and Case turned out to be one of the heroes of the night, because after Ray Kennedy had given Liverpool some hope by scoring just inside the hour, Case struck two minutes later, to level the score. And then the night air was rent by a crescendo of sound three minutes after that when Liverpool were awarded a penalty and Keegan made no mistake from the spot.

The final result was Liverpool 3, FC Bruges 2 . . . and after the match, chairman John Smith confided that when the half-time whistle went, he would have been happy to feel that the result after 90 minutes was going to be a draw, never mind a 3–2 victory. That lead was slender enough to take to Belgium, but it was a great deal better than Liverpool might have expected, after their two-goal setback of the first half. In between the two legs of the final, there was another cliffhanger of a match – the League game against Wolves at Molineux, where a win would ensure the Championship for the men from Anfield. It looked ominous again, though, as Steve Kindon struck to put Wolves in the driving seat, and the scoreline remained 1–0 until the last quarter of an hour. Then Liverpool braced themselves for one final effort, and they produced three goals to win the game and secure the title. The marksmen: Keegan, Toshack and Kennedy.

So Liverpool flew out to Belgium as the Champions of the English League and, as in season 1972-73, they were going for a double of League title and UEFA Cup. Was the single-goal lead against Bruges going to prove enough? The answer came in the first half of the match . . . shortly after Bruges had made the aggregate score 3–3, thanks to a penalty goal from Lambert inside quarter of an hour. Instead of being rocked on their heels by that spot-kick, Liverpool rapidly hit back. Skipper Emlyn Hughes took a free-kick and pushed the ball square to Kevin Keegan, who hammered in a shot which flew past 'keeper Birger Jensen. So it was 1–1 on the day, 4–3 to Liverpool on aggregate . . . and the men from Merseyside kept their heads and held out to claim the trophy.

European Cup 1976-77

As the League Champions, of course, Liverpool competed in the European Cup the following season, and if the spring of 1976 had produced a stirring finale, the spring of 1977 eclipsed what had gone before, as Liverpool drove onwards in their efforts to retain the Championship, win the FA Cup and capture the European Cup. That

they failed to achieve this tantalising treble could not detract one iota from their feat in holding on to the Championship and coming back from defeat at Wembley to carry off the most coveted prize in European football.

The European campaign started in September, with a so-called easy tie against Irish League club Crusaders, and after a 7–0 aggregate success over the two legs Liverpool were on their way to uncharted territory as they were paired with a Turkish club called Trabzonspor. Nobody knew anything about these Turks, but Liverpool did their homework as well as possible, sending Tom Saunders on a spying mission. And that meant travelling to the Black Sea coast, not far from the borders of Georgia, in Soviet Russia. It was a trip which lasted five days, from start to finish, and when Tom returned to Anfield he didn't minimise the problems Liverpool would encounter. Hotel accommodation was not of the highest standard, catering problems had to be sorted out, and apart from these details there was the organisation of travel for what would be a 5,000-mile round trip.

As for the little matter of the match, that was something else. The ground could accommodate around 13,000 fans – and they would be giving fanatical support to the home side – while the pitch itself was grassy, but not up to the standard of Anfield . . . not, indeed, by a long way.

A couple of days before their departure, Liverpool had beaten Everton in the Anfield derby game, to remain on course for the League title; now, as Bob Paisley admitted, Liverpool were 'going into the unknown.' The trip to Turkey involved a five-hour flight to the capital, Ankara, an overnight stay there and a 500-mile hop to Trabzon for the game, which would be sandwiched between two nights in the Turkish town. Then there would be the return trip to Ankara and the long flight home.

Liverpool had a couple of injury problems – Phil Neal had been hurt in the derby game, while Ian Callaghan had been hit by an attack of fibrositis. In the event, Tommy Smith took over from Neal – who thus missed his first European match – and Callaghan was ruled fit to play. All that Liverpool had to do now was beat the Turks. It was no score at half-time, but after an hour Trabzonspor fans were chanting their team's name as Rumanian referee Nicolai Rainea awarded a penalty against Liverpool. Skipper Cemil decided he was the man to take it, and he sidefooted the ball towards goal . . . but he miskicked. As Ray Clemence dived to one side, the ball hit the opposite upright and crossed the line for a goal which could only be rated as lucky. That was the end of the scoring, and Liverpool returned home, weary but confident that it would be a different story when the Turks visited Anfield. By which time Liverpool had shot into a

INTERNATIONALS AT ANFIELD

DIEGO MARADONA'S infamous 'Hand of God' goal for Argentina against England in the 1986 World Cup wasn't the first occasion such an incident caused controversy . . . a similar thing happened at Anfield in 1977, when Scotland played Wales in a World Cup qualifying match. Joe Jordan of Scotland was the central figure involved in the arguments, as Scotland won and went on to Argentina. That game was played on the night of Wednesday, 12 October 1977 – ironically, it was a 'home' game for Wales, but the Scottish supporters seemed to far outnumber the fans from 'down the road'.

Liverpool players in the Welsh squad were John Toshack and Joey Jones, and in Scotland's team that fateful night was one Kenny Dalglish who, of course, was to claim a record number of international caps (102) . . . which brings us back to Anfield as the venue for international matches. And while Wales and Scotland were competing there for the first time in that World Cup qualifying game, England have played five times on Liverpool's ground.

The first full international was way back in 1883, when England beat Ireland 7–0. Then, in March 1905, England defeated Wales 3–1. There was another game against Wales in March 1922, when England scored the only goal. Then in October 1926, England and Ireland shared half a dozen goals and in November 1931, it was England versus Wales again, with the Welsh on the losing end of a 3–1 scoreline.

Apart from Kenny Dalglish, John Toshack and Joey Jones, Liverpool have had other players in action at Anfield for their respective countries. In 1905 George Latham played for Wales; in 1922 Tommy Bromilow wore England's colours; and in 1926 Elisha Scott was Ireland's last line of defence. Ernie Blenkinsop and Tom Cooper were England's full-back pairing for the 1931 game – though Blenkinsop was then with Sheffield Wednesday and Cooper with Derby County, both played for Liverpool later.

There was an unofficial international between England and Wales during the Second World War, in September 1944, and Ray Lambert and Cyril Sidlow played for Wales, who held England to a 2–2 draw. Sidlow joined Liverpool from Wolves soon after that match at Anfield.

Liverpool players have skippered

■ Football's honours came thick and fast for Kenny Dalglish during his career with Liverpool and Glasgow Celtic – not to mention Scotland. Indeed, he became his country's most-capped player, as he collected no fewer than 102 caps.

■ Included in the England line-up against Wales in 1921 were Liverpool's Tommy Bromilow (far right, back row) and Harry Chambers (second right, front row).

England over the years. The great Ephraim Longworth led his country to a 2–0 victory over Belgium in Brussels in May 1921 (when Harry Chambers scored one of the goals), and in more recent times players such as Emlyn Hughes, Kevin Keegan, Phil Thompson, Ray Clemence and Phil Neal were honoured, while Sammy Lee captained England's Under-21 team. Kenny Dalglish skippered Scotland, too.

There is a lengthy list of Liverpool players who have been capped by their respective countries, and there have been occasions when Liverpool have fielded virtually an all-international side at club level. Indeed, there was one time when England's team consisted mainly of players from Liverpool Football Club, and men from

Anfield have represented their countries in World Cup matches.

Billy Liddell was honoured by being chosen for a Great Britain side which took on the Rest of Europe in Glasgow in 1947, when the hosts won 6–1. There was a similar match – in Belfast in 1955

– when the Rest of Europe won 4–1, and Liddell and Stanley Matthews were the only two players to take part in both games.

During the 1966 World Cup tournament, Liverpool had seven players in the original, 40-strong England squad, with Roger Hunt, Ian Callaghan and Gerry Byrne making the final 22; and four years later, Emlyn Hughes and Peter Thompson were in England's final 22. Later still, England called up the bulk of the Liverpool side, when players such as Phil Neal, Phil Thompson, Hughes, Clemence, Callaghan, Ray Kennedy and Terry McDermott claimed international honours.

As a matter of interest, in January 1991, when Liverpool met Blackburn Rovers in an FA Cup replay, their side was composed entirely of internationals . . . Bruce Grobbelaar (Zimbabwe), Glenn Hysen (Sweden), Jan Molby (Denmark), Ronny Rosenthal (Israel), Ian Rush (Wales), Ray Houghton and Steve Staunton (Republic of Ireland), Steve Nicol and Gary Gillespie (Scotland), and John Barnes and Steve McMahon (England).

■ During his Liverpool career Emlyn Hughes was capped 59 times, with three more caps to come after he had moved to Wolves.

three-point lead at the top of the First Division.

Trabzonspor had a following of around 3,000 Turkish fans at Anfield, but it was the Liverpool faithful who were cheering as goals from Steve Heighway, David Johnson and Kevin Keegan put paid to the opposition in a 20-minute scoring spree. All that Liverpool needed to know after that was the name of their quarter-final opponents . . . and they turned out to be *Les Verts*, The Greens, of St Etienne, from France.

Only the previous season St Etienne had gone to the final of the competition, and though they had lost 1–0 to Bayern Munich, they had won many admirers by the style of their play. Now, for the first time, Liverpool had to find a way of outwitting them. If Liverpool had Keegan, *Les Verts* had Dominique Rocheteau, and he admitted that he couldn't wait to play in front of that soccer institution known as The Kop, although the first leg was to be at St Etienne. There were other fascinating aspects of this duel between two top clubs – such as how John Toshack would fare in his confrontation with the Argentinian international, Osvaldo Piazza; how Steve Heighway would compare with Gerard Janvion, his direct opponent; how St Etienne's Yugoslav-international goalkeeper, Curkovic, would rate against Ray Clemence and how much influence French-international midfield ace Jean-Michel Larqué would be able to wield.

St Etienne had a home reputation which was as formidable as that of Liverpool at Anfield – they had not lost a match on their own ground in four years. And on the eve of the first leg they were boosted by the news that, while Rocheteau had recovered from injury and would play, Keegan had suffered a ligament pull and would not be in the Liverpool line-up. So Terry McDermott went into the side.

Liverpool played it cool, they played it defensively, as St Etienne strove to break them down with one foray after another. But half the game had gone by without *Les Verts* having made a breakthrough. There were fewer than 15 minutes to go when St Etienne finally scored – a corner found Janvion, who mis-hit his shot but saw the ball go to Bathenay. He got his left foot to the ball and it was 1–0 for the French team.

The lead was slender, but St Etienne were noted for being miserly when it came to conceding goals – only one had beaten their 'keeper in nine European Cup games. So they arrived at Anfield in hope, despite the absence of Piazza, who was suspended after his first-match caution. Backing the French were 7,000 fans, and they certainly made themselves heard . . . though the Kop outdid them, especially when Liverpool got their name on the scoresheet.

Only two minutes of the match had gone by when Kevin Keegan struck, and it was still 1–0 at half-time, 1–1 on aggregate. The second half brought three more goals – one of them to St Etienne . . . but one just wasn't enough. Ray Kennedy made it two for Liverpool just inside the hour, to cancel out Bathenay's strike which still kept the French on course for the semi-finals; but with just over five minutes to go the man they called 'Supersub', David Fairclough, exploded into scoring action.

The red-headed Fairclough, a scourge of English defences so often, made his mark when he had been in the game for little more than ten minutes, as he chested the ball down, then zig-zagged his way forward for some 40 yards and sent a shot whistling past the advancing Curkovic. And so the match was won and lost, the score 3–1 on the night and 3–2 over both legs. Liverpool could look forward to their second semi-final in the European Cup, and this time the opposition was regarded as easier than it had been in 1965.

Instead of the mighty Inter-Milan, Liverpool had to account for surprise contenders from Switzerland, FC Zurich, who were rated as the weakest side left in the tournament – though, true to form, Liverpool didn't under-rate them. When they travelled to Switzerland for the first leg, they did a supremely professional job by winning 3–1, with two goals from Phil Neal (one a penalty) and one from Steve Heighway. And on home ground, Liverpool didn't sit back – they knocked in three more goals, with Jimmy Case on target twice and Kevin Keegan also scoring.

Now it was a case of history repeating itself, because Liverpool's opponents in the final – to be staged in Rome – were Borussia Moenchengladbach, whom they had conquered in the 1973 final of the UEFA Cup. But before they met Borussia, Liverpool had a Wembley date with Manchester United in the final of the FA Cup. The title was already theirs, after a scoreless draw against West Ham United at Anfield on Saturday, 14 May – just one week before the Wembley date – and that 0–0 result meant that Liverpool were the Champions for a record tenth time, after they had seen off the challenge of Manchester City and Ipswich Town.

At Wembley, half-time arrived with the score-line reading 0–0, but the final burst into nail-biting goal action early in the second half, as Stuart Pearson put United ahead and Jimmy Case rifled an equaliser. But United got their noses in front again when a Lou Macari effort took a deflection off Jimmy Greenhoff and left Ray Clemence stranded. Time ran out for the Anfield Reds. They were still the Champions, but they had lost the Cup – could they now brace themselves for the test in Rome the following week?

It was a subdued Liverpool party that headed away from Wembley stadium for the railway

station at Watford. A police escort paved the way, and as everyone stood waiting on the platform for the Liverpool-bound train to arrive, few people knew what to say about the bitter disappointment of the afternoon. Yet once aboard the train, and with a meal being served, Ray Clemence set the tone when he started to grin and joke with his team-mates, and before long the atmosphere had brightened considerably.

By the time the players had reached Liverpool – while thousands of their supporters were already making the overland trek to Rome – there was a feeling that the European Cup could still be carried off to Anfield, if everyone put their backs into the final task. Bob Paisley summed it up as he reminded people that Liverpool were bidding to become the first English club to achieve a League-European Cup double.

On Monday, Liverpool trained; on Tuesday they boarded the plane for Rome; and on the Wednesday night, in Rome's Olympic stadium, they lined up for the final against Borussia Moenchengladbach, with Bob Paisley indicating that he was prepared to call upon 13 players to do the job. John Toshack, an absentee from the side for several weeks, was in the 16-man squad, and Borussia – now under the management of Udo Lattek – had good cause to remember him from the 1973 UEFA Cup final.

On the other hand Borussia, having just clocked up a hat-trick of League Championship successes, had every reason to feel confident themselves, and they could call upon stars such as Berti Vogts, Rainer Bonhof, Allan Simonsen, their Danish ace, Uli Stielike and Jupp Heynckes – in fact, their whole team consisted of players who were household names. It was while Liverpool were still airborne that Bob Paisley named his team – the same players who had finished the game against Manchester United at Wembley, with Toshack, David Johnson, Alec Lindsay, David Fairclough and reserve 'keeper Peter McDonnell on the bench. Match day dawned, and with it came the bad news . . . after training, John Toshack was out – so Alan Waddle became the 16th member of the squad.

Of the 57,000 fans who flocked to the Olympic stadium, it was reckoned that 26,000 had come from Liverpool – by car, coach, van, train, plane . . . some had even hitch-hiked their way across the Continent to be there on the big day. And how they cheered when Liverpool's players emerged into the arena to line up like this: Clemence, Neal, Jones, Smith, Kennedy, Hughes, Keegan, Case, Heighway, Callaghan, McDermott.

The referee was a Frenchman, Robert Wurtz, one of the most experienced in Europe, and he found himself in charge of an exciting, absorbing final which was played in the right spirit, as the teams sparred for an opening. The first one came

when Bonhof got a sight of goal, and Borussia could easily have been one up . . . but Bonhof's fierce drive cannoned off a post. Then the Germans had another bit of bad luck – Herbert Wimmer was injured, so he had to go off, with Christian Kulik taking his place. Just inside the half-hour, fortune favoured Liverpool yet again as Callaghan robbed Bonhof and got Heighway going upfield. He picked his moment, then slid a pass straight into the space for McDermott to connect and send a right-footer past 'keeper Wolfgang Kneib. So at half-time Liverpool led 1–0, and they resumed the action confident that they could keep Borussia at bay . . . but mere minutes later they were having to think again.

A pass from Case went astray, and it was snapped up by Simonsen, who didn't waste this golden opportunity – quick as a flash, he was cutting inside from the left and hammering the ball into the top corner, leaving Clemence clawing at air. Suddenly, it was 1–1 and the game was balanced on a knife-edge. The Liverpool fans began to wonder if, after all, this was going to be another Wembley.

Keegan had certainly been giving Vogts, his marker, a chasing; and Heighway, too, had been posing plenty of problems. But after referee Wurtz had waved play on, when Vogts seemed to have downed Keegan, the action switched to the other end as Simonsen sent over a cross which was met by Stielike, and a goal looked certain. Yet there was Clemence, Liverpool's saviour more than once in previous European ties, coming to the rescue again as he blocked the shot.

Inside another five minutes, Liverpool fans were going delirious with delight, because Tommy Smith was making the scoreline 2–1. Liverpool had won a corner on the left, and as Heighway delivered a pinpoint cross from the

■ The scene is the Olympic stadium in Rome, on a spring night in 1977, and Liverpool are meeting Borussia Moenchengladbach in the final of the European Cup. Tommy Smith scores Liverpool's second goal, with a devastating header.

flag-kick, Smith raced in by the near post to meet the ball and steer an unstoppable header past Kneib. Smith was entitled to celebrate – this was his 600th game in a Liverpool jersey, and he was on the verge of hanging up his boots at Anfield.

When Bonhof and Heighway tangled soon afterwards, Liverpool fans roared for a penalty . . . but again referee Wurtz turned a deaf ear. However, he finally did blow his whistle and point to the spot after Vogts had sent Keegan crashing inside the box. Up stepped Phil Neal, and he kept

■ The smile on the face of the tiger . . . and this particular 'tiger' is Tommy Smith, being embraced by coach Ronnie Moran after Liverpool have seen off Borussia Moenchengladbach in the 1977 final of the European Cup in Rome.

his nerve while all around him people found their hearts pounding . . . with fear or eager anticipation, depending upon whose side you were on. As Neal despatched that spot-kick past Kneib, it seemed that everyone in the stadium knew that the die had been finally cast, and that victory was going to Liverpool. The final whistle confirmed that Liverpool had beaten Borussia 3–1, and there was a carnival atmosphere as Liverpool's management team, the players and the fans rejoiced together. When captain Emlyn Hughes lifted the

glittering European Cup aloft in triumph, it was the signal for a crescendo of sound from the massed ranks of the supporters from Merseyside.

The remainder of the night – and the early hours of the morning – passed all too swiftly, but they will be remembered for ever by those who were there. The champagne flowed, the fans joined in the celebrations, and while there was some sympathy to spare for Borussia, no-one doubted that on the night, victory had gone to the better team. Liverpool had thoroughly earned their moment of European glory.

The one sad thing about it was that this tremendous victory marked the farewell appearance of Kevin Keegan, and there was a touch of irony in the fact that he would be joining a West German club, Sportverein Hamburg. His departure, of course, posed the question . . . how would Liverpool replace him? He had scored 100 goals for the club he joined from Scunthorpe, he had become a key man for the Anfield Reds, and now he would be moving on. No-one begrudged him his success, or his desire to seek a new challenge on the Continent; but everyone pondered on what difference his absence might make to Liverpool.

Bob Paisley had been pondering, too, and he was about to come up with the answer – a player called Kenny Dalglish, who in turn was to inspire Liverpool to even more glory on the playing fields of Europe, as well as in the domestic competitions. With Dalglish in their side, Liverpool were to capture the European Cup on three more occasions, and they were to reach the final for a fifth time . . . although that would be overwhelmed by tragedy.

For now, the glory that was Rome remained uppermost in people's minds – and when season 1977-78 came around and Dalglish had become a British record signing at £440,000, Liverpool started out once more on the trail of the European Cup. They had it on the sideboard at Anfield; they had every intention of keeping it there, too. And they did.

European Cup 1977-78

Once again, when Liverpool embarked upon their defence of the European Cup in season 1977-78, they had to contend with the East Germans from Dynamo Dresden, but in the first leg of the first-round tie at Anfield, Liverpool scored a nap hand of goals while conceding only one, and if they lost the return 2–1, it didn't really matter. They were through the tie and looking forward to taking on the Eagles of Lisbon, Benfica, in their own Stadium of Light.

There was a crowd of 70,000 for the first leg in Lisbon, and Liverpool proved that they were more than a match for the most famous team in

Portugal, as they held Benfica to a 1–1 draw in the first 45 minutes (thanks to a Jimmy Case goal), then took the lead through Emlyn Hughes with just over quarter of an hour to go. The return at Anfield became a formality, as Benfica crumbled beneath the weight of the Liverpool onslaught . . . goals from Ian Callaghan (after only six minutes), Kenny Dalglish (17), Terry McDermott (78) and Phil Neal (88) brought a 6–2 aggregate victory.

If that quarter-final tie had turned out to be much easier than anticipated, Liverpool knew they were up against stiffer opposition in their semi-final – The Colts of Borussia Moenchenglad-bach, who were clearly aiming to avenge their final defeat of the previous season. This was a match which had every promise of being another nail-biting affair, and by the end of the first leg in Germany it was certainly turning out that way.

The 66,000 fans packed into the stadium saw Borussia score in the first half, and again in the second . . . and then, two minutes from the final whistle, Liverpool rustled up an attacking move which saw David Johnson sticking the ball into the net, to alter the complexion of the game. With a final score of 2–1 to Borussia, Liverpool at least had a fighting chance when the teams met again Anfield.

It was another of those famous European nights when the battle was resumed on Wednesday, 12 April, 1978. Liverpool needed the tonic of a quick goal, and Ray Kennedy provided it, when he struck with the match just six minutes old. Ten minutes before half-time, Kenny Dalglish became a scoring hero as he put Liverpool 2–0 up on the night and 3–2 ahead on aggregate, and when Jimmy Case scored just inside the hour, Borussia were out for the count. The 51,000 fans went home – most of them, at any rate – rejoicing in Liverpool's success, and they looked forward to watching them play in their second successive final – and, hopefully, to seeing them retain the European Cup. The venue this time didn't involve a trek across the Continent . . . for Liverpool fans, there was the simple matter of a drive down the motorway to Wembley, where their favourites would be meeting FC Bruges . . .

■ **Terry McDermott shows why he became one of Liverpool's most feared marksmen against Continental opposition, as he weaves his way between these two Bruges defenders in the European Cup final at Wembley in 1978.**

who, like Borussia Moenchengladbach, no doubt felt they had something to prove, after their UEFA Cup final defeat in 1976.

It seemed that Liverpool were fated to keep on coming up against opponents they had met and mastered in previous finals, and the more superstitious wondered if this time fortune would favour the Belgians. The final took place on 10 May, and 92,000 people flocked down Wembley Way to watch this latest confrontation. Bruges were still a force to be reckoned with, and as the minutes went by, they showed that they were not just there to make up the numbers.

Half-time came and went, and there wasn't a goal in sight; the first hour passed by, and still it was a scoreless stalemate; and then, with the match 65 minutes old, Liverpool got their chance to nail the opposition. It was a goal fashioned by midfield maestro Graeme Souness, as he drilled a defence-splitting pass forward and to the right. It was his fellow-Scot, Kenny Dalglish, who seized upon the ball and then, with clinical precision,

the Football League. Somewhere along the line, it seemed, these two giants of English football might well clash in the European Cup . . . and they did.

When the draw for the first round of the European Cup was made, it could not have been more cruel, so far as Liverpool and Forest were concerned, because events conspired to ensure that the names of these two English clubs came out of the bag together. So Bob Paisley and Brian Clough knew at the outset that one of them was going to see his side make its exit at the very outset of the competition. The draw decreed that Liverpool had to travel to Nottingham and meet Forest first at the City Ground, and there was a gate of more than 38,000 for this battle. By half-time, Forest had forged a slender, one-goal lead; by the end of 90 minutes they had made the scoreline 2–0, and Liverpool were clearly in trouble. That didn't deter 51,000 people from going to Anfield for the return, and they saw Liverpool give it everything they'd got.

They hammered away at Forest, they sent on

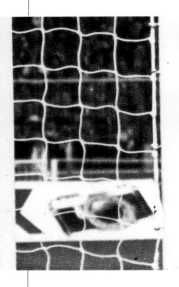

■ The goal that kept the European Cup at Anfield in 1978, as Graeme Souness drilled a defence-splitting pass for Kenny Dalglish to take, and the reaction of the Bruges defender is plain to see, as the ball goes into the net. It was glanced home by Dalglish with a deft touch.

curled it across and into the net. The goal was typical – it bore the Dalglish trademark of incisive thinking, swift and accurate action, and it turned out to be the match-winner. Kenny had scored on his League debut for Liverpool that season, he had shown he could fill the boots of the departed Kevin Keegan as he had become the new hero of the Anfield faithful . . . and now he had climaxed his first campaign in a red jersey by ensuring that the European Cup would be staying at Anfield. What more could anyone have asked?

European Cup 1978-79

As the holders, of course, Liverpool entered the European Cup competition the following season – and so did Nottingham Forest, who had finished the previous campaign as the new Champions of

David Fairclough and David Johnson as substitutes for Jimmy Case and Terry McDermott, but even Supersub couldn't find a way through the Forest defence on the night. Forest, indeed, rode their luck and they defended superbly, as well, to defy everything that Liverpool could throw at them, and when the final whistle was blown they had ridden the storm . . . it was 0–0 on the night, 2–0 to Forest on aggregate. So Liverpool were out – and, as the season went on, Forest became the club who succeeded them as European Champions.

European Cup 1979-80

So Liverpool had to wait and see what happened; and what happened was that they claimed the Championship of the Football League at the end

of season 1978-79 to stake their claims to another run in the European Cup the following term. Once more, however, they drew the short straw, because while they avoided Forest in the first-round draw, they found they were up against the Soviet champions, Dynamo Tbilisi, which meant a journey into the unknown again, this time to Georgia. But first, Liverpool had to see what their opponents were made of, in the first leg at Anfield.

They discovered that Dynamo Tbilisi were no pushover, although Liverpool scored two goals during the first half. But while they were grateful to see David Johnson and Jimmy Case on the mark, they were also unhappy about the goal they conceded. There were no more goals in the second half, so it was a case of waiting to see if Liverpool had done enough to ensure that they got through the return game. They hadn't – not by a long chalk; in Tbilisi, the Soviet Champions turned on a power-packed display which left Liverpool well beaten, although they held Dynamo to a 0–0 scoreline up to half-time. But in the second period Dynamo cut loose and scored three goals, to take the tie 4–2 on aggregate. Once more, Liverpool made their exit from the European Cup before they had even got going.

European Cup 1980-81

Yet once more, also, they claimed the First Division Championship, to assure them of another crack at the European Cup, and by the end of season 1980-81 they had achieved a hat-trick of successes in the competition . . . though they didn't win too many plaudits after their first match, which was in Finland. The opposition was named Oulu Palloseura, and the players were all part-timers. At the end of the first leg, after Terry McDermott had given Liverpool the lead in the first quarter of an hour, the score was 1–1, so the Reds had to demonstrate that they could win well at Anfield.

On the night there, the goals began to flow . . . Liverpool started with one and finished with ten, as Oulu's 'keeper found himself being bombarded from all angles. Afterwards, he said, with feeling, that he was glad he didn't have to face Liverpool every week! Two of the Liverpool players – Graeme Souness and Terry McDermott – claimed hat-tricks, David Fairclough hit a brace of goals, and the others came from Sammy Lee and Ray Kennedy, to make the final result Liverpool 10 Oulu 1, and the aggregate 11–2.

The next round, however, brought Liverpool into conflict with sterner opposition – Aberdeen, with the first leg at Pittodrie. The Dons were experienced campaigners in Europe, they had a side packed with Scottish internationals, and they had a shrewd tactician in manager Alex Ferguson.

But they didn't get the result they wanted – and certainly needed – at Pittodrie, because Terry McDermott put Liverpool ahead after only five minutes, then the men from Anfield shut up shop. They returned home with a 1–0 lead, and they increased this at Anfield as they scored four more goals without reply. Willie Miller was the unlucky victim of an own goal shortly before half-time, and a few minutes later Phil Neal struck. In the second half, Kenny Dalglish and Alan Hansen wrapped it up.

It was ironic that Aberdeen had suffered at the hands of the Liverpool Scots, but over the two legs Liverpool had shown how it should be done, and when they came up against CSKA Sofia, from Bulgaria, in the next round, they showed them the way home, as well. In the first leg at Anfield, Souness hit another hat-trick, as Liverpool scored a resounding 5–1 victory; and when they went the Sofia, Terry McDermott's goal brought a 1–0 result, to make it 6–1 on aggregate and send Liverpool into the semi-finals.

They found they were up against Bayern Munich, whom they had met in the old Fairs Cup and in the European Cup-Winners' Cup, and so far it was honours even, because Liverpool had knocked Bayern out of the Fairs Cup but been beaten by the Germans in the European Cup-Winners' Cup. Now it was the European Cup, with a place in the final at stake; and Liverpool knew that when they met Bayern in the first leg at Anfield, a great deal would hinge upon the result.

The 44,000 spectators looked in vain for a goal – from either side – as Bayern defended tenaciously while Liverpool struggled to find a way through. It was 0–0 at half-time, 0–0 at the final whistle, and the Bayern players clearly felt that they had done the difficult bit – indeed, one of them indicated that he believed he and his team-mates were already on their way to the final.

When the return game was played in Munich, close on 78,000 people went to watch the battle, and Bayern were the favourites to win it. But at half-time neither side had managed to break the stalemate, and while Bayern did score during the second period, so did Liverpool – a late strike from Ray Kennedy which gave his team the edge. The final result was 1–1, which meant that Liverpool went through on the ruling that their away goal counted double.

The final was scheduled for the famous Parc des Princes stadium in Paris, and as for the opposition . . . well, there was no bigger name in football than that of Real Madrid, the Spanish club which had made a habit of winning the trophy year after year during the days of Puskas, Di Stefano and company. Real now were not quite the force they had been, but they were aiming to show that they were still the masters in Europe. So the stage was set for a thriller of a game in Paris.

■ *Right:* **Victory for Liverpool in the European Cup final of 1981, as they overcome Real Madrid in the Parc des Princes stadium in Paris. And here's the match-winner, Alan Kennedy, who scored the only goal of the game.**

■ *Below:* **A joyful Phil Thompson holds the glittering trophy aloft in triumph.**

If the final turned out to be something less than a showgame, it certainly ended on a satisfactory note for Liverpool, although when the last ten minutes arrived it looked for all the world as if the spectators were going to be kept waiting for even one goal. Then, with nine minutes left on the clock, the issue was settled by a player who, at the outset, would not have been tagged the favourite to open the scoring . . . left-back Alan Kennedy. The man the Liverpool fans loved to call Barney Rubble, after *The Flintstones* television character, earned their gratitude, as well as their affection, as he struck the goal that brought victory for his side and took the European Cup to Anfield for the third time in the club's history. And once again Liverpool could look forward to having another go in season 1981-82 . . . by which time they had an up-and-coming striker in their ranks by the name of Ian Rush.

European Cup 1981-82

However, the following term didn't produce the expected success for Liverpool, although their three matches were not without their moments of drama. The first round paired Liverpool with the Finns of Oulu Palloseura again, and a late goal from Kenny Dalglish won the away game; then the Finns suffered a seven-goal onslaught at Anfield, where Rush got his name on the score-sheet. The second round brought Liverpool into opposition with a new name for them – AZ '67

Alkmaar, from Holland, and on paper the Anfield men had little reason to fear their fate, especially after they had come away from Holland with a 2–2 draw to their credit. Whatever might happen at Anfield, those two away goals were in the bag and would probably stand as good credit, if need be.

Perhaps the home fans thought that Alkmaar wouldn't be up to much; at any rate, the gate for the Anfield return was not quite 30,000. Yet as the minutes ticked away, a note of anxiety began to appear, as Liverpool found themselves being held by the Dutch side. Three minutes from half-time Liverpool did get a goal – thanks to a penalty decision which was followed by an accurate spot-

On the evidence of what had happened the previous time these clubs had met, there were few who feared for Liverpool's safety – indeed, hopes were high that Liverpool would score five goals again when the Bulgarians tried their luck at Anfield. On the night, however, Liverpool ended up thankful that Ronnie Whelan was on target, because this goal, after 65 minutes, was all that separated the sides. Even then, there were few who believed that Liverpool would go down in Sofia – but 60,000 fans turned up to see if CSKA could turn the tables on their exalted opponents. At half-time there was no score, but in the second half the Bulgarians got a goal, to make it 1–1 on aggregate and take the tie into extra time. It was

E U R O P E A N
N I G H T S O F
G L O R Y

■ A dramatic, last-minute winner in the European Cup-tie against AZ'67 Alkmaar at Anfield in 1981, after Liverpool had drawn 2–2 in Holland. This Alan Hansen effort meant that Liverpool had won 3–2 on the night and 5–4 overall.

kick from the reliable Terry McDermott.

So it was 1–0 at half-time, 3–2 overall as the second half began and Liverpool's fans looked for more goals. They got them, too – a couple from Alkmaar, a goal from Rush . . . and, almost at the death, a goal from Alan Hansen.

During that second half, nerves were evident both on the pitch and around the terraces and stands, as Alkmaar made Liverpool sweat for their victory, and the final whistle came as a great relief to the home fans and players. Alkmaar may have started out as seeming no-hopers, but by the end of their stint at Anfield they were being accorded real respect for their performance. Still, that round was behind Liverpool, and the next one brought them face to face again with CSKA Sofia.

then that Liverpool gave away another goal, and it proved to be costly, because they couldn't recover from that setback, and so they lost 2–0; which meant that they went out on a 2–1 aggregate result.

European Cup 1982-83

Yet again, however, they remained in the European Cup the following season, because they had finished as League Champions, and they made short work of Dundalk, their opponents from the League of Ireland – it was 4–1 away, 1–0 at Anfield. Then the second round brought Liverpool up against supposedly weak opposition

again, in the shape of JK Helsinki . . . who promptly shocked the world of football by beating Liverpool 1–0 in Finland. The second leg, at Anfield, was a formality, though, as Liverpool raced into a 3–0 first-half lead and wound up winning 5–0, to take the tie 5–1 on aggregate. This meant that a trip to Poland figured next on the agenda for Liverpool, who were drawn against Widzew Lodz. They were not widely regarded as being one of the top clubs in Europe, and Liverpool were expected to get through this third-round tie.

As on previous occasions, though, the football fates demonstrated that you're there to be shot at and knocked down, just when people are thinking you've got it made. Dundalk, JK Helsinki, Widzew Lodz . . . by general consent, Liverpool were being given a comfortable ride towards the final; but in Poland they were stopped in their tracks as Widzew scored two second-half goals to put a huge question mark against the outcome of the Anfield return.

When Phil Neal scored from the penalty spot inside the first quarter of an hour at Anfield, the home supporters started to breathe more easily; but by half-time the scoreline read 1–1, and Liverpool had just 45 minutes in which to pull something special out of the hat. To their credit, they tried . . . how they tried . . . but though late goals from Ian Rush and David Hodgson made the final result 3–2 on the night, it wasn't quite good enough . . . the Poles had won 4–3 overall.

European Cup 1983-84

Yet again, Liverpool had finished season 1982-83 as Champions, so they competed for the European Cup the following term, and they wound up winning the coveted trophy for a fourth time as the spring came around. Their first test, however, came in the shape of BK Odense, from Denmark, and a Kenny Dalglish goal won the away leg, then Liverpool hammered in five goals at Anfield. So far, so good – though after the previous two seasons, no-one was taking anything for granted.

The second round brought Liverpool up against Athletic Bilbao, whom they had previously met in the Fairs Cup . . . and lost the tie on the toss of a coin. This time out, Liverpool hoped for better fortune, but when Bilbao held them to a scoreless draw in the first leg at Anfield, there were some worried faces. The one man who didn't appear to be fazed by this result was manager Joe Fagan; he maintained his usual, smiling image as he pointed out that if Liverpool hadn't scored, neither had the Spaniards – and so, if Joe's team got a goal in the return, it would put Bilbao under pressure. They appeared to be brave words, even though his listeners acknowledged the truth of

what Joe was saying. But Liverpool hadn't been able to break Bilbao down at Anfield, and this tie was now going to switch to Spain. The odds, surely, were in favour of the home team.

Those who went to Spain for the second leg found that their hopes of seeing Liverpool triumph were starting to revive, as the half-time whistle went with neither side having scored a goal. So far, this was a repeat of the Anfield duel, and Liverpool were not being given the run-around. In the second half, it was Bilbao who cracked, as Liverpool went forward and Ian Rush delivered the goods – in the shape of a goal – with just over 20 minutes to go.

Bilbao's efforts to pierce the Liverpool rear-guard became more and more desperate, and Liverpool clung to that single-goal lead as if their lives depended upon it, while at the same time making their opponents worry about losing yet another one. The Rush-job proved sufficient . . . and he did another one when Liverpool traded punches with Benfica at Anfield in the first leg of the quarter-finals. Once again, the question was whether or not Liverpool had done enough – and

once again, Joe Fagan reminded people that now Liverpool were going to Portugal with this one-goal lead, and that Benfica hadn't scored at Anfield. In the Stadium of Light, the return match turned out to be no contest, because while Benfica pulled a goal back, Liverpool struck again, and again, and again . . . and again. On the night they won 4–1, with Rush a marksman once more, two goals from Ronnie Whelan, and one from Craig Johnston.

Dinamo Bucharest barred Liverpool's path to the final, and after a 1–0 victory at Anfield, where Sammy Lee's goal gave Liverpool the edge, it was on to Bucharest and a stern test in front of a 60,000 crowd. Inside the first 15 minutes Ian Rush had scored, and though it was 1–1 at half-time, Rush struck again six minutes from the final whistle, to give Liverpool an aggregate 3–1 victory. That success was heartening, indeed . . . but Liverpool still faced the hardest part, because in the final not only were they to meet AS Roma . . . they had to meet them in their own Olympic stadium.

There was a crowd of close on 70,000, and the Italians, with the majority of the supporters on their side, kicked off as 13–8 favourites. Yet when Phil Neal gave Liverpool the lead with the match only 14 minutes old, the fans from Merseyside began to have visions of their team returning home with the European Cup. Roma, however, managed an equaliser on the stroke of half-time, through Roberto Pruzzo, but neither side could get another goal during the second period of play. So the game went into extra time.

Even then, the sides were so evenly matched – and no-one wanted to make a mistake – that the 30 minutes came and went without another goal . . . so when the whistle went, everyone accepted that it would be settled in a sudden-death shoot-out. Penalties would decide the destination of the European Cup, and the contestants had better get on with it.

The atmosphere was electric, as the respective goalkeepers took it in turn to try to save the spot-kicks, and the men deputed to take them for Liverpool were Phil Neal, Graeme Souness, Ian Rush, Alan Kennedy and Steve Nicol. Neal was the sole survivor of the 1977 European Cup final . . . Souness had scored the goal which had

■ Another European night at Anfield, and the Poles of Widzew Lodz provide the opposition in the third round of the European Cup 1982-83. Liverpool's first goal is scored by Phil Neal from the penalty spot, but though Liverpool won 3–2 on the night, it wasn't enough to see them through on aggregate.

■ **Phil Neal puts the Anfield Reds ahead against Roma, but with a final scoreline of 1–1, a penalty shoot-out was required to settle the match.**

won the Milk Cup for Liverpool, and he had also skippered them to the title, so he was bidding to make it a treble before he signed off and joined Sampdoria, in Italy. And Nicol, who had gone on as a substitute against Roma, had also volunteered to take one of the penalties, if things worked out that way.

Now they had done, and Nicol was first to take aim. He was one of the youngest players on the park, facing one of the most experienced 'keepers in Franco Tancredi, who hadn't missed a European tie for Roma. As Steve stepped up to strike the ball, you could have heard a pin drop – then there was a roar from the Italian fans as Tancredi, going to his right, saw the ball rising and skimming over the bar.

The drama had only just begun, though. Phil Neal kept his nerve for Liverpool's second spot-kick, and as he rammed the ball into the net Tancredi was left stranded and lying on the ground. Roma then missed a kick, putting the ball over the bar, so it was all square again. Then it was the turn of Souness, and as Tancredi dived to his left, the ball fairly zipped into the top corner . . . which left Rush and Kennedy as the men on the spot. And Rush sent Roma's 'keeper completely the wrong way, when he despatched the ball low to Tancredi's left while the 'keeper hurled himself to his right.

At this stage, the final was still finely balanced, but Roma then put another penalty over the bar. The destination of the trophy now hinged upon the efforts of Liverpool's last man, left-back Alan Kennedy, whose goal in the Parc des Princes stadium in Paris had beaten Real Madrid and

won the European Cup for Liverpool in 1981.

Now the stadium had a deathly hush about it, as the fans – no matter which side they supported – just held their breath. Apart from the thousands inside the Olympic stadium, there were millions of television viewers waiting to see the outcome of the shoot-out. At this stage it was Liverpool 3, AS Roma 2, with each team having one more strike . . . but if Kennedy could beat Tancredi, Roma's last chance would have vanished. Once again, Tancredi guessed wrong, as he started to go to his left, because Alan Kennedy's shot was going the other way . . . and going past him and into the net. The stadium exploded as the Liverpool supporters finally raised the roof with their cheers, and the players raced up to congratulate Alan Kennedy, the man who had so coolly kept his nerve when all around him were people who had hardly dared to look.

The man whose goal won the European Cup for Liverpool a second time said simply: 'I didn't even look at the 'keeper . . . I knew where I was going to put it, and I was confident about it.' And Joe Fagan summed up: 'My feeling when that one

went in was one of relief. I'd always seen Alan put his kick to the goalkeeper's left before . . . this time, he put it to his right.'

So Liverpool achieved a sensational treble, and Joe Fagan was rewarded by being named Manager of the Year. Twelve months hence, as his team met another crack Italian club in the final of the European Cup, there was more drama, but this time the overwhelming sensation was one of tragedy, as people lost their lives in the Heysel stadium in Brussels.

European Cup 1984-85

It all started out smoothly enough, during season 1984-85, as Liverpool met the Poles from Lech Poznan and overcame them without difficulty – John Wark, signed from Ipswich Town, scored the only goal of the game in the away leg, then rattled in a hat-trick as Liverpool won the Anfield return 4–0. Once again, Benfica provided the next obstacle, but they were sent packing, thanks to a Rush hat-trick at Anfield, though the aggregate

■ The teams take the field for the final of the European Cup in 1984.

EUROPEAN
NIGHTS OF
GLORY

result was close enough . . . 3–2 for Liverpool.

Now the third-round opponents came from Vienna – they were called Austria Memphis – and Liverpool drew 1–1 away then swamped them 4–1 at Anfield, to reach the semi-finals. Their opponents in the penultimate round were former European Cup finalists, Panathinaikos, from Athens, and the Greeks went down 4–0 in the first leg at Anfield, then lost 1–0 on their own ground.

So, once again, Liverpool had gone all the way to the final and, once again, they had to face up to opposition from Italy. They had beaten Borussia

Moenchengladbach in Rome in 1977, FC Bruges at Wembley in 1978, Real Madrid in Paris in 1981, and AS Roma in Rome in 1984 . . . now, 12 months on, they were about to try conclusions with Juventus, from Turin, in the Heysel stadium in Brussels. Juventus had a long-playing record in Europe which was as impressive as that of Liverpool, for they had embarked upon their first European tie back in 1958. They had met the best, as well – Real Madrid, Benfica, Ajax, Borussia Moenchengladbach, FC Bruges, Anderlecht, Barcelona, Atletico Madrid, Paris St Germain,

Ferencvaros, Red Star and Partizan Belgrade, Manchester United, Arsenal, Glasgow Celtic and Glasgow Rangers, and they had won the UEFA Cup in 1977 and the European Cup-Winners' Cup in 1984. Now, in 1985, they were aiming to create footballing history by becoming the first club to have captured all three major European trophies.

For Liverpool, the night of Wednesday, 29 May 1985, also marked a watershed in the club's history, because after 21 successive seasons of competing in Europe, they were going for the

European Cup for the fifth time and, they hoped, they would be rewarded by being allowed to keep the trophy, should they succeed. But the events that preceded the 1985 final put a totally different complexion on the whole affair.

Crowd trouble erupted even before the game had begun, and with fans feuding and damage being caused inside the Heysel stadium, there was an air of pandemonium as millions of people saw – via live television – the horrific scenes unfolding in front of their very eyes. There was doubt as to whether or not the game would even get under way, discussion as to whether or not the final should be postponed or cancelled; but after a lengthy delay, the decision was taken – the game would go on. And so the teams came out to contest the European Cup final; a final which had already become virtually meaningless, overshadowed as it was by the tragedy on the terraces.

Right the way through, as the players did their best to make a game of it, there was an unreal atmosphere, a feeling that the participants were really just going through the motions. Most people, in fact, could hardly wait for the proceedings to come to an end. There were no goals at half-time, and when Juventus did score in the second half, it scarcely seemed to matter; the heart had been taken out of the players on both sides by what had gone before.

That goal remained the only one of the night, and while Juventus took the Cup the celebrations were muted indeed. As for Liverpool, they returned home to learn that they were banned, along with other English clubs, from competing in Europe, and Joe Fagan's reign as manager came to a dramatic and totally unwanted end. Joe had been ready to hand over the reins in any event, but no-one would have wished this to happen in the way it had. His retirement should have been an occasion for smiles, not tears, after the way he had steered the club to success in his short spell as the team boss.

Liverpool had finished as First Division runners-up and so, although they had lost out in the European Cup, they had already qualified for the UEFA Cup in season 1985-86; but, voluntarily, they withdrew, even before the sanctions had been applied. Their tremendous run of 21 years had come to an end, and no-one knew when they would be readmitted to the European fold. Not until the start of the 1990s, indeed, did English football rehabilitate itself sufficiently to gain a foothold in the European Cup-Winners' Cup and the UEFA Cup, when Manchester United and Aston Villa pioneered the way.

Liverpool, meanwhile, had won their League Championship for a record 18th time, they had won the FA Cup twice . . . and as 1991 progressed, they learned that in 1991-92 they could once more be part of European football again.

■ *Opposite:* **The start of the ill-fated European Cup final in the Heysel stadium in Brussels, in 1985, as Liverpool's captain, Phil Neal, exchanges pennants with his opposite number from Juventus. The Italians won, by the only goal, but after the tragedy on the terraces, the result really didn't matter.**

THE following is a list of all Liverpool's major games from their first season in 1892-93 until the 1990-91 season. Listed are the dates, opponents, venue, result and score of all games, together with a summary of Liverpool's final position in the League table compared to that of the Division winners.

The number of appearances (which includes appearances as a substitute) and of goals scored is given for each player in each competition from 1919-20 onwards. In Cup competitions, the figure after the name of the opponent indicates the round: P means preliminary round, R means replay, PO play-off, SF semi-final and F final. The venue of a match on neutral ground (N) is given in parenthesis, and A in the result column means abandoned.

Liverpool's Record Season by Season

SEASON 1892-93

LANCASHIRE LEAGUE

3 Sep	Higher Walton	H	W	8-0
24 Sep	Bury	H	W	4-0
1 Oct	West Manchester	H	W	3-1
22 Oct	Higher Walton	A	W	5-0
5 Nov	Blackpool	A	L	0-3
12 Nov	Fleetwood R	A	W	4-1
26 Nov	Rossendale U	A	W	2-0
3 Dec	Fleetwood R	H	W	7-0
17 Dec	Blackpool	H	L	0-2
24 Dec	South Shore	A	W	1-0
31 Dec	Heywood Central	H	W	6-2
2 Jan	Fairfield	A	W	4-1
7 Jan	Heywood Central	A	W	2-1
14 Jan	West Manchester	A	D	0-0
11 Feb	Bury	A	L	0-3
18 Feb	Nelson	A	W	3-2
25 Feb	Southport Cen	H	W	2-0
4 Mar	Nelson	H	W	3-0
16 Mar	Fairfield	H	W	5-0
18 Mar	South Shore	H	W	4-1
25 Mar	Rossendale U	H	W	2-1
15 Apr	Southport Cen	A	D	1-1

Final League Position

	P	W	D	L	F	A	Pts	
Liverpool	22	17	2	3	66	19	36	1st

FA CUP

15 Oct	Nantwich (Q)	A	W	4-0
29 Oct	Newtown (Q)	H	W	9-0
19 Nov	Northwich Vic (Q)	A	L	1-2

SEASON 1893-94

FOOTBALL LEAGUE (DIVISION 2)

2 Sep	Middlesbrough I	A	W	2-0
9 Sep	Lincoln City	H	W	4-0
16 Sep	Ardwick	A	W	1-0
23 Sep	Small Heath	H	W	3-1
30 Sep	Notts County	A	D	1-1
7 Oct	Middlesbrough I	H	W	6-0
14 Oct	Small Heath	A	W	4-3
21 Oct	Burton Swifts	A	D	1-1
28 Oct	Royal Arsenal	A	W	5-0
4 Nov	Newcastle U	H	W	5-1
11 Nov	Walsall T Swifts	A	D	1-1
18 Nov	Notts County	H	W	2-1
25 Nov	Newcastle U	A	D	0-0
2 Dec	Ardwick	H	W	3-0
9 Dec	Walsall T Swifts	H	W	3-0
28 Dec	Crewe Alexandra	A	W	5-0
30 Dec	Grimsby T	H	W	2-0
1 Jan	Royal Arsenal	H	W	2-0
6 Jan	Rotherham T	A	W	4-1
13 Jan	Rotherham T	H	W	5-1
3 Feb	Northwich Vic	H	W	4-0
3 Mar	Burton Swifts	H	W	3-1
17 Mar	Lincoln C	A	D	1-1
24 Mar	Crewe Alexandra	H	W	2-0
28 Mar	Northwich Vic	A	W	3-2
31 Mar	Grimsby T	A	W	1-0
7 Apr	Burslem Port Vale	A	D	2-2
14 Apr	Burslem Port Vale	H	W	2-1

Final League Position

	P	W	D	L	F	A	Pts	
Liverpool	28	22	6	0	77	18	50	1st

Test Match

28 Apr	Newton Heath	H	W	2-0

(Liverpool promoted to Division 1)

FA CUP

27 Jan	Grimsby T (1)	H	W	3-0
10 Feb	Preston NE (2)	H	W	3-2
24 Feb	Bolton W (3)	A	L	0-3

SEASON 1894-95

FOOTBALL LEAGUE (DIVISION 1)

1 Sep	Blackburn R	A	D	1-1
3 Sep	Burnley	A	D	3-3
8 Sep	Aston Villa	H	L	1-2
13 Sep	Bolton W	H	L	1-2
15 Sep	West Brom	A	L	0-5
22 Sep	Blackburn R	H	D	2-2
29 Sep	Wolverhampton W	A	L	1-3
6 Oct	Sheffield U	H	D	2-2
13 Oct	Everton	A	L	0-3
20 Oct	Stoke C	H	W	2-0
27 Oct	Aston Villa	A	L	0-5
3 Nov	Burnley	H	L	0-3
10 Nov	Stoke C	A	L	1-3
17 Nov	Everton	H	D	2-2
24 Nov	Sunderland	A	L	2-3
1 Dec	Wolverhampton W	H	D	3-3
8 Dec	Sheffield U	A	D	2-2
15 Dec	Small Heath	H	W	3-1
25 Dec	Bolton W	A	L	0-1
29 Dec	Small Heath	A	L	0-3
1 Jan	West Brom	H	W	4-0
5 Jan	Sheffield W	A	L	0-5
9 Jan	Derby County	A	W	1-0
12 Jan	Nottingham F	H	W	5-0
2 Mar	Derby County	H	W	5-1
25 Mar	Sunderland	H	L	2-3
30 Mar	Sheffield W	H	W	4-2
6 Apr	Nottingham F	A	L	0-3
12 Apr	Preston NE	A	D	2-2
20 Apr	Preston NE	H	L	2-5

Final League Position

	P	W	D	L	F	A	Pts	
Sunderland	30	21	5	4	80	37	47	1st
Liverpool	30	7	8	15	51	70	22	16th

Test Match (at Blackburn)

27 Apr	Bury		L	0-1

(Liverpool relegated to Division 2)

FA CUP

2 Feb	Barnsley St P (1)	A	D	1-1
11 Feb	Barnsley St P (1R)	H	W	4-0
16 Feb	Nottingham F (2)	H	L	0-2

SEASON 1895-96

FOOTBALL LEAGUE (DIVISION 2)

7 Sep	Notts County	A	W	3-2
14 Sep	Newcastle U	H	W	5-1
21 Sep	Loughborough T	A	W	4-2
28 Sep	Burslem Port Vale	H	W	5-1
30 Sep	Burton W	H	W	4-1
5 Oct	Newcastle U	A	L	0-1
7 Oct	Crewe Alexandra	H	W	6-1
12 Oct	Newton Heath	H	W	7-1
19 Oct	Grimsby T	A	L	0-1
21 Oct	Burslem Port Vale	A	L	4-5
26 Oct	Notts County	H	W	3-0
2 Nov	Newton Heath	A	L	2-5
9 Nov	Leicester Fosse	H	W	3-1
16 Nov	Royal Arsenal	A	W	2-0
23 Nov	Darwen	H	D	0-0
30 Nov	Leicester Fosse	A	L	0-2
7 Dec	Loughborough T	H	W	1-0
14 Dec	Darwen	A	W	4-0
21 Dec	Lincoln C	A	W	1-0
1 Jan	Manchester C	H	W	3-1
4 Jan	Rotherham T	A	W	5-0
11 Jan	Royal Arsenal	H	W	3-0
25 Jan	Lincoln C	H	W	6-1
18 Feb	Rotherham T	H	W	10-1
22 Feb	Grimsby T	H	W	3-1
29 Feb	Burton Swifts	A	W	7-0
7 Mar	Burton W	A	L	1-2
21 Mar	Burton Swifts	H	W	3-0
28 Mar	Crewe Alexandra	A	W	7-0
3 Apr	Manchester C	A	D	1-1

Final League Position

	P	W	D	L	F	A	Pts	
Liverpool	30	22	2	6	106	32	46	1st

Test Matches

18 Apr	Small Heath	H	W	4-0
20 Apr	Small Heath	A	D	0-0
25 Apr	West Brom	H	W	2-0
27 Apr	West Brom	A	L	0-2

(Liverpool promoted to Division 1)

FA CUP

1 Feb	Millwall Ath (1)	H	W	4-1
15 Feb	Wolverhampton W (2)	A	L	0-2

SEASON 1896-97

FOOTBALL LEAGUE (DIVISION 1)

1 Sep	Sheffield W	A	W	2-1
5 Sep	Blackburn R	A	L	0-1
7 Sep	Bolton W	H	L	0-2
12 Sep	Derby County	H	W	2-0
19 Sep	Bury	A	W	2-1
26 Sep	West Brom	H	D	0-0
3 Oct	Everton	A	L	1-2
10 Oct	Nottingham F	H	W	3-0
17 Oct	Sunderland	A	L	3-4
19 Oct	Sheffield U	H	D	1-1
24 Oct	Blackburn R	H	W	4-0
31 Oct	West Brom	A	W	1-0
7 Nov	Sunderland	H	W	3-0
14 Nov	Preston NE	A	D	1-1

21 Nov	Everton	H	D	0–0
28 Nov	Nottingham F	A	L	0–2
12 Dec	Bury	H	W	3–1
19 Dec	Derby County	A	L	2–3
25 Dec	Aston Villa	H	D	3–3
26 Dec	Burnley	A	L	1–4
1 Jan	Bolton W	A	W	4–1
2 Jan	Sheffield U	H	D	0–0
9 Jan	Wolverhampton W	A	W	2–1
16 Jan	Stoke C	H	W	1–0
16 Feb	Stoke C	A	L	1–6
4 Mar	Wolverhampton W	H	W	3–0
13 Mar	Aston Villa	A	D	0–0
27 Mar	Burnley	H	L	1–2
3 Apr	Sheffield W	H	D	2–2
10 Apr	Preston NE	H	D	0–0

Final League Position

	P	W	D	L	F	A	Pts	
Aston Villa	30	21	5	4	73	38	47	1st
Liverpool	30	12	9	9	46	38	33	5th

FA CUP

1 Feb	Burton Swifts (1)	H	W	4–3
13 Feb	West Brom (2)	A	W	2–1
27 Feb	Nottingham F (3)	H	D	1–1
3 Mar	Nottingham F (3R)	A	W	1–0
20 Mar	Aston Villa (SF)	N	L	0–3
(Bramall Lane)				

SEASON 1897-98

FOOTBALL LEAGUE (DIVISION 1)

4 Sep	Stoke C	A	D	2–2
11 Sep	Preston NE	H	D	0–0
18 Sep	Sheffield W	A	L	2–4
25 Sep	Everton	H	W	3–1
2 Oct	Preston NE	A	D	1–1
9 Oct	Stoke C	H	W	4–0
16 Oct	Everton	A	L	0–3
23 Oct	Derby County	H	W	4–2
30 Oct	Aston Villa	A	L	1–3
6 Nov	Nottingham F	H	L	1–2
13 Nov	West Brom	A	L	1–2
20 Nov	Wolverhampton W	H	W	1–0
27 Nov	Nottingham F	A	W	3–2
11 Dec	Wolverhampton W	A	L	1–2
18 Dec	Blackburn R	H	L	0–1
25 Dec	Bolton W	A	W	2–0
27 Dec	Sunderland	H	L	0–2
29 Dec	Sheffield U	A	W	2–1
1 Jan	West Brom	H	D	1–1
8 Jan	Blackburn R	A	L	1–2
22 Jan	Sunderland	A	L	0–1
5 Feb	Sheffield U	H	L	0–4
12 Mar	Notts County	H	W	2–0
19 Mar	Bolton W	H	D	1–1
26 Mar	Bury	A	W	2–0
31 Mar	Bury	H	D	2–2
2 Apr	Notts County	A	L	2–3
11 Apr	Sheffield W	H	W	4–0
12 Apr	Derby County	A	L	1–3
16 Apr	Aston Villa	H	W	4–0

Final League Position

	P	W	D	L	F	A	Pts	
Sheffield U	30	17	8	5	56	31	42	1st
Liverpool	30	11	6	13	48	45	28	9th

FA CUP

29 Jan	Hucknall St J (1)	H	W	2–0
12 Feb	Newton Heath (2)	A	D	0–0
16 Feb	Newton Heath (2R)	H	W	2–1
25 Feb	Derby County (3)	A	D	1–1
2 Mar	Derby County (3R)	H	L	1–5

SEASON 1898-99

FOOTBALL LEAGUE (DIVISION 1)

3 Sep	Sheffield W	H	W	4–0
10 Sep	Sunderland	A	L	0–1
17 Sep	Wolverhampton W	H	W	1–0
24 Sep	Everton	A	W	2–1
1 Oct	Notts County	H	D	0–0
8 Oct	Stoke C	A	L	1–2
15 Oct	Aston Villa	H	L	0–3
22 Oct	Burnley	A	L	1–2
29 Oct	Sheffield U	H	W	2–1
5 Nov	Newcastle U	A	L	0–3
12 Nov	Preston NE	H	W	3–1
19 Nov	Bury	A	L	0–3
26 Nov	Nottingham F	A	W	3–0
3 Dec	Bolton W	H	W	2–0
10 Dec	Derby County	A	L	0–1
17 Dec	West Brom	H	D	2–2
24 Dec	Blackburn R	A	W	3–1
26 Dec	West Brom	A	W	1–0
27 Dec	Notts County	A	D	1–1
31 Dec	Sheffield W	A	W	3–0
2 Jan	Sheffield U	A	W	2–0
7 Jan	Sunderland	H	D	0–0
14 Jan	Wolverhampton W	A	D	0–0
21 Jan	Everton	H	W	2–0
4 Feb	Stoke C	H	W	1–0
18 Feb	Burnley	H	W	2–0
11 Mar	Preston NE	A	W	2–1
25 Mar	Nottingham F	H	L	0–1
1 Apr	Bolton W	A	L	1–2
3 Apr	Newcastle U	H	W	3–2
8 Apr	Derby County	H	W	4–0
20 Apr	Bury	H	W	1–0
22 Apr	Blackburn R	H	W	2–0
29 Apr	Aston Villa	A	L	0–5

Final League Position

	P	W	D	L	F	A	Pts	
Aston Villa	34	19	7	8	76	40	45	1st
Liverpool	34	19	5	10	49	33	43	2nd

FA CUP

28 Jan	Blackburn R (1)	H	W	2–0
11 Feb	Newcastle U (2)	A	W	3–1
25 Feb	West Brom (3)	A	W	2–0
18 Mar	Sheffield U (SF)	N	D	2–2
(Nottingham)				
23 Mar	Sheffield U (SFR)	N	D	4–4
(Bolton)				
27 Mar	Sheffield U (SFR)	N	A	1–0
(Fallowfield)				
30 Mar	Sheffield U (SFR)	N	L	0–1
(Derby)				

SEASON 1899-1900

FOOTBALL LEAGUE (DIVISION 1)

2 Sep	Stoke C	A	L	2–3
9 Sep	Sunderland	H	L	0–2
16 Sep	West Brom	A	L	0–2
23 Sep	Everton	H	L	1–2
30 Sep	Blackburn R	A	L	0–2
5 Oct	Notts County	A	L	1–2
7 Oct	Derby County	H	L	0–2
14 Oct	Bury	A	L	1–2
21 Oct	Notts County	H	W	3–1
28 Oct	Manchester C	A	W	1–0
4 Nov	Sheffield U	H	D	2–2
11 Nov	Newcastle U	A	D	1–1
18 Nov	Aston Villa	H	D	3–3
25 Nov	Wolverhampton W	H	D	1–1
2 Dec	Burnley	A	L	1–2
9 Dec	Preston NE	H	W	1–0
16 Dec	Nottingham F	A	L	0–1
23 Dec	Glossop	H	W	5–2
25 Dec	Derby County	A	L	2–3
30 Dec	Stoke C	H	D	0–0
1 Jan	Sunderland	A	L	0–1
13 Jan	West Brom	H	W	2–0
20 Jan	Everton	A	L	1–3
3 Feb	Blackburn R	H	W	3–1
3 Mar	Manchester C	H	W	5–2
10 Mar	Sheffield U	A	W	2–1
17 Mar	Newcastle U	H	W	2–0
24 Mar	Aston Villa	A	L	0–1
31 Mar	Wolverhampton W	A	W	1–0
7 Apr	Burnley	H	L	0–1
9 Apr	Bury	H	W	2–0
14 Apr	Preston NE	A	W	3–1
21 Apr	Nottingham F	H	W	1–0
28 Apr	Glossop	A	W	2–1

Final League Position

	P	W	D	L	F	A	Pts	
Aston Villa	34	22	6	6	77	35	50	1st
Liverpool	34	14	5	15	49	45	33	10th

FA CUP

27 Jan	Stoke C (1)	H	D	0–0
1 Feb	Stoke C (1R)	A	W	1–0
17 Feb	West Brom (2)	A	D	1–1
21 Feb	West Brom (2R)	H	L	1–2

SEASON 1900-01

FOOTBALL LEAGUE (DIVISION 1)

1 Sep	Blackburn R	H	W	3–0
8 Sep	Stoke C	A	W	2–1
15 Sep	West Brom	H	W	5–0
22 Sep	Everton	A	D	1–1
29 Sep	Sunderland	H	L	1–2
6 Oct	Derby County	A	W	3–2
13 Oct	Bolton W	H	W	2–1
20 Oct	Notts County	A	L	0–3
27 Oct	Preston NE	H	W	3–2
3 Nov	Wolverhampton W	A	L	1–2
10 Nov	Aston Villa	H	W	5–1
17 Nov	Sheffield W	A	L	2–3
24 Nov	Newcastle U	A	D	1–1
1 Dec	Sheffield U	H	L	1–2
8 Dec	Manchester C	A	W	4–3
15 Dec	Bury	H	W	1–0
22 Dec	Nottingham F	A	D	0–0
25 Dec	Derby County	H	D	0–0
29 Dec	Blackburn R	A	L	1–3
1 Jan	Stoke C	H	W	3–1
19 Jan	Everton	H	L	1–2
2 Feb	Bolton W	A	L	0–1
23 Feb	Sunderland	A	W	1–0
2 Mar	Preston NE	A	D	2–2
9 Mar	Wolverhampton W	H	W	1–0
16 Mar	Aston Villa	A	W	2–0
23 Mar	Sheffield W	H	D	1–1
30 Mar	Newcastle U	H	W	3–0
8 Apr	Notts County	H	W	1–0
13 Apr	Manchester C	H	W	3–1
20 Apr	Bury	A	D	0–0
22 Apr	Sheffield U	A	W	2–0
27 Apr	Nottingham F	H	W	2–0
29 Apr	West Brom	A	W	1–0

Final League Position

	P	W	D	L	F	A	Pts	
Liverpool	34	19	7	8	59	35	45	1st

FA CUP

9 Feb	Notts County (1)	A	L	0–2

SEASON 1901-02

FOOTBALL LEAGUE (DIVISION 1)

2 Sep	Small Heath	A	D	0–0
7 Sep	Stoke C	A	L	0–1
14 Sep	Everton	H	D	2–2
21 Sep	Sunderland	A	D	1–1
28 Sep	Small Heath	H	W	3–1
5 Oct	Derby County	A	D	1–1
12 Oct	Sheffield W	H	L	1–2
19 Oct	Notts County	A	D	2–2
26 Oct	Bolton W	H	D	1–1
2 Nov	Manchester C	A	W	3–2
9 Nov	Wolverhampton W	H	W	4–1
23 Nov	Newcastle U	A	L	0–1
30 Nov	Aston Villa	H	W	1–0
7 Dec	Sheffield U	A	L	1–2
14 Dec	Nottingham F	H	L	0–2
26 Dec	Sunderland	H	L	0–1
28 Dec	Blackburn R	H	W	1–0
4 Jan	Stoke C	H	W	7–0
11 Jan	Everton	A	L	0–4
1 Feb	Bury	A	D	0–0
15 Feb	Notts County	H	L	0–1
22 Feb	Bolton W	A	L	0–1
1 Mar	Manchester C	H	W	4–0
8 Mar	Wolverhampton W	A	L	1–3
15 Mar	Grimsby T	A	D	1–1
22 Mar	Newcastle U	H	L	0–1
29 Mar	Aston Villa	A	W	1–0
1 Apr	Sheffield W	A	D	1–1
5 Apr	Sheffield U	H	W	1–0
12 Apr	Nottingham F	A	D	1–1
14 Apr	Derby County	H	L	0–2
19 Apr	Bury	H	W	1–0
21 Apr	Grimsby T	H	D	2–2
26 Apr	Blackburn R	A	D	1–1

Final League Position

	P	W	D	L	F	A	Pts	
Sunderland	34	19	6	9	50	35	44	1st
Liverpool	34	10	12	12	42	38	32	11th

FA CUP

25 Jan	Everton (1)	H	D	2–2
30 Jan	Everton (1R)	A	W	2–0
8 Feb	Southampton (2)	A	L	1–4

SEASON 1902-03

FOOTBALL LEAGUE (DIVISION 1)

6 Sep	Blackburn R	H	W	5–2
13 Sep	Sunderland	A	L	1–2
20 Sep	Stoke C	H	D	1–1
27 Sep	Everton	A	L	1–3
4 Oct	Sheffield W	H	W	4–2
11 Oct	West Brom	A	W	2–1
18 Oct	Notts County	H	L	0–2
25 Oct	Bolton W	A	D	1–1
1 Nov	Middlesbrough	H	W	5–0
8 Nov	Newcastle U	A	W	2–1
15 Nov	Wolverhampton W	H	W	4–1
22 Nov	Derby County	A	L	1–2
29 Nov	Sheffield U	A	L	0–2
6 Dec	Grimsby T	H	W	9–2
13 Dec	Aston Villa	A	W	2–1
20 Dec	Nottingham F	H	W	2–1
25 Dec	Bolton W	H	W	5–1
27 Dec	Bury	A	L	1–3
1 Jan	West Brom	H	L	0–2
3 Jan	Blackburn R	A	L	1–3
17 Jan	Stoke C	A	L	0–1
31 Jan	Sheffield W	A	L	1–3
14 Feb	Notts County	A	W	2–1
28 Feb	Middlesbrough	A	W	2–0
7 Mar	Newcastle U	H	W	3–0
23 Mar	Derby County	H	W	3–1
28 Mar	Sheffield U	H	L	2–4
30 Mar	Sunderland	H	D	1–1
4 Apr	Grimsby T	A	L	1–3
10 Apr	Everton	H	D	0–0
11 Apr	Aston Villa	H	W	2–1
18 Apr	Nottingham F	A	L	0–1
25 Apr	Bury	H	W	2–0
27 Apr	Wolverhampton W	A	W	2–0

Final League Position

	P	W	D	L	F	A	Pts	
Sheffield W	34	19	4	11	54	36	42	1st
Liverpool	34	17	4	13	68	49	38	5th

FA CUP

7 Feb	Manchester U (1)	A	L	1–2

SEASON 1903-04

FOOTBALL LEAGUE (DIVISION 1)

5 Sep	Nottingham F	A	L	1–2
12 Sep	Sheffield W	H	L	1–3
19 Sep	Sunderland	A	L	1–2
26 Sep	West Brom	H	L	1–3
1 Oct	Notts County	A	L	2–4
3 Oct	Small Heath	A	W	2–1
10 Oct	Everton	H	D	2–2
17 Oct	Stoke C	A	L	2–5
24 Oct	Derby County	H	W	3–1
31 Oct	Manchester C	A	L	2–3
7 Nov	Notts County	H	W	2–1
14 Nov	Sheffield U	A	L	1–2
21 Nov	Newcastle U	H	W	1–0
28 Nov	Aston Villa	A	L	1–2
12 Dec	Wolverhampton W	H	L	1–2
19 Dec	Bury	A	D	2–2
25 Dec	Derby County	A	L	0–2
26 Dec	Blackburn R	H	L	1–2
28 Dec	Wolverhampton W	A	L	2–4
1 Jan	Nottingham F	H	D	0–0
9 Jan	Sheffield W	A	L	1–2
16 Jan	Sunderland	H	W	2–1
23 Jan	West Brom	A	D	2–2
30 Jan	Small Heath	H	L	0–2
13 Feb	Stoke C	H	D	0–0
22 Feb	Middlesbrough	H	W	1–0
27 Feb	Manchester C	H	D	2–2
12 Mar	Sheffield U	H	W	3–0
19 Mar	Newcastle U	A	D	1–1
26 Mar	Aston Villa	H	D	1–1
1 Apr	Everton	A	L	2–5
2 Apr	Middlesbrough	A	L	0–1
16 Apr	Bury	H	W	3–0
23 Apr	Blackburn R	A	W	3–2

Final League Position

	P	W	D	L	F	A	Pts	
Sheffield W	34	20	7	7	48	28	47	1st
Liverpool	34	9	8	17	49	62	26	17th

(Relegated to Division 2)

FA CUP

6 Feb	Blackburn R (1)	A	L	1–3

SEASON 1904-05

FOOTBALL LEAGUE (DIVISION 2)

1 Sep	Burton United	H	W	2–0
3 Sep	Glossop NE	H	D	2–2
10 Sep	Chesterfield T	A	D	1–1
17 Sep	Bradford C	H	W	4–1
24 Sep	Lincoln C	A	W	2–0
1 Oct	Leicester Fosse	H	W	4–0
8 Oct	Barnsley	A	W	2–0
15 Oct	West Brom	H	W	3–2
22 Oct	Burnley	A	W	2–0
29 Oct	Grimsby T	H	W	5–0
5 Nov	Blackpool	A	W	3–0
12 Nov	Burslem Port Vale	H	W	2–1
19 Nov	Gainsborough Tr	A	W	2–1
3 Dec	Bolton W	A	L	0–2
17 Dec	Bristol C	H	W	3–1
24 Dec	Manchester U	A	L	1–3
26 Dec	Barnsley	H	W	2–1
31 Dec	Glossop NE	A	W	2–0
7 Jan	Chesterfield T	H	W	6–1
21 Jan	Lincoln C	H	D	1–1
28 Jan	Leicester Fosse	A	W	3–0
11 Feb	West Brom	A	W	2–0

25 Feb	Grimsby T	A	W	1–0
4 Mar	Blackpool	H	W	5–0
7 Mar	Bradford C	A	W	4–2
11 Mar	Doncaster R	A	W	4–1
18 Mar	Gainsborough Tr	H	W	6–1
25 Mar	Burton U	A	L	1–2
1 Apr	Bolton W	H	D	1–1
8 Apr	Burslem Port Vale	H	W	8–1
15 Apr	Bristol C	A	W	1–0
21 Apr	Doncaster R	H	W	1–0
22 Apr	Manchester U	H	W	4–0
29 Apr	Burnley	H	W	3–0

Final League Position

	P	W	D	L	F	A	Pts	
Liverpool	34	27	4	3	93	25	58	1st

(Promoted to Division 1)

FA CUP

4 Feb	Everton (1)	H	D	1–1
8 Feb	Everton (1R)	A	L	1–2

SEASON 1905-06

FOOTBALL LEAGUE (DIVISION 1)

2 Sep	Woolwich Arsenal	A	L	1–3
9 Sep	Blackburn R	H	L	1–3
11 Sep	Aston Villa	A	L	0–5
16 Sep	Sunderland	A	W	2–1
23 Sep	Birmingham C	H	W	2–0
30 Sep	Everton	A	L	2–4
7 Oct	Derby County	H	W	4–1
14 Oct	Sheffield W	A	L	2–3
21 Oct	Nottingham F	H	W	4–1
28 Oct	Manchester C	A	W	1–0
4 Nov	Bury	H	W	3–1
11 Nov	Middlesbrough	A	W	5–1
18 Nov	Preston NE	H	D	1–1
25 Nov	Newcastle U	H	W	3–2
2 Dec	Aston Villa	H	W	3–0
9 Dec	Wolverhampton W	H	W	4–0
16 Dec	Sheffield U	A	W	2–1
23 Dec	Notts County	H	W	2–0
25 Dec	Bolton W	H	D	2–2
26 Dec	Stoke C	A	L	1–2
30 Dec	Woolwich Arsenal	H	W	3–0
1 Jan	Stoke C	H	W	3–1
6 Jan	Blackburn R	A	D	0–0
20 Jan	Sunderland	H	W	2–0
27 Jan	Birmingham C	A	L	0–1
10 Feb	Derby County	A	W	3–0
17 Feb	Sheffield W	H	W	2–1
3 Mar	Manchester C	H	L	0–1
14 Mar	Nottingham F	A	W	2–1
17 Mar	Middlesbrough	H	W	6–1
21 Mar	Notts County	A	L	0–3
24 Mar	Preston NE	A	W	2–1
2 Apr	Bury	A	D	0–0
9 Apr	Newcastle U	H	W	3–0
13 Apr	Everton	H	D	1–1
14 Apr	Wolverhampton W	A	W	2–0
16 Apr	Bolton W	A	L	2–3
21 Apr	Sheffield U	H	W	3–1

Final League Position

	P	W	D	L	F	A	Pts	
Liverpool	38	23	5	10	79	46	51	1st

FA CUP

13 Jan	Leicester Fosse (1)	H	W	2–1
3 Feb	Barnsley (2)	H*	W	1–0
24 Feb	Brentford (3)	H	W	2–0
10 Mar	Southampton (4)	H	W	3–0
31 Mar	Everton (SF)	N	L	0–2

(Villa Park)

*Tie against Barnsley originally scheduled for Oakwell, was switched to Anfield.

SEASON 1906-07

FOOTBALL LEAGUE (DIVISION 1)

1 Sep	Stoke C	H	W	1–0
8 Sep	Blackburn R	A	D	1–1
10 Sep	Bury	H	D	2–2
15 Sep	Sunderland	H	L	1–2
22 Sep	Birmingham C	A	L	1–2
29 Sep	Everton	H	L	1–2
6 Oct	Woolwich Arsenal	A	L	1–2
13 Oct	Sheffield W	H	L	1–2
20 Oct	Bury	A	W	3–1
27 Oct	Manchester C	H	W	5–4
3 Nov	Middlesbrough	A	W	1–0
10 Nov	Preston NE	H	W	6–1
17 Nov	Newcastle U	A	L	0–2
24 Nov	Aston Villa	H	W	5–2
1 Dec	Derby County	A	W	1–0
8 Dec	Bristol C	A	L	1–3
15 Dec	Notts County	H	W	5–1
22 Dec	Sheffield U	A	L	0–1
25 Dec	Manchester U	A	D	0–0
26 Dec	Bolton W	H	L	0–2
1 Jan	Bolton W	A	L	0–3
5 Jan	Blackburn R	H	L	0–2
19 Jan	Sunderland	A	D	5–5
26 Jan	Birmingham C	H	W	2–0
9 Feb	Woolwich Arsenal	H	W	4–0
16 Feb	Sheffield W	A	W	3–2
2 Mar	Manchester C	A	L	0–1
11 Mar	Stoke C	A	D	1–1
16 Mar	Preston NE	A	L	1–3
23 Mar	Newcastle U	H	W	4–1
29 Mar	Everton	A	D	0–0
30 Mar	Aston Villa	A	L	0–4
1 Apr	Manchester U	H	L	0–1
6 Apr	Derby County	H	W	2–0
13 Apr	Bristol C	H	L	2–4
17 Apr	Middlesbrough	H	L	2–4
20 Apr	Notts County	A	L	0–2
27 Apr	Sheffield U	H	D	2–2

Final League Position

	P	W	D	L	F	A	Pts	
Newcastle U	38	22	7	9	74	46	51	1st
Liverpool	38	13	7	18	64	65	33	15th

FA CUP

12 Jan	Birmingham C (1)	H	W	2–1
2 Feb	Oldham A (2)	A	W	1–0
23 Feb	Bradford C (3)	H	W	1–0
9 Mar	Sheffield W (4)	A	L	0–1

SEASON 1907-08

FOOTBALL LEAGUE (DIVISION 1)

2 Sep	Nottingham F	A	L	1–3
7 Sep	Manchester U	A	L	0–4
14 Sep	Blackburn R	H	W	2–0
16 Sep	Sheffield U	A	D	0–0
21 Sep	Bolton W	A	W	4–0
28 Sep	Birmingham C	H	L	3–4
5 Oct	Everton	A	W	4–2
12 Oct	Sunderland	H	W	1–0
19 Oct	Woolwich Arsenal	A	L	1–2
26 Oct	Sheffield W	H	W	3–0
2 Nov	Bristol C	A	L	0–2
9 Nov	Notts County	H	W	6–0
16 Nov	Manchester C	A	D	1–1
23 Nov	Preston NE	H	L	1–2
7 Dec	Newcastle U	H	W	5–0
14 Dec	Newcastle U	H	L	1–5
21 Dec	Middlesbrough	A	L	1–3
25 Dec	Chelsea	H	L	1–4
28 Dec	Sheffield U	H	W	3–0
1 Jan	Nottingham F	H	W	2–0
18 Jan	Bolton W	A	W	1–0
25 Jan	Birmingham C	A	D	1–1
8 Feb	Sunderland	A	L	0–1
15 Feb	Woolwich Arsenal	H	W	4–1
29 Feb	Bristol C	H	W	3–1
7 Mar	Notts County	A	D	2–2
9 Mar	Sheffield W	A	W	2–1
14 Mar	Manchester C	H	L	0–1
21 Mar	Preston NE	A	L	0–3
25 Mar	Manchester U	H	W	7–4
28 Mar	Bury	A	L	1–3
4 Apr	Aston Villa	A	L	1–5
6 Apr	Blackburn R	A	W	3–1
11 Apr	Newcastle U	A	L	1–3
17 Apr	Everton	H	D	0–0
18 Apr	Middlesbrough	H	L	0–1
20 Apr	Chelsea	H	W	2–0
27 Apr	Bury	H	W	2–1

Final League Position

	P	W	D	L	F	A	Pts	
Manchester U	38	23	6	9	81	48	52	1st
Liverpool	38	16	6	16	68	61	38	8th

FA CUP

11 Jan	Derby County (1)	H	W	4–2
1 Feb	Brighton & HA (2)	H	D	1–1
5 Feb	Brighton & HA (2R)	A	W	3–0
22 Feb	Newcastle U (3)	A	L	1–3

SEASON 1908-09

FOOTBALL LEAGUE (DIVISION 1)

1 Sep	Aston Villa	H	W	3–2
5 Sep	Chelsea	H	W	2–1
12 Sep	Blackburn R	A	L	0–1
14 Sep	Sheffield U	A	W	2–0
19 Sep	Bradford C	H	W	4–0
26 Sep	Manchester U	A	L	2–3
1 Oct	Nottingham F	A	L	1–5
3 Oct	Everton	H	L	0–1
10 Oct	Leicester F	A	L	2–3

■ The 1905-06 Liverpool squad that secured the Championship for the second time in the club's history: J. Carlin (1), A. West (2), C. Wilson (3), S. Hardy (4), J. Doig (5), W. Dunlop (6), D. Murray (7), J. Hewitt (8), W. Connell (trainer) (9), James Hughes (10), G. Latham (11), John Hughes (12), M. Parry (13), A. Raisbeck (captain) (14), G. Fleming (15), T. Chorlton (16), T. Watson (secretary) (17), G. Robinson (18), J. Gorman (19), A. Goddard (20), R. Robinson (21), J. Parkinson (22), S. Raybould (23), J. Cox (24), J. Garside (25).

17 Oct	Woolwich Arsenal	H	D	2-2
24 Oct	Notts County	A	W	2-1
31 Oct	Newcastle U	H	W	2-1
7 Nov	Bristol C	A	L	0-1
14 Nov	Preston NE	H	W	2-1
21 Nov	Middlesbrough	A	L	0-1
28 Nov	Manchester C	H	L	1-3
5 Dec	Sheffield W	A	W	3-2
12 Dec	Bury	A	L	1-2
19 Dec	Sheffield U	H	W	2-1
25 Dec	Aston Villa	A	D	1-1
26 Dec	Nottingham F	H	D	1-1
1 Jan	Sunderland	A	W	4-1
2 Jan	Chelsea	A	L	0-3
9 Jan	Blackburn R	H	D	1-1
23 Jan	Bradford C	A	W	2-0
30 Jan	Manchester U	H	W	3-1
13 Feb	Leicester F	H	W	4-1
20 Feb	Woolwich Arsenal	A	L	0-5
27 Feb	Notts County	H	D	1-1
13 Mar	Bristol C	H	L	1-2
20 Mar	Preston NE	A	L	0-2
27 Mar	Middlesbrough	H	L	1-2
3 Apr	Manchester C	A	L	0-4
9 Apr	Everton	A	L	0-5
10 Apr	Sheffield W	H	L	1-2
12 Apr	Sunderland	H	W	3-0
17 Apr	Bury	H	D	2-2
30 Apr	Newcastle U	A	W	1-0

Final League Position

	P	W	D	L	F	A	Pts	
Newcastle U	38	24	5	9	65	41	53	1st
Liverpool	38	15	6	17	57	65	36	16th

FA CUP

16 Jan	Lincoln C (1)	H	W	5-1
6 Feb	Norwich C (2)	H	L	2-3

SEASON 1909-10

FOOTBALL LEAGUE (DIVISION 1)

4 Sep	Chelsea	A	L	1-2
6 Sep	Bolton W	A	W	2-1
11 Sep	Blackburn R	H	W	3-1
18 Sep	Nottingham F	A	W	4-1
25 Sep	Sunderland	H	L	1-4
2 Oct	Everton	A	W	3-2
9 Oct	Manchester U	H	W	3-2

16 Oct	Bradford C	A	W	2-1
23 Oct	Sheffield W	H	W	3-1
30 Oct	Bristol C	A	W	1-0
6 Nov	Bury	H	D	2-2
13 Nov	Tottenham H	A	L	0-1
20 Nov	Preston NE	H	W	2-0
27 Nov	Notts County	A	L	1-3
4 Dec	Newcastle U	H	W	6-5
11 Dec	Middlesbrough	H	D	0-0
18 Dec	Aston Villa	A	L	1-3
25 Dec	Bolton W	H	W	3-0
27 Dec	Woolwich Arsenal	A	D	1-1
28 Dec	Sheffield U	A	L	2-4
1 Jan	Woolwich Arsenal	H	W	5-1
8 Jan	Chelsea	H	W	5-1
22 Jan	Blackburn R	A	D	1-1
12 Feb	Everton	H	L	0-1
19 Feb	Manchester U	A	W	4-3
26 Feb	Bradford C	H	W	1-0
5 Mar	Sheffield W	A	L	0-3
12 Mar	Bristol C	H	L	0-1
19 Mar	Bury	A	W	2-1
25 Mar	Sheffield U	H	D	0-0
26 Mar	Tottenham H	H	W	2-0
28 Mar	Sunderland	A	L	1-2
2 Apr	Preston NE	A	L	0-2
9 Apr	Notts County	H	W	2-1
16 Apr	Newcastle U	A	W	3-1
20 Apr	Nottingham F	H	W	7-3
23 Apr	Middlesbrough	A	D	2-2
30 Apr	Aston Villa	H	W	2-0

Final League Position

	P	W	D	L	F	A	Pts	
Aston Villa	38	23	7	8	84	42	53	1st
Liverpool	38	21	6	11	78	57	48	2nd

FA CUP

15 Jan	Bristol C (1)	A	L	0-2

SEASON 1910-11

FOOTBALL LEAGUE (DIVISION 1)

3 Sep	Bradford C	H	L	1-2
10 Sep	Blackburn R	A	W	2-1
17 Sep	Nottingham F	H	L	2-3
19 Sep	Sheffield U	A	L	0-2
24 Sep	Manchester C	A	W	2-1
1 Oct	Everton	H	L	0-2

8 Oct	Sheffield W	A	L	0-1
15 Oct	Bristol C	H	W	4-0
22 Oct	Newcastle U	A	L	1-6
29 Oct	Tottenham H	H	L	1-2
5 Nov	Middlesbrough	A	D	2-2
12 Nov	Preston NE	H	W	3-0
19 Nov	Notts County	A	L	0-1
26 Nov	Manchester U	H	W	3-2
3 Dec	Oldham A	A	L	1-3
10 Dec	Bury	A	L	0-3
17 Dec	Sheffield U	H	W	2-0
24 Dec	Aston Villa	A	D	1-1
26 Dec	Sunderland	H	L	1-2
27 Dec	Everton	A	W	1-0
31 Dec	Bradford C	A	W	3-1
2 Jan	Sunderland	A	L	0-4
7 Jan	Blackburn R	H	D	2-2
21 Jan	Nottingham F	A	L	0-2
28 Jan	Manchester City	H	D	1-1
11 Feb	Sheffield W	H	W	3-0
18 Feb	Bristol C	A	D	1-1
27 Feb	Newcastle U	H	W	3-0
4 Mar	Tottenham H	A	L	0-1
11 Mar	Middlesbrough	H	W	3-0
18 Mar	Preston NE	A	L	1-2
25 Mar	Notts County	H	W	2-1
1 Apr	Manchester U	A	L	0-2
8 Apr	Oldham A	H	W	1-0
14 Apr	Woolwich Arsenal	A	D	0-0
15 Apr	Bury	H	W	2-0
17 Apr	Woolwich Arsenal	H	D	1-1
29 Apr	Aston Villa	H	W	3-1

Final League Position

	P	W	D	L	F	A	Pts	
Manchester U	38	22	8	8	72	40	52	1st
Liverpool	38	15	7	16	53	53	37	13th

FA CUP

14 Jan	Gainsborough Tr (1)	H	W	3-2
4 Feb	Everton (2)	A	L	1-2

SEASON 1911-12

FOOTBALL LEAGUE (DIVISION 1)

2 Sep	Woolwich Arsenal	A	D	2-2
4 Sep	Bolton W	A	L	1-2
9 Sep	Manchester C	H	D	2-2
16 Sep	Everton	A	L	1-2

23 Sep	West Brom	H	L	1-3
30 Sep	Sunderland	A	W	2-1
7 Oct	Blackburn R	H	L	1-2
14 Oct	Sheffield W	A	D	2-2
21 Oct	Bury	H	D	1-1
28 Oct	Middlesbrough	A	W	3-0
4 Nov	Notts County	H	L	0-2
11 Nov	Tottenham H	A	L	0-2
18 Nov	Manchester U	H	W	3-2
25 Nov	Preston NE	H	L	0-1
2 Dec	Newcastle U	H	L	0-1
9 Dec	Sheffield U	A	L	1-3
16 Dec	Oldham A	H	W	1-0
23 Dec	Bolton W	H	W	1-0
30 Dec	Woolwich Arsenal	A	W	4-1
1 Jan	Bradford C	H	W	1-0
6 Jan	Manchester C	A	W	3-2
20 Jan	Everton	H	L	1-3
27 Jan	West Brom	A	L	0-1
10 Feb	Blackburn R	A	L	0-1
17 Feb	Sheffield W	H	D	1-1
24 Feb	Bury	A	D	2-2
2 Mar	Middlesbrough	H	D	1-1
9 Mar	Notts County	A	D	0-0
16 Mar	Tottenham H	H	L	1-2
23 Mar	Manchester U	A	D	1-1
30 Mar	Preston NE	A	L	1-2
5 Apr	Sunderland	H	W	2-1
6 Apr	Aston Villa	H	L	1-2
8 Apr	Bradford C	A	W	2-0
13 Apr	Newcastle U	A	D	1-1
20 Apr	Sheffield U	H	W	2-0
27 Apr	Oldham A	A	W	1-0

....

■ For the first time in their history, Liverpool reached the final of the FA Cup when they went to Crystal Palace in 1914. They met Burnley, and lost by the only goal. It was a final graced by the reigning monarch, King George V.

Final League Position

	P	W	D	L	F	A	Pts	
Blackburn R	38	20	9	9	60	43	49	1st
Liverpool	38	12	10	16	49	55	34	17th

FA CUP

13 Jan	Leyton (1)	H	W	1–0
3 Feb	Fulham (2)	A	L	0–3

SEASON 1912-13

FOOTBALL LEAGUE (DIVISION 1)

4 Sep	Oldham A	H	W	2–0
7 Sep	Woolwich Arsenal	H	W	3–0
9 Sep	Chelsea	A	W	2–1
14 Sep	Bradford C	A	L	0–2
21 Sep	Manchester C	H	L	1–2
28 Sep	West Brom	A	L	1–3
5 Oct	Everton	H	L	0–2
12 Oct	Sheffield W	A	L	0–1
14 Oct	Sheffield U	A	L	1–4
19 Oct	Blackburn R	H	W	4–1
26 Oct	Derby County	A	L	2–4
2 Nov	Tottenham H	H	W	4–1
9 Nov	Middlesbrough	A	W	4–3
16 Nov	Notts County	H	D	0–0
23 Nov	Manchester U	A	L	1–3
30 Nov	Aston Villa	H	W	2–0
7 Dec	Sunderland	A	L	0–7
14 Dec	Bolton W	A	D	1–1
21 Dec	Sheffield U	H	D	2–2
26 Dec	Newcastle U	H	W	2–1
28 Dec	Woolwich Arsenal	A	D	1–1
1 Jan	Newcastle U	A	D	0–0
4 Jan	Bradford C	H	W	2–1
18 Jan	Manchester C	A	L	1–4
25 Jan	West Brom	H	W	2–1
8 Feb	Everton	A	W	2–0
10 Feb	Oldham A	A	L	1–3
15 Feb	Sheffield W	H	W	2–1
1 Mar	Derby County	H	W	2–1
8 Mar	Tottenham H	A	L	0–1
10 Mar	Blackburn R	A	L	1–5
15 Mar	Middlesbrough	H	W	4–2
22 Mar	Notts County	A	L	0–3
24 Mar	Chelsea	H	L	1–2
29 Mar	Manchester U	H	L	0–2
5 Apr	Aston Villa	A	W	3–1
12 Apr	Sunderland	H	L	2–5
19 Apr	Bolton W	H	W	5–0

Final League Position

	P	W	D	L	F	A	Pts	
Sunderland	38	25	4	9	86	43	54	1st
Liverpool	38	16	5	17	61	71	37	12th

FA CUP

15 Jan	Bristol C (1)	H	W	3–0
1 Feb	Woolwich Arsenal (2)	A	W	4–1
22 Feb	Newcastle U (3)	H	D	1–1
26 Feb	Newcastle U (3R)	A	L	0–1

SEASON 1913-14

FOOTBALL LEAGUE (DIVISION 1)

1 Sep	Derby County	A	D	1–1
6 Sep	Blackburn R	A	L	2–6
13 Sep	Sunderland	H	L	1–3
20 Sep	Everton	A	W	2–1
27 Sep	West Brom	H	D	0–0
4 Oct	Sheffield W	A	L	1–4
11 Oct	Bolton W	H	W	2–1
18 Oct	Chelsea	A	L	0–3
25 Oct	Oldham A	H	L	0–3
1 Nov	Manchester U	A	L	0–3
8 Nov	Burnley	H	D	1–1
15 Nov	Preston NE	A	W	1–0
22 Nov	Newcastle U	H	D	0–0
29 Nov	Tottenham H	H	W	2–1
6 Dec	Aston Villa	A	L	1–2
13 Dec	Middlesbrough	H	W	2–1
20 Dec	Sheffield U	A	W	1–0
25 Dec	Manchester C	H	W	4–2
26 Dec	Manchester C	A	L	0–1
27 Dec	Blackburn R	H	D	3–3
1 Jan	Bradford C	H	L	0–1
3 Jan	Sunderland	A	W	2–1
17 Jan	Everton	H	L	1–2
24 Jan	West Brom	A	W	1–0
2 Feb	Sheffield W	H	L	1–2
14 Feb	Bolton W	A	L	1–2
28 Feb	Oldham A	A	D	2–2
14 Mar	Burnley	A	L	2–5
18 Mar	Chelsea	H	W	3–0
21 Mar	Preston NE	H	W	3–1
1 Apr	Newcastle U	A	W	2–1
4 Apr	Tottenham H	A	D	0–0
10 Apr	Derby County	H	W	1–0
11 Apr	Aston Villa	H	L	0–1
13 Apr	Bradford C	A	L	0–1
15 Apr	Manchester U	H	L	1–2
18 Apr	Middlesbrough	A	L	0–4
27 Apr	Sheffield U	H	W	2–1

Final League Position

	P	W	D	L	F	A	Pts	
Blackburn R	38	20	11	7	78	42	51	1st
Liverpool	38	14	7	17	46	62	35	16th

FA CUP

10 Jan	Barnsley (1)	H	D	1–1
15 Jan	Barnsley (1R)	A	W	1–0
31 Jan	Gillingham (2)	H	W	2–0
21 Feb	West Ham U (3)	A	D	1–1
25 Feb	West Ham U (3R)	H	W	5–1
7 Mar	QPR (4)	H	W	2–1
28 Mar	Aston Villa (SF) (White Hart Lane)	N	W	2–0
25 Apr	Burnley (F) (Crystal Palace)	N	L	0–1

SEASON 1914-15

FOOTBALL LEAGUE (DIVISION 1)

2 Sep	Bolton W	H	W	4–3
5 Sep	Notts County	H	D	1–1
12 Sep	Sunderland	A	D	2–2
19 Sep	Sheffield W	H	W	2–1
21 Sep	Blackburn R	A	L	2–4
26 Sep	West Brom	A	L	0–4
3 Oct	Everton	H	L	0–5
10 Oct	Chelsea	A	L	1–3
17 Oct	Bradford C	H	W	2–1
24 Oct	Burnley	A	L	0–3
31 Oct	Tottenham H	H	W	7–2
7 Nov	Newcastle U	A	D	0–0
14 Nov	Middlesbrough	H	D	1–1
21 Nov	Sheffield U	A	L	1–2
28 Nov	Aston Villa	H	L	3–6
5 Dec	Manchester C	A	D	1–1
12 Dec	Bradford PA	A	L	0–1
19 Dec	Oldham A	H	L	1–2
25 Dec	Bolton W	A	W	1–0
26 Dec	Manchester U	H	D	1–1
2 Jan	Notts County	A	L	1–3
16 Jan	Sunderland	H	W	2–1
23 Jan	Sheffield W	A	L	1–2
6 Feb	Everton	A	W	3–1
13 Feb	Chelsea	H	D	3–3
27 Feb	Burnley	H	W	3–0
6 Mar	Tottenham H	A	D	1–1
10 Mar	Bradford C	A	L	2–3
13 Mar	Manchester C	H	W	3–2
20 Mar	Middlesbrough	A	L	0–3
24 Mar	West Brom	H	W	3–1
29 Mar	Newcastle U	H	D	2–2
2 Apr	Manchester U	A	L	0–2
3 Apr	Aston Villa	A	L	2–6
5 Apr	Blackburn R	H	W	3–0
12 Apr	Sheffield U	H	W	2–1
17 Apr	Bradford PA	H	W	2–1
24 Apr	Oldham A	A	W	2–0

Final League Position

	P	W	D	L	F	A	Pts	
Everton	38	19	8	11	76	47	46	1st
Liverpool	38	14	9	15	65	75	37	14th

FA CUP

9 Jan	Stockport County (1)	H	W	3–0
30 Jan	Sheffield U (2)	A	L	0–1

SEASON 1919-20

FOOTBALL LEAGUE (DIVISION 1)

30 Aug	Bradford C	A	W	3–1
1 Sep	Arsenal	H	L	2–3
6 Sep	Bradford C	H	W	2–1
8 Sep	Arsenal	A	L	0–1
13 Sep	Aston Villa	H	W	2–1
20 Sep	Aston Villa	A	W	1–0
27 Sep	Newcastle U	H	D	1–1
4 Oct	Newcastle U	A	L	0–3
11 Oct	Chelsea	A	L	0–1
18 Oct	Chelsea	H	L	0–1
25 Oct	Burnley	A	W	2–1
1 Nov	Burnley	H	L	0–1
8 Nov	Bradford PA	A	W	2–1
15 Nov	Bradford PA	H	D	3–3
22 Nov	Preston NE	A	L	1–2
29 Nov	Preston NE	H	L	1–2
6 Dec	Middlesbrough	A	L	2–3
13 Dec	Middlesbrough	H	W	1–0
20 Dec	Everton	A	D	0–0
25 Dec	Sunderland	H	W	3–2
26 Dec	Manchester U	A	D	0–0
27 Dec	Everton	H	W	3–1
1 Jan	Manchester U	H	D	0–0
3 Jan	Sheffield U	A	L	2–3
17 Jan	Sheffield U	H	W	2–0
24 Jan	Bolton W	A	W	3–0
4 Feb	Bolton W	H	W	2–0
7 Feb	Blackburn R	A	W	2–0
14 Feb	Blackburn R	H	W	3–0
26 Feb	Notts County	A	L	0–1
28 Feb	Notts County	H	W	3–0
10 Mar	Sheffield W	H	W	1–0
13 Mar	Sheffield W	A	D	2–2
20 Mar	Manchester C	H	W	1–0
27 Mar	Manchester C	A	L	1–2
2 Apr	Oldham A	A	D	1–1
3 Apr	Derby County	H	W	3–0
5 Apr	Oldham A	H	D	2–2
10 Apr	Derby County	A	L	0–3
17 Apr	West Brom	H	D	0–0
24 Apr	West Brom	A	D	1–1
1 May	Sunderland	A	W	1–0

Final League Position

	P	W	D	L	F	A	Pts	
West Brom	42	28	4	10	104	47	60	1st
Liverpool	42	19	10	13	59	44	48	4th

League Appearances (goals)

Armstrong 1 · Bamber 24 (1) · Bennett 1
Bromilow 23 (1) · Campbell 32 · Chambers 34 (15)
Forshaw 23 (7) · Jenkinson 13 · Johnson 1
Lacey 32 (3) · Lewis 23 (7) · Longworth 27 · Lowe 5
Lucas 16 · McKinlay 41 (4) · McNab 2 · Matthews 1
J. Miller 8 · T. Miller 20 (11) · Pagnam 8 (4)
Pearson 34 (4) · Pursell 2 · Scott 9 · Sheldon 37 (1)
Speakman 4 · H. Wadsworth 8 · W. Wadsworth 33
Own goals (1)

FA CUP

10 Jan	South Shields (1)	A	D	1–1
14 Jan	South Shields (1R)	H	W	2–0
31 Jan	Luton T (2)	A	W	2–0
21 Feb	Birmingham C (3)	H	W	2–0
6 Mar	Huddersfield T (4)	A	L	1–2

FA Cup Appearances (goals)

Bamber 5 · Bromilow 5 · Campbell 5 · Lacey 5 (2)
Lewis 5 (2) · Longworth 5 · McKinlay 5
T. Miller 5 (2) · Pearson 5 · Sheldon 5 (2)
W. Wadsworth 5

SEASON 1920-21

FOOTBALL LEAGUE (DIVISION 1)

28 Aug	Manchester C	H	W	4–2
1 Sep	West Brom	A	D	1–1
4 Sep	Manchester C	A	L	2–3
6 Sep	West Brom	H	D	0–0
11 Sep	Oldham A	H	W	5–2
18 Sep	Oldham A	A	D	0–0
25 Sep	Preston NE	H	W	6–0
2 Oct	Preston NE	A	W	3–2
9 Oct	Sheffield U	H	D	2–2
16 Oct	Sheffield U	A	W	1–0
23 Oct	Everton	H	W	1–0
30 Oct	Everton	A	W	3–0
6 Nov	Bradford PA	H	L	0–1
13 Nov	Bradford PA	A	W	3–1
20 Nov	Newcastle U	A	L	0–2
27 Nov	Newcastle U	H	L	0–1
4 Dec	Burnley	H	D	0–0
11 Dec	Burnley	A	L	0–1
18 Dec	Aston Villa	H	W	4–1
25 Dec	Chelsea	A	D	1–1
27 Dec	Chelsea	H	W	2–1
1 Jan	Aston Villa	A	W	2–0
15 Jan	Sunderland	H	D	0–0
22 Jan	Sunderland	A	L	1–2
5 Feb	Manchester U	A	D	1–1
9 Feb	Manchester U	H	W	2–0
12 Feb	Bradford C	H	W	2–1
19 Feb	Bradford C	A	D	0–0
26 Feb	Huddersfield T	H	W	4–1
5 Mar	Huddersfield T	A	W	2–1
12 Mar	Middlesbrough	H	D	0–0
19 Mar	Middlesbrough	A	W	1–0
25 Mar	Tottenham H	H	D	1–1
26 Mar	Blackburn R	A	D	1–1
28 Mar	Tottenham H	A	L	0–1
2 Apr	Blackburn R	H	W	2–0
9 Apr	Derby County	A	D	0–0
16 Apr	Derby County	H	D	1–1
23 Apr	Bolton W	A	L	0–1
30 Apr	Bolton W	H	L	2–3
2 May	Arsenal	A	D	0–0
7 May	Arsenal	H	W	3–0

Final League Position

	P	W	D	L	F	A	Pts	
Burnley	42	23	13	6	79	36	59	1st
Liverpool	42	18	15	9	63	35	51	4th

League Appearances (goals)

Bamber 30 (1) · Bromilow 40 · Chambers 40 (22)
Cunningham 2 · Forshaw 27 (9) · Harrington 4
Johnson 26 (13) · Lacey 22 (1) · Lewis 17 (2)
Longworth 24 · Lucas 29 · McKinlay 35 (2)
McKinney 3 (1) · McNab 1 · McNaughton 1
Matthews 1 · T. Miller 4 (3) · Mitchell 15 · Parry 2
Pearson 10 · Penman 1 · Scott 26 · Sheldon 35 (1)
H. Wadsworth 25 (3) · W. Wadsworth 42 (5)

FA CUP

8 Jan	Manchester U (1)	H	D	1–1
12 Jan	Manchester U (1R)	A	W	2–1
29 Jan	Newcastle U (2)	A	L	0–1

FA Cup Appearances (goals)

Bamber 3 · Bromilow 3 · Chambers 3 (2) · Johnson 1
Lacey 2 (1) · Lewis 3 · Lucas 3 · McKinlay 3
Pearson 3 · Scott 3 · Sheldon 3 · W. Wadsworth 3

SEASON 1921-22

FOOTBALL LEAGUE (DIVISION 1)

27 Aug	Sunderland	A	L	0–3
31 Aug	Manchester C	H	W	3–2
3 Sep	Sunderland	H	W	2–1
7 Sep	Manchester C	A	D	1–1
10 Sep	Sheffield U	A	W	1–0
17 Sep	Sheffield U	H	D	1–1
24 Sep	Chelsea	A	W	1–0
1 Oct	Chelsea	H	D	1–1
8 Oct	Preston NE	A	D	1–1
15 Oct	Preston NE	H	W	4–0
22 Oct	Tottenham H	A	W	1–0
29 Oct	Tottenham H	H	D	1–1
5 Nov	Everton	A	D	1–1
12 Nov	Everton	H	D	1–1
19 Nov	Middlesbrough	H	W	4–0
26 Nov	Middlesbrough	A	L	1–3
3 Dec	Aston Villa	A	D	1–1
10 Dec	Aston Villa	H	W	2–0
17 Dec	Manchester U	H	W	2–1
24 Dec	Manchester U	A	D	0–0
26 Dec	Newcastle U	H	W	1–0
27 Dec	Huddersfield T	H	W	2–0
31 Dec	Bradford C	A	D	0–0
2 Jan	Newcastle U	A	D	1–1
14 Jan	Bradford C	H	W	2–1
21 Jan	Huddersfield T	A	W	1–0
4 Feb	Birmingham C	A	W	2–0
11 Feb	Birmingham C	H	W	1–0
25 Feb	Arsenal	H	W	4–0
4 Mar	Blackburn R	A	D	0–0
11 Mar	Blackburn R	H	W	2–0
18 Mar	Bolton W	H	L	0–2
22 Mar	Arsenal	A	L	0–1
25 Mar	Bolton W	A	W	3–1
1 Apr	Oldham A	H	W	2–0
8 Apr	Oldham A	A	L	0–4
14 Apr	Burnley	A	D	1–1
15 Apr	Cardiff C	H	W	5–1
17 Apr	Burnley	H	W	2–1
22 Apr	Cardiff C	A	L	0–2
29 Apr	West Brom	H	L	1–2
6 May	West Brom	A	W	4–1

Final League Position

	P	W	D	L	F	A	Pts	
Liverpool	42	22	13	7	63	36	57	1st

League Appearances (goals)

Bamber 8 · Beadles 11 (6) · Bromilow 40 (2)
Chambers 32 (19) · Checkland 5 · Cunningham 1
Forshaw 42 (17) · Gilhespy 2 (1) · Hopkin 42
Lacey 39 (1) · Lewis 19 (1) · Longworth 26
Lucas 27 (2) · McKinlay 29 (1) · McNab 29 (2)
Matthews 7 (4) · Mitchell 3 · Parry 7 · Scott 39
Shone 15 (6) · H. Wadsworth 1 · W. Wadsworth 38
Own goals (1)

FA CUP

7 Jan	Sunderland (1)	A	D	1–1
11 Jan	Sunderland (1R)	H	W	5–0
28 Jan	West Brom (2)	H	L	0–1

FA Cup Appearances (goals)

Bromilow 3 · Chambers 3 (2) · Forshaw 3 (3)
Hopkin 3 · Lacey 3 · Lewis 3 · Lucas 3 · McKinlay 3
McNab 3 · Scott 3 · W. Wadsworth 3 (1)

SEASON 1922-23

FOOTBALL LEAGUE (DIVISION 1)

26 Aug	Arsenal	H	W	5–2
30 Aug	Sunderland	A	L	0–1
2 Sep	Arsenal	A	L	0–1
6 Sep	Sunderland	H	W	5–1
9 Sep	Preston NE	A	W	3–1
16 Sep	Preston NE	H	W	5–2
23 Sep	Burnley	H	W	3–0
30 Sep	Burnley	A	L	0–2

Date	Opponent			Score
7 Oct	Everton	H	W	5–1
14 Oct	Everton	A	W	1–0
21 Oct	Cardiff C	H	W	3–1
28 Oct	Cardiff C	A	L	0–3
4 Nov	Tottenham H	A	W	4–2
11 Nov	Tottenham H	H	D	0–0
18 Nov	Aston Villa	H	W	3–0
25 Nov	Aston Villa	A	W	1–0
2 Dec	Newcastle U	H	L	0–2
9 Dec	Newcastle U	A	W	1–0
16 Dec	Nottingham F	H	W	2–1
23 Dec	Nottingham F	A	W	3–1
25 Dec	Oldham A	A	W	2–0
26 Dec	Oldham A	H	W	2–1
30 Dec	Chelsea	A	D	0–0
6 Jan	Chelsea	H	W	1–0
20 Jan	Middlesbrough	A	W	2–0
27 Jan	Middlesbrough	H	W	2–0
7 Feb	West Brom	H	W	2–0
10 Feb	West Brom	A	D	0–0
17 Feb	Blackburn R	H	W	3–0
3 Mar	Bolton W	H	W	2–1
12 Mar	Blackburn R	A	L	0–1
17 Mar	Manchester C	A	L	0–1
24 Mar	Manchester C	H	W	2–0
30 Mar	Sheffield U	H	W	2–1
31 Mar	Birmingham C	A	W	1–0
2 Apr	Sheffield U	A	L	1–4
7 Apr	Birmingham C	H	D	0–0
14 Apr	Huddersfield T	A	D	0–0
18 Apr	Bolton W	A	D	1–1
21 Apr	Huddersfield T	H	D	1–1
28 Apr	Stoke C	A	D	0–0
5 May	Stoke C	H	W	1–0

Final League Position

	P	W	D	L	F	A	Pts	
Liverpool	42	26	8	8	70	31	60	1st

League Appearances (goals)
Bamber 4 · Beadles 4 · Bromilow 41 (3)
Chambers 39 (22) · Forshaw 42 (19)
Gilhespy 10 (2) · Hopkin 40 (1) · Johnson 37 (14)
Lacey 30 (1) · Longworth 41 · Lucas 1
McKinlay 42 (5) · McNab 39 (1) · Pratt 7
Sambrooke 2 · Scott 42 · Shone 1 · H. Wadsworth 3
W. Wadsworth 37 (2)

FA CUP

13 Jan	Arsenal (1)	H	D	0–0
17 Jan	Arsenal (1R)	A	W	4–1
3 Feb	Wolverhampton W (2)	A	W	2–0
24 Feb	Sheffield U (3)	H	L	1–2

FA Cup Appearances (goals)
Bromilow 4 · Chambers 4 (3) · Forshaw 4 (1)
Hopkin 4 · Johnson 4 (2) · Lacey 4 · Longworth 4
McKinley 4 (1) · McNab 4 · Scott 4 · W. Wadsworth 4

SEASON 1923-24

FOOTBALL LEAGUE (DIVISION 1)

25 Aug	West Brom	A	L	0–2
29 Aug	Birmingham C	H	W	6–2
1 Sep	West Brom	H	D	0–0
5 Sep	Birmingham C	A	L	1–2
8 Sep	Preston NE	A	W	1–0
15 Sep	Preston NE	H	W	3–1
22 Sep	Burnley	A	L	0–2
29 Sep	Burnley	H	W	1–0
6 Oct	Everton	A	L	0–1
13 Oct	Everton	H	L	1–2
20 Oct	Nottingham F	H	W	4–2
27 Oct	Nottingham F	A	W	1–0
3 Nov	Huddersfield T	H	D	1–1
10 Nov	Huddersfield T	A	L	1–3
17 Nov	Aston Villa	H	D	0–0
24 Nov	Aston Villa	A	L	0–1
1 Dec	Sheffield U	A	D	1–1
8 Dec	Sheffield U	H	L	2–3
15 Dec	Cardiff C	H	L	0–2
22 Dec	Cardiff C	A	L	0–2
25 Dec	Newcastle U	H	L	0–1
26 Dec	Newcastle U	A	L	1–2
29 Dec	West Ham U	H	W	2–0
1 Jan	Chelsea	H	W	3–1
5 Jan	West Ham U	A	L	0–1
19 Jan	Manchester C	A	W	1–0
26 Jan	Manchester C	H	D	0–0
9 Feb	Bolton W	H	W	3–1
16 Feb	Sunderland	A	D	0–0
1 Mar	Arsenal	A	L	1–3
12 Mar	Bolton W	A	L	1–4
15 Mar	Blackburn R	H	D	0–0
19 Mar	Sunderland	H	W	4–2
22 Mar	Blackburn R	A	D	0–0
29 Mar	Tottenham H	H	W	1–0
2 Apr	Arsenal	H	D	0–0
5 Apr	Tottenham H	A	D	1–1
12 Apr	Middlesbrough	H	W	3–1
18 Apr	Chelsea	A	L	1–2
19 Apr	Middlesbrough	A	D	1–1

■ **Another era, but success has come Liverpool's way, as this team picture illustrates, with the old-time players having a trophy to show for their efforts.**

....

26 Apr	Notts County	H	W	1–0
3 May	Notts County	A	W	2–1

Final League Position

	P	W	D	L	F	A	Pts	
Huddersfield T	42	23	11	8	60	33	57	1st
Liverpool	42	15	11	16	49	48	41	12th

League Appearances (goals)
Bamber 6 · Beadles 2 · Bromilow 27
Chambers 30 (13) · Forshaw 39 (5) · Gilhespy 5
Hopkin 33 · Johnson 2 · Keetley 9 (3) · Lacey 8
Lawson 10 · Longworth 14 · Lucas 28 · McDevitt 3
McKinlay 39 (6) · McNab 30 · Parry 3 · Pratt 15
Rawlings 11 · Scott 42 · Shone 15 (5)
H. Wadsworth 17 · W. Wadsworth 37
Walsh 37 (16) · Own goals (1)

FA CUP

12 Jan	Bradford C (1)	H	W	2–1
2 Feb	Bolton W (2)	A	W	4–1
23 Feb	Southampton (3)	A	D	0–0
27 Feb	Southampton (3R)	H	W	2–0
8 Mar	Newcastle U (4)	A	L	0–1

FA Cup Appearances (goals)
Bromilow 5 · Chambers 5 (4) · Forshaw 5 (1)
Hopkin 5 · Lacey 1 · Lawson 4 · Lucas 5 · McKinley 5
McNab 4 · Scott 5 · Shone 1 · W. Wadsworth 5
Walsh 5 (3)

SEASON 1924-25

FOOTBALL LEAGUE (DIVISION 1)

30 Aug	Aston Villa	H	L	2–4
6 Sep	Arsenal	A	L	0–2
13 Sep	Manchester C	H	W	5–3
15 Sep	Blackburn R	A	L	1–3
20 Sep	Bury	A	D	0–0
27 Sep	Nottingham F	H	W	3–0
4 Oct	Everton	A	W	1–0
11 Oct	Newcastle U	A	D	0–0
15 Oct	Blackburn R	H	D	0–0
18 Oct	Sheffield U	H	W	4–1
25 Oct	Sunderland	H	W	3–1
8 Nov	Preston NE	H	W	3–1
12 Nov	Huddersfield T	H	L	2–3
15 Nov	Burnley	A	L	1–2
22 Nov	Leeds U	H	W	1–0
29 Nov	Birmingham C	A	L	2–5

6 Dec	West Brom	H	D	1–1
13 Dec	Tottenham H	A	D	1–1
15 Dec	Cardiff C	A	W	3–1
20 Dec	Bolton W	H	D	0–0
25 Dec	Notts County	A	W	2–1
26 Dec	Notts County	H	W	1–0
3 Jan	Arsenal	H	W	2–1
17 Jan	Manchester C	A	L	0–5
21 Jan	Aston Villa	A	W	4–1
24 Jan	Bury	H	W	4–0
4 Feb	Nottingham F	A	W	1–0
7 Feb	Everton	H	W	3–1
14 Feb	Newcastle U	H	D	1–1
28 Feb	Sunderland	A	L	0–3
14 Mar	Preston NE	A	L	0–4
16 Mar	Sheffield U	A	W	1–0
21 Mar	Burnley	H	W	3–0
28 Mar	Leeds U	A	L	1–4
4 Apr	Birmingham C	H	D	1–1
10 Apr	West Ham U	H	W	2–0
11 Apr	West Brom	A	D	0–0
13 Apr	West Ham U	A	W	1–0
18 Apr	Tottenham H	H	W	1–0
25 Apr	Bolton W	A	L	0–2
29 Apr	Cardiff C	H	L	1–2
2 May	Huddersfield T	A	D	1–1

Final League Position

	P	W	D	L	F	A	Pts	
Huddersfield T	42	21	16	5	69	28	58	1st
Liverpool	42	20	10	12	63	55	50	4th

League Appearances (goals)
Baron 9 (5) · Bromilow 22 · Chalmers 2
Chambers 27 (7) · Cockburn 17 · Forshaw 37 (19)
Garner 4 · Gilhespy 2 · Hopkin 26 (1)
Johnson 12 (1) · Jones 4 · Lawson 2 · Longworth 22
Lucas 37 · McKinlay 41 (2)
McNab 29 (2) · Parry 1 · Pratt 26 · Rawlings 40 (7)
E. Scott 38 · T. Scott 6 (1) · Shone 42 (12)
W. Wadsworth 25 · Walsh 3 (3) · Own goals (1)

FA CUP

10 Jan	Leeds U (1)	H	W	3–0
31 Jan	Bristol C (2)	A	W	1–0
21 Feb	Birmingham C (3)	H	W	2–1
7 Mar	Southampton (4)	A	L	0–1

FA Cup Appearances (goals)
Bromilow 2 · Chambers 4 · Cockburn 1 · Forshaw 3
Hopkin 4 (1) · Longworth 2 · Lucas 4 · McKinlay 2
McNab 2 · Pratt 4 · Rawlings 4 (2) · E. Scott 4
Shone 4 (3) · W. Wadsworth 3 · Walsh 1

SEASON 1925-26

FOOTBALL LEAGUE (DIVISION 1)

29 Aug	Leicester C	A	L	1–3
2 Sep	Notts County	H	W	2–0
5 Sep	West Ham U	H	D	0–0
12 Sep	Arsenal	A	D	1–1
19 Sep	Manchester U	H	W	5–0

26 Sep	Everton	H	W	5–1
1 Oct	Notts County	A	W	2–1
3 Oct	Burnley	A	L	1–2
10 Oct	Leeds U	H	D	1–1
17 Oct	Manchester C	H	W	2–1
24 Oct	Tottenham H	A	L	1–3
31 Oct	Sunderland	H	D	2–2
14 Nov	West Brom	H	W	2–0
21 Nov	Birmingham C	A	L	0–2
25 Nov	Huddersfield T	A	D	0–0
28 Nov	Bury	H	L	0–1
5 Dec	Blackburn R	H	D	1–1
12 Dec	Cardiff C	H	L	0–2
19 Dec	Sheffield U	A	L	1–5
25 Dec	Newcastle U	H	W	6–3
26 Dec	Newcastle U	A	L	0–3
1 Jan	Aston Villa	H	W	3–1
2 Jan	Leicester C	H	L	0–3
16 Jan	West Ham U	A	W	2–1
23 Jan	Arsenal	H	W	3–0
6 Feb	Everton	A	D	3–3
13 Feb	Burnley	H	W	3–2
20 Feb	Leeds U	A	D	1–1
27 Feb	Manchester C	A	D	1–1
6 Mar	Tottenham H	H	D	0–0
10 Mar	Manchester U	A	D	3–3
13 Mar	Sunderland	A	L	2–3
20 Mar	Huddersfield T	H	L	1–2
27 Mar	West Brom	A	W	3–0
2 Apr	Bolton W	A	W	1–0
3 Apr	Birmingham C	H	D	2–2
5 Apr	Bolton W	H	D	2–2
6 Apr	Aston Villa	A	L	0–3
10 Apr	Bury	A	W	1–0
17 Apr	Blackburn R	H	D	2–2
24 Apr	Cardiff C	A	D	2–2
1 May	Sheffield U	H	D	2–2

Final League Position

	P	W	D	L	F	A	Pts	
Huddersfield T	42	23	11	8	92	60	57	1st
Liverpool	42	14	16	12	70	63	44	7th

League Appearances (goals)
Baron 10 (2) · Bromilow 29 (1) · Chambers 42 (17)
Cockburn 37 · Forshaw 32 (27) · Garner 1
Hodgson 12 (4) · Hopkin 33 (1) · Jackson 12
Longworth 4 · Lucas 39 · McKinlay 41 (2)
McMullan 10 · McNab 34 · Oxley 31 (6) · Pratt 15 (1)
Rawlings 12 (1) · Reid 1 (2) · Riley 3 · E. Scott 39
T. Scott 4 (1) · Shears 2 · Shone 3 · W. Wadsworth 4
Walsh 12 (3) · Own goals (2)

FA CUP

9 Jan	Southampton (3)	A	D	0–0
13 Jan	Southampton (3R)	H	W	1–0
30 Jan	Fulham (4)	A	L	1–3

FA Cup Appearances (goals)
Bromilow 3 · Chambers 3 · Cockburn 3
Forshaw 3 (3) · Jackson 2 · Longworth 2 · Lucas 1
McKinlay 3 · McMullan 3 · McNab 3 · Oxley 3
E. Scott 3 · T. Scott 1

SEASON 1926-27

FOOTBALL LEAGUE (DIVISION 1)

28 Aug	Manchester U	H	W	4–2
30 Aug	Aston Villa	A	D	1–1
4 Sep	Derby County	A	L	1–2
8 Sep	Aston Villa	H	W	2–1
11 Sep	Sheffield U	H	W	5–1
18 Sep	Arsenal	A	L	0–2
25 Sep	Everton	A	L	0–1
2 Oct	Leeds U	H	L	2–4
9 Oct	Newcastle U	A	L	0–1
16 Oct	Sheffield W	A	L	2–3
23 Oct	Leicester C	H	W	1–0
30 Oct	Blackburn R	A	L	1–2
6 Nov	Huddersfield T	H	L	2–3
13 Nov	Sunderland	A	L	1–2
20 Nov	West Brom	H	W	2–1
27 Nov	Bury	A	W	2–0
4 Dec	Birmingham C	H	W	2–1
11 Dec	Tottenham H	A	W	2–1
18 Dec	West Ham U	H	D	0–0
25 Dec	Burnley	A	L	0–4
27 Dec	Burnley	H	D	2–2
28 Dec	Bolton W	H	W	3–2
1 Jan	Bolton W	A	L	1–2
15 Jan	Manchester U	A	W	1–0
22 Jan	Derby County	H	W	3–2
5 Feb	Arsenal	H	W	3–0
7 Feb	Sheffield U	A	W	4–1
12 Feb	Everton	H	W	1–0
23 Feb	Leeds U	A	D	0–0
26 Feb	Newcastle U	H	L	1–2
5 Mar	Sheffield W	H	W	3–0
12 Mar	Leicester C	A	L	2–3
19 Mar	Blackburn R	H	D	2–2
26 Mar	Huddersfield T	A	L	0–1
2 Apr	Sunderland	H	L	1–2
9 Apr	West Brom	A	W	1–0
15 Apr	Cardiff C	H	W	5–0
16 Apr	Bury	H	D	2–2
18 Apr	Cardiff C	A	L	0–2
23 Apr	Birmingham C	A	L	0–3
30 Apr	Tottenham H	H	W	1–0
7 May	West Ham U	A	D	3–3

Final League Position

	P	W	D	L	F	A	Pts	
Newcastle U	42	25	6	11	96	58	56	1st
Liverpool	42	18	7	17	69	61	43	9th

League Appearances (goals)

Baron 1 · Bromilow 40 · Chambers 42 (17) Cockburn 9 · Devlin 1 (1) · Done 2 · Edmed 38 (6) Forshaw 24 (14) · Hodgson 36 (16) · Hopkin 36 Jackson 19 · Longworth 15 · Lucas 39 (1) McKinlay 28 (1) · McMullan 2 · McNab 29 · Pither 6 Pratt 14 · Reid 20 (12) · Riley 10 · E. Scott 32 T. Scott 4 (1) · Shears 8 · Walsh 7

FA CUP

8 Jan	Bournemouth (3)	A	D	1–1
12 Jan	Bournemouth (3R)	H	W	4–1
29 Jan	Southport (4)	H	W	3–1
19 Feb	Arsenal (5)	A	L	0–2

FA Cup Appearances (goals)

Bromilow 4 · Chambers 4 (4) · Edmed 4 (1) Forshaw 3 · Hodgson 4 (2) · Hopkin 4 (1) · Lucas 4 McKinlay 4 · McNab 4 · Pratt 4 · Reid 1 · E. Scott 4

SEASON 1927-28

FOOTBALL LEAGUE (DIVISION 1)

27 Aug	Sheffield U	A	D	1–1
31 Aug	Bury	H	W	5–1
3 Sep	Aston Villa	H	D	0–0
10 Sep	Sunderland	A	L	1–2
17 Sep	Derby County	H	W	5–2
19 Sep	Bury	A	L	2–5
24 Sep	West Ham U	A	L	1–3
1 Oct	Portsmouth	H	W	8–2
8 Oct	Leicester C	A	D	1–1
15 Oct	Everton	A	D	1–1
22 Oct	Bolton W	A	L	1–2
29 Oct	Blackburn R	H	W	4–2
5 Nov	Cardiff C	A	D	1–1
12 Nov	Sheffield W	H	W	5–2
19 Nov	Middlesbrough	A	D	1–1
26 Nov	Huddersfield T	H	W	4–2
3 Dec	Newcastle U	A	D	1–1
10 Dec	Birmingham C	H	L	2–3
17 Dec	Tottenham H	A	L	1–3
24 Dec	Manchester U	H	W	2–0
27 Dec	Arsenal	H	L	0–2
31 Dec	Sheffield U	H	W	2–1
2 Jan	Burnley	H	D	2–2
7 Jan	Aston Villa	A	W	4–3
21 Jan	Sunderland	H	L	2–5
4 Feb	West Ham U	H	L	1–3
11 Feb	Portsmouth	A	L	0–1
15 Feb	Derby County	A	W	3–2
25 Feb	Everton	H	D	3–3
3 Mar	Bolton W	H	W	4–2
7 Mar	Arsenal	A	L	3–6
10 Mar	Blackburn R	A	L	1–2
17 Mar	Cardiff C	H	L	1–2
24 Mar	Sheffield W	A	L	0–4
31 Mar	Middlesbrough	H	D	1–1
6 Apr	Burnley	A	D	2–2
7 Apr	Huddersfield T	A	W	4–2
14 Apr	Newcastle U	H	D	0–0
21 Apr	Birmingham C	A	L	0–2
25 Apr	Leicester C	H	D	1–1
28 Apr	Tottenham H	H	W	2–0
5 May	Manchester U	A	L	1–6

Final League Position

	P	W	D	L	F	A	Pts	
Everton	42	20	13	9	102	66	53	1st
Liverpool	42	13	13	16	84	87	39	16th

League Appearances (goals)

Bromilow 42 (3) · Chambers 24 (3) · Clarke 2 Devlin 18 (14) · Done 4 · Edmed 42 (14) Hodgson 32 (23) · Hopkin 36 (3) · Jackson 40 (1) Longworth 1 · Lucas 28 · McBain 10 · McKinlay 40 McMullan 19 · McNab 7 (1) · Morrison 15 · Murray 2 Pither 6 (1) · Race 11 (2) · Reid 25 (15) · Riley 25 E. Scott 17 · T. Scott 3 (1) · Shears 4 · Walsh 9 (2) Own goals (1)

FA CUP

14 Jan	Darlington (3)	H	W	1–0
28 Jan	Cardiff C (4)	A	L	1–2

FA Cup Appearances (goals)

Bromilow 2 · Chambers 2 (1) · Edmed 2 (1) Hopkin 2 · Jackson 2 · Lucas 2 · McKinlay 2 McMullan 1 · McNab 1 · Reid 2 · Riley 2 · Walsh 2

SEASON 1928-29

FOOTBALL LEAGUE (DIVISION 1)

25 Aug	Bury	H	W	3–0
1 Sep	Aston Villa	A	L	1–3
5 Sep	Sheffield U	H	L	1–2
8 Sep	Leicester C	H	W	6–3
10 Sep	Sheffield U	A	W	3–1
15 Sep	Manchester U	A	D	2–2
22 Sep	Leeds U	H	D	1–1
29 Sep	Everton	A	L	0–1
6 Oct	West Ham U	A	D	1–1
13 Oct	Newcastle U	H	W	2–1
20 Oct	Huddersfield T	H	L	2–3
27 Oct	Arsenal	A	D	4–4
3 Nov	Birmingham C	H	L	1–2
10 Nov	Portsmouth	A	W	1–0
17 Nov	Bolton W	H	W	3–0
24 Nov	Sheffield W	A	L	2–3
1 Dec	Derby County	H	W	3–0
8 Dec	Sunderland	A	L	1–2
15 Dec	Blackburn R	H	D	1–1
22 Dec	Manchester C	A	W	3–2
25 Dec	Burnley	A	L	2–3
26 Dec	Burnley	H	W	8–0
29 Dec	Bury	A	D	2–2
5 Jan	Aston Villa	H	W	4–0
19 Jan	Leicester C	A	L	0–2
2 Feb	Leeds U	A	D	2–2
9 Feb	Everton	H	L	1–2
13 Feb	Manchester U	H	L	2–3
23 Feb	Newcastle U	A	D	2–2
9 Mar	Arsenal	H	L	2–4
13 Mar	West Ham U	H	W	2–1
16 Mar	Birmingham C	A	D	0–0
29 Mar	Cardiff C	H	W	2–0
30 Mar	Bolton W	A	D	0–0
1 Apr	Cardiff C	A	W	2–1
6 Apr	Sheffield W	H	W	3–2
10 Apr	Huddersfield T	A	W	3–1
13 Apr	Derby County	A	W	5–2
17 Apr	Portsmouth	H	D	0–0
20 Apr	Sunderland	H	W	5–2
27 Apr	Blackburn R	A	L	1–2
4 May	Manchester C	H	D	1–1

Final League Position

	P	W	D	L	F	A	Pts	
Sheffield W	42	21	10	11	86	62	52	1st
Liverpool	42	17	12	13	90	64	46	5th

League Appearances (goals)

Bromilow 28 (1) · Clarke 32 (9) · Davidson 36 (1) Done 37 (5) · Edmed 39 (16) · Gray 1 Hodgson 38 (30) · Hopkin 22 · Jackson 42 Lindsay 10 (1) · Lucas 5 · McBain 2 McDougall 36 (8) · McFarlane 1 · McKinlay 2 Miller 3 (2) · Morrison 42 · Race 13 (9) · Reid 5 (2) Riley 20 · Salisbury 16 (2) · E. Scott 22 · Shears 2 Whitehurst 8 (2) · Own goals (2)

FA CUP

12 Jan	Bristol C (3)	A	W	2–0
26 Jan	Bolton W (4)	H	D	0–0
30 Jan	Bolton W (4R)	A	L	2–5

FA Cup Appearances (goals)

Bromilow 2 · Clarke 3 · Davidson 3 · Done 3 Edmed 3 · Hodgson 3 (2) · Jackson 3 · Lindsay 2 (1) McDougall 3 · Morrison 3 · Reid 1 · Riley 3 Salisbury 1 (1)

SEASON 1929-30

FOOTBALL LEAGUE (DIVISION 1)

31 Aug	Middlesbrough	A	L	0–5
4 Sep	Huddersfield T	H	W	3–0
7 Sep	Everton	H	L	0–3
14 Sep	West Ham U	H	W	3–1
16 Sep	Huddersfield T	A	L	0–3
21 Sep	Manchester U	A	W	2–1
28 Sep	Grimsby T	H	W	2–0
5 Oct	Leicester C	A	L	1–2
9 Oct	Blackburn R	H	D	1–1
12 Oct	Birmingham C	H	D	1–1
19 Oct	Derby County	A	D	2–2
26 Oct	Manchester C	H	L	1–6
2 Nov	Portsmouth	A	D	3–3
9 Nov	Bolton W	H	W	3–0
16 Nov	Aston Villa	A	W	3–2
23 Nov	Leeds U	H	W	1–0
30 Nov	Sheffield W	A	L	1–2
7 Dec	Burnley	H	L	1–3
14 Dec	Sunderland	A	W	3–2
21 Dec	Arsenal	H	W	1–0
25 Dec	Sheffield U	A	L	0–4
26 Dec	Sheffield U	H	W	2–0
28 Dec	Middlesbrough	H	W	5–2
4 Jan	Everton	A	D	3–3
18 Jan	West Ham U	A	L	1–4
25 Jan	Manchester U	H	W	1–0
1 Feb	Grimsby T	A	L	2–3
8 Feb	Leicester C	H	D	1–1
15 Feb	Birmingham C	A	L	0–1
22 Feb	Derby County	H	D	2–2
1 Mar	Manchester C	A	L	3–4
8 Mar	Portsmouth	H	W	2–0
15 Mar	Bolton W	A	W	2–0
22 Mar	Aston Villa	H	W	2–0
29 Mar	Leeds U	A	D	1–1
2 Apr	Arsenal	A	W	1–0
5 Apr	Sheffield W	H	L	1–3
12 Apr	Burnley	A	L	1–4
18 Apr	Newcastle U	A	L	1–3
19 Apr	Sunderland	H	L	0–6
21 Apr	Newcastle U	H	D	0–0
3 May	Blackburn R	A	L	0–1

Final League Position

	P	W	D	L	F	A	Pts	
Sheffield W	42	26	8	8	105	57	60	1st
Liverpool	42	16	9	17	63	79	41	12th

League Appearances (goals)

Barton 11 · Bradshaw 17 · Bromilow 9 · Clarke 5 (1) Davidson 22 (1) · Done 13 · Edmed 29 (4) · Gardner 5 Gunson 10 (1) · Hodgson 36 (14) · Hopkin 31 (2) Jackson 40 · Lindsay 4 (1) · Lucas 31 McDougall 34 (1) · McFarlane 1 · McPherson 25 (5) Morrison 36 · Murray 2 (1) · Race 19 (7) · Riley 34 A. Scott 1 · E. Scott 8 · Smith 37 (23) · Thompson 1 Wright 1 · Own goals (2)

FA CUP

11 Jan	Cardiff C (3)	H	L	1–2

FA Cup Appearances (goals)

Davidson 1 · Edmed 1 · Hodgson 1 · Hopkin 1 Jackson 1 · Lucas 1 · McDougall 1 · McPherson 1 (1) Morrison 1 · Riley 1 · Smith 1

SEASON 1930-31

FOOTBALL LEAGUE (DIVISION 1)

30 Aug	Blackburn R	H	W	2–1
1 Sep	West Ham U	A	L	0–7
6 Sep	Middlesbrough	A	D	3–3
10 Sep	Bolton W	H	W	7–2
13 Sep	Huddersfield T	H	L	1–4
20 Sep	Aston Villa	A	L	2–4
27 Sep	Chelsea	H	W	3–1
4 Oct	Newcastle U	A	W	4–0
11 Oct	Sheffield W	H	L	1–2
18 Oct	Leeds U	H	W	2–0
25 Oct	Blackpool	A	W	3–1
1 Nov	Manchester C	H	L	0–2
8 Nov	Derby County	A	D	2–2
15 Nov	Leicester C	H	W	3–1
22 Nov	Portsmouth	A	L	0–4
29 Nov	Sheffield U	H	W	6–1
6 Dec	Sunderland	A	L	5–6
13 Dec	Arsenal	H	D	1–1
20 Dec	Birmingham C	A	L	0–2
25 Dec	Grimsby T	A	D	0–0
26 Dec	Grimsby T	H	D	1–1
27 Dec	Blackburn R	A	D	3–3
3 Jan	Middlesbrough	H	W	3–1
14 Jan	Bolton W	A	L	0–2
17 Jan	Huddersfield T	A	L	1–2
24 Jan	Aston Villa	H	D	1–1
31 Jan	Chelsea	A	D	2–2
7 Feb	Newcastle U	H	W	4–2
14 Feb	Sheffield W	A	W	5–3
21 Feb	Leeds U	A	W	2–1
28 Feb	Blackpool	H	W	5–2
7 Mar	Manchester C	A	D	1–1
14 Mar	Derby County	H	D	0–0
21 Mar	Leicester C	A	L	2–3
28 Mar	Portsmouth	H	W	3–1
3 Apr	Manchester U	H	D	1–1
4 Apr	Sheffield U	A	L	1–4
6 Apr	Manchester U	A	L	1–4
11 Apr	Sunderland	H	L	2–4
15 Apr	Birmingham C	H	D	0–0
18 Apr	Arsenal	A	L	1–3
2 May	West Ham U	H	W	2–0

Final League Position

	P	W	D	L	F	A	Pts	
Arsenal	42	28	10	4	127	59	66	1st
Liverpool	42	15	12	15	86	85	42	9th

League Appearances (goals)

Aitken 1 · Barkas 4 · Barton 25 (4) · Bradshaw 35 Buxton 1 · Clarke 1 (1) · Done 14 (2) · Edmed 12 (4) Gunson 8 (1) · Hodgson 40 (36) · Hopkin 36 (1) Ireland 1 · Jackson 28 · James 7 · Lucas 42 McDougall 40 (1) · McPherson 42 (10) McRorie 3 (1) · Morrison 39 (1) · Riley 27 A. Scott 2 (2) · E. Scott 14 · Smith 21 (14) Thompson 4 · Wright 15 (6) · Own goals (2)

FA CUP

Jan 10	Birmingham C (3)	H	L	0–2

FA Cup Appearances (goals)

Bradshaw 1 · Gunson 1 · Hodgson 1 · Hopkin 1 Jackson 1 · Lucas 1 · McPherson 1 · Morrison 1 Riley 1 · A. Scott 1 · Thompson 1

SEASON 1931-32

FOOTBALL LEAGUE (DIVISION 1)

29 Aug	Newcastle U	A	W	1–0
2 Sep	Bolton W	H	D	2–2
5 Sep	Aston Villa	H	W	2–0
9 Sep	Middlesbrough	A	L	1–4
12 Sep	Leicester C	A	L	1–2
16 Sep	Middlesbrough	H	W	7–2
19 Sep	Everton	H	L	1–3
26 Sep	Grimsby T	H	W	4–0
3 Oct	Chelsea	A	L	0–2
10 Oct	West Ham U	H	D	2–2
17 Oct	West Brom	A	W	2–1
24 Oct	Blackpool	H	W	3–2
31 Oct	Sheffield U	A	L	0–3
7 Nov	Blackburn R	H	W	4–2
14 Nov	Sunderland	A	W	3–1
21 Nov	Manchester C	H	W	4–3
28 Nov	Arsenal	A	L	0–6
5 Dec	Birmingham C	H	W	4–3
12 Dec	Portsmouth	A	L	0–2
19 Dec	Derby County	H	D	1–1
25 Dec	Sheffield W	H	W	3–1
26 Dec	Sheffield W	A	D	1–1
2 Jan	Newcastle U	H	W	4–2
16 Jan	Aston Villa	A	L	1–6
27 Jan	Leicester C	H	D	3–3
30 Jan	Everton	A	L	1–2
6 Feb	Grimsby T	A	L	1–5
20 Feb	West Ham U	A	L	0–1
2 Mar	West Brom	H	W	4–1
5 Mar	Blackpool	A	D	2–2
12 Mar	Sheffield U	H	W	2–1
19 Mar	Blackburn R	A	W	3–1
26 Mar	Sunderland	H	L	1–2
28 Mar	Huddersfield T	H	L	0–3
29 Mar	Huddersfield T	A	L	3–4
2 Apr	Manchester C	A	W	1–0
6 Apr	Chelsea	H	W	2–1
9 Apr	Arsenal	H	W	2–1
16 Apr	Birmingham C	A	L	1–3
23 Apr	Portsmouth	H	L	1–3
30 Apr	Derby County	A	W	2–1
7 May	Bolton W	A	L	1–8

Final League Position

	P	W	D	L	F	A	Pts	
Everton	42	26	4	12	116	64	56	1st
Liverpool	42	19	6	17	81	93	44	10th

League Appearances (goals)

Barkas 1 · Barton 24 (8) · Bradshaw 42 · Bruton 1

ıarlton 3 · Done 26 (3) · Gunson 42 (17)
ancock 9 (2) · Henderson 5 · Hodgson 39 (26)
ackson 17 · Lucas 16 · McDougall 39
cPherson 28 (2) · McRorie 25 (5) · Morrison 35 (1)
ley 5 · Roberts 1 · Savage 7 (2) · E. Scott 37
nith 3 (1) · Steel 22 · Wright 35 (13)
wn goals (1)

CUP

Jan	Everton (3)	A	W	2–1
Jan	Chesterfield (4)	A	W	4–2
Feb	Grimsby T (5)	H	W	1–0
Feb	Chelsea (6)	H	L	0–2

Cup Appearances (goals)
rton 4 (4) · Bradshaw 4 · Bruton 1 · Gunson 4 (2)
odgson 4 (1) · Jackson 3 · Lucas 1 · McDougall 4
cPherson 1 · McRorie 2 · Morrison 4 · E. Scott 4
eel 4 · Wright 4

EASON 1932-33

OTBALL LEAGUE (DIVISION 1)

Aug	Wolverhampton W	H	W	5–1
Aug	Sheffield U	A	L	2–6
Sep	Newcastle U	A	L	3–4
Sep	Sheffield U	H	D	2–2
Sep	Aston Villa	H	D	0–0
Sep	Middlesbrough	A	W	1–0
Sep	Bolton W	A	L	0–1
Oct	Everton	H	L	1–3
Oct	Leicester C	A	W	2–1
Oct	Portsmouth	H	W	4–3
Oct	Arsenal	H	L	2–3
Oct	Manchester C	A	D	1–1
Nov	Leeds U	H	L	0–1
Nov	Blackburn R	A	D	2–2
Nov	Derby County	H	W	6–1
Nov	Blackpool	A	L	1–4
Dec	Sunderland	H	D	3–3
Dec	Birmingham C	A	L	0–3
Dec	West Brom	H	W	2–0
Dec	Sheffield W	A	L	0–3
Dec	Chelsea	H	W	3–0
Dec	Chelsea	A	W	2–0
Dec	Wolverhampton W	A	L	1–3
Jan	Newcastle U	H	W	3–0
Jan	Aston Villa	A	L	2–5
Feb	Middlesbrough	H	L	1–3
Feb	Bolton W	A	D	3–3
Feb	Everton	H	W	7–4
Feb	Leicester C	H	L	1–2
Feb	Portsmouth	A	L	1–2
Mar	Arsenal	A	W	1–0
Mar	Manchester C	H	D	1–1
Mar	Leeds U	A	L	0–5
Mar	Blackburn R	H	D	2–2
Apr	Derby County	A	D	1–1
Apr	Blackpool	H	W	4–3
Apr	Huddersfield T	H	D	2–2
Apr	Sunderland	A	D	0–0
Apr	Huddersfield T	A	L	1–3
Apr	Birmingham C	H	W	1–0
Apr	West Brom	A	L	1–2
May	Sheffield W	H	W	4–1

nal League Position

	P	W	D	L	F	A	Pts	
senal	42	25	8	9	118	61	58	1st
verpool	42	14	11	17	79	84	39	14th

ague Appearances (goals)
rton 34 (13) · Bradshaw 39 (3) · Bruton 6 (1)
awford 7 (4) · Done 29 (1) · Gunson 21 (5)
anson 11 (2) · Hodgson 38 (24) · Jackson 14 (1)
mes 1 · Lucas 3 · McDougall 26
cPherson 24 (1) · McRorie 5 · Morrison 32 (1)
ey 15 · Roberts 25 (6) · Savage 11 · E. Scott 27
eel 42 · Taylor 22 (2) · Wright 30 (14)
vn goals (1)

CUP

Jan	West Brom (3)	A	L	0–2

Cup Appearances (goals)
rton 1 · Bradshaw 1 · Bruton 1 · Done 1 · Gunson 1
odgson 1 · McDougall 1 · Morrison 1 · E. Scott 1
eel 1 · Wright 1

EASON 1933-34

OTBALL LEAGUE (DIVISION 1)

Aug	Wolverhampton W	A	L	2–3
Aug	Stoke C	H	D	1–1
Sep	Sheffield U	H	W	3–2
Sep	Stoke C	A	D	1–1
Sep	Aston Villa	A	L	2–4
Sep	Leicester C	H	L	1–3
Sep	Tottenham H	A	W	3–0
Sep	Everton	H	W	3–2
7 Oct	Chelsea	H	W	3–0
14 Oct	Sunderland	A	L	1–4
21 Oct	Middlesbrough	A	L	1–4
28 Oct	Blackburn R	H	W	4–0
4 Nov	Birmingham C	A	W	2–1
11 Nov	Leeds U	H	W	4–3
18 Nov	Derby County	A	L	1–3
25 Nov	West Brom	H	D	1–1
2 Dec	Arsenal	A	L	1–2
9 Dec	Sheffield W	H	L	1–3
16 Dec	Manchester C	A	L	1–2
23 Dec	Newcastle U	H	L	1–2
25 Dec	Portsmouth	H	D	2–2
26 Dec	Portsmouth	A	L	0–1
30 Dec	Wolverhampton W	H	D	1–1
1 Jan	Newcastle U	A	L	2–9
6 Jan	Sheffield U	A	D	2–2
20 Jan	Aston Villa	H	L	2–3
1 Feb	Leicester C	A	L	0–1
3 Feb	Tottenham H	H	W	3–1
10 Feb	Everton	A	D	0–0
21 Feb	Chelsea	A	L	0–2
24 Feb	Sunderland	H	D	1–1
3 Mar	Middlesbrough	H	W	6–2
10 Mar	Blackburn R	A	L	1–3
17 Mar	Birmingham C	H	W	4–1
24 Mar	Leeds U	A	L	1–5
30 Mar	Huddersfield T	H	D	2–2
31 Mar	Derby County	H	W	4–2
3 Apr	Huddersfield T	A	W	2–0
7 Apr	West Brom	A	D	2–2
14 Apr	Arsenal	H	L	2–3
21 Apr	Sheffield W	A	W	2–1
2 May	Manchester C	H	W	3–2

Final League Position

	P	W	D	L	F	A	Pts	
Arsenal	42	25	9	8	75	47	59	1st
Liverpool	42	14	10	18	79	87	38	18th

League Appearances (goals)
Barton 6 · Blenkinsop 9 · Bradshaw 39 · Bush 2
Carr 2 · Dabbs 1 · Done 21 (2) · English 28 (19)
Hanson 36 (12) · Hodgson 37 (23) · Johnson 11 (2)
McDougall 32 · McPherson 9 · Morrison 33 (1)
Nieuwenhuys 34 (9) · Riley 32 · J. Roberts 1
S. Roberts 13 (3) · Savage 15 · E. Scott 10
Steel 40 · Taylor 19 (3) · Tennant 13
D. Wright 12 (2) · E. Wright 7 (2) · Own goals (1)

FA CUP

13 Jan	Fulham (3)	H	D	1–1
17 Jan	Fulham (3R)	A	W	3–2†
27 Jan	Tranmere R (4)	H*	W	3–1
17 Feb	Bolton W (5)	H	L	0–3

†after extra time
*Tranmere drawn at home, but match switched to Anfield

FA Cup Appearances (goals)
Barton 1 · Bradshaw 4 (1) · Done 4 · English 3 (2)
Hanson 3 (1) · Hodgson 3 (1) · McDougall 4
Morrison 4 · Nieuwenhuys 4 (1) · Roberts 2 (1)
E. Scott 4 · Steel 3 · Taylor 2 · Tennant 1 · S. Wright 2

SEASON 1934-35

FOOTBALL LEAGUE (DIVISION 1)

25 Aug	Blackburn R	H	W	2–0
29 Aug	Manchester C	A	L	1–3
1 Sep	Arsenal	A	L	1–8
5 Sep	Manchester C	H	W	2–1
8 Sep	Portsmouth	H	L	0–1
15 Sep	Everton	A	L	0–1
22 Sep	Leeds U	A	W	3–0
29 Sep	West Brom	H	W	3–2
6 Oct	Sheffield W	A	L	1–4
13 Oct	Birmingham C	H	W	5–4
20 Oct	Grimsby T	H	D	1–1
27 Oct	Preston NE	A	D	2–2
3 Nov	Wolverhampton W	H	W	2–1
10 Nov	Huddersfield T	A	L	0–8
17 Nov	Leicester C	H	W	5–1
24 Nov	Derby County	A	W	2–1
1 Dec	Aston Villa	H	W	3–1
8 Dec	Chelsea	A	L	1–4
15 Dec	Tottenham H	H	W	4–1
22 Dec	Sunderland	A	W	3–2
26 Dec	Middlesbrough	H	D	2–2
29 Dec	Blackburn R	A	W	2–0
1 Jan	Middlesbrough	A	L	0–2
5 Jan	Arsenal	H	L	0–2
19 Jan	Portsmouth	A	W	2–1
2 Feb	Leeds U	H	W	4–2
9 Feb	West Brom	A	D	1–1
20 Feb	Sheffield W	H	L	1–2
23 Feb	Birmingham C	A	W	3–1
2 Mar	Grimsby T	A	L	2–3
9 Mar	Preston NE	H	D	0–0
16 Mar	Wolverhampton W	A	L	3–5
20 Mar	Everton	H	W	2–1
23 Mar	Huddersfield T	H	W	3–2
30 Mar	Leicester C	A	L	1–3
6 Apr	Derby County	H	L	1–3
13 Apr	Aston Villa	A	L	2–4
19 Apr	Stoke C	H	W	5–0
20 Apr	Chelsea	H	W	6–0
22 Apr	Stoke C	A	D	1–1
27 Apr	Tottenham H	A	L	1–5
4 May	Sunderland	H	D	2–2

Final League Position

	P	W	D	L	F	A	Pts	
Arsenal	42	23	12	7	115	46	58	1st
Liverpool	42	19	7	16	85	88	45	7th

League Appearances (goals)
Blenkinsop 16 · Bradshaw 31 · Browning 3
Carr 8 (2) · Cooper 23 · Dabbs 2 · Done 1
English 19 (6) · Hanson 35 (9) · Hodgson 34 (27)
Howe 6 (3) · Johnson 20 (5) · Kane 3 · Low 11
McDougall 38 (1) · McPherson 2 · Morrison 8
Nieuwenhuys 29 (10) · Riley 39 · S. Roberts 10 (1)
Rogers 5 · Savage 27 · Steel 16 · Taylor 14 (1)
Tennant 26 · E. Wright 36 (19) · Own goals (1)

FA CUP

12 Jan	Yeovil & Petters (3)	A	W	6–2
26 Jan	Blackburn R (4)	A	L	0–1

FA Cup Appearances (goals)
Bradshaw 2 · Cooper 2 · Hanson 2 · Hodgson 2 (2)
McDougall 2 · Nieuwenhuys 2 (1) · Riley 2
Roberts 2 (2) · Savage 2 · Tennant 2 · Wright 2 (1)

SEASON 1935-36

FOOTBALL LEAGUE (DIVISION 1)

31 Aug	Chelsea	A	D	2–2
4 Sep	Manchester C	H	L	0–2
7 Sep	Everton	H	W	6–0
11 Sep	Manchester C	A	L	0–6
14 Sep	Grimsby T	H	W	7–2
18 Sep	Stoke C	H	W	2–0
21 Sep	Leeds U	A	L	0–1
28 Sep	West Brom	H	W	5–0
5 Oct	Sunderland	A	L	0–2
12 Oct	Birmingham C	H	L	1–2
19 Oct	Bolton W	A	D	0–0
26 Oct	Huddersfield T	H	W	3–0
2 Nov	Middlesbrough	A	D	2–2
9 Nov	Aston Villa	H	W	3–2
16 Nov	Wolverhampton W	A	L	1–3
23 Nov	Derby County	H	D	0–0
30 Nov	Portsmouth	A	L	1–2
7 Dec	Preston NE	H	W	2–1
14 Dec	Brentford	A	W	2–1
21 Dec	Sheffield W	H	W	1–0
25 Dec	Arsenal	H	L	0–1
26 Dec	Arsenal	A	W	2–1
28 Dec	Chelsea	H	L	2–3
4 Jan	Everton	A	D	0–0
18 Jan	Grimsby	A	D	0–0
1 Feb	West Brom	A	L	1–6
8 Feb	Sunderland	H	L	0–3
15 Feb	Birmingham C	A	L	0–2
22 Feb	Bolton W	H	D	1–1
29 Feb	Aston Villa	A	L	0–3
7 Mar	Portsmouth	H	W	2–0
14 Mar	Huddersfield T	A	L	0–1
18 Mar	Leeds U	H	W	2–1
21 Mar	Wolverhampton W	H	L	0–2
28 Mar	Derby County	A	D	2–2
4 Apr	Middlesbrough	H	D	2–2
10 Apr	Blackburn R	A	D	2–2
11 Apr	Preston NE	A	L	1–3
13 Apr	Blackburn R	H	W	4–1
18 Apr	Brentford	H	D	0–0
25 Apr	Sheffield W	A	D	0–0
2 May	Stoke C	A	L	1–2

Final League Position

	P	W	D	L	F	A	Pts	
Sunderland	42	25	6	11	109	74	56	1st
Liverpool	42	13	12	17	60	64	38	19th

League Appearances (goals)
Balmer 17 (3) · Blenkinsop 37 · Bradshaw 41
Browning 6 · Busby 11 (1) · Carr 21 (6) · Collins 6
Cooper 26 · Dabbs 13 · Glassey 8 (4) · Hanson 5
Harley 8 · Hartill 5 · Hodgson 17 (9) · Howe 34 (17)
Johnson 6 (1) · Kane 3 · Low 1 · McDougall 38 (1)
Nieuwenhuys 39 (10) · Riley 39 · Roberts 6
Rogers 2 · Savage 27 · Shield 1 · H. Taylor 13
P. Taylor 7 (2) · Wright 25 (6)

FA CUP

11 Jan	Swansea T (3)	H	W	1–0
25 Jan	Arsenal (4)	H	L	0–2

FA Cup Appearances (goals)
Bradshaw 2 · Carr 2 · Cooper 2 · Dabbs 2 · Howe 2
Johnson 2 · McDougall 2 · Nieuwenhuys 2 · Riley 2
Savage 2 · Wright 2 (1)

SEASON 1936-37

FOOTBALL LEAGUE (DIVISION 1)

29 Aug	Stoke C	H	W	2–1
2 Sep	Portsmouth	A	L	2–6
5 Sep	Charlton A	A	D	1–1
9 Sep	Portsmouth	H	D	0–0
12 Sep	Grimsby T	H	W	7–1
16 Sep	Chelsea	A	L	0–2
19 Sep	Everton	A	L	0–2
26 Sep	Leeds U	A	L	0–2
3 Oct	Birmingham C	H	W	2–0
10 Oct	Middlesbrough	A	D	3–3
17 Oct	Bolton W	H	D	0–0
24 Oct	Brentford	A	L	2–5
31 Oct	Arsenal	H	W	2–1
7 Nov	Preston NE	A	L	1–3
14 Nov	Sheffield W	H	D	2–2
21 Nov	Manchester U	A	W	5–2
28 Nov	Derby County	H	D	3–3
5 Dec	Wolverhampton W	A	L	0–2
12 Dec	Sunderland	H	W	4–0
19 Dec	Huddersfield T	A	L	0–4
25 Dec	West Brom	A	L	1–3
26 Dec	Stoke C	A	D	1–1
29 Dec	West Brom	H	L	1–2
2 Jan	Charlton A	H	L	1–2
9 Jan	Grimsby T	A	L	1–2
23 Jan	Everton	H	W	3–2
30 Jan	Leeds U	H	W	3–0
6 Feb	Birmingham C	A	L	0–5
13 Feb	Middlesbrough	H	L	0–2
24 Feb	Bolton W	A	W	1–0
27 Feb	Brentford	H	D	2–2
10 Mar	Arsenal	A	L	0–1
13 Mar	Preston NE	H	D	1–1
20 Mar	Sheffield W	A	W	2–1
26 Mar	Manchester C	H	L	0–5
27 Mar	Manchester U	H	W	2–0
29 Mar	Manchester C	A	L	1–5
3 Apr	Derby County	A	L	1–4
10 Apr	Wolverhampton W	H	W	1–0
17 Apr	Sunderland	A	L	2–4
24 Apr	Huddersfield T	H	D	1–1
1 May	Chelsea	H	D	1–1

Final League Position

	P	W	D	L	F	A	Pts	
Manchester C	42	22	13	7	107	61	57	1st
Liverpool	42	12	11	19	62	84	35	18th

League Appearances (goals)
Balmer 33 (8) · Blenkinsop 7 · Bradshaw 31
Browning 3 · Busby 29 (1) · Bush 9 · Collins 1
Cooper 39 · Dabbs 32 · Eastham 22 (2) · Glassey 1
Hanson 42 (13) · Harley 4 · Hobson 25
Howe 40 (16) · Kemp 7 · Low 1 · McDougall 39
Nieuwenhuys 40 (13) · Riley 10 · Roberts 2
Rogers 9 · Savage 8 · H. Taylor 1 · P. Taylor 14 (3)
Wright 13 (4) · Own goals (2)

FA CUP

16 Jan	Norwich C (3)	A	L	0–3

FA Cup Appearances (goals)
Balmer 1 · Busby 1 · Cooper 1 · Eastham 1
Hanson 1 · Harley 1 · Hobson 1 · Howe 1
McDougall 1 · Nieuwenhuys 1 · Savage 1

SEASON 1937-38

FOOTBALL LEAGUE (DIVISION 1)

28 Aug	Chelsea	A	L	1–6
1 Sep	Portsmouth	H	W	3–2
4 Sep	Charlton A	H	L	1–2
8 Sep	Portsmouth	A	D	1–1
11 Sep	Preston NE	A	L	1–4
15 Sep	Stoke C	H	W	3–0
18 Sep	Grimsby T	H	W	2–1
25 Sep	Leeds U	A	L	0–2
2 Oct	Everton	H	L	1–2
9 Oct	West Brom	H	L	0–1
16 Oct	Wolverhampton W	A	L	0–2
23 Oct	Leicester C	H	D	1–1
30 Oct	Sunderland	A	W	3–2
6 Nov	Brentford	H	L	3–4
13 Nov	Manchester C	A	W	3–1
20 Nov	Huddersfield T	H	L	0–1
27 Nov	Blackpool	A	W	1–0
4 Dec	Derby County	H	L	3–4
11 Dec	Bolton W	A	D	0–0
18 Dec	Arsenal	H	W	2–0
27 Dec	Birmingham C	A	D	2–2
1 Jan	Chelsea	H	D	2–2
15 Jan	Charlton A	A	L	0–3
29 Jan	Grimsby T	A	D	0–0
2 Feb	Preston NE	H	D	2–2
5 Feb	Leeds U	H	D	1–1
16 Feb	Everton	A	W	3–1
19 Feb	West Brom	A	L	1–5

26 Feb	Wolverhampton W	H	L	0–1
5 Mar	Leicester C	A	D	2–2
12 Mar	Sunderland	H	W	4–0
19 Mar	Brentford	A	W	3–1
26 Mar	Manchester C	H	W	2–0
2 Apr	Huddersfield T	A	W	2–1
6 Apr	Birmingham C	H	W	3–2
9 Apr	Blackpool	H	W	4–2
15 Apr	Middlesbrough	A	D	1–1
16 Apr	Derby County	A	L	1–4
18 Apr	Middlesbrough	H	D	1–1
23 Apr	Bolton W	H	W	2–1
30 Apr	Arsenal	A	L	0–2
7 May	Stoke C	A	L	0–2

Final League Position

	P	W	D	L	F	A	Pts	
Arsenal	42	21	10	11	77	44	52	1st
Liverpool	42	15	11	16	65	71	41	11th

League Appearances (goals)

Balmer 30 (13) · Blenkinsop 2 · Bradshaw 2
Browning 5 · Busby 33 · Bush 24 · Cooper 26
Dabbs 6 · Eastham 15 · Fagan 31 (8)
Hanson 37 (14) · Harley 33 · Harston 5 (3)
Hobson 1 · Hood 3 · Howe 9 · Jones 2 (1) · Kemp 13
McDougall 17 · McInnes 11 (1)
Nieuwenhuys 40 (13) · Ramsden 14 · Riley 28
Rogers 24 · Savage 5 · Shafto 13 (6) · Smith 1
P. Taylor 29 (6) · Van den Berg 3

FA CUP

8 Jan	Crystal Palace (3)	A	D	0–0
12 Jan	Crystal Palace (3R)	H	W	3–1*
22 Jan	Sheffield U (4)	A	D	1–1

26 Jan	Sheffield U (4R)	H	W	1–0
12 Feb	Huddersfield T (5)	H	L	0–1

*after extra time

FA Cup Appearances (goals)

Balmer 1 · Busby 3 · Bush 5 · Cooper 5 · Fagan 5 (1)
Eastham 1 · Hanson 5 (1) · Harley 5 · Howe 2
Nieuwenhuys 5 · Ramsden 1 · Riley 5 · Rogers 4
Shafto 3 (1) · Taylor 5 · Own goals (2)

SEASON 1938-39

FOOTBALL LEAGUE (DIVISION 1)

27 Aug	Chelsea	H	W	2–1
3 Sep	Preston NE	A	L	0–1
7 Sep	Manchester U	H	W	1–0
10 Sep	Charlton A	H	W	1–0
14 Sep	Middlesbrough	H	W	3–1
17 Sep	Bolton W	A	L	1–3
24 Sep	Leeds U	H	W	3–0
1 Oct	Everton	A	L	1–2
8 Oct	Leicester C	A	D	2–2
15 Oct	Aston Villa	H	W	3–0
22 Oct	Wolverhampton W	A	D	2–2
29 Oct	Huddersfield T	H	D	3–3
5 Nov	Portsmouth	A	D	1–1
12 Nov	Arsenal	H	D	2–2
19 Nov	Brentford	A	L	1–2
26 Nov	Blackpool	H	W	1–0
3 Dec	Derby County	A	D	2–2
10 Dec	Grimsby T	H	D	2–2
17 Dec	Sunderland	A	W	3–2
24 Dec	Chelsea	A	L	1–4

Final League Position

	P	W	D	L	F	A	Pts	
Everton	42	27	5	10	88	52	59	1st
Liverpool	42	14	14	14	62	63	42	11th

League Appearances (goals)

Balmer 42 (10) · Browning 2 · Busby 42 (1)
Bush 23 (1) · Cooper 36 · Eastham 7 (1)
Fagan 39 (14) · Fitzsimmon 1 · Harley 31 · Jones 3
Kemp 7 · Kinghorn 19 (4) · McInnes 34
Nieuwenhuys 39 (14) · Patterson 2 · Peters 1
Ramsden 10 · Riley 35 · Rogers 30 · Shafto 4
Taylor 39 (14) · Van den Berg 16 (3)

FA CUP

7 Jan	Luton T (3)	H	W	3–0
21 Jan	Stockport County (4)	H	W	5–1
11 Feb	Wolverhampton W (5)	A	L	1–4

FA Cup Appearances (goals)

Balmer 3 (4) · Busby 3 · Bush 2 · Eastham 2 (1)
Fagan 3 (1) · Harley 3 · Kemp 3 · McInnes 3
Nieuwenhuys 3 (2) · Patterson 1 (1) · Ramsden 3
Rogers 1 · Taylor 3

26 Dec	Stoke C	A	L	1–3
27 Dec	Stoke C	H	W	1–0
31 Dec	Preston NE	H	W	4–1
2 Jan	Middlesbrough	A	L	0–3
14 Jan	Charlton A	A	W	3–1
25 Jan	Bolton W	H	L	1–2
28 Jan	Leeds U	A	D	1–1
4 Feb	Everton	H	L	0–3
18 Feb	Aston Villa	A	L	0–2
25 Feb	Wolverhampton W	H	L	0–2
4 Mar	Leicester C	H	D	1–1
11 Mar	Portsmouth	H	D	4–4
15 Mar	Huddersfield T	A	D	1–1
18 Mar	Arsenal	A	L	0–2
25 Mar	Brentford	H	W	1–0
1 Apr	Blackpool	A	D	1–1
7 Apr	Birmingham C	H	W	4–0
8 Apr	Derby County	H	W	2–1
10 Apr	Birmingham C	A	D	0–0
15 Apr	Grimsby T	A	L	1–2
22 Apr	Sunderland	H	D	1–1
6 May	Manchester U	A	L	0–2

SEASON 1946-47

FOOTBALL LEAGUE (DIVISION 1)

31 Aug	Sheffield U	A	W	1–0
4 Sep	Middlesbrough	H	L	0–1
7 Sep	Chelsea	H	W	7–4
11 Sep	Manchester U	A	L	0–5
14 Sep	Bolton W	A	W	3–1
21 Sep	Everton	H	D	0–0
28 Sep	Leeds U	H	W	2–0
5 Oct	Grimsby T	A	W	6–1
9 Oct	Middlesbrough	A	D	2–2
12 Oct	Charlton A	H	D	1–1
19 Oct	Huddersfield T	A	W	4–1
26 Oct	Brentford	H	W	1–0
2 Nov	Blackburn R	A	D	0–0
9 Nov	Portsmouth	H	W	3–0
16 Nov	Derby County	A	W	4–1
23 Nov	Arsenal	H	W	4–2
30 Nov	Blackpool	A	W	4–1
7 Dec	Wolverhampton W	H	L	1–5
14 Dec	Sunderland	A	W	4–1
21 Dec	Aston Villa	H	W	4–1
25 Dec	Stoke C	A	L	1–2
26 Dec	Stoke C	H	W	2–0
28 Dec	Sheffield U	H	L	1–2
4 Jan	Chelsea	A	L	1–3
18 Jan	Bolton W	H	L	0–3
29 Jan	Everton	A	L	0–1
1 Feb	Leeds U	A	W	2–1
12 Feb	Grimsby T	H	W	5–0
22 Feb	Huddersfield T	H	W	1–0
8 Mar	Blackburn R	H	W	2–1
15 Mar	Portsmouth	A	W	2–1
22 Mar	Derby County	H	D	1–1
4 Apr	Preston NE	A	D	0–0
5 Apr	Blackpool	H	L	2–3
7 Apr	Preston NE	H	W	3–0
19 Apr	Sunderland	H	W	1–0
26 Apr	Aston Villa	A	W	2–1
3 May	Manchester U	H	W	1–0
10 May	Charlton A	A	W	3–1
17 May	Brentford	A	D	1–1
24 May	Arsenal	H	W	2–1
31 May	Wolverhampton W	A	W	2–1

....

■ Liverpool's FA Cup semi-final side of season 1946-47, as they prepared to meet Burnley. Manager George Kay is standing on the left, chairman Bill McConnell is seated in the middle of the front row. *Back row:* **Harley, Taylor, Lambert, Sidlow, Paisley, Jones, Liddell and trainer Albert Shelley;** *front row:* **Fagan, Balmer, Stubbins and Done.**

Final League Position

	P	W	D	L	F	A	Pts	
Liverpool	42	25	7	10	84	52	57	1st

League Appearances (goals)
Ashcroft 2 · Balmer 39 (24) · Bush 3 · Carney 2 (1) · Done 17 (10) · Easdale 2 · Eastham 19 · Fagan 18 (7) · Harley 17 · Hughes 30 · Jones 26 (2) · Kaye 1 · Lambert 36 · Liddell 35 (7) · McLeod 3 · Minshull 6 · Nieuwenhuys 15 (5) · Paisley 33 · Polk 6 · Priday 8 (2) · Ramsden 23 · Sidlow 34 · Spicer 10 · Stubbins 36 (24) · Taylor 35 (1) · Watkinson 6 (1)

FA CUP

11 Jan	Walsall (3)	A	W	5–2
25 Jan	Grimsby T (4)	H	W	2–0
8 Feb	Derby County (5)	H	W	1–0
1 Mar	Birmingham C (6)	H	W	4–1
29 Mar	Burnley (SF)	N	D	0–0*
(Ewood Park)				
12 Apr	Burnley (SFR)	N	L	0–1
(Maine Road)				

*after extra time

FA Cup Appearances (goals)
Balmer 6 (4) · Done 6 (2) · Eastham · Fagan 4 · Harley 4 · Hughes 1 · Jones 6 · Lambert 6 · Liddell 6 (1) · Paisley 6 · Ramsden 1 · Sidlow 6 · Stubbins 6 (4) · Taylor 6

SEASON 1947-48

FOOTBALL LEAGUE (DIVISION 1)

23 Aug	Preston NE	H	W	3–1
27 Aug	Manchester U	A	L	0–2
30 Aug	Stoke C	A	W	2–0
3 Sep	Manchester U	H	D	2–2
6 Sep	Burnley	H	D	1–1
8 Sep	Sheffield U	A	L	1–3
13 Sep	Portsmouth	A	L	0–1
17 Sep	Charlton A	A	L	0–2
20 Sep	Bolton W	H	D	0–0
27 Sep	Everton	A	W	3–0
4 Oct	Middlesbrough	A	L	1–3
11 Oct	Chelsea	H	W	3–0
18 Oct	Huddersfield T	A	D	1–1
25 Oct	Derby County	H	D	2–2
1 Nov	Blackpool	A	L	0–2
8 Nov	Grimsby T	H	W	3–1
15 Nov	Sunderland	A	L	1–5
26 Nov	Blackburn R	H	W	2–1
29 Nov	Manchester C	A	L	0–2
6 Dec	Aston Villa	H	D	3–3
13 Dec	Wolverhampton W	A	W	2–1
20 Dec	Preston NE	A	D	3–3
25 Dec	Arsenal	H	L	1–3
27 Dec	Arsenal	A	W	2–1
1 Jan	Charlton A	H	L	2–3
3 Jan	Stoke C	H	D	0–0
17 Jan	Burnley	A	L	0–3
31 Jan	Portsmouth	H	L	0–3
7 Feb	Bolton W	A	L	0–3
21 Feb	Middlesbrough	H	L	0–1
28 Feb	Chelsea	A	L	1–3
6 Mar	Huddersfield T	H	W	4–0
20 Mar	Blackpool	H	W	2–0
26 Mar	Sheffield U	H	W	4–0
27 Mar	Grimsby T	A	W	2–0
31 Mar	Derby County	A	W	3–0
3 Apr	Sunderland	H	D	0–0
10 Apr	Blackburn R	A	W	2–1
17 Apr	Manchester C	H	D	1–1
21 Apr	Everton	H	W	4–0
24 Apr	Aston Villa	A	L	1–2
1 May	Wolverhampton W	H	W	2–1

Final League Position

	P	W	D	L	F	A	Pts	
Arsenal	42	23	13	6	81	32	59	1st
Liverpool	42	16	10	16	65	61	42	11th

League Appearances (goals)
Balmer 40 (15) · Baron 6 (2) · Brierley 10 (1) · Carney 4 · Done 4 · Fagan 15 (5) · Harley 21 · Hughes 32 · Jones 41 (1) · Lambert 30 · Liddell 37 (10) · McAvoy 1 · Minshull 13 · Muir 4 · Paisley 37 (1) · Polk 7 · Priday 21 (4) · Ramsden 10 · Shannon 1 · Sidlow 29 · Spicer 14 (2) · Stubbins 40 (24) · Taylor 34 · Watkinson 11

FA CUP

10 Jan	Nottingham F (3)	H	W	4–1
24 Jan	Manchester U (4)	A	L	0–3
(Goodison Park)				

FA Cup Appearances (goals)
Balmer 1 · Done 2 · Hughes 2 · Jones 2 · Lambert 2 · Liddell 2 (1) · Minshull 2 · Paisley 2 · Priday 2 (1) · Spicer 1 · Stubbins 2 (2) · Taylor 2

SEASON 1948-49

FOOTBALL LEAGUE (DIVISION 1)

21 Aug	Aston Villa	A	L	1–2
25 Aug	Sheffield U	H	D	3–3
28 Aug	Sunderland	H	W	4–0
30 Aug	Sheffield U	A	W	2–1
4 Sep	Wolverhampton W	A	D	0–0
8 Sep	Arsenal	A	D	1–1
11 Sep	Bolton W	H	L	0–1
15 Sep	Arsenal	H	L	0–1
18 Sep	Everton	A	D	1–1
25 Sep	Blackpool	A	L	0–1
2 Oct	Derby County	H	D	0–0
9 Oct	Chelsea	H	D	1–1
16 Oct	Birmingham C	A	W	1–0
23 Oct	Middlesbrough	H	W	4–0
30 Oct	Newcastle U	A	L	0–1
6 Nov	Portsmouth	H	W	3–1
13 Nov	Manchester C	A	W	4–2
20 Nov	Charlton A	H	D	1–1
27 Nov	Stoke C	A	L	0–3
4 Dec	Burnley	H	D	1–1
11 Dec	Preston NE	A	L	2–3
18 Dec	Aston Villa	H	D	1–1
25 Dec	Manchester U	A	D	0–0
27 Dec	Manchester U	H	L	0–2
1 Jan	Sunderland	A	W	2–0
22 Jan	Bolton W	A	W	3–0
5 Feb	Everton	H	D	0–0
19 Feb	Blackpool	H	D	1–1
5 Mar	Chelsea	A	L	1–2
12 Mar	Birmingham C	H	W	1–0
19 Mar	Charlton A	A	L	1–2
26 Mar	Stoke C	H	W	4–0
2 Apr	Portsmouth	A	L	2–3
6 Apr	Wolverhampton W	H	D	0–0
9 Apr	Manchester C	H	L	0–1
15 Apr	Huddersfield T	H	L	0–1
16 Apr	Middlesbrough	A	W	1–0
18 Apr	Huddersfield T	A	W	1–0
23 Apr	Newcastle U	H	D	1–1
30 Apr	Burnley	A	W	2–0
4 May	Derby County	A	L	0–3
7 May	Preston NE	H	L	0–2

Final League Position

	P	W	D	L	F	A	Pts	
Portsmouth	42	25	8	9	84	42	58	1st
Liverpool	42	13	14	15	53	43	40	12th

League Appearances (goals)
Balmer 42 (14) · Baron 6 (2) · Brierley 13 · Done 24 (11) · Fagan 13 (2) · Hughes 12 · Jones 38 · Kippax 1 · Lambert 41 · Liddell 38 (8) · McAvoy 1 · McLeod 4 · Minshull 4 · Paisley 36 (1) · Payne 35 (3) · Priday 4 · Shannon 10 (1) · Shepherd 41 · Sidlow 38 · Spicer 4 · Stubbins 15 (6) · Taylor 30 (1) · Watkinson 6 (1) · Williams 6 · Own goals (3)

FA CUP

8 Jan	Nottingham F (3)	A	D	2–2*
15 Jan	Nottingham F (3R)	H	W	4–0
29 Jan	Notts County (4)	H	W	1–0
12 Feb	Wolverhampton W (5)	A	L	1–3

*after extra time

FA Cup Appearances (goals)
Balmer 4 (2) · Brierley 1 · Done 4 (1) · Fagan 1 (1) · Jones 4 · Lambert 4 · Liddell 4 (1) · Minshull 1 · Paisley 4 (1) · Payne 3 (1) · Shepherd 4 · Sidlow 3 · Stubbins 3 (1) · Taylor 4

SEASON 1949-50

FOOTBALL LEAGUE (DIVISION 1)

20 Aug	Sunderland	H	W	4–2
22 Aug	Stoke C	A	D	0–0
27 Aug	Everton	A	D	0–0
31 Aug	Stoke C	H	D	1–1
3 Sep	Arsenal	A	W	2–1
7 Sep	Manchester U	H	D	1–1
10 Sep	Bolton W	H	D	1–1
17 Sep	Birmingham C	A	W	3–2
24 Sep	Derby County	H	W	3–1
1 Oct	West Brom	A	W	1–0
8 Oct	Middlesbrough	A	W	2–0
15 Oct	Blackpool	A	D	0–0
22 Oct	Newcastle U	H	D	2–2

■ This was Liverpool at the start of the 1950s, as the club reached the final of the FA Cup. Bob Paisley is pictured on the far right (back row), but when the Anfield Reds met Arsenal at Wembley he was omitted.

29 Oct	Fulham	A	W	1–0
5 Nov	Manchester C	H	W	4–0
12 Nov	Charlton A	A	W	3–1
19 Nov	Aston Villa	H	W	2–1
26 Nov	Wolverhampton W	A	D	1–1
3 Dec	Portsmouth	H	D	2–2
10 Dec	Huddersfield T	A	L	2–3
17 Dec	Sunderland	A	L	2–3
24 Dec	Everton	H	W	3–1
26 Dec	Chelsea	A	D	1–1
27 Dec	Chelsea	H	D	2–2
31 Dec	Arsenal	H	W	2–0
14 Jan	Bolton W	A	L	2–3
21 Jan	Birmingham C	H	W	2–0
4 Feb	Derby County	A	D	2–2
18 Feb	West Brom	H	W	2–1
25 Feb	Middlesbrough	A	L	1–4
8 Mar	Blackpool	H	L	0–1
11 Mar	Aston Villa	A	L	0–2
15 Mar	Manchester U	A	D	0–0
18 Mar	Wolverhampton W	H	L	0–2
29 Mar	Manchester C	A	W	2–1
1 Apr	Charlton A	H	W	1–0
7 Apr	Burnley	A	W	2–0
8 Apr	Newcastle U	A	L	1–5
10 Apr	Burnley	H	L	0–1
15 Apr	Fulham	H	D	1–1
22 Apr	Portsmouth	A	L	1–2
3 May	Huddersfield T	H	L	2–3

Final League Position

	P	W	D	L	F	A	Pts	
Portsmouth	42	22	9	11	74	38	53	1st
Liverpool	42	17	14	11	64	54	48	8th

League Appearances (goals)
Balmer 9 (1) · Baron 38 (7) · Brierley 11 (5)
Christie 4 · Done 14 (5) · Fagan 35 (11) · Hughes 35
Jones 26 · Lambert 41 (1) · Liddell 41 (18)
Minshull 5 · Paisley 23 (1) · Payne 32 (5)
Shepherd 6 · Shields 1 · Sidlow 37 · Spicer 37
Stubbins 29 (10) · Taylor 37 · Watkinson 1

FA CUP

7 Jan	Blackburn R (3)	A	D	0–0
11 Jan	Blackburn R (3R)	H	W	2–1
28 Jan	Exeter C (4)	H	W	3–1
11 Feb	Stockport County (5)	A	W	2–1
4 Mar	Blackpool (6)	H	W	2–1
25 Mar	Everton (SF) (Maine Road)	N	W	2–0
29 Apr	Arsenal (F) (Wembley)	N	L	0–2

FA Cup Appearances (goals)
Baron 7 (1) · Fagan 7 (4) · Hughes 6 · Jones 3
Lambert 7 · Liddell 7 (2) · Paisley 5 (1) · Payne 7 (2)
Sidlow 7 · Spicer 7 · Stubbins 7 (1) · Taylor 7

SEASON 1950-51

FOOTBALL LEAGUE (DIVISION 1)

19 Aug	Wolverhampton W	A	L	0–2
23 Aug	Manchester U	H	W	2–1
26 Aug	Sunderland	H	W	4–0
30 Aug	Manchester U	A	L	0–1
2 Sep	Aston Villa	A	D	1–1
6 Sep	Tottenham H	H	W	2–1
9 Sep	Derby County	H	W	1–0
16 Sep	Everton	A	W	3–1
23 Sep	Fulham	A	L	1–2
30 Sep	Bolton W	H	D	3–3
7 Oct	Stoke C	H	D	0–0
14 Oct	West Brom	A	D	1–1
21 Oct	Middlesbrough	H	D	0–0
28 Oct	Sheffield W	A	L	1–4
4 Nov	Newcastle U	H	L	2–4
11 Nov	Huddersfield T	A	D	2–2
18 Nov	Arsenal	H	L	1–3
25 Nov	Burnley	A	D	1–1
2 Dec	Chelsea	H	W	1–0
9 Dec	Portsmouth	A	W	3–1
16 Dec	Wolverhampton W	H	L	1–4
23 Dec	Sunderland	A	L	1–2
25 Dec	Blackpool	A	L	0–3
26 Dec	Blackpool	H	W	1–0
13 Jan	Derby County	A	W	2–1
20 Jan	Everton	H	L	0–2
27 Jan	Charlton A	A	L	0–1
3 Feb	Fulham	H	W	2–0
10 Feb	Portsmouth	H	W	2–1
17 Feb	Bolton W	A	L	1–2
24 Feb	Stoke C	A	W	3–2
3 Mar	West Brom	H	D	1–1
10 Mar	Middlesbrough	A	D	1–1
17 Mar	Sheffield W	H	W	2–1
23 Mar	Charlton A	H	W	1–0
24 Mar	Newcastle U	A	D	1–1
31 Mar	Huddersfield T	H	L	1–4
7 Apr	Arsenal	A	W	2–1
14 Apr	Burnley	H	W	1–0
21 Apr	Chelsea	A	L	0–1
25 Apr	Aston Villa	H	D	0–0
5 May	Tottenham H	A	L	1–3

Final League Position

	P	W	D	L	F	A	Pts	
Tottenham H	42	25	10	7	82	44	60	1st
Liverpool	42	16	11	15	53	59	43	9th

League Appearances (goals)
Ashcroft 7 · Balmer 35 (10) · Baron 6 (1)
Brierley 3 · Cadden 4 · Crossley 24 · Done 24 (3)
Fagan 4 · Heydon 13 · Hughes 24 · Haigh 8 (3)
Jones 38 (4) · Lambert 34 · Liddell 36 (15)
Paisley 41 (1) · Payne 39 (6) · Shepherd 5
Sidlow 11 · Spicer 42 · Stubbins 23 (6)
Taylor 36 (2) · Williams 3 · Woan 2

FA CUP

6 Jan	Norwich C	A	L	1–3

FA Cup Appearances (goals)
Balmer 1 (1) · Crossley 1 · Done 1 · Heydon 1
Jones 1 · Lambert 1 · Liddell 1 · Paisley 1 · Payne 1
Stubbins 1 · Spicer 1

SEASON 1951-52

FOOTBALL LEAGUE (DIVISION 1)

18 Aug	Portsmouth	H	L	0–2
21 Aug	Burnley	A	D	0–0
25 Aug	Chelsea	A	W	3–1
29 Aug	Burnley	H	W	3–1
1 Sep	Huddersfield T	H	W	2–1
5 Sep	Arsenal	A	D	0–0
8 Sep	Wolverhampton W	A	L	1–2
12 Sep	Arsenal	H	D	0–0
15 Sep	Sunderland	H	D	2–2
22 Sep	Aston Villa	A	L	0–2
29 Sep	Derby County	H	W	2–0
6 Oct	Charlton A	A	L	0–2
13 Oct	Fulham	H	W	4–0
20 Oct	Middlesbrough	A	D	3–3
27 Oct	West Brom	H	L	2–5
3 Nov	Newcastle U	A	D	1–1
10 Nov	Bolton W	H	D	1–1
17 Nov	Stoke C	A	W	2–1
24 Nov	Manchester U	H	D	0–0
1 Dec	Tottenham H	A	W	3–2
8 Dec	Preston NE	H	D	2–2
15 Dec	Portsmouth	A	W	3–1
22 Dec	Chelsea	H	D	1–1
25 Dec	Blackpool	H	D	1–1
26 Dec	Blackpool	A	L	0–2
29 Dec	Huddersfield T	A	W	2–1
5 Jan	Wolverhampton W	H	D	1–1
19 Jan	Sunderland	A	L	0–3
26 Jan	Aston Villa	H	L	1–2
9 Feb	Derby County	A	D	1–1
16 Feb	Charlton A	H	D	1–1
1 Mar	Fulham	A	D	1–1
8 Mar	Middlesbrough	H	D	1–1
15 Mar	West Brom	A	D	3–3
22 Mar	Newcastle U	H	W	3–0
29 Mar	Bolton W	A	D	1–1
5 Apr	Stoke C	H	W	2–1
11 Apr	Manchester C	A	W	2–1
12 Apr	Manchester U	A	L	0–4
14 Apr	Manchester C	H	L	1–2
19 Apr	Tottenham H	H	D	1–1
26 Apr	Preston NE	A	L	0–4

Final League Position

	P	W	D	L	F	A	Pts	
Manchester U	42	23	11	8	95	52	57	1st
Liverpool	42	12	19	11	57	61	43	11th

League Appearances (goals)
Ashcroft 34 · Balmer 2 · Baron 40 (6)
Brierley 11 (1) · Crossley 8 · Done 10 (3) · Fagan 3
Haigh 3 · Heydon 27 · Hughes 25 (1)
Jackson 14 (1) · Jones M 3 · Jones W 37 (2)
Lambert 32 · Liddell 40 (19) · Paisley 37 (2) · Parr 16
Payne 35 (9) · Shepherd 1 · Smith 27 (6)
Stubbins 13 (5) · Taylor 24 (1) · Whitworth 9
Williams 11 (1)

FA CUP

12 Jan	Workington T (3)	H	W	1–0
2 Feb	Wolverhampton W (4)	H	W	2–1
23 Feb	Burnley (5)	A	L	0–2

FA Cup Appearances (goals)
Ashcroft 1 · Balmer 2 · Baron 1 · Cadden 1
Crossley 2 · Done 2 (1) · Heydon 2 · Hughes 1
Jackson 1 · Jones W 3 · Lambert 3 · Liddell 3
Paisley 3 (1) · Payne 3 (1) · Smith 1 · Taylor 2
Williams 2

SEASON 1952-53

FOOTBALL LEAGUE (DIVISION 1)

23 Aug	Preston NE	A	D	1–1
27 Aug	Sheffield W	H	W	1–0
30 Aug	Stoke C	H	W	3–2
3 Sep	Sheffield W	A	W	2–0
6 Sep	Manchester C	A	W	2–0
10 Sep	Tottenham H	H	W	2–1
13 Sep	Portsmouth	H	D	1–1
15 Sep	Tottenham H	A	L	1–3
20 Sep	Middlesbrough	H	W	4–1
27 Sep	West Brom	A	L	0–3
4 Oct	Newcastle U	H	W	5–3
11 Oct	Bolton W	A	D	2–2
18 Oct	Aston Villa	H	L	0–2
25 Oct	Sunderland	A	L	1–3
1 Nov	Wolverhampton W	H	W	2–1
8 Nov	Charlton A	A	L	2–3
15 Nov	Arsenal	H	L	1–5
22 Nov	Derby County	A	L	2–3
29 Nov	Blackpool	H	D	2–2
13 Dec	Manchester U	H	L	1–2
20 Dec	Preston NE	H	D	2–2
25 Dec	Burnley	A	L	0–2
26 Dec	Burnley	H	D	1–1
3 Jan	Stoke C	A	L	1–3
17 Jan	Manchester C	H	L	0–1
24 Jan	Portsmouth	A	L	1–3
7 Feb	Middlesbrough	A	W	3–2
14 Feb	West Brom	H	W	3–0
21 Feb	Newcastle U	A	W	2–1
4 Mar	Bolton W	H	D	0–0
7 Mar	Aston Villa	A	L	0–4
14 Mar	Sunderland	H	W	2–0
21 Mar	Wolverhampton W	A	L	0–3
23 Mar	Chelsea	A	L	0–3
28 Mar	Charlton A	H	L	1–2
3 Apr	Cardiff C	H	W	2–1
4 Apr	Arsenal	A	L	3–5
6 Apr	Cardiff C	A	L	0–4
11 Apr	Derby County	H	D	1–1
18 Apr	Blackpool	A	L	1–3
20 Apr	Manchester U	A	L	1–3
25 Apr	Chelsea	H	W	2–0

Final League Position

	P	W	D	L	F	A	Pts	
Arsenal	42	21	12	9	97	64	54	1st
Liverpool	42	14	8	20	61	82	36	17th

League Appearances (goals)
A'Court 12 (2) · Anderson 1 · Ashcroft 24
Baron 27 (10) · Bimpson 8 (3) · Brierley 10 (1)
Crossley 18 · Gerhardi 6 · Heydon 23 · Hughes 11
Jackson 5 · Jones M 1 · Jones W 26 (2) · Lambert 36
Liddell 39 (13) · Maloney 6 · Moran 11
Paisley 26 (2) · Payne 33 (7) · Parr 4 · Rowley 11
Saunders 13 · Smith 27 (8) · Smyth 19 (7)
Spicer 28 · Stubbins 5 · Taylor 21 (2)
Williams 11 (4)

FA CUP

10 Jan	Gateshead (3)	A	L	0–1

FA Cup Appearances (goals)
Baron 1 · Crossley 1 · Heydon 1 · Jones M 1
Jones W 1 · Lambert 1 · Liddell 1 · Moran 1
Saunders 1 · Smith 1 · Williams 1

SEASON 1953-54

FOOTBALL LEAGUE (DIVISION 1)

19 Aug	Portsmouth	H	W	3–1
22 Aug	Manchester U	H	D	4–4
26 Aug	Newcastle U	H	D	2–2
29 Aug	Bolton W	A	L	0–2
2 Sep	Newcastle U	A	L	0–4
5 Sep	Preston NE	H	L	1–5
7 Sep	Wolverhampton W	A	L	1–2
12 Sep	Tottenham H	A	L	1–2
16 Sep	Wolverhampton W	H	D	1–1
19 Sep	Burnley	H	W	4–0
26 Sep	Charlton A	A	L	0–6
3 Oct	Sheffield W	H	D	2–2
10 Oct	Aston Villa	H	W	6–1
17 Oct	Huddersfield T	A	L	0–2
24 Oct	Sheffield U	H	W	3–0
31 Oct	Chelsea	A	L	2–5
7 Nov	Manchester C	H	D	2–2
14 Nov	Sunderland	A	L	2–3
21 Nov	Arsenal	H	L	1–2
28 Nov	Cardiff C	A	L	1–3
5 Dec	Blackpool	H	W	5–2
12 Dec	Portsmouth	A	L	1–5
19 Dec	Manchester U	A	L	1–5
25 Dec	West Brom	A	L	2–5
26 Dec	West Brom	H	D	0–0
2 Jan	Bolton W	H	L	1–2
16 Jan	Preston NE	A	L	1–2
23 Jan	Tottenham H	H	D	2–2
6 Feb	Burnley	A	D	1–1
13 Feb	Charlton A	H	L	2–3
24 Feb	Sheffield W	A	D	1–1
27 Feb	Aston Villa	A	L	1–2
6 Mar	Huddersfield T	H	L	1–3
13 Mar	Sheffield U	A	L	1–3
20 Mar	Chelsea	H	D	1–1
3 Apr	Sunderland	H	W	4–3
7 Apr	Manchester C	A	W	2–0
10 Apr	Arsenal	A	L	0–3
16 Apr	Middlesbrough	A	W	1–0
17 Apr	Cardiff C	H	L	0–1
19 Apr	Middlesbrough	H	W	4–1
24 Apr	Blackpool	A	L	0–3

Final League Position

	P	W	D	L	F	A	Pts	
Wolverhampton W	42	25	7	10	96	56	57	1st
Liverpool	42	9	10	23	68	97	28	22nd

League Appearances (goals)
A'Court 16 (3) · Anderson 13 (5) · Arnell 3 (1)
Ashcroft 6 · Baron 17 (4) · Bimpson 24 (13)
Campbell 2 · Childs 2 · Crossley 18 · Evans 16 (5)
Hughes 27 · Jones H 1 · Jones W 25 (6)
Jackson 27 (4) · Lambert 20 (1) · Liddell 36 (6)
Lock 18 · Maloney 6 · Moran 1 · McNulty 12
Paisley 20 (2) · Payne 17 (3) · Rowley 2 (1)
Saunders 19 · Smith 3 · Smyth 26 (13) · Spicer 23
Taylor 6 · Twentyman 20 · Wilkinson 18
Underwood 18 · Own goals (1)

FA CUP

9 Jan	Bolton W	A	L	0–1

FA Cup Appearances (goals)
Crossley 1 · Evans 1 · Hughes 1 · Jackson 1
Jones W 1 · Lambert 1 · Liddell 1 · Lock 1 · Payne 1
Taylor 1 · Wilkinson 1

SEASON 1954-55

FOOTBALL LEAGUE (DIVISION 2)

21 Aug	Doncaster R	H	W	3–2
23 Aug	Plymouth Argyle	A	L	0–1
28 Aug	Derby County	A	L	2–3
1 Sep	Plymouth Argyle	H	D	3–3
4 Sep	West Ham U	H	L	1–2
6 Sep	Bristol R	A	L	0–3
11 Sep	Blackburn R	A	L	3–4
15 Sep	Bristol R	H	W	5–3
18 Sep	Fulham	H	W	4–1
25 Sep	Swansea T	A	L	2–3
2 Oct	Notts County	H	W	3–1
9 Oct	Rotherham U	H	W	3–1
16 Oct	Stoke C	A	L	0–2
23 Oct	Bury	H	D	1–1
30 Oct	Lincoln C	A	D	3–3
6 Nov	Hull C	H	W	2–1
13 Nov	Luton T	A	L	2–3
20 Nov	Nottingham F	H	W	1–0
27 Nov	Leeds U	A	D	2–2
4 Dec	Middlesbrough	H	W	3–1
11 Dec	Birmingham C	A	L	1–9
18 Dec	Doncaster R	A	L	1–4
25 Dec	Ipswich T	H	W	6–2
27 Dec	Ipswich T	A	L	0–2
1 Jan	Derby County	H	W	2–0
22 Jan	Blackburn R	H	W	4–1
5 Feb	Fulham	A	W	2–1
12 Feb	Swansea T	H	D	1–1
3 Mar	Notts County	A	W	3–0
5 Mar	Stoke C	H	L	2–4
12 Mar	Bury	A	W	4–3
19 Mar	Lincoln C	H	L	2–4
26 Mar	Hull C	A	D	2–2
2 Apr	Luton T	H	D	4–4
8 Apr	Port Vale	A	L	3–4
9 Apr	Nottingham F	A	L	1–3
11 Apr	Port Vale	H	D	1–1
16 Apr	Leeds U	H	D	2–2
23 Apr	Middlesbrough	A	W	2–1
26 Apr	West Ham U	A	W	3–0
30 Apr	Birmingham C	H	D	2–2
2 May	Rotherham U	A	L	1–6

Final League Position

	P	W	D	L	F	A	Pts	
Birmingham C	42	22	10	10	92	47	54	1st
Liverpool	42	16	10	16	92	96	42	11th

League Appearances (goals)
A'Court 30 (2) · Anderson 32 (9) · Arnell 7 (3)
Ashcroft 14 · Bimpson 8 (2) · Burkinshaw 1
Campbell 12 · Evans 38 (29) · Hughes 26
Jackson 23 (3) · Lambert 28 · Lock 23
Liddell 40 (30) · McNulty 19 · Moran 17
Payne 17 (2) · Rowley 13 (8) · Rudham 22
Saunders 28 · South 6 (1) · Tomley 2
Twentyman 35 (3) · Underwood 6 · Wilkinson 15

FA CUP

8 Jan	Lincoln C (3)	A	D	1-1
12 Jan	Lincoln C (3R)	H	W	1-0*
29 Jan	Everton (4)	A	W	4-0
19 Feb	Huddersfield T (5)	H	L	0-2

*after extra time

FA Cup Appearances (goals)

A'Court 3 (1) · Anderson 3 · Arnell 1 · Ashcroft 1
Bimpson 1 · Evans 4 (4) · Hughes 3 · Jackson 3
Lambert 4 · Liddell 4 (1) · Moran 4 · Payne 1
Rudham 3 · Saunders 4 · South 1 · Twentyman 4

SEASON 1955-56

FOOTBALL LEAGUE (DIVISION 2)

20 Aug	Nottingham F	A	W	3-1
24 Aug	Sheffield W	H	L	0-3
27 Aug	Hull C	H	W	3-0
31 Aug	Sheffield W	A	D	1-1
3 Sep	Blackburn R	A	D	3-3
7 Sep	Bristol R	H	L	0-2
10 Sep	Lincoln C	H	W	2-1
17 Sep	Leicester C	A	L	1-3
24 Sep	Middlesbrough	H	D	1-1
1 Oct	Plymouth Argyle	H	W	4-1
8 Oct	Bristol C	A	L	1-2
15 Oct	West Ham U	H	W	3-1
22 Oct	Bury	A	W	4-1
29 Oct	Rotherham U	H	W	2-0
5 Nov	Swansea T	A	L	1-2
12 Nov	Notts County	H	W	2-1
19 Nov	Leeds U	A	L	2-4
26 Nov	Fulham	H	W	7-0
3 Dec	Port Vale	A	D	1-1
10 Dec	Burnley	H	D	1-1
17 Dec	Nottingham F	H	W	5-2
24 Dec	Hull C	A	W	2-1
26 Dec	Stoke C	H	D	2-2
27 Dec	Stoke C	A	L	2-3
31 Dec	Blackburn R	H	L	1-2
21 Jan	Leicester C	H	W	3-1
4 Feb	Middlesbrough	A	W	2-1
11 Feb	Plymouth Argyle	A	L	0-4
25 Feb	West Ham U	A	L	1-2
29 Feb	Leeds U	H	W	1-0
3 Mar	Bury	H	W	4-2
10 Mar	Barnsley	A	W	5-0
17 Mar	Swansea T	H	W	4-1
24 Mar	Notts County	A	L	1-2
30 Mar	Doncaster R	A	L	0-1
31 Mar	Bristol C	H	W	2-1
2 Apr	Doncaster R	H	L	1-2
7 Apr	Fulham	A	L	1-3
14 Apr	Port Vale	H	W	4-1
21 Apr	Rotherham U	A	W	1-0
28 Apr	Bristol R	A	W	2-1
2 May	Lincoln C	A	L	0-2

Final League Position

	P	W	D	L	F	A	Pts	
Sheffield W	42	21	13	8	101	62	55	1st
Liverpool	42	21	6	15	85	63	48	3rd

League Appearances (goals)

A'Court 40 (6) · Anderson 20 (6) · Arnell 23 (13)
Bimpson 8 · Dickson 6 (3) · Evans 31 (13)
Hughes 39 · Jackson 15 · Lambert 10
Liddell 39 (28) · Melia 4 (1) · McNulty 1
Molyneux 32 · Moran 39 · Payne 16 (2) · Perry 1
Price 1 · Rowley 7 (6) · Rudham 21 · Saunders 37
Twentyman 42 (7) · Underwood 21 · White 8
Wilkinson 1

FA CUP

7 Jan	Accrington S (3)	H	W	2-0
28 Jan	Scunthorpe U (4)	H	D	3-3
6 Feb	Scunthorpe U (4R)	A	W	2-1*
18 Feb	Manchester C (5)	A	D	0-0
22 Feb	Manchester C (5R)	H	L	1-2

*after extra time

FA Cup Appearances (goals)

A'Court 5 · Arnell 4 (2) · Bimpson 1 · Evans 5
Hughes 5 · Liddell 5 (5) · Molyneux 5 · Moran 5
Payne 5 (1) · Saunders 5 · Twentyman 5
Underwood 5

SEASON 1956-57

FOOTBALL LEAGUE (DIVISION 2)

18 Aug	Huddersfield T	H	L	2-3
23 Aug	Notts County	A	D	1-1
25 Aug	Bury	A	W	2-0
29 Aug	Notts County	H	D	3-3
1 Sep	Grimsby T	H	W	3-2
3 Sep	West Ham U	A	D	1-1
8 Sep	Doncaster R	A	D	1-1
15 Sep	Stoke C	H	L	0-2
22 Sep	Middlesbrough	A	D	1-1
29 Sep	Leicester C	H	W	2-0
6 Oct	Blackburn R	H	L	2-3
13 Oct	Bristol C	A	L	1-2
20 Oct	Fulham	H	W	4-3
27 Oct	Barnsley	A	L	1-4
3 Nov	Port Vale	H	W	4-1
10 Nov	Rotherham U	A	D	2-2
17 Nov	Lincoln C	H	W	4-0
24 Nov	Swansea T	A	D	1-1
1 Dec	Sheffield U	H	W	5-1
8 Dec	Nottingham F	A	L	0-1
15 Dec	Huddersfield T	A	W	3-0
22 Dec	Bury	H	W	2-0
25 Dec	Leyton Orient	H	W	1-0
26 Dec	Leyton Orient	A	W	4-0
29 Dec	Grimsby T	A	D	0-0
12 Jan	Doncaster R	H	W	2-1
19 Jan	Stoke C	A	L	0-1
2 Feb	Middlesbrough	H	L	1-2
9 Feb	Leicester C	A	L	2-3
16 Feb	Blackburn R	A	D	2-2
2 Mar	Fulham	A	W	2-1
9 Mar	Barnsley	H	W	2-1
16 Mar	Port Vale	A	W	2-1
23 Mar	Rotherham U	H	W	4-1
30 Mar	Lincoln C	A	D	3-3
6 Apr	Swansea T	H	W	2-0
13 Apr	Sheffield U	A	L	0-3
19 Apr	Bristol R	H	W	4-1
20 Apr	Nottingham F	H	W	3-1
22 Apr	Bristol R	A	D	0-0
27 Apr	West Ham U	H	W	1-0
1 May	Bristol C	H	W	2-1

Final League Position

	P	W	D	L	F	A	Pts	
Leicester C	42	25	11	6	109	67	61	1st
Liverpool	42	21	11	10	82	54	53	3rd

League Appearances (goals)

A'Court 38 (10) · Anderson 7 (1) · Arnell 14 (10)
Bimpson 21 (6) · Campbell 6 (1) · Evans 11 (2)
Hughes 41 · Jackson 19 (2) · Liddell 41 (21)
McNulty 2 · Melia 26 (6) · Molyneux 40 · Moran 42
Rowley 14 (7) · Rudham 2 · Saunders 27 (1)
Twentyman 30 (3) · Wheeler 28 (10) · White 5
Wilkinson 8 · Younger 40

FA CUP

5 Jan	Southend U (3)	A	L	1-2

FA Cup Appearances (goals)

A'Court 1 · Arnell 1 · Hughes 1 · Liddell 1 · Melia 1
Molyneux 1 · Moran 1 · Saunders 1 · Twentyman 1
Wheeler 1 (1) · Younger 1

SEASON 1957-58

FOOTBALL LEAGUE (DIVISION 2)

24 Aug	Bristol C	A	W	2-1
28 Aug	Huddersfield T	H	D	1-1
31 Aug	Cardiff C	H	W	3-0
4 Sep	Huddersfield T	A	L	1-2
7 Sep	Fulham	A	D	2-2
14 Sep	Middlesbrough	A	D	2-2
19 Sep	Rotherham U	A	D	2-2
21 Sep	Leyton Orient	H	W	3-0
23 Sep	Stoke C	A	W	2-1
28 Sep	Charlton A	A	L	1-5
5 Oct	Doncaster R	H	W	5-0
12 Oct	Swansea T	H	W	4-0
19 Oct	Derby County	A	L	1-2
26 Oct	Bristol R	H	W	2-0
2 Nov	Lincoln C	A	W	1-0
9 Nov	Notts County	H	W	4-0
16 Nov	Ipswich T	A	L	1-3
23 Nov	Blackburn R	H	W	2-0
27 Nov	Rotherham U	H	W	2-0
30 Nov	Sheffield U	A	D	1-1
7 Dec	West Ham U	H	D	1-1
14 Dec	Barnsley	A	L	1-2
21 Dec	Bristol C	H	W	4-3
25 Dec	Grimsby T	A	L	1-3
26 Dec	Grimsby T	H	W	3-2

■ The Liverpool playing squad in season 1957-58, when Bob Paisley had stepped up to become the club's chief coach. Liverpool were still in the Second Division, but the arrival of Bill Shankly the following year was to bring about a change in the club's fortunes.

28 Dec	Cardiff C	A	L	1–6
11 Jan	Fulham	H	W	2–1
18 Jan	Middlesbrough	H	L	0–2
1 Feb	Leyton Orient	A	L	0–1
8 Feb	Charlton A	H	W	3–1
19 Feb	Doncaster R	A	D	1–1
22 Feb	Blackburn R	A	D	3–3
5 Mar	Derby County	H	W	2–0
8 Mar	Bristol R	A	L	1–3
15 Mar	Lincoln C	H	W	1–0
22 Mar	Notts County	A	W	2–0
29 Mar	Ipswich T	H	W	3–1
5 Apr	Swansea T	A	W	2–0
7 Apr	Stoke C	H	W	3–0
12 Apr	Sheffield U	H	W	1–0
19 Apr	West Ham U	A	D	1–1
26 Apr	Barnsley	H	D	1–1

Final League Position

	P	W	D	L	F	A	Pts	
West Ham U	42	23	11	8	101	54	57	1st
Liverpool	42	22	10	10	79	54	54	4th

League Appearances (goals)

A'Court 40 (6) · Arnell 8 (1) · Bimpson 6 (4) · Byrne 1 · Campbell D 27 (1) · Harrower 12 (2) · Hughes 1 · Jackson 21 (2) · Liddell 35 (22) · McNamara 10 (3) · McNulty 2 · Melia 35 (10) · Molyneux 40 · Moran 41 · Morrissey 2 · Murdoch 15 (5) · Rowley 24 (16) · Rudham 3 · Saunders 4 · Twentyman 7 (1) · Wheeler 38 (5) · White 41 · Wilkinson 10 · Younger 39

FA CUP

4 Jan	Southend U (3)	H	D	1–1
8 Jan	Southend U (3R)	A	W	3–2
25 Jan	Northampton T (4)	H	W	3–1
15 Feb	Scunthorpe U (5)	A	W	1–0
1 Mar	Blackburn R (6)	A	L	1–2

FA Cup Appearances (goals)

A'Court 5 · Bimpson 3 (1) · Campbell D 1 · Harrower 2 · Jackson 2 · Liddell 5 (1) · McNamara 1 · Melia 2 · Molyneux 5 (1) · Moran 5 · Murdoch 2 (2) · Rowley 3 (1) · Saunders 1 · Twentyman 3 · Wheeler 5 · White 5 (1) · Younger 5 · Own goals (2)

SEASON 1958-59

FOOTBALL LEAGUE (DIVISION 2)

23 Aug	Grimsby T	H	D	3–3
30 Aug	Sunderland	A	L	1–2
3 Sep	Brighton & HA	H	W	5–0
6 Sep	Middlesbrough	A	L	1–2
10 Sep	Sheffield U	H	W	2–1
13 Sep	Charlton A	H	W	3–0
15 Sep	Sheffield U	A	L	0–2
20 Sep	Bristol C	A	W	3–1
24 Sep	Brighton & HA	A	D	2–2
27 Sep	Cardiff C	H	L	1–2
4 Oct	Huddersfield T	A	L	0–5
11 Oct	Lincoln C	H	W	3–2
18 Oct	Fulham	A	W	1–0
25 Oct	Sheffield W	H	W	3–2
1 Nov	Stoke C	A	W	2–0
8 Nov	Leyton Orient	H	W	3–0
15 Nov	Derby County	A	L	2–3
22 Nov	Bristol R	H	W	2–1
29 Nov	Ipswich T	A	L	0–2
6 Dec	Swansea T	H	W	4–0
13 Dec	Scunthorpe U	A	W	2–1
20 Dec	Grimsby T	A	W	3–2
26 Dec	Rotherham U	A	W	1–0
27 Dec	Rotherham U	H	W	4–0
3 Jan	Sunderland	H	W	3–1
31 Jan	Charlton A	A	W	3–2
7 Feb	Bristol C	H	W	3–2
14 Feb	Cardiff C	A	L	0–3
21 Feb	Huddersfield T	H	D	2–2
28 Feb	Leyton Orient	A	W	3–1
7 Mar	Fulham	H	D	0–0
20 Mar	Stoke C	H	L	3–4
27 Mar	Barnsley	H	W	3–2
28 Mar	Lincoln C	A	L	1–2
30 Mar	Barnsley	A	W	2–0
4 Apr	Derby County	H	W	3–0
8 Apr	Middlesbrough	H	L	1–2
11 Apr	Bristol R	A	L	0–3
14 Apr	Sheffield W	A	L	0–1
18 Apr	Ipswich T	H	W	3–1
22 Apr	Scunthorpe U	H	W	3–0
25 Apr	Swansea T	A	D	3–3

Final League Position

	P	W	D	L	F	A	Pts	
Sheffield W	42	28	6	8	106	48	62	1st
Liverpool	42	24	5	13	87	62	53	4th

League Appearances (goals)

A'Court 39 (7) · Arnell 12 (5) · Banks 3 (2) · Bimpson 15 (11) · Byrne 1 · Campbell D 10 (1) · Harrower 37 (6) · Liddell 19 (14) · Melia 39 (21) · Morris 40 (12) · Moran 40 · Molyneux 37 (1) · Morrissey 2 · Murdoch 2 · Rudham 1 · Saunders 4 · Twentyman 25 (4) · Wheeler 41 (1) · White 42 · Wilkinson 12 · Younger 41 · Own goals (2)

FA CUP

15 Jan	Worcester C (3)	A	L	1–2

FA Cup Appearances (goals)

A'Court 1 · Bimpson 1 · Harrower 1 · Melia 1 · Molyneux 1 · Moran 1 · Morris 1 · Wheeler 1 · White 1 · Twentyman 1 (1) · Younger 1

SEASON 1959-60

FOOTBALL LEAGUE (DIVISION 2)

22 Aug	Cardiff C	A	L	2–3
26 Aug	Bristol C	H	W	4–2
29 Aug	Hull C	H	W	5–3
1 Sep	Bristol C	A	L	0–1
5 Sep	Sheffield U	A	L	1–2
9 Sep	Scunthorpe U	H	W	2–0
12 Sep	Middlesbrough	H	L	1–2
17 Sep	Scunthorpe U	A	D	1–1
19 Sep	Derby County	A	W	2–1
26 Sep	Plymouth Argyle	H	W	4–1
3 Oct	Swansea T	A	L	4–5
10 Oct	Brighton & HA	H	D	2–2
17 Oct	Stoke C	A	D	1–1
24 Oct	Portsmouth	H	D	1–1
31 Oct	Sunderland	A	D	1–1
7 Nov	Aston Villa	H	W	2–1
14 Nov	Lincoln C	A	L	2–4
21 Nov	Leyton Orient	H	W	4–3
28 Nov	Huddersfield T	A	L	0–1
5 Dec	Ipswich T	H	W	3–1
12 Dec	Bristol R	A	W	2–0
19 Dec	Cardiff C	H	L	0–4
26 Dec	Charlton A	A	L	0–3
28 Dec	Charlton A	H	W	2–0
1 Jan	Hull C	A	W	1–0
16 Jan	Sheffield U	H	W	3–0
23 Jan	Middlesbrough	A	D	3–3
13 Feb	Plymouth Argyle	A	D	1–1
20 Feb	Swansea T	H	W	4–1
27 Feb	Brighton & HA	A	W	2–1
5 Mar	Stoke C	H	W	5–1
12 Mar	Portsmouth	A	L	1–2
19 Mar	Huddersfield T	H	D	2–2
30 Mar	Aston Villa	A	D	4–4
2 Apr	Lincoln C	H	L	1–3
6 Apr	Derby County	H	W	4–1
9 Apr	Leyton Orient	A	L	0–2
16 Apr	Bristol R	H	W	4–0
18 Apr	Rotherham U	H	W	3–0
19 Apr	Rotherham U	A	D	2–2
23 Apr	Ipswich T	A	W	1–0
30 Apr	Sunderland	H	W	3–0

Final League Position

	P	W	D	L	F	A	Pts	
Aston Villa	42	25	9	8	89	43	59	1st
Liverpool	42	20	10	12	90	66	50	3rd

League Appearances (goals)

A'Court 42 (8) · Arnell 1 · Bimpson 5 · Blore 1 · Byrne 5 · Callaghan 4 · Campbell D 13 (1) · Carlin 1 · Harrower 26 (5) · Hickson 27 (21) · Hunt 36 (21) · Jones A 1 · Leishman 15 · Liddell 17 (5) · Melia 34 (14) · Molyneux 38 (1) · Moran 42 (5) · Morris 7 (2) · Morrissey 9 (1) · Nicholson 1 · Rudham 14 · Slater 28 · Twentyman 11 · Wheeler 29 (2) · White 41 · Wilkinson 14 · Own goals (4)

FA CUP

9 Jan	Leyton Orient (3)	H	W	2–1
30 Jan	Manchester U (4)	H	L	1–3

FA Cup Appearances (goals)

A'Court 2 · Harrower 2 · Hickson 2 · Hunt 2 (2) · Leishman 2 · Melia 2 · Molyneux 2 · Moran 2 · Slater 2 · Wheeler 2 (1) · White 2

SEASON 1960-61

FOOTBALL LEAGUE (DIVISION 2)

20 Aug	Leeds U	H	W	2–0
24 Aug	Southampton	A	L	1–4
27 Aug	Middlesbrough	A	D	1–1
31 Aug	Southampton	H	L	0–1
3 Sep	Brighton & HA	H	W	2–0
7 Sep	Luton T	H	D	2–2
10 Sep	Ipswich T	A	L	0–1
14 Sep	Luton T	A	L	1–2
17 Sep	Scunthorpe U	H	W	3–2
24 Sep	Leyton Orient	A	W	3–1
1 Oct	Derby County	H	W	1–0
8 Oct	Lincoln C	A	W	2–1
15 Oct	Portsmouth	H	D	3–3
22 Oct	Huddersfield T	A	W	4–2
29 Oct	Sunderland	H	D	1–1
5 Nov	Plymouth Argyle	A	W	4–0
12 Nov	Norwich C	H	W	2–1
19 Nov	Charlton A	A	W	3–1
26 Nov	Sheffield U	H	W	4–2
10 Dec	Swansea T	H	W	4–0
17 Dec	Leeds U	A	D	2–2
26 Dec	Rotherham U	H	W	2–1
27 Dec	Rotherham U	A	L	0–1
31 Dec	Middlesbrough	H	L	3–4
14 Jan	Brighton & HA	A	L	1–3
21 Jan	Ipswich T	H	D	1–1
4 Feb	Scunthorpe U	A	W	3–2
11 Feb	Leyton Orient	H	W	5–0
18 Feb	Derby County	A	W	4–1
25 Feb	Lincoln C	H	W	2–0
4 Mar	Portsmouth	A	D	2–2
11 Mar	Huddersfield T	H	W	3–1
18 Mar	Swansea T	A	L	0–2
24 Mar	Plymouth Argyle	H	D	1–1
31 Mar	Bristol R	H	W	3–0
1 Apr	Sheffield U	A	D	1–1
4 Apr	Bristol R	A	L	3–4
8 Apr	Charlton A	H	W	2–1
15 Apr	Norwich C	A	L	1–2
22 Apr	Stoke C	H	W	3–0
29 Apr	Sunderland	A	D	1–1
3 May	Stoke C	A	L	1–3

Final League Position

	P	W	D	L	F	A	Pts	
Ipswich T	42	26	7	9	100	55	59	1st
Liverpool	42	21	10	11	87	58	52	3rd

League Appearances (goals)

A'Court 33 (7) · Arnell 1 · Banks 5 (4) · Byrne 33 · Callaghan 3 · Campbell R 1 · Harrower 21 (8) · Hickson 33 (16) · Hunt 32 (15) · Leishman 40 (4) · Lewis 32 (19) · Liddell 1 · Melia 26 (3) · Milne 16 · Molyneux 39 · Moran 12 (2) · Morrissey 23 (5) · Slater 42 · Wheeler 27 (3) · White 42

FA CUP

7 Jan	Coventry C (3)	H	W	3–2
28 Jan	Sunderland (4)	H	L	0–2

FA Cup Appearances (goals)

A'Court 2 · Byrne 2 · Harrower 1 (1) · Hickson 2 · Hunt 1 (1) · Leishman 2 · Lewis 2 (1) · Melia 1 · Milne 1 · Molyneux 2 · Morrissey 1 · Slater 2 · Wheeler 1 · White 2

LEAGUE CUP

19 Oct	Luton T (2)	H	D	1–1
24 Oct	Luton T (2R)	A	W	5–2
16 Nov	Southampton (3)	H	L	1–2

League Cup Appearances (goals)

A'Court 2 · Byrne 3 · Callaghan 2 · Harrower 3 · Hickson 3 (1) · Hunt 3 (3) · Leishman 3 (1) · Lewis 2 (2) · Molyneux 3 · Slater 3 · Wheeler 3 · White 3

SEASON 1961-62

FOOTBALL LEAGUE (DIVISION 2)

19 Aug	Bristol R	A	W	2–0
23 Aug	Sunderland	H	W	3–0
26 Aug	Leeds U	H	W	5–0
30 Aug	Sunderland	A	W	4–1
2 Sep	Norwich C	A	W	2–1
9 Sep	Scunthorpe U	H	W	2–1
16 Sep	Brighton & HA	A	D	0–0
20 Sep	Newcastle U	A	W	2–1
23 Sep	Bury	H	W	5–0
30 Sep	Charlton A	A	W	4–0
4 Oct	Newcastle U	H	W	2–0
7 Oct	Middlesbrough	A	L	0–2
14 Oct	Walsall	H	W	6–1
21 Oct	Derby County	A	L	0–2
28 Oct	Leyton Orient	H	D	3–3
4 Nov	Preston NE	A	W	3–1
11 Nov	Luton T	H	D	1–1
18 Nov	Huddersfield T	A	W	2–1
25 Nov	Swansea T	H	W	5–0
2 Dec	Southampton	A	L	0–2
9 Dec	Plymouth Argyle	H	W	2–1
16 Dec	Bristol R	H	W	2–0
23 Dec	Leeds U	A	L	0–1
26 Dec	Rotherham U	A	L	0–1
13 Jan	Norwich C	H	W	5–4
20 Jan	Scunthorpe U	A	D	1–1
3 Feb	Brighton & HA	H	W	3–1
10 Feb	Bury	A	W	3–0
24 Feb	Middlesbrough	H	W	5–1
3 Mar	Walsall	A	D	1–1
10 Mar	Derby County	H	W	4–1
17 Mar	Leyton Orient	A	D	2–2
24 Mar	Preston NE	H	W	4–1
28 Mar	Rotherham U	H	W	4–1
31 Mar	Luton T	A	L	0–1
7 Apr	Huddersfield T	H	D	1–1
21 Apr	Southampton	H	W	2–0
23 Apr	Stoke C	H	W	2–1
24 Apr	Stoke C	A	D	0–0
28 Apr	Plymouth Argyle	A	W	3–2
30 Apr	Charlton A	H	W	2–1
4 May	Swansea T	A	L	2–4

■ **This was the team which brought Liverpool promotion in season 1961-62.** ***Back row:*** **Ronnie Moran, Gordon Milne, Tommy Lawrence, Ron Yeats, Gerry Byrne, Willie Stevenson.** ***Front row:*** **Ian Callaghan, Roger Hunt, Ian St John, Jimmy Melia and Kevin Lewis.**

Final League Position

	P	W	D	L	F	A	Pts	
Liverpool	42	27	8	7	99	43	62	1st

League Appearances (goals)

A'Court 42 (8) · Arrowsmith 1 · Byrne 42 (1) · Callaghan 24 (1) · Furnell 13 · Hunt 41 (41) · Leishman 41 (1) · Lewis 20 (10) · Melia 42 (12) · Milne 42 (2) · Moran 16 (1) · Molyneux 3 · Slater 29 · St John 40 (18) · Wheeler 1 · White 24 · Yeats 41 · Own goals (4)

FA CUP

6 Jan	Chelsea (3)	H	W	4–3
27 Jan	Oldham A (4)	A	W	2–1
17 Feb	Preston NE (5)	H	D	0–0
20 Feb	Preston NE (5R)	A	D	0–0*
26 Feb	Preston NE (5R) (Old Trafford)	N	L	0–1

*after extra time

FA Cup Appearances (goals)

A'Court 5 (1) · Byrne 5 · Callaghan 5 · Hunt 5 (1) · Leishman 5 · Melia 5 · Milne 5 · Moran 3 · Molyneux 1 · Slater 5 · St John 5 (4) · White 1 · Yeats 5

SEASON 1962-63

FOOTBALL LEAGUE (DIVISION 1)

18 Aug	Blackpool	H	L	1–2
22 Aug	Manchester C	A	D	2–2
26 Aug	Blackburn R	A	L	0–1
29 Aug	Manchester C	H	W	4–1
1 Sep	Sheffield U	H	W	2–0
3 Sep	West Ham U	A	L	0–1
8 Sep	Nottingham F	A	L	1–3
12 Sep	West Ham U	H	W	2–1
15 Sep	Ipswich T	H	D	1–1
22 Sep	Everton	A	D	2–2
29 Sep	Wolverhampton W	A	L	2–3
6 Oct	Bolton W	H	W	1–0
13 Oct	Leicester C	A	L	0–3
27 Oct	West Brom	A	L	0–1
3 Nov	Burnley	H	L	1–2
10 Nov	Manchester U	A	D	3–3
14 Nov	Arsenal	H	W	2–1
17 Nov	Leyton Orient	H	W	5–0
24 Nov	Birmingham C	A	W	2–0
1 Dec	Fulham	H	W	2–1
8 Dec	Sheffield W	A	W	2–0
15 Dec	Blackpool	A	W	2–1
22 Dec	Blackburn R	H	W	3–1
13 Feb	Aston Villa	H	W	4–0
16 Feb	Wolverhampton W	H	W	4–1
2 Mar	Leicester C	H	L	0–2
5 Mar	Ipswich T	A	D	2–2
9 Mar	Arsenal	A	D	2–2
20 Mar	West Brom	H	D	2–2
23 Mar	Burnley	A	W	3–1
8 Apr	Everton	H	D	0–0
12 Apr	Tottenham H	H	W	5–2
13 Apr	Manchester U	H	W	1–0
15 Apr	Tottenham H	A	L	2–7
18 Apr	Nottingham F	H	L	0–2
20 Apr	Fulham	A	D	0–0
29 Apr	Sheffield W	H	L	0–2
2 May	Leyton Orient	A	L	1–2
8 May	Birmingham C	H	W	5–1
11 May	Sheffield U	A	D	0–0
13 May	Bolton W	A	L	0–1
18 May	Aston Villa	A	L	0–2

Final League Position

	P	W	D	L	F	A	Pts	
Everton	42	25	11	6	84	42	61	1st
Liverpool	42	17	10	15	71	59	44	8th

League Appearances (goals)
A'Court 23 (2) · Arrowsmith 3 · Byrne 38
Callaghan 37 (2) · Ferns 5 · Furnell 13 · Hunt 42 (24)
Jones 4 · Lawler 6 · Lawrence 29 · Leishman 11 (1)
Lewis 19 (10) · Melia 39 (5) · Milne 41
Moran 34 (5) · Smith 1 · Stevenson 28 (2)
St John 40 (19) · Thomson 4 · Wallace 7 (1)
Yeats 38

FA CUP

9 Jan	Wrexham (3)	A	W	3–0
26 Jan	Burnley (4)	A	D	1–1
21 Feb	Burnley (4R)	H	W	2–1*
16 Mar	Arsenal (5)	A	W	2–1
30 Mar	West Ham U (6)	H	W	1–0
27 Apr	Leicester C (SF)	N	L	0–1

(Hillsborough)
*after extra time

FA Cup Appearances (goals)
Byrne 6 · Callaghan 6 · Hunt 6 (2) · Lawler 1
Lawrence 6 · Lewis 6 (2) · Melia 5 (2) · Milne 6
Moran 6 (2) · Stevenson 6 · St John 6 (1) · Yeats 6

SEASON 1963-64

FOOTBALL LEAGUE (DIVISION 1)

24 Aug	Blackburn R	A	W	2–1
28 Aug	Nottingham F	H	L	1–2
31 Aug	Blackpool	H	L	1–2
3 Sep	Nottingham F	A	D	0–0
7 Sep	Chelsea	A	W	3–1
9 Sep	Wolverhampton W	A	W	3–1
14 Sep	West Ham U	H	L	1–2
16 Sep	Wolverhampton W	H	W	6–0
21 Sep	Sheffield U	A	L	0–3
28 Sep	Everton	H	W	2–1
5 Oct	Aston Villa	H	W	5–2
9 Oct	Sheffield W	H	W	3–1
19 Oct	West Brom	H	W	1–0
26 Oct	Ipswich T	A	W	2–1
2 Nov	Leicester C	H	L	0–1
9 Nov	Bolton W	A	W	2–1
16 Nov	Fulham	H	W	2–0
23 Nov	Manchester U	A	W	1–0

30 Nov	Burnley	H	W	2–0
7 Dec	Arsenal	A	D	1–1
14 Dec	Blackburn R	H	L	1–2
21 Dec	Blackpool	A	W	1–0
26 Dec	Stoke C	H	W	6–1
11 Jan	Chelsea	H	W	2–1
18 Jan	West Ham U	A	L	0–1
1 Feb	Sheffield U	H	W	6–1
8 Feb	Everton	A	L	1–3
19 Feb	Aston Villa	A	D	2–2
22 Feb	Birmingham C	H	W	2–1
4 Mar	Sheffield W	A	D	2–2
7 Mar	Ipswich T	H	W	6–0
14 Mar	Fulham	A	L	0–1
20 Mar	Bolton W	H	W	2–0
27 Mar	Tottenham H	A	W	3–1
28 Mar	Leicester C	A	W	2–0
30 Mar	Tottenham H	H	W	3–1
4 Apr	Manchester U	H	W	3–0
14 Apr	Burnley	A	W	3–0
18 Apr	Arsenal	H	W	5–0
22 Apr	Birmingham C	A	L	1–3
25 Apr	West Brom	A	D	2–2
29 Apr	Stoke C	A	L	1–3

Final League Position

	P	W	D	L	F	A	Pts
Liverpool	42	26	5	11	92	45	57	1st

League Appearances (goals)
Arrowsmith 20 (15) · Byrne 33 · Callaghan 42 (8)
Ferns 18 · Furnell 2 · Hunt 41 (31) · Lawler 6
Lawrence 40 · Melia 24 (4) · Milne 42 (3)
Moran 35 (1) · Stevenson 38 (1) · St John 40 (21)
Thompson 42 (6) · Thomson 2 · Wallace 1
Yeats 36 (1) · Own goals (1)

FA CUP

4 Jan	Derby County (3)	H	W	5–0
25 Jan	Port Vale (4)	H	D	0–0
27 Jan	Port Vale (4R)	A	W	2–1*
15 Feb	Arsenal (5)	A	W	1–0
29 Feb	Swansea T (6)	H	L	1–2

*after extra time

FA Cup Appearances (goals)
Arrowsmith 4 (4) · Byrne 4 · Callaghan 5 · Ferns 1
Hunt 5 (2) · Lawrence 5 · Melia 1 · Milne 5 · Moran 4

Stevenson 5 · St John 5 (1) · Thompson 5 (2)
Thomson 1 · Yeats 5

SEASON 1964-65

FOOTBALL LEAGUE (DIVISION 1)

22 Aug	Arsenal	H	W	3–2
26 Aug	Leeds U	A	L	2–4
29 Aug	Blackburn R	A	L	2–3
2 Sep	Leeds U	H	W	2–1
5 Sep	Blackpool	H	W	2–1
9 Sep	Leicester C	A	L	0–2
12 Sep	Sheffield W	A	L	0–1
19 Sep	Everton	H	L	1–4
26 Sep	Aston Villa	H	W	5–1
7 Oct	Sheffield U	A	W	3–1
10 Oct	Birmingham C	A	D	0–0
13 Oct	Leicester C	H	L	0–1
17 Oct	West Ham U	H	D	2–2
24 Oct	West Brom	A	L	0–3
31 Oct	Manchester U	H	L	0–2
7 Nov	Fulham	A	D	1–1
14 Nov	Nottingham F	H	W	2–0
21 Nov	Stoke C	A	D	1–1
28 Nov	Tottenham H	H	D	1–1
5 Dec	Burnley	A	W	5–1
12 Dec	Arsenal	A	D	0–0
19 Dec	Blackburn R	H	W	3–2
26 Dec	Sunderland	A	W	3–2
28 Dec	Sunderland	H	D	0–0
2 Jan	Blackpool	A	W	3–2
16 Jan	Sheffield W	H	W	4–2
6 Feb	Aston Villa	A	W	1–0
13 Feb	Wolverhampton W	H	W	2–1
24 Feb	Birmingham C	H	W	4–3
27 Feb	West Ham U	A	L	1–2
13 Mar	Sheffield U	A	L	0–3
20 Mar	Fulham	H	W	3–2
1 Apr	Nottingham F	A	D	2–2
3 Apr	Stoke C	H	W	3–2
6 Apr	West Brom	A	L	0–3
9 Apr	Tottenham H	A	L	0–3
12 Apr	Everton	A	L	1–2
16 Apr	Chelsea	A	L	0–4

17 Apr	Burnley	H	D	1–1
19 Apr	Chelsea	H	W	2–0
24 Apr	Manchester U	A	L	0–3
26 Apr	Wolverhampton W	A	W	3–1

Final League Position

	P	W	D	L	F	A	Pts
Manchester U	42	26	9	7	89	39	61	1st
Liverpool	42	17	10	15	67	73	44	7th

League Appearances (goals)
Arrowsmith 7 (1) · Byrne 40 · Callaghan 37 (6)
Chisnall 6 (1) · Ferns 4 (1) · Graham 14 (4)
Hignett 1 · Hunt 40 (25) · Lawler 33 (2)
Lawrence 41 · Lowry 1 · Milne 34 (5) · Molyneux 1
Moran 13 · Sealey 1 (1) · Smith 25 (4)
St John 27 (3) · Stevenson 39 (3) · Strong 13 (3)
Thompson 39 (5) · Wallace 11 (2) · Yeats 35

FA CUP

9 Jan	West Brom (3)	A	W	2–1
30 Jan	Stockport County (4)	H	D	1–1
3 Feb	Stockport County (4R)	A	W	2–0
20 Feb	Bolton W (5)	A	W	1–0
6 Mar	Leicester C (6)	A	D	0–0
10 Mar	Leicester C (6R)	H	W	1–0
27 Mar	Chelsea (SF)	N	W	2–0

(Villa Park)

1 May	Leeds U (F)	N	W	2–1*

(Wembley)
*after extra time

FA Cup Appearances (goals)
Arrowsmith 1 · Byrne 8 · Callaghan 8 (1) · Hunt 8 (5)
Lawler 8 · Lawrence 8 · Milne 6 (1) · Smith 8
Stevenson 8 (1) · St John 8 (2) · Strong 1
Thompson 8 (1) · Yeats 8

EUROPEAN CUP

17 Aug	Reykjavik (P)	A	W	5–0
14 Sep	Reykjavik (P)	H	W	6–1
25 Nov	Anderlecht (1)	H	W	3–0
16 Dec	Anderlecht (1)	A	W	1–0
10 Feb	FC Cologne (2)	A	D	0–0
17 Mar	FC Cologne (2)	H	D	0–0
24 Mar	FC Cologne (PO)	N	D	2–2*

(Rotterdam)

4 May	Inter Milan (SF)	H	W	3–1

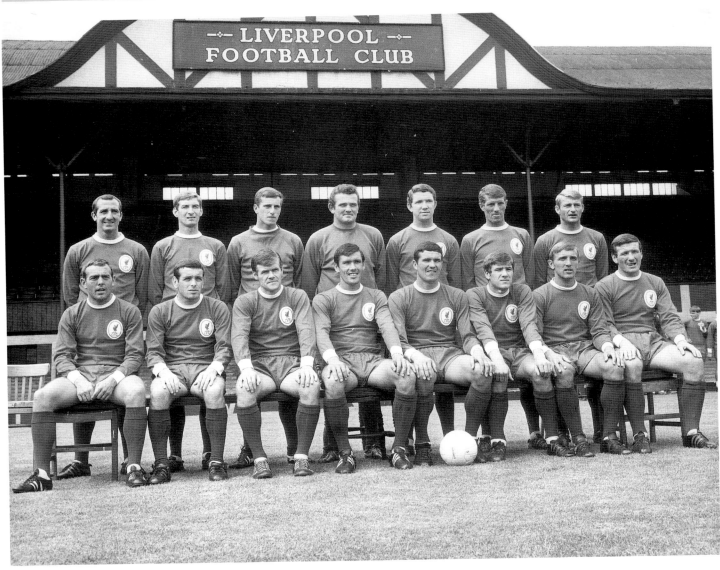

12 May	Inter Milan (SF)	A	L	0–3

*Liverpool won on toss of disc

European Appearances (goals)
A'Court 1 · Byrne 7 (1) · Callaghan 9 (1) ·
Chisnall 1 (1) · Graham 1 (1) · Hunt 9 (7) · Lawler 7 ·
Lawrence 9 · Milne 7 · Moran 4 · Smith 7 ·
Stevenson 9 (1) · St John 8 (5) · Strong 2 ·
Thompson 8 · Wallace 1 (2) · Yeats 9 (1)

SEASON 1965-66

FOOTBALL LEAGUE (DIVISION 1)

21 Aug	Leicester C	A	W	3–1
25 Aug	Sheffield U	H	L	0–1
1 Sep	Sheffield U	A	D	0–0
4 Sep	Blackpool	A	W	3–2
6 Sep	West Ham U	A	W	5–1
11 Sep	Fulham	H	W	2–1
15 Sep	West Ham U	H	D	1–1
18 Sep	Tottenham H	A	L	1–2
25 Sep	Everton	H	W	5–0
2 Oct	Aston Villa	H	W	3–1
9 Oct	Manchester U	A	L	0–2
16 Oct	Newcastle U	H	W	2–0
23 Oct	West Brom	A	L	0–3
30 Oct	Nottingham F	H	W	4–0
6 Nov	Sheffield W	A	W	2–0
13 Nov	Northampton T	H	W	5–0
17 Nov	Blackburn R	H	W	5–2
20 Nov	Stoke C	A	D	0–0
27 Nov	Burnley	H	W	2–1
4 Dec	Chelsea	A	W	1–0
11 Dec	Arsenal	H	W	4–2

18 Dec	Newcastle U	A	D	0–0
27 Dec	Leeds U	H	L	0–1
28 Dec	Leeds U	A	W	1–0
1 Jan	Manchester U	H	W	2–1
8 Jan	Arsenal	A	W	1–0
15 Jan	West Brom	H	D	2–2
29 Jan	Leicester C	H	W	1–0
5 Feb	Blackburn R	A	W	4–1
12 Feb	Sunderland	H	W	4–0
19 Feb	Blackpool	H	W	4–1
26 Feb	Fulham	A	L	0–2
12 Mar	Tottenham H	H	W	1–0
19 Mar	Everton	A	D	0–0
26 Mar	Aston Villa	A	W	3–0
6 Apr	Sheffield W	H	W	1–0
9 Apr	Northampton T	A	D	0–0
11 Apr	Sunderland	A	D	2–2
16 Apr	Stoke C	H	W	2–0
23 Apr	Burnley	A	L	0–2
30 Apr	Chelsea	H	W	2–1
10 May	Nottingham F	A	D	1–1

Final League Position

	P	W	D	L	F	A	Pts	
Liverpool	42	26	9	7	79	34	61	1st

League Appearances (goals)
Arrowsmith 5 (1) · Byrne 42 (1) · Callaghan 42 (5) ·
Graham 1 · Hunt 37 (30) · Lawler 40 (5) ·
Lawrence 42 · Milne 28 (7) · Smith 42 (3) ·
Stevenson 41 · St John 41 (10) · Strong 22 (5) ·
Thompson 40 (5) · Yeats 42 (2)

FA CUP

22 Jan	Chelsea (3)	H	L	1–2

FA Cup Appearances (goals)
Byrne 1 · Callaghan 1 · Hunt 1 (1) · Lawler 1 ·
Lawrence 1 · Milne 1 · Smith 1 · Stevenson 1 ·
St John 1 · Thompson 1 · Yeats 1

EUROPEAN CUP-WINNERS' CUP

29 Sep	Juventus (P)	A	L	0–1
13 Oct	Juventus (P)	H	W	2–0
1 Dec	Standard Liege (1)	H	W	3–1
15 Dec	Standard Liege (1)	A	W	2–1
1 Mar	Honved (2)	A	D	0–0
8 Mar	Honved (2)	H	W	2–0
14 Apr	Celtic (SF)	A	L	0–1
19 Apr	Celtic (SF)	H	W	2–0
5 May	Borussia Dortmund (F)	N	L	1–2*

(Hampden Park)
*after extra time

European Appearances (goals)
Arrowsmith 1 · Byrne 9 · Callaghan 9 · Chisnall 1 ·
Hunt 7 (2) · Lawler 8 (4) · Lawrence 9 · Milne 6 ·
Smith 9 (1) · Stevenson 9 · St John 9 (2) ·
Strong 4 (2) · Thompson 9 (1) · Yeats 9

SEASON 1966-67

FOOTBALL LEAGUE (DIVISION 1)

20 Aug	Leicester C	H	W	3–2
24 Aug	Manchester C	A	L	1–2
27 Aug	Everton	A	L	1–3
30 Aug	Manchester C	H	W	3–2
3 Sep	West Ham U	A	D	1–1
5 Sep	Blackpool	A	W	2–1
10 Sep	Sheffield W	H	D	1–1

■ The men who served Liverpool so well during the 1960s, as Bill Shankly steered the club to Championships and FA Cup glory. Tommy Lawrence in goal, Ron Yeats at centre-half, Ian St John and Roger Hunt spearheading the attack . . . so the team took shape, packed with skill and strength.

17 Sep	Southampton	A	W	2–1
24 Sep	Sunderland	H	D	2–2
1 Oct	Aston Villa	A	W	3–2
8 Oct	Fulham	H	D	2–2
15 Oct	Nottingham F	A	D	1–1
29 Oct	Stoke C	A	L	0–2
5 Nov	Nottingham F	H	W	4–0
9 Nov	Burnley	H	W	2–0
12 Nov	Newcastle U	A	W	2–0
19 Nov	Leeds U	H	W	5–0
26 Nov	West Brom	A	L	1–2
3 Dec	Sheffield U	H	W	1–0
10 Dec	Manchester U	A	D	2–2
24 Dec	Chelsea	A	W	2–1
26 Dec	Chelsea	H	W	2–1
31 Dec	Everton	H	D	0–0

7 Jan	West Ham U	H	W	2–0
14 Jan	Sheffield W	A	W	1–0
18 Jan	Leicester C	A	L	1–2
21 Jan	Southampton	H	W	2–1
4 Feb	Sunderland	A	D	2–2
11 Feb	Aston Villa	H	W	1–0
25 Feb	Fulham	A	D	2–2
4 Mar	Stoke C	H	W	2–1
18 Mar	Burnley	A	L	0–1
25 Mar	Manchester U	H	D	0–0
27 Mar	Arsenal	H	D	0–0
28 Mar	Arsenal	A	D	1–1
1 Apr	Tottenham H	A	L	1–2
7 Apr	Newcastle U	H	W	3–1
22 Apr	West Brom	H	L	0–1
28 Apr	Sheffield U	A	W	1–0
3 May	Leeds U	A	L	1–2
6 May	Tottenham H	H	D	0–0
13 May	Blackpool	H	L	1–3

Final League Position

	P	W	D	L	F	A	Pts	
Manchester U	42	24	12	6	84	45	60	1st
Liverpool	42	19	13	10	64	47	51	5th

League Appearances (goals)
Arrowsmith 8 (2) · Byrne 9 · Callaghan 40 (4)
Graham 3 (1) · Hughes 10 · Hunt 39 (14)
Lawler 42 (4) · Lawrence 41 · Milne 33 (1) · Ogston 1
Ross 1 · St John 39 (9) · Smith 42 (1)
Stevenson 41 (3) · Strong 36 (11)
Thompson 42 (10) · Wilson 1 · Yeats 40 (2)
Own goals (2)

FA CUP

28 Jan	Watford (3)	A	D	0–0
1 Feb	Watford (3R)	H	W	3–1
18 Feb	Aston Villa (4)	H	W	1–0
11 Mar	Everton (5)	A	L	0–1

FA Cup Appearances (goals)
Byrne 2 · Callaghan 4 · Hunt 3 (1) · Lawler 4 (1)
Lawrence 4 · Milne 4 · St John 4 (2) · Strong 3
Thompson 4 · Smith 4 · Stevenson 4 · Yeats 4

EUROPEAN CUP

28 Sep	Petrolul Ploesti (1)	H	W	2–0
12 Oct	Petrolul Ploesti (1)	A	L	1–3
19 Oct	Petrolul Ploesti (PO) (Brussels)	N	W	2–0
7 Dec	Ajax Amsterdam (2)	A	L	1–5
14 Dec	Ajax Amsterdam (2)	H	D	2–2

European Appearances (goals)
Callaghan 5 (1) · Graham 2 · Hunt 5 (3) · Lawler 5 (1)
Lawrence 5 · Milne 3 · Smith 5 · St John 5 (2)
Stevenson 5 · Strong 5 · Thompson 5 (1) · Yeats 5

SEASON 1967-68

FOOTBALL LEAGUE (DIVISION 1)

19 Aug	Manchester C	A	D	0–0
22 Aug	Arsenal	H	W	2–0
26 Aug	Newcastle U	H	W	6–0
28 Aug	Arsenal	A	L	0–2
2 Sep	West Brom	A	W	2–0
5 Sep	Nottingham F	A	W	1–0
9 Sep	Chelsea	H	W	3–1
16 Sep	Southampton	A	L	0–1
23 Sep	Everton	H	W	1–0
30 Sep	Stoke C	H	W	2–1
7 Oct	Leicester C	A	L	1–2
14 Oct	West Ham U	H	W	3–1
24 Oct	Burnley	A	D	1–1
28 Oct	Sheffield W	H	W	1–0
4 Nov	Tottenham H	A	D	1–1
11 Nov	Manchester U	H	L	1–2
18 Nov	Sunderland	A	D	1–1
25 Nov	Wolverhampton W	H	W	2–1
2 Dec	Fulham	A	D	1–1
9 Dec	Leeds U	H	W	2–0
16 Dec	Manchester C	H	D	1–1
23 Dec	Newcastle U	A	D	1–1
26 Dec	Coventry C	A	D	1–1
30 Dec	Coventry C	H	W	1–0
6 Jan	West Brom	H	W	4–1
20 Jan	Southampton	H	W	2–0
3 Feb	Everton	A	L	0–1
12 Feb	Chelsea	A	L	1–3
24 Feb	Leicester C	H	W	3–1
2 Mar	Wolverhampton W	A	D	1–1
16 Mar	Burnley	H	W	3–2
23 Mar	Sheffield W	A	W	2–1
6 Apr	Manchester U	A	W	2–1
12 Apr	Sheffield U	H	L	1–2
13 Apr	Sunderland	H	W	2–1
15 Apr	Sheffield U	A	D	1–1
20 Apr	West Ham U	A	L	0–1
27 Apr	Fulham	H	W	4–1
29 Apr	Tottenham H	H	D	1–1
4 May	Leeds U	A	W	2–1
11 May	Nottingham F	H	W	6–1
15 May	Stoke C	A	L	1–2

Final League Position

	P	W	D	L	F	A	Pts	
Manchester C	42	26	6	10	86	43	58	1st
Liverpool	42	22	11	9	71	40	55	3rd

League Appearances (goals)
Arrowsmith 3 (1) · Byrne 27 · Callaghan 41 (3)
Graham 4 (1) · Hateley 38 (16) · Hughes 39 (2)
Hunt 40 (25) · Lawler 42 (3) · Lawrence 42
Livermore 1 · Ross 4 · Smith 36 (3) · St John 41 (5)
Stevenson 1 (1) · Strong 19 (5) · Thompson 41 (2)
Wall 9 · Yeats 38 (2) · Own goals (2)

FA CUP

27 Jan	Bournemouth (3)	A	D	0–0
30 Jan	Bournemouth (3R)	H	W	4–1
17 Feb	Walsall (4)	A	D	0–0
19 Feb	Walsall (4R)	H	W	5–2
9 Mar	Tottenham H (5)	A	D	1–1
12 Mar	Tottenham H (5R)	H	W	2–1
30 Mar	West Brom (6)	A	D	0–0
8 Apr	West Brom (6R)	H	D	1–1*
18 Apr	West Brom (6R) (Maine Road)	N	L	1–2

*after extra time

FA Cup Appearances (goals)
Arrowsmith 1 · Byrne 1 · Callaghan 9 · Hateley 7 (8)
Hughes 9 · Hunt 9 (2) · Lawler 9 (1) · Lawrence 9
Ross 2 · Smith 7 (1) · St John 9 · Strong 9 (1)
Thompson 9 (1) · Yeats 9

LEAGUE CUP

13 Sep	Bolton W (2)	H	D	1–1
27 Sep	Bolton W (2R)	A	L	2–3

League Cup Appearances (goals)
Byrne 2 · Callaghan 2 (1) · Hateley 2 · Hughes 2
Hunt 2 · Lawler 2 · Lawrence 2 · Smith 2 (1)
St John 2 · Thompson 2 (1) · Yeats 2

EUROPEAN FAIRS CUP

19 Sep	Malmo (1)	A	W	2–0
4 Oct	Malmo (1)	H	W	2–1
7 Nov	TSV Munchen 1860 (2)	H	W	8–0
14 Nov	TSV Munchen 1860 (2)	A	L	1–2
28 Nov	Ferencvaros (3)	A	L	0–1
9 Jan	Ferencvaros (3)	H	L	0–1

European Appearances (goals)
Byrne 6 · Callaghan 6 (3) · Hateley 5 (3) · Hughes 6
Hunt 6 (3) · Lawler 6 · Lawrence 6 · Smith 6 (1)
St John 4 (1) · Stevenson 3 · Strong 1
Thompson 6 (1) · Yeats 6 (1)

SEASON 1968-69

FOOTBALL LEAGUE (DIVISION 1)

10 Aug	Manchester C	H	W	2–1
14 Aug	Southampton	A	L	0–2
17 Aug	Arsenal	A	D	1–1
20 Aug	Stoke C	H	W	2–1
24 Aug	Sunderland	H	W	4–1
27 Aug	Everton	A	D	0–0
31 Aug	Leeds U	A	L	0–1
7 Sep	QPR	H	W	2–0
14 Sep	Ipswich T	A	W	2–0
21 Sep	Leicester C	H	W	4–0
28 Sep	Wolverhampton W	A	W	6–0
5 Oct	Burnley	A	W	4–0
8 Oct	Everton	H	D	1–1
12 Oct	Manchester U	H	W	2–0
19 Oct	Tottenham H	A	L	1–2
26 Oct	Newcastle U	H	W	2–1
2 Nov	West Brom	A	D	0–0
9 Nov	Chelsea	H	W	2–1
16 Nov	Sheffield W	A	W	2–1
23 Nov	Coventry C	H	W	2–0
30 Nov	Nottingham F	A	W	1–0
3 Dec	Southampton	H	W	1–0
7 Dec	West Ham U	H	W	2–0
14 Dec	Manchester U	A	L	0–1
21 Dec	Tottenham H	H	W	1–0
26 Dec	Burnley	H	D	1–1
11 Jan	West Brom	H	W	1–0
18 Jan	Chelsea	A	W	2–1
1 Feb	Sheffield W	H	W	1–0
15 Feb	Nottingham F	H	L	0–2
22 Feb	West Ham U	A	D	1–1
15 Mar	Sunderland	A	W	2–0
29 Mar	QPR	A	W	2–1
31 Mar	Arsenal	H	W	1–1
5 Apr	Wolverhampton W	H	W	1–0
7 Apr	Stoke C	A	D	0–0
12 Apr	Leicester C	A	W	2–1
19 Apr	Ipswich T	H	W	4–0
22 Apr	Coventry C	A	D	0–0
28 Apr	Leeds U	H	D	0–0
12 May	Manchester C	A	L	0–1
17 May	Newcastle U	A	D	1–1

Final League Position

	P	W	D	L	F	A	Pts	
Leeds U	42	27	13	2	66	26	67	1st
Liverpool	42	25	11	6	63	24	61	2nd

League Appearances (goals)
Byrne 3 · Callaghan 42 (8) · Evans 33 (7)
Graham 12 (5) · Hall 2 · Hateley 4 (1) · Hughes 40 (3)
Hunt 38 (13) · Lawler 42 (3) · Lawrence 42 · Ross 3
Smith 42 (6) · St John 41 (4) · Strong 31 (2)
Thompson 42 (8) · Wall 13 · Yeats 39 (2)
Own goals (1)

FA CUP

4 Jan	Doncaster R (3)	H	W	2–0
25 Jan	Burnley (4)	H	W	2–1
1 Mar	Leicester C (5)	A	D	0–0
3 Mar	Leicester C (5R)	H	L	0–1

FA Cup Appearances (goals)
Callaghan 4 (1) · Evans 4 · Graham 1 · Hughes 4 (1)
Hunt 4 (1) · Lawler 4 · Lawrence 4 · Smith 4 (1)
St John 4 · Strong 4 · Thompson 4 · Yeats 4

LEAGUE CUP

4 Sep	Sheffield U (2)	H	W	4–0
25 Sep	Swansea T (3)	H	W	2–0
15 Oct	Arsenal (4)	A	L	1–2

League Cup Appearances (goals)
Callaghan 3 (1) · Clemence 1 · Evans 1 · Graham 1
Hughes 3 · Hunt 3 (2) · Lawler 3 (3) · Lawrence 2
Smith 3 · St John 3 · Strong 2 · Thompson 3 (1)
Wall 2 · Yeats 3

EUROPEAN FAIRS CUP

18 Sep	Athletic Bilbao (1)	A	L	1–2
2 Oct	Athletic Bilbao (1)	H	W	2–1*

*after extra time. Liverpool lost on toss of disc

European Appearances (goals)
Callaghan 2 · Evans 1 · Graham 1 · Hunt 2 (1)
Hughes 2 (1) · Lawler 2 (1) · Lawrence 2 · Ross 1
Smith 2 · St John 2 · Strong 1 · Thompson 2 · Wall 2
Yeats 2

SEASON 1969-70

FOOTBALL LEAGUE (DIVISION 1)

9 Aug	Chelsea	H	W	4–1
12 Aug	Manchester C	H	W	3–2
16 Aug	Tottenham H	A	W	2–0
20 Aug	Manchester C	A	W	2–0
23 Aug	Burnley	H	D	3–3
27 Aug	Crystal Palace	A	W	3–1
30 Aug	Sheffield W	A	D	1–1
6 Sep	Coventry C	H	W	2–1
9 Sep	Sunderland	H	W	2–0
13 Sep	Manchester U	A	L	0–1
20 Sep	Stoke C	H	W	3–1
27 Sep	West Brom	A	D	2–2
4 Oct	Nottingham F	H	D	1–1
7 Oct	Tottenham H	H	D	0–0
11 Oct	Newcastle U	A	L	0–1
18 Oct	Ipswich T	A	D	2–2
25 Oct	Southampton	H	W	4–1
1 Nov	Derby County	A	L	0–4
8 Nov	Wolverhampton W	H	D	0–0
15 Nov	West Ham U	H	W	2–0
22 Nov	Leeds U	A	D	1–1
29 Nov	Arsenal	H	L	0–1
6 Dec	Everton	A	W	3–0
13 Dec	Manchester U	H	L	1–4
26 Dec	Burnley	A	W	5–1
10 Jan	Stoke C	A	W	2–0
17 Jan	West Brom	H	D	1–1
31 Jan	Nottingham F	A	L	0–1
16 Feb	Newcastle U	H	D	0–0
28 Feb	Derby County	H	L	0–2
3 Mar	Coventry C	A	W	3–2
7 Mar	Leeds U	H	D	0–0
11 Mar	Southampton	A	W	1–0
14 Mar	Arsenal	A	L	1–2
16 Mar	Sheffield W	H	W	3–0
21 Mar	Everton	H	L	0–2
24 Mar	Ipswich T	H	W	2–0
28 Mar	West Ham U	A	L	0–1
30 Mar	Wolverhampton W	A	W	1–0
3 Apr	Crystal Palace	H	W	3–0
15 Apr	Sunderland	A	W	1–0
18 Apr	Chelsea	A	L	1–2

Final League Position

	P	W	D	L	F	A	Pts	
Everton	42	29	8	5	72	34	66	1st
Liverpool	42	20	11	11	65	42	51	5th

League Appearances (goals)
Boersma 4 · Callaghan 41 (3) · Clemence 14
Evans A 19 (3) · Evans R 3 · Graham 42 (13) · Hall 1
Hughes 41 (7) · Hunt 18 (6) · Lawler 42 (10)
Lawrence 28 · Lloyd 8 · Lindsay 6 (1) · Livermore 14
McLaughlin 1 · Peplow 2 · Ross 7 (1) · Smith 36 (4)
St John 26 (5) · Strong 34 (3) · Thompson 39 (3)
Wall 9 · Yeats 37 (3) · Own goals (3)

FA CUP

7 Jan	Coventry C (3)	A	D	1–1
12 Jan	Coventry C (3R)	H	W	3–0
24 Jan	Wrexham (4)	H	W	3–1
7 Feb	Leicester C (5)	H	D	0–0
11 Feb	Leicester C (5R)	A	W	2–0
21 Feb	Watford (6)	A	L	0–1

FA Cup Appearances (goals)
Callaghan 6 · Clemence 1 · Evans A 1 (2)
Graham 6 (4) · Hughes 6 · Lawler 6 · Lawrence 5
Ross 5 (1) · Smith 3 · Strong 6 · St John 6 (1)
Thompson 4 (1) · Wall 6 · Yeats 6

LEAGUE CUP

3 Sep	Watford (2)	A	W	2–1
24 Sep	Manchester C (3)	A	L	2–3

League Cup Appearances (goals)
Boersma 1 · Callaghan 2 · Evans A 1 (1)
Graham 2 (1) · Hughes 2 · Lawler 2 · Lawrence 2
Smith 2 · Strong 2 · St John 1 (1) · Thompson 2
Yeats 2 · Own goals (1)

EUROPEAN FAIRS CUP

16 Sep	Dundalk (1)	H	W	10–0
30 Sep	Dundalk (1)	A	W	4–0
12 Nov	Vitoria Setubal (2)	A	L	0–1
26 Nov	Vitoria Setubal (2)	H	W	3–2*

*Liverpool lost on away goals

European Appearances (goals)
Boersma 1 · Callaghan 1 (2) · Clemence 2
Evans A 3 (3) · Graham 4 (3) · Hunt 2 (1) · Hughes 4
Lawler 4 (1) · Lawrence 2 · Lloyd 1 · Lindsay 1 (1)
Peplow 1 · Ross 1 · Smith 4 (3) · St John 2
Strong 4 · Thompson 4 (3) · Wall 1 · Yeats 3

SEASON 1970-71

FOOTBALL LEAGUE (DIVISION 1)

15 Aug	Burnley	A	W	2–1
17 Aug	Blackpool	A	D	0–0
22 Aug	Huddersfield T	H	W	4–0
25 Aug	Crystal Palace	H	D	1–1
29 Aug	West Brom	A	D	1–1
5 Sep	Manchester U	H	D	1–1
12 Sep	Newcastle U	A	D	0–0
19 Sep	Nottingham F	H	W	3–0
26 Sep	Southampton	A	L	0–1
3 Oct	Chelsea	H	W	1–0
10 Oct	Tottenham H	A	L	0–1
17 Oct	Burnley	H	W	2–0
24 Oct	Ipswich T	A	L	0–1
31 Oct	Wolverhampton W	H	W	2–0
7 Nov	Derby County	A	D	0–0
14 Nov	Coventry C	H	D	0–0
21 Nov	Everton	H	W	3–2
28 Nov	Arsenal	A	L	0–2
5 Dec	Leeds U	H	D	1–1
12 Dec	West Ham U	A	W	2–1
19 Dec	Huddersfield T	A	D	0–0
26 Dec	Stoke C	H	D	0–0
9 Jan	Blackpool	H	D	2–2
12 Jan	Manchester C	H	D	0–0
16 Jan	Crystal Palace	A	L	0–1
30 Jan	Arsenal	H	W	2–0
6 Feb	Leeds U	A	W	1–0
16 Feb	West Ham U	H	W	1–0
20 Feb	Everton	A	D	0–0
27 Feb	Wolverhampton W	A	L	0–1
13 Mar	Coventry C	A	L	0–1
20 Mar	Derby County	H	W	2–0
29 Mar	Ipswich T	H	W	2–1
2 Apr	West Brom	H	D	1–1
6 Apr	Newcastle U	H	D	1–1
10 Apr	Stoke C	A	W	1–0
12 Apr	Chelsea	A	L	0–1
17 Apr	Tottenham H	H	D	0–0
19 Apr	Manchester U	A	W	2–0
24 Apr	Nottingham F	A	W	1–0
26 Apr	Manchester C	A	D	2–2
1 May	Southampton	H	W	1–0

Final League Position

	P	W	D	L	F	A	Pts	
Arsenal	42	29	7	6	71	29	65	1st
Liverpool	42	17	17	8	42	24	51	5th

League Appearances (goals)
Arnold 1 · Boersma 14 (1) · Callaghan 22
Clemence 41 · Evans A 21 (10) · Evans R 4 · Fagan 1
Graham 14 (5) · Hall 33 (1) · Heighway 31 (4)
Hughes 39 (2) · Lawler 41 (3) · Lawrence 1
Lindsay 21 · Livermore 1 · Lloyd 40
McLaughlin 33 (2) · Ross 12 · Smith 41 (2)
St John 1 · Thompson 27 (2) · Toshack 21 (5)
Whitham 6 (1) · Yeats 12 (1) · Own goals (3)

FA CUP

2 Jan	Aldershot (3)	H	W	1–0

23 Jan	Swansea T (4)	H	W	3–0
13 Feb	Southampton (5)	H	W	1–0
6 Mar	Tottenham H (6)	H	D	0–0
16 Mar	Tottenham H (6R)	A	W	1–0
27 Mar	Everton (SF)	N	W	2–1
(Old Trafford)				
8 May	Arsenal (F)	N	L	1–2*
(Wembley)				

*after extra time

FA Cup Appearances (goals)
Boersma 3 · Callaghan 5 · Clemence 7 · Evans A 4 (1)
Hall 7 (1) · Heighway 7 (2) · Hughes 7 · Lawler 7 (2)
Lindsay 4 · Lloyd 7 · McLaughlin 4 (1) · Smith 7
St John 1 (1) · Thompson 2 · Toshack 7 (1) · Yeats 2

LEAGUE CUP

8 Sep	Mansfield T (2)	A	D	0–0
22 Sep	Mansfield T (2R)	H	W	3–2*
6 Oct	Swindon T (3)	A	L	0–2

*after extra time

League Cup Appearances (goals)
Callaghan 1 · Clemence 3 · Evans A 3 (1) · Evans R 1
Graham 2 · Hall 3 · Heighway 2 · Hughes 3 (1)
Lawler 3 · Lindsay 2 · Livermore 1 · Lloyd 3
McLaughlin 1 · Smith 3 (1) · Thompson 1
Whitham 1

EUROPEAN FAIRS CUP

15 Sep	Ferencvaros (1)	H	W	1–0
29 Sep	Ferencvaros (1)	A	D	1–1
21 Oct	Dinamo Bucharest (2)	H	W	3–0
4 Nov	Dinamo Bucharest (2)	A	D	1–1
9 Dec	Hibernian (3)	A	W	1–0
22 Dec	Hibernian (3)	H	W	2–0
10 Mar	Bayern Munich (4)	H	W	3–0
24 Mar	Bayern Munich (4)	A	D	1–1
14 Apr	Leeds U (SF)	H	L	0–1
28 Apr	Leeds U (SF)	A	D	0–0

European Appearances (goals)
Boersma 3 (2) · Callaghan 5 · Clemence 10
Evans A 6 (3) · Evans R 1 · Graham 2 (1) · Hall 8
Heighway 7 (1) · Hughes 10 (2) · Lawler 10 (1)
Lindsay 8 (1) · Lloyd 10 · McLaughlin 7 · Ross 2 (1)
Smith 10 · St John 1 · Thompson 7 · Toshack 5 (1)
Yeats 2

SEASON 1971-72

FOOTBALL LEAGUE (DIVISION 1)

14 Aug	Nottingham F	H	W	3–1
17 Aug	Wolverhampton W	H	W	3–2
21 Aug	Newcastle U	A	L	2–3
24 Aug	Crystal Palace	A	W	1–0
28 Aug	Leicester C	H	W	3–2
1 Sep	Manchester C	A	L	0–1
4 Sep	Tottenham H	A	L	0–2
11 Sep	Southampton	H	W	1–0
18 Sep	Leeds U	A	L	0–1
25 Sep	Manchester U	H	D	2–2
2 Oct	Stoke C	A	D	0–0
9 Oct	Chelsea	H	D	0–0
16 Oct	Nottingham F	A	W	3–2
23 Oct	Huddersfield T	H	W	2–0
30 Oct	Sheffield U	A	D	1–1
6 Nov	Arsenal	H	W	3–2
13 Nov	Everton	A	L	0–1
20 Nov	Coventry C	A	W	2–0
27 Nov	West Ham U	H	W	1–0
4 Dec	Ipswich T	A	D	0–0
11 Dec	Derby County	H	W	3–2
18 Dec	Tottenham H	H	D	0–0
27 Dec	West Brom	A	L	0–1
1 Jan	Leeds U	H	L	0–2
8 Jan	Leicester C	A	L	0–1
22 Jan	Wolverhampton W	A	D	0–0
29 Jan	Crystal Palace	H	W	4–1
12 Feb	Huddersfield T	A	W	1–0
19 Feb	Sheffield U	H	W	2–0
26 Feb	Manchester C	H	W	3–0
4 Mar	Everton	H	W	4–0
11 Mar	Chelsea	A	D	0–0
18 Mar	Newcastle U	H	W	5–0
25 Mar	Southampton	A	W	1–0
28 Mar	Stoke C	H	W	2–1
1 Apr	West Brom	H	W	2–0
3 Apr	Manchester U	A	W	3–0
8 Apr	Coventry C	H	W	3–1
15 Apr	West Ham U	A	W	2–0
22 Apr	Ipswich T	H	W	2–0
1 May	Derby County	A	L	0–1
8 May	Arsenal	A	D	0–0

Final League Position

	P	W	D	L	F	A	Pts	
Derby County	42	24	10	8	69	33	58	1st
Liverpool	42	24	9	9	64	30	57	3rd

League Appearances (goals)
Boersma 6 · Callaghan 41 (2) · Clemence 42
Evans A 6 (1) · Graham 11 (2) · Hall 26 (1)
Heighway 40 (5) · Hughes 42 (8) · Keegan 35 (9)
Lawler 42 (6) · Lindsay 38 · Lloyd 33 (1)
McLaughlin 5 · Ross 21 (1) · Smith 37 (6)
Thompson P 10 · Thompson P B 1 · Toshack 29 (13)
Whitham 9 (6)

FA CUP

15 Jan	Oxford U (3)	A	W	3–0
5 Feb	Leeds U (4)	H	D	0–0
9 Feb	Leeds U (4R)	A	L	0–2

FA Cup Appearances (goals)
Boersma 1 · Callaghan 3 · Clemence 3 · Evans A 1
Graham 2 · Hall 1 · Heighway 3 · Hughes 3
Keegan 3 (2) · Lawler 3 · Lindsay 3 (1) · Lloyd 2
Ross 3 · Smith 3 · Toshack 1 · Thompson P 1

LEAGUE CUP

9 Sep	Hull C (2)	H	W	3–0
5 Oct	Southampton (3)	H	W	1–0
27 Oct	West Ham U	A	L	1–2

League Cup Appearances (goals)
Callaghan 3 · Clemence 3 · Evans A 2 · Graham 3 (1)
Hall 2 (1) · Heighway 3 · Hughes 3 · Keegan 3
Lawler 3 (1) · Lindsay 1 · Lloyd 3 · McLaughlin 1
Ross 3 · Smith 1 · Thompson P 1 · Toshack 1

EUROPEAN CUP-WINNERS CUP

15 Sep	Servette Geneva (1)	A	L	1–2
29 Sep	Servette Geneva (1)	H	W	2–0
20 Oct	Bayern Munich (2)	H	D	0–0
3 Nov	Bayern Munich (2)	A	L	1–3

European Appearances (goals)
Callaghan 4 · Clemence 4 · Evans A 3 (1) · Graham 3
Hall 3 · Heighway 4 (1) · Hughes 4 (1) · Keegan 3

Lawler 4 (1) · Lloyd 4 · Lindsay 2 · Ross 4 · Smith 3
Thompson P 2 · Toshack 2

SEASON 1972-73

FOOTBALL LEAGUE (DIVISION 1)

12 Aug	Manchester C	H	W	2–0
15 Aug	Manchester U	H	W	2–0
19 Aug	Crystal Palace	A	D	1–1
23 Aug	Chelsea	A	W	2–1
26 Aug	West Ham U	H	W	3–2
30 Aug	Leicester C	A	L	2–3
2 Sep	Derby County	A	L	1–2
9 Sep	Wolverhampton W	H	W	4–2
16 Sep	Arsenal	H	D	0–0
23 Sep	Sheffield U	H	W	5–0
30 Sep	Leeds U	A	W	2–1
7 Oct	Everton	H	W	1–0
14 Oct	Southampton	A	D	1–1
21 Oct	Stoke C	H	W	2–1
28 Oct	Norwich C	A	D	1–1
4 Nov	Chelsea	H	W	3–1
11 Nov	Manchester U	A	L	0–2

■ Shankly's team of the 1970s combined experience and youth. The old brigade was represented by men like Tommy Smith, Peter Thompson, Chris Lawler and Ian Callaghan . . . the new boys included Steve Heighway, Brian Hall, Ray Clemence, John Toshack and Larry Lloyd.

18 Nov	Newcastle U	H	W	3–2
25 Nov	Tottenham H	A	W	2–1
2 Dec	Birmingham C	H	W	4–3
9 Dec	West Brom	A	D	1–1
16 Dec	Ipswich T	A	D	1–1
23 Dec	Coventry C	H	W	2–0
26 Dec	Sheffield U	A	W	3–0
30 Dec	Crystal Palace	H	W	1–0
6 Jan	West Ham U	A	W	1–0
20 Jan	Derby County	H	D	1–1
27 Jan	Wolverhampton W	A	L	1–2
10 Feb	Arsenal	H	L	0–2
17 Feb	Manchester C	A	D	1–1
24 Feb	Ipswich T	H	W	2–1
3 Mar	Everton	A	W	2–0
10 Mar	Southampton	H	W	3–2
17 Mar	Stoke C	A	W	1–0
24 Mar	Norwich C	H	W	3–1
31 Mar	Tottenham H	H	D	1–1
7 Apr	Birmingham C	A	L	1–2
14 Apr	West Brom	H	W	1–0
17 Apr	Coventry C	A	W	2–1
21 Apr	Newcastle U	A	L	1–2
23 Apr	Leeds U	H	W	2–0
28 Apr	Leicester C	H	D	0–0

Final League Position

	P	W	D	L	F	A	Pts	
Liverpool	42	25	10	7	72	42	60	1st

League Appearances (goals)
Boersma 19 (7) · Callaghan 42 (3) · Clemence 41 · Cormack 30 (8) · Hall 21 (2) · Heighway 38 (6) · Hughes 41 (7) · Keegan 41 (13) · Lane 1 · Lawler 42 (3) · Lindsay 37 (4) · Lloyd 42 (2) · Smith 33 (2) · Storton 4 · Thompson 14 · Toshack 22 (13) · Own goals (2)

FA CUP

13 Jan	Burnley (3)	A	D	0–0
16 Jan	Burnley (3R)	H	W	3–0
4 Feb	Manchester C (4)	H	D	0–0
7 Feb	Manchester C (4R)	A	L	0–2

FA Cup Appearances (goals)
Boersma 1 · Callaghan 4 · Clemence 4 · Cormack 4 (1) · Heighway 4 · Hughes 4 · Keegan 4 · Lawler 4 · Lindsay 4 · Lloyd 4 · Smith 2 · Thompson 2 · Toshack 4 (2)

LEAGUE CUP

5 Sep	Carlisle U (2)	A	D	1–1
19 Sep	Carlisle U (2R)	H	W	5–1
3 Oct	West Brom (3)	A	D	1–1
10 Oct	West Brom (3R)	H	W	2–1*
31 Oct	Leeds U (4)	H	D	2–2
22 Nov	Leeds U (4R)	A	W	1–0
4 Dec	Tottenham H (5)	H	D	1–1
6 Dec	Tottenham H (5R)	A	L	1–3

*after extra time

League Cup Appearances (goals)
Boersma 3 (2) · Callaghan 8 (1) · Clemence 7 · Cormack 8 · Hall 2 · Heighway 8 (2) · Hughes 8 (2) · Keegan 8 (5) · Lane 1 · Lawler 8 (1) · Lindsay 7 · Lloyd 8 · Smith 4 · Storton 4 · Thompson 1 · Toshack 6 (1)

UEFA CUP

12 Sep	Eintracht Frankfurt (1)	H	W	2–0
26 Sep	Eintracht Frankfurt (1)	A	D	0–0
24 Oct	A E K Athens (2)	H	W	3–0
7 Nov	A E K Athens (2)	A	W	3–1
29 Nov	Dynamo Berlin (3)	A	D	0–0
13 Dec	Dynamo Berlin (3)	H	W	3–1
7 Mar	Dynamo Dresden (4)	H	W	2–0
21 Mar	Dynamo Dresden (4)	A	W	1–0
10 Apr	Tottenham H (SF)	H	W	1–0
25 Apr	Tottenham H (SF)	A	L	1–2*
10 May	Borussia M'gladbach (F)	H	W	3–0
23 May	Borussia M'gladbach (F)	A	L	0–2

(Liverpool won Cup 3–2 on aggregate)
*Liverpool won on away goals

European Appearances (goals)
Boersma 8 (4) · Callaghan 12 · Clemence 12 · Cormack 10 (1) · Hall 7 (1) · Heighway 12 (2) · Hughes 12 (3) · Keegan 11 (4) · Lawler 12 · Lindsay 11 (1) · Lloyd 12 (1) · Smith 10 (1) · Storton 2 · Thompson P 3 · Toshack 8 (1) · Whitham 1

SEASON 1973-74

FOOTBALL LEAGUE (DIVISION 1)

25 Aug	Stoke C	H	W	1–0
28 Aug	Coventry C	A	L	0–1
1 Sep	Leicester C	A	D	1–1
4 Sep	Derby County	H	W	2–0
8 Sep	Chelsea	H	W	1–0
12 Sep	Derby County	A	L	1–3
15 Sep	Birmingham C	A	D	1–1
22 Sep	Tottenham H	H	W	3–2
29 Sep	Manchester U	A	D	0–0
6 Oct	Newcastle U	H	W	2–1
13 Oct	Southampton	A	L	0–1
20 Oct	Leeds U	A	L	0–1
27 Oct	Sheffield U	H	W	1–0
3 Nov	Arsenal	A	W	2–0
10 Nov	Wolverhampton W	H	W	1–0
17 Nov	Ipswich T	H	W	4–2
24 Nov	QPR	A	D	2–2
1 Dec	West Ham U	H	W	1–0
8 Dec	Everton	A	W	1–0
15 Dec	Norwich C	A	D	1–1
22 Dec	Manchester U	H	W	2–0
26 Dec	Burnley	A	L	1–2
29 Dec	Chelsea	A	W	1–0
1 Jan	Leicester C	H	D	1–1
12 Jan	Birmingham C	H	W	3–2
19 Jan	Stoke C	A	D	1–1
2 Feb	Norwich C	H	W	1–0
5 Feb	Coventry C	H	W	2–1
23 Feb	Newcastle U	A	D	0–0
26 Feb	Southampton	H	W	1–0
2 Mar	Burnley	H	W	1–0
16 Mar	Leeds U	H	W	1–0
23 Mar	Wolverhampton W	A	W	1–0
6 Apr	QPR	H	W	2–1
8 Apr	Sheffield U	A	L	0–1
12 Apr	Manchester C	A	D	1–1
13 Apr	Ipswich T	A	D	1–1
16 Apr	Manchester C	H	W	4–0
20 Apr	Everton	H	D	0–0
24 Apr	Arsenal	H	L	0–1
27 Apr	West Ham U	A	D	2–2
8 May	Tottenham H	A	D	1–1

Final League Position

	P	W	D	L	F	A	Pts	
Leeds U	42	24	14	4	66	31	62	1st
Liverpool	42	22	13	7	52	31	57	2nd

League Appearances (goals)
Boersma 15 (3) · Brownbill 1 · Callaghan 42 · Clemence 42 · Cormack 42 (9) · Evans R 2 · Hall 22 (4) · Heighway 36 (5) · Hughes 42 (2) · Keegan 42 (12) · Lawler 18 (2) · Lindsay 36 (4) · Lloyd 27 (1) · McLaughlin 1 · Smith 34 (1) · Storton 1 · Thompson M 1 · Thompson PB 35 (2) · Toshack 19 (5) · Waddle 11 (1) · Own goals (1)

FA CUP

5 Jan	Doncaster R (3)	H	D	2–2
8 Jan	Doncaster R (3R)	A	W	2–0
26 Jan	Carlisle U (4)	H	D	0–0
29 Jan	Carlisle U (4R)	A	W	2–0
16 Feb	Ipswich T (5)	H	W	2–0
9 Mar	Bristol C (6)	A	W	1–0
30 Mar	Leicester C (SF) (Old Trafford)	N	D	0–0
3 Apr	Leicester C (SFR) (Villa Park)	N	W	3–1
4 May	Newcastle U (F) (Wembley)	N	W	3–0

FA Cup Appearances (goals)
Boersma 5 (1) · Callaghan 9 · Clemence 9 · Cormack 8 (1) · Hall 8 (2) · Heighway 6 (2) · Hughes 9 · Keegan 9 (6) · Lindsay 9 · Lloyd 3 · Rylands 1 · Smith 7 · Storton 1 · Thompson 9 · Toshack 6 (3) · Waddle 2

LEAGUE CUP

8 Oct	West Ham U (2)	A	D	2–2
29 Oct	West Ham U (2R)	H	W	1–0
21 Nov	Sunderland (3)	A	W	2–0
27 Nov	Hull C (4)	A	D	0–0
4 Dec	Hull C (4R)	H	W	3–1
19 Dec	Wolverhampton W (5)	A	L	0–1

League Cup Appearances (goals)
Callaghan 6 (3) · Clemence 6 · Cormack 6 (1) · Hall 1 · Heighway 6 (1) · Hughes 6 · Keegan 6 (1) · Lawler 3 · Lindsay 6 · Lloyd 6 · Smith 5 · Thompson 4 · Toshack 2 (2) · Waddle 3

EUROPEAN CUP

19 Sep	Jeunesse D'Esch (1)	A	D	1–1
3 Oct	Jeunesse D'Esch (1)	H	W	2–0
24 Oct	Red Star Belgrade (2)	A	L	1–2
6 Nov	Red Star Belgrade (2)	H	L	1–2

European Appearances (goals)
Boersma 2 · Callaghan 4 · Clemence 4 · Cormack 1 · Hall 3 (1) · Heighway 4 · Hughes 4 · Keegan 4 · Lawler 4 (2) · Lloyd 4 · Lindsay 3 · McLaughlin 1 · Smith 3 · Thompson 2 · Toshack 3 (1) · Own goals (1)

SEASON 1974-75

FOOTBALL LEAGUE (DIVISION 1)

17 Aug	Luton T	A	W	2–1
20 Aug	Wolverhampton W	A	D	0–0
24 Aug	Leicester C	H	W	2–1
27 Aug	Wolverhampton W	H	W	2–0
31 Aug	Chelsea	A	W	3–0
7 Sep	Tottenham H	H	W	5–2
14 Sep	Manchester C	A	L	0–2
21 Sep	Stoke C	H	W	3–0
24 Sep	Burnley	H	L	0–1
28 Sep	Sheffield U	A	L	0–1
5 Oct	Carlisle U	A	W	1–0
12 Oct	Middlesbrough	H	W	2–0
19 Oct	QPR	A	W	1–0
26 Oct	Leeds U	H	W	1–0
2 Nov	Ipswich T	A	L	0–1
9 Nov	Arsenal	H	L	1–3
16 Nov	Everton	A	D	0–0
23 Nov	West Ham U	H	D	1–1
30 Nov	Coventry C	A	D	1–1
7 Dec	Derby County	H	D	2–2
14 Dec	Luton T	H	W	2–0
21 Dec	Birmingham C	A	L	1–3
26 Dec	Manchester C	H	W	4–1
11 Jan	Derby County	A	L	0–2
18 Jan	Coventry C	H	W	2–1
1 Feb	Arsenal	A	L	0–2
8 Feb	Ipswich T	H	W	5–2
12 Feb	Newcastle U	A	L	1–4
19 Feb	West Ham U	A	D	0–0
22 Feb	Everton	H	D	0–0
1 Mar	Chelsea	H	D	2–2
8 Mar	Burnley	A	D	1–1
15 Mar	Sheffield U	H	D	0–0
19 Mar	Leicester	A	D	1–1
22 Mar	Tottenham H	A	W	2–0
25 Mar	Newcastle U	H	W	4–0
29 Mar	Birmingham C	H	W	1–0
31 Mar	Stoke C	A	L	0–2
5 Apr	Leeds U	A	W	2–0
12 Apr	Carlisle U	H	W	2–0
19 Apr	Middlesbrough	A	L	0–1
26 Apr	QPR	H	W	3–1

Final League Position

	P	W	D	L	F	A	Pts	
Derby County	42	21	11	10	67	49	53	1st
Liverpool	42	20	11	11	60	39	51	2nd

League Appearances (goals)
Boersma 21 (6) · Callaghan 41 (1) · Case 1 · Clemence 42 · Cormack 36 (3) · Hall 35 (5) · Heighway 35 (9) · Hughes 42 (1) · Keegan 33 (10) · Kennedy 25 (5) · Lawler 10 · Lindsay 25 (3) · McDermott 15 (2) · Neal 23 · Smith 36 (2) · Thompson 32 · Toshack 21 (12) · Waddle 5 · Own goals (1)

FA CUP

4 Jan	Stoke C (3)	H	W	2–0
25 Jan	Ipswich T (4)	A	L	0–1

FA Cup Appearances (goals)
Callaghan 2 · Clemence 2 · Cormack 2 · Hall 2 · Heighway 2 (1) · Hughes 2 · Keegan 2 (1) · Lindsay 2 · Neal 2 · Toshack 2 · Thompson 2

LEAGUE CUP

10 Sep	Brentford (2)	H	W	2–1
8 Oct	Bristol C (3)	A	D	0–0
16 Oct	Bristol C (3R)	H	W	4–0
12 Nov	Middlesbrough (4)	H	L	0–1

League Cup Appearances (goals)
Boersma 3 (1) · Callaghan 3 · Clemence 4 · Cormack 3 · Hall 3 · Heighway 4 (2) · Hughes 4 · Keegan 3 · Kennedy 4 (3) · Lawler 3 · Lindsay 4 · McLaughlin 1 · Smith 4 · Thompson 1

EUROPEAN CUP-WINNERS CUP

17 Sep	Stromgodset Drammen (1)	H	W	11–0
1 Oct	Stromgodset Drammen (1)	A	W	1–0
23 Oct	Ferencvaros (2)	H	D	1–1
5 Nov	Ferencvaros (2)	A	D	0–0*

*Liverpool lost on away goals

European Appearances (goals)
Boersma 4 (2) · Callaghan 4 (1) · Clemence 4 · Cormack 3 (1) · Hall 4 · Heighway 4 (1) · Hughes 4 (1) · Keegan 3 (1) · Kennedy 4 (2) · Lawler 3 · Lindsay 4 (1) · Smith 4 (1) · Thompson 1 (2) · Toshack 2

SEASON 1975-76

FOOTBALL LEAGUE (DIVISION 1)

16 Aug	QPR	A	L	0–2
19 Aug	West Ham U	H	D	2–2
23 Aug	Tottenham H	H	W	3–2
26 Aug	Leeds U	A	W	3–0
30 Aug	Leicester C	A	D	1–1
6 Sep	Sheffield U	H	W	1–0
13 Sep	Ipswich T	A	L	0–2
20 Sep	Aston Villa	H	W	3–0
27 Sep	Everton	A	D	0–0
4 Oct	Wolverhampton W	H	W	2–0
11 Oct	Birmingham C	H	W	3–1
18 Oct	Coventry C	A	D	0–0
25 Oct	Derby County	H	D	1–1
1 Nov	Middlesbrough	A	W	1–0
8 Nov	Manchester U	H	W	3–1
15 Nov	Newcastle U	A	W	2–1
22 Nov	Coventry C	H	D	1–1
29 Nov	Norwich C	H	L	1–3
2 Dec	Arsenal	H	D	2–2
6 Dec	Burnley	A	D	0–0
13 Dec	Tottenham H	A	W	4–0
20 Dec	QPR	H	W	2–0
26 Dec	Stoke C	A	D	1–1
27 Dec	Manchester C	H	W	1–0
10 Jan	Ipswich T	H	D	3–3
17 Jan	Sheffield U	A	D	0–0
31 Jan	West Ham U	A	W	4–0
7 Feb	Leeds U	H	W	2–0
18 Feb	Manchester U	A	D	0–0
21 Feb	Newcastle U	H	W	2–0
24 Feb	Arsenal	A	L	0–1
28 Feb	Derby County	A	D	1–1
6 Mar	Middlesbrough	H	L	0–2
13 Mar	Birmingham C	A	W	1–0
20 Mar	Norwich C	A	W	1–0
27 Mar	Burnley	H	W	2–0
3 Apr	Everton	H	W	1–0
6 Apr	Leicester C	H	W	1–0
10 Apr	Aston Villa	A	D	0–0
17 Apr	Stoke C	H	W	5–3
19 Apr	Manchester C	A	W	3–0
4 May	Wolverhampton W	A	W	3–1

Final League Position

	P	W	D	L	F	A	Pts	
Liverpool	42	23	14	5	66	31	60	1st

League Appearances (goals)
Boersma 3 · Callaghan 40 (3) · Case 27 (6) · Clemence 42 · Cormack 17 (1) · Fairclough 14 (7) · Hall 13 (2) · Heighway 39 (4) · Hughes 41 (2) · Jones 13 · Keegan 41 (12) · Kennedy 30 (6) · Kettle 1 · Lindsay 6 · McDermott 9 (1) · Neal 42 (6) · Smith 24 · Thompson 41 · Toshack 35 (16)

FA CUP

3 Jan	West Ham U (3)	A	W	2–0
24 Jan	Derby County (4)	A	L	0–1

FA Cup Appearances (goals)
Callaghan 2 · Case 2 · Clemence 2 · Hall 1 · Heighway 2 · Hughes 2 · Keegan 2 (1) · Kennedy 2 · Neal 2 · Smith 2 · Thompson 2 · Toshack 2 (1)

LEAGUE CUP

10 Sep	York City (2)	A	W	1–0
7 Oct	Burnley (3)	H	D	1–1
14 Oct	Burnley (3R)	A	L	0–1

League Cup Appearances (goals)
Boersma 1 · Callaghan 3 · Clemence 3 · Case 1 (1) · Cormack 3 · Hall 2 · Heighway 2 · Hughes 3 · Keegan 3 · Kennedy 1 · Lindsay 3 (1) · McDermott 1 · Neal 3 · Thompson 3 · Toshack 2

UEFA CUP

17 Sep	Hibernian (1)	A	L	0–1
30 Sep	Hibernian (1)	H	W	3–1
22 Oct	Real Sociedad (2)	A	W	3–1
4 Nov	Real Sociedad (2)	H	W	6–0
26 Nov	Slask Wroclaw (3)	A	W	2–1
10 Dec	Slask Wroclaw (3)	H	W	3–0
3 Mar	Dynamo Dresden (4)	A	D	0–0
17 Mar	Dynamo Dresden (4)	H	W	2–1
30 Mar	Barcelona (SF)	A	W	1–0
14 Apr	Barcelona (SF)	H	D	1–1
28 Apr	F C Bruges (F)	H	W	3–2
19 May	F C Bruges (F)	A	D	1–1

Liverpool won Cup 4–3 on aggregate

UEFA Cup Appearances (goals)
Boersma 1 · Callaghan 12 (1) · Clemence 12 · Case 9 (5) · Cormack 4 · Fairclough 5 (1) · Hall 9 · Heighway 11 (2) · Hughes 11 · Keegan 11 (3) · Kettle 1 · Jones 1 · Kennedy 10 (4) · Lawler 1 · Lindsay 2 · Neal 12 (1) · Smith 9 · Thompson M 1 · Thompson PB 11 (2) · Toshack 11 (6)

SEASON 1976-77

FOOTBALL LEAGUE (DIVISION 1)

21 Aug	Norwich C	H	W	1–0
25 Aug	West Brom	A	W	1–0
28 Aug	Birmingham C	A	L	1–2
4 Sep	Coventry C	H	W	3–1
11 Sep	Derby County	A	W	3–2
18 Sep	Tottenham H	H	W	2–0
25 Sep	Newcastle U	A	L	0–1
2 Oct	Middlesbrough	H	D	0–0
16 Oct	Everton	H	W	3–1
23 Oct	Leeds U	A	D	1–1
27 Oct	Leicester C	A	W	1–0
30 Oct	Aston Villa	H	W	3–0
6 Nov	Sunderland	A	W	1–0
9 Nov	Leicester C	H	W	5–1
20 Nov	Arsenal	A	D	1–1

27 Nov	Bristol C	H	W	2–1
4 Dec	Ipswich T	A	L	0–1
11 Dec	QPR	H	W	3–1
15 Dec	Aston Villa	A	L	1–5
18 Dec	West Ham U	A	L	0–2
27 Dec	Stoke C	H	W	4–0
29 Dec	Manchester C	A	D	1–1
1 Jan	Sunderland	H	W	2–0
15 Jan	West Brom	H	D	1–1
22 Jan	Norwich C	A	L	1–2
5 Feb	Birmingham C	H	W	4–1
16 Feb	Manchester U	A	D	0–0
19 Feb	Derby County	H	W	3–1
5 Mar	Newcastle U	H	W	1–0
9 Mar	Tottenham H	A	L	0–1
12 Mar	Middlesbrough	A	W	1–0
22 Mar	Everton	A	D	0–0
2 Apr	Leeds U	H	W	3–1
9 Apr	Manchester C	H	W	2–1
11 Apr	Stoke C	A	D	0–0
16 Apr	Arsenal	H	W	2–0
30 Apr	Ipswich T	H	W	2–1
3 May	Manchester U	H	W	1–0
7 May	QPR	A	D	1–1
10 May	Coventry C	A	D	0–0
14 May	West Ham U	H	D	0–0
16 May	Bristol C	A	L	1–2

Final League Position

	P	W	D	L	F	A	Pts	
Liverpool	42	23	11	8	62	33	57	1st

League Appearances (goals)
Callaghan 33 (1) · Clemence 42 · Case 27 (1)
Fairclough 20 (3) · Heighway 39 (8) · Hughes 42 (1)
Johnson 26 (5) · Jones 39 (3) · Keegan 38 (12)
Kennedy 41 (7) · Kettle 2 · Lindsay 1
McDermott 26 (1) · Neal 42 (7) · Smith 16
Thompson 26 (2) · Toshack 22 (10) · Own goals (1)

FA CUP

8 Jan	Crystal Palace (3)	H	D	0–0
11 Jan	Crystal Palace (3R)	A	W	3–2
29 Jan	Carlisle U (4)	H	W	3–0
26 Feb	Oldham A (5)	H	W	3–1
19 Mar	Middlesbrough (6)	H	W	2–0
23 Apr	Everton (SF) (Maine Road)	N	D	2–2
27 Apr	Everton (SFR) (Maine Road)	N	W	3–0
21 May	Manchester U (F) (Wembley)	N	L	1–2

FA Cup Appearances (goals)
Callaghan 5 · Case 7 (4) · Clemence 8
Fairclough 5 (1) · Heighway 7 (3) · Hughes 8
Johnson 4 · Jones 8 · Keegan 8 (4) · Kennedy R 8 (1)
McDermott 5 (1) · Neal 8 (2) · Smith 4
Thompson 4 · Toshack 2 (1)

LEAGUE CUP

31 Aug	West Brom (2)	H	D	1–1
6 Sep	West Brom (2R)	A	L	0–1

League Cup Appearances (goals)
Callaghan 2 (1) · Case 1 · Clemence 2 · Fairclough 1
Heighway 2 · Hughes 2 · Johnson 2 · Jones 2
Keegan 2 · Kennedy 2 · Neal 2 · Thompson 2
Toshack 1

EUROPEAN CUP

14 Sep	Crusaders (1)	H	W	2–0
28 Sep	Crusaders (1)	A	W	5–0
20 Oct	Trabzonspor (2)	A	L	0–1
3 Nov	Trabzonspor (2)	H	W	3–0
2 Mar	St Etienne (3)	A	L	0–1
16 Mar	St Etienne (3)	H	W	3–1
6 Apr	F C Zurich (SF)	A	W	3–1
20 Apr	F C Zurich (SF)	H	W	3–0
25 May	Borussia M'gladbach (F) (Rome)	N	W	3–1

European Cup Appearances (goals)
Callaghan 7 · Case 6 (2) · Clemence 9
Fairclough 3 (1) · Heighway 9 (3) · Hughes 9
Johnson 5 (3) · Jones 9 · Keegan 8 (4)
Kennedy 9 (1) · McDermott 7 (2) · Neal 8 (4)
Smith 8 (1) · Thompson 3 · Toshack 4 (1) · Waddle 1

SEASON 1977-78

FOOTBALL LEAGUE (DIVISION 1)

20 Aug	Middlesbrough	A	D	1–1
23 Aug	Newcastle U	H	W	2–0
27 Aug	West Brom	H	W	3–0
3 Sep	Birmingham C	A	W	1–0
10 Sep	Coventry C	H	W	2–0
17 Sep	Ipswich T	A	D	1–1
24 Sep	Derby County	H	W	1–0
1 Oct	Manchester U	A	L	0–2
4 Oct	Arsenal	A	D	0–0
8 Oct	Chelsea	H	W	2–0
15 Oct	Leeds U	A	W	2–1
22 Oct	Everton	H	D	0–0
29 Oct	Manchester C	A	L	1–3
5 Nov	Aston Villa	H	L	1–2
12 Nov	QPR	A	L	0–2
19 Nov	Bristol C	H	D	1–1
26 Nov	Leicester C	A	W	4–0
3 Dec	West Ham U	H	W	2–0
10 Dec	Norwich C	A	L	1–2
17 Dec	QPR	H	W	1–0
26 Dec	Nottingham F	A	D	1–1
27 Dec	Wolverhampton W	H	W	1–0
31 Dec	Newcastle U	A	W	2–0
2 Jan	Middlesbrough	H	W	2–0
14 Jan	West Brom	A	W	1–0
21 Jan	Birmingham C	H	L	2–3
4 Feb	Coventry C	A	L	0–1
25 Feb	Manchester U	H	W	3–1
4 Mar	Chelsea	A	L	1–3
8 Mar	Derby County	A	L	2–4
11 Mar	Leeds U	H	W	1–0
25 Mar	Wolverhampton W	A	W	3–1
1 Apr	Aston Villa	A	W	3–0
5 Apr	Everton	A	W	1–0
8 Apr	Leicester C	H	W	3–2
15 Apr	Bristol C	A	D	1–1
18 Apr	Ipswich T	H	D	2–2
22 Apr	Norwich C	H	W	3–0
25 Apr	Arsenal	H	W	1–0
29 Apr	West Ham U	A	W	2–0
1 May	Manchester C	H	W	4–0
4 May	Nottingham F	H	D	0–0

Final League Position

	P	W	D	L	F	A	Pts	
Nottingham F	42	25	14	3	69	24	64	1st
Liverpool	42	24	9	9	65	34	57	2nd

League Appearances (goals)
Callaghan 26 · Clemence 40 · Case 33 (5)
Dalglish 42 (20) · Fairclough 29 (10) · Hansen 18
Heighway 28 (5) · Hughes 39 · Johnson 11 (3)
Jones 20 · Kennedy 41 (4) · Kewley 1 · Lee 2 (1)
McDermott 37 (4) · Neal 42 (4) · Ogrizovic 2
Smith 22 (2) · Souness 15 (2) · Thompson 27 (3)
Toshack 3 · Own goals (2)

FA CUP

7 Jan	Chelsea (3)	A	L	2–4

FA Cup Appearances (goals)
Callaghan 1 · Clemence 1 · Dalglish 1 (1)
Fairclough 1 · Hansen 1 · Heighway 1 · Hughes 1
Johnson 1 (1) · Jones 1 · Kennedy 1 · Neal 1
Thompson 1

LEAGUE CUP

30 Aug	Chelsea (2)	H	W	2–0
26 Oct	Derby County (3)	H	W	2–0
29 Nov	Coventry C (4)	H	D	2–2
20 Dec	Coventry C (4R)	A	W	2–0
17 Jan	Wrexham (5)	A	W	3–1
7 Feb	Arsenal (SF)	H	W	2–1
14 Feb	Arsenal (SF)	A	D	0–0
18 Mar	Nottingham F (F) (Wembley)	N	D	0–0*
22 Mar	Nottingham F (FR) (Old Trafford)	N	L	0–1

*after extra time

League Cup Appearances (goals)
Callaghan 7 · Case 8 (2) · Clemence 9 · Dalglish 9 (6)
Fairclough 7 (3) · Hansen 3 · Heighway 8 · Hughes 9
Johnson 1 · Jones 2 · Kennedy 9 (1) · McDermott 8
Neal 9 (1) · Smith 6 · Toshack 1

EUROPEAN CUP

19 Oct	Dynamo Dresden (2)	H	W	5–1
2 Nov	Dynamo Dresden (2)	A	L	1–2
1 Mar	Benfica (3)	A	W	2–1
15 Mar	Benfica (3)	H	W	4–1
29 Mar	Borussia M'gladbach (SF)	A	L	1–2
12 Apr	Borussia M'gladbach (SF)	H	W	3–0
10 May	FC Bruges (F) (Wembley)	N	W	1–0

European Cup Appearances (goals)
Callaghan 5 (1) · Case 7 (4) · Clemence 7
Dalglish 7 (3) · Fairclough 2 · Hansen 4 (1)
Heighway 7 (1) · Hughes 7 (1) · Jones 2
Johnson 1 (1) · Kennedy 7 (2) · McDermott 6 (1)
Neal 7 (2) · Smith 4 · Souness 3 · Thompson 5
Toshack 1

EUROPEAN SUPER CUP

22 Nov	SV Hamburg	A	D	1–1
6 Dec	SV Hamburg	H	W	6–0

European Super Cup Appearances (goals)
Callaghan 1 · Case 2 · Clemence 2 · Dalglish 2 (1)
Fairclough 2 (2) · Heighway 2 · Hughes 2 · Jones 1
Johnson 2 · Kennedy 2 · McDermott 1 (3) · Neal 2
Smith 2 · Thompson 2 (1)

SEASON 1978-79

FOOTBALL LEAGUE (DIVISION 1)

19 Aug	QPR	H	W	2–1
22 Aug	Ipswich T	A	W	3–0
26 Aug	Manchester C	A	W	4–1
2 Sep	Tottenham H	H	W	7–0
9 Sep	Birmingham C	A	W	3–0
16 Sep	Coventry C	H	W	1–0
23 Sep	West Brom	A	D	1–1
30 Sep	Bolton W	H	W	3–0
7 Oct	Norwich C	A	W	4–1
14 Oct	Derby County	H	W	5–0
21 Oct	Chelsea	H	W	2–0
28 Oct	Everton	A	L	0–1
4 Nov	Leeds U	H	D	1–1
11 Nov	QPR	A	W	3–1
18 Nov	Manchester C	H	W	1–0
22 Nov	Tottenham H	A	D	0–0
25 Nov	Middlesbrough	H	W	2–0
2 Dec	Arsenal	A	L	0–1
9 Dec	Nottingham F	H	W	2–0
16 Dec	Bristol C	A	L	0–1
26 Dec	Manchester U	A	W	3–0
3 Feb	West Brom	H	W	2–1
13 Feb	Birmingham C	H	W	1–0
21 Feb	Norwich C	H	W	6–0
24 Feb	Derby County	A	W	2–0
3 Mar	Chelsea	A	D	0–0
6 Mar	Coventry C	A	D	0–0
13 Mar	Everton	H	D	1–1
20 Mar	Wolverhampton W	H	W	2–0
24 Mar	Ipswich T	H	W	2–0
7 Apr	Arsenal	H	W	3–0
10 Apr	Wolverhampton W	A	W	1–0
14 Apr	Manchester U	H	W	2–0
16 Apr	Aston Villa	A	L	1–3
21 Apr	Bristol C	H	W	1–0
24 Apr	Southampton	A	D	1–1
28 Apr	Nottingham F	A	D	0–0
1 May	Bolton W	A	W	4–1
5 May	Southampton	H	W	2–0
8 May	Aston Villa	H	W	3–0
11 May	Middlesbrough	A	W	1–0
17 May	Leeds U	A	W	3–0

Final League Position

	P	W	D	L	F	A	Pts	
Liverpool	42	30	8	4	85	16	68	1st

League Appearances (goals)
Case 37 (7) · Clemence 42 · Dalglish 42 (21)
Fairclough 4 (2) · Hansen 34 (1) · Heighway 28 (4)
Hughes 16 · Johnson 30 (16) · Kennedy A 37 (3)
Kennedy R 42 (10) · Lee 2 · McDermott 37 (8)
Neal 42 (5) · Souness 41 (8) · Thompson 39

FA CUP

10 Jan	Southend U (3)	A	D	0–0
17 Jan	Southend U (3R)	H	W	3–0
30 Jan	Blackburn R (4)	H	W	1–0
28 Feb	Burnley (5)	H	W	3–0
10 Mar	Ipswich T (6)	A	W	1–0
31 Mar	Manchester U (SF) (Maine Road)	N	D	2–2
4 Apr	Manchester U (SF) (Goodison Park)	N	L	0–1

FA Cup Appearances (goals)
Case 6 (1) · Clemence 7 · Dalglish 7 (4) · Fairclough 3
Hansen 6 (1) · Heighway 5 · Hughes 7
Johnson 4 (2) · Kennedy A 2 · Kennedy R 7 (1)
McDermott 7 · Neal 7 · Souness 7 (1) · Thompson 6

LEAGUE CUP

28 Aug	Sheffield U (2)	A	L	0–1

League Cup Appearances (goals)
Case 1 · Clemence 1 · Dalglish 1 · Fairclough 1
Heighway 1 · Hughes 1 · Kennedy A 1 · Kennedy R 1
McDermott 1 · Neal 1 · Souness 1 · Thompson 1

EUROPEAN CUP

13 Sep	Nottingham F (1)	A	L	0–2
27 Sep	Nottingham F (1)	H	D	0–0

European Cup Appearances (goals)
Case 2 · Clemence 2 · Dalglish 2 · Fairclough 1
Heighway 2 · Hughes 2 · Johnson 2 · Kennedy A 2
Kennedy R 2 · McDermott 2 · Neal 2 · Souness 2
Thompson 2

EUROPEAN SUPER CUP

4 Dec	Anderlecht	A	L	1–3
19 Dec	Anderlecht	H	W	2–1

European Super Cup Appearances (goals)
Case 2 (1) · Clemence 1 · Dalglish 2 · Fairclough 1 (1)
Hansen 2 · Heighway 1 · Hughes 2 (1) · Johnson 1
Kennedy A 1 · Kennedy R 2 · McDermott 2 · Neal 2
Ogrizovic 1 · Souness 2 · Thompson 1

SEASON 1979-80

FOOTBALL LEAGUE (DIVISION 1)

21 Aug	Bolton W	H	D	0–0
25 Aug	West Brom	H	W	3–1
1 Sep	Southampton	A	L	2–3
8 Sep	Coventry C	H	W	4–0
15 Sep	Leeds U	A	D	1–1
22 Sep	Norwich C	H	D	0–0
29 Sep	Nottingham F	A	L	0–1
6 Oct	Bristol C	H	W	4–0
9 Oct	Bolton W	A	D	1–1
13 Oct	Ipswich T	A	W	2–1
20 Oct	Everton	H	D	2–2
27 Oct	Manchester C	A	W	4–0
3 Nov	Wolverhampton W	H	W	3–0
10 Nov	Brighton & HA	A	W	4–1
17 Nov	Tottenham H	H	W	2–1
24 Nov	Arsenal	A	D	0–0
1 Dec	Middlesbrough	H	W	4–0
8 Dec	Aston Villa	A	W	3–1
15 Dec	Crystal Palace	H	W	3–0
22 Dec	Derby County	A	W	3–1
26 Dec	Manchester U	H	W	2–0
29 Dec	West Brom	A	W	2–0
12 Jan	Southampton	H	D	1–1
19 Jan	Coventry C	A	L	0–1
9 Feb	Norwich C	A	W	5–3
19 Feb	Nottingham F	H	W	2–0
23 Feb	Ipswich T	H	D	1–1
26 Feb	Wolverhampton W	A	L	0–1
3 Mar	Everton	A	W	2–1
11 Mar	Manchester C	H	W	2–0
15 Mar	Bristol C	A	W	3–1
19 Mar	Leeds U	H	W	3–0
22 Mar	Brighton & HA	H	W	1–0
29 Mar	Tottenham H	A	L	0–2
1 Apr	Stoke C	H	W	1–0
5 Apr	Manchester U	A	L	1–2
8 Apr	Derby County	H	W	3–0
19 Apr	Arsenal	H	D	1–1
23 Apr	Stoke C	A	W	2–0
26 Apr	Crystal Palace	A	D	0–0
3 May	Aston Villa	H	W	4–1
6 May	Middlesbrough	A	L	0–1

Final League Position

	P	W	D	L	F	A	Pts	
Liverpool	42	25	10	7	81	30	60	1st

League Appearances (goals)
Case 37 (3) · Clemence 41 · Cohen 4 (1)
Dalglish 42 (16) · Fairclough 14 (5) · Hansen 38 (4)
Heighway 9 · Irwin 8 (2) · Johnson 37 (21)
Kennedy A 37 (1) · Kennedy R 40 (9) · Lee 7
McDermott 37 (11) · Neal 42 (1) · Ogrizovic 1
Souness 41 (1) · Thompson 42 · Own goals (6)

FA CUP

5 Jan	Grimsby T (3)	H	W	5–0
26 Jan	Nottingham F (4)	A	W	2–0
16 Feb	Bury (5)	H	W	2–0
8 Mar	Tottenham H (6)	A	W	1–0
12 Apr	Arsenal (SF) (Hillsborough)	N	D	0–0
16 Apr	Arsenal (SFR) (Villa Park)	N	D	1–1*
28 Apr	Arsenal (SFR) (Villa Park)	N	D	1–1*
1 May	Arsenal (SFR) (Highfield Road)	N	L	0–1

*after extra time

FA Cup Appearances (goals)
Case 5 (1) · Clemence 8 · Cohen 1 · Dalglish 8 (2)
Fairclough 5 (3) · Hansen 8 · Irwin 2 · Johnson 8 (3)
Kennedy A 5 · Kennedy R 8 · Lee 4 · McDermott 6 (2)
Neal 8 · Souness 8 (1) · Thompson 8

LEAGUE CUP

29 Aug	Tranmere R (2)	A	D	0–0
4 Sep	Tranmere R (2)	H	W	4–0
25 Sep	Chesterfield (3)	H	W	3–1
30 Oct	Exeter C (4)	H	W	2–0
5 Dec	Norwich C (5)	A	W	3–1
22 Jan	Nottingham F (SF)	A	L	0–1
12 Feb	Nottingham F (SF)	H	D	1–1

League Cup Appearances (goals)
Case 7 · Clemence 7 · Dalglish 7 (4) · Fairclough 5 (5)
Hansen 5 · Heighway 1 · Irwin 2 · Johnson 6 (2)
Kennedy A 7 · Kennedy R 6 · McDermott 7 (1)
Neal 7 · Souness 7 · Thompson 7 (1)

EUROPEAN CUP

19 Sep	Dynamo Tbilisi (1)	H	W	2–1
3 Oct	Dynamo Tbilisi (1)	A	L	0–3

European Cup Appearances (goals)
Case 2 (1) · Clemence 2 · Dalglish 2 · Fairclough 2
Hansen 1 · Heighway 1 · Irwin 2 · Johnson 2 (1)
Kennedy A 1 · Kennedy R 1 · McDermott 2 · Neal 2
Souness 2 · Thompson 2

SEASON 1980-81

FOOTBALL LEAGUE (DIVISION 1)

16 Aug	Crystal Palace	H	W	3–0
19 Aug	Coventry C	A	D	0–0
23 Aug	Leicester C	A	L	0–2
30 Aug	Norwich C	H	W	4–1
6 Sep	Birmingham C	A	D	1–1

13 Sep	West Brom	H	W	4–0
20 Sep	Southampton	A	D	2–2
27 Sep	Brighton & HA	H	W	4–1
4 Oct	Manchester C	A	W	3–0
7 Oct	Middlesbrough	H	W	4–2
11 Oct	Ipswich T	H	D	1–1
18 Oct	Everton	A	D	2–2
25 Oct	Arsenal	H	D	1–1
1 Nov	Stoke C	A	D	2–2
8 Nov	Nottingham F	H	D	0–0
11 Nov	Coventry C	A	W	2–1
15 Nov	Crystal Palace	A	D	2–2
22 Nov	Aston Villa	H	W	2–1
25 Nov	Wolverhampton W	A	L	1–4
29 Nov	Sunderland	A	W	4–2
6 Dec	Tottenham H	H	W	2–1
13 Dec	Ipswich T	A	D	1–1
20 Dec	Wolverhampton W	H	W	1–0
26 Dec	Manchester U	A	D	0–0
27 Dec	Leeds U	H	D	0–0
10 Jan	Aston Villa	A	L	0–2
17 Jan	Norwich C	A	W	1–0
31 Jan	Leicester C	H	L	1–2
7 Feb	West Brom	A	L	0–2
14 Feb	Birmingham C	H	D	2–2
21 Feb	Brighton & HA	A	D	2–2
28 Feb	Southampton	H	W	2–0
21 Mar	Everton	H	W	1–0
28 Mar	Arsenal	A	L	0–1
3 Apr	Stoke C	H	W	3–0
11 Apr	Nottingham F	A	D	0–0
14 Apr	Manchester U	H	L	0–1
18 Apr	Leeds U	A	D	0–0
25 Apr	Tottenham H	A	D	1–1
2 May	Sunderland	H	L	0–1
5 May	Middlesbrough	A	W	2–1
14 May	Manchester C	H	W	1–0

Final League Position

	P	W	D	L	F	A	Pts	
Aston Villa	42	26	8	8	72	40	60	1st
Liverpool	42	17	17	8	62	42	51	5th

League Appearances (goals)
Clemence 41 · Ogrizovic 1 · Neal 42 (2)
Hansen 36 (1) · Thompson 25 · A. Kennedy 19 (2)
Irwin 21 (1) · Cohen 14 · Money 14

McDermott 40 (13) · R. Kennedy 41 (8)
Souness 37 (6) · Lee 37 (4) · Case 24 (1)
Whelan 1 (1) · Dalglish 34 (8) · Johnson 29 (8)
Fairclough 9 (4) · Rush 7 · Heighway 6 · Sheedy 1
Gayle 4 (1) · Russell 1

FA CUP

3 Jan	Altrincham (3)	H	W	4–1
24 Jan	Everton (4)	A	L	1–2

FA Cup Appearances (goals)
Clemence 2 · Neal 2 · Thompson 1 · Irwin 2
A. Kennedy 1 · Money 1 · Cohen 1 · McDermott 2 (1)
Case 2 (1) · R. Kennedy 2 (1) · Souness 1 · Lee 2
Dalglish 2 (2) · Fairclough 1 · Johnson 1

LEAGUE CUP

27 Aug	Bradford C (2)	A	L	0–1
2 Sep	Bradford C (2)	H	W	4–0
23 Sep	Swindon T (3)	H	W	5–0
28 Oct	Portsmouth (4)	H	W	4–1
2 Dec	Birmingham C (5)	H	W	3–1
14 Jan	Manchester C (SF)	A	W	1–0
10 Feb	Manchester C (SF)	H	D	1–1
14 Mar	West Ham U (F)	N	D	1–1*

(Wembley) *after extra time

1 Apr	West Ham U (FR)	N	W	2–1

(Villa Park)

League Cup Appearances (goals)
Clemence 9 · Neal 9 · Hansen 8 (1)
A. Kennedy 7 (1) · Thompson 6 · Irwin 4 · Cohen 1
Money 1 · R. Kennedy 9 (2) · McDermott 9 (1)
Souness 8 (1) · Lee 7 (2) · Case 4 · Dalglish 8 (7)
Johnson 5 (4) · Fairclough 4 (1) · Heighway 1 · Rush 1

EUROPEAN CUP

17 Sep	Oulou Palloseura (1)	A	D	1–1
1 Oct	Oulou Palloseura (1)	H	W	10–1
22 Oct	Aberdeen (2)	A	W	1–0
5 Nov	Aberdeen (2)	H	W	4–0
4 Mar	CSKA Sofia (3)	H	W	5–1
18 Mar	CSKA Sofia (3)	A	W	1–0
8 Apr	Bayern Munich (SF)	H	D	0–0
22 Apr	Bayern Munich (SF)	A	D	1–1*
27 May	Real Madrid (F)	N	W	1–0

(Paris)
*won on away goals

European Cup Appearances (goals)
Clemence 9 · Neal 9 (1) · Hansen 9 (1) · Thompson 7
A. Kennedy 6 (1) · Irwin 3 · Cohen 3 · Money 1
Lee 9 (2) · R. Kennedy 9 (2) · Souness 8 (6)
McDermott 8 (6) · Case 5 · Dalglish 9 (1)
Johnson 5 (1) · Heighway 3 · Fairclough 2 (2)
Rush 1 · Gayle 1

SEASON 1981-82

FOOTBALL LEAGUE (DIVISION 1)

29 Aug	Wolverhampton W	A	L	0–1
1 Sep	Middlesbrough	H	D	1–1
5 Sep	Arsenal	H	W	2–0
12 Sep	Ipswich T	A	L	0–2
19 Sep	Aston Villa	H	D	0–0
22 Sep	Coventry C	A	W	2–1
26 Sep	West Ham U	A	D	1–1
3 Oct	Swansea C	H	D	2–2
10 Oct	Leeds U	H	W	3–0
17 Oct	Brighton & HA	A	D	3–3
24 Oct	Manchester U	H	L	1–2
31 Oct	Sunderland	A	W	2–0
7 Nov	Everton	H	W	3–1
21 Nov	West Brom	A	D	1–1
28 Nov	Southampton	H	L	0–1
5 Dec	Nottingham F	A	W	2–0
26 Dec	Manchester C	H	L	1–3
5 Jan	West Ham U	H	W	3–0
16 Jan	Wolverhampton W	H	W	2–1
26 Jan	Notts County	A	W	4–0
30 Jan	Aston Villa	A	W	3–0
6 Feb	Ipswich T	H	W	4–0
16 Feb	Swansea C	A	L	0–2
20 Feb	Coventry C	H	W	4–0
27 Feb	Leeds U	A	W	2–0
9 Mar	Stoke C	A	W	5–1
20 Mar	Sunderland	H	W	1–0
27 Mar	Everton	A	W	1–0
30 Mar	Birmingham C	H	W	3–1
2 Apr	Notts County	H	W	1–0
7 Apr	Manchester U	A	W	1–0
10 Apr	Manchester C	A	W	5–0
13 Apr	Stoke C	H	W	2–0

■ It's not unusual . . . the scene is Wembley, and once again Liverpool are celebrating success. This time it's the 1982 Milk Cup final, and Tottenham Hotspur have been on the losing end. So Liverpool retain the trophy.

17 Apr	West Brom	H	W	1–0
24 Apr	Southampton	A	W	3–2
1 May	Nottingham F	H	W	2–0
3 May	Tottenham H	A	D	2–2
8 May	Birmingham C	A	W	1–0
11 May	Arsenal	A	D	1–1
15 May	Tottenham H	H	W	3–1
18 May	Middlesbrough	A	D	0–0

Final League Position

	P	W	D	L	F	A	Pts	
Liverpool	42	26	9	7	80	32	87	1st

League Appearances (goals)
Grobbelaar 42 · Neal 42 (2) · Lawrenson 38 (2)
A. Kennedy 34 (3) · Hansen 35 · Thompson 34
Souness 35 (5) · Lee 35 (3) · Whelan 32 (10)
McDermott 29 (14) · R. Kennedy 15 (3)
Johnston 19 (6) · Sheedy 2 · Dalglish 42 (13)
Rush 32 (17) · Johnson 15 (2)

FA CUP

2 Jan	Swansea C (3)	A	W	4–0
23 Jan	Sunderland (4)	A	W	3–0
13 Feb	Chelsea (5)	A	L	0–2

FA Cup Appearances (goals)
Grobbelaar 3 · Neal 3 · A. Kennedy 3
Lawrenson 3 (1) · Hansen 3 (1) · Thompson 1
Whelan 3 · McDermott 3 · Souness 3 · Lee 2
Johnston 1 · Rush 3 (3) · Dalglish 3 (2) · Johnson 1

LEAGUE CUP

7 Oct	Exeter C (2)	H	W	5–0
28 Oct	Exeter C (2)	A	W	6–0
10 Nov	Middlesbrough (3)	H	W	4–1
1 Dec	Arsenal (4)	A	D	0–0
8 Dec	Arsenal (4R)	H	W	3–0
12 Jan	Barnsley (5)	H	D	0–0
19 Jan	Barnsley (5R)	A	W	3–1
2 Feb	Ipswich T (SF)	A	W	2–0
9 Feb	Ipswich T (SF)	H	D	2–2
13 Mar	Tottenham H (F)	N	W	3–1*

(Wembley)
*After extra time

League Cup Appearances (goals)
Grobbelaar 10 · Neal 10 (1) · Lawrenson 10
Hansen 8 · Thompson 7 · A. Kennedy 6
McDermott 10 (3) · Souness 9 (1) · Lee 6
R. Kennedy 3 · Johnston 2 (1) · Sheedy 2 (2)
Whelan 8 (3) · Rush 10 (8) · Dalglish 10 (5)
Johnson 5 (3)

EUROPEAN CUP

16 Sep	Oulou Palloseura (1)	A	W	1–0
30 Sep	Oulou Palloseura (1)	H	W	7–0
21 Oct	AZ 67 Alkmaar (2)	A	D	2–2
4 Nov	AZ 67 Alkmaar (2)	H	W	3–2
3 Mar	CSKA Sofia (3)	H	W	1–0
17 Mar	CSKA Sofia (3)	A	L	0–2

European Cup Appearances (goals)
Grobbelaar 6 · Neal 6 · Lawrenson 6 (1)
Hansen 5 (1) · Thompson 5 · A. Kennedy 4
Souness 6 · McDermott 5 (3) · R. Kennedy 4 (1)
Lee 5 (1) · Whelan 4 (1) · Johnston 1 · Dalglish 6 (2)
Rush 4 (2) · Johnson 4 (2)

WORLD CLUB CHAMPIONSHIP

13 Dec	Flamengo	N	L	0–3

(Tokyo)

World Club Championship Appearances (goals)
Grobbelaar 1 · Neal 1 · Lawrenson 1 · Thompson 1
R. Kennedy 1 · Hansen 1 · Dalglish 1 · Lee 1
Johnston 1 . McDermott 1 · Souness 1 · Johnson 1

SEASON 1982-83

FOOTBALL LEAGUE (DIVISION 1)

28 Aug	West Brom	H	W	2–0
31 Aug	Birmingham C	A	D	0–0
4 Sep	Arsenal	A	W	2–0
7 Sep	Nottingham F	H	W	4–3
11 Sep	Luton T	H	D	3–3
18 Sep	Swansea C	A	W	3–0
25 Sep	Southampton	H	W	5–0
2 Oct	Ipswich T	A	L	0–1
9 Oct	West Ham U	A	L	1–3
16 Oct	Manchester U	H	D	0–0
23 Oct	Stoke C	A	D	1–1
30 Oct	Brighton & HA	H	W	3–1
6 Nov	Everton	A	W	5–0
13 Nov	Coventry C	H	W	4–0
20 Nov	Notts County	A	W	2–1
27 Nov	Tottenham H	H	W	3–0
4 Dec	Norwich C	A	L	0–1
11 Dec	Watford	H	W	3–1
18 Dec	Aston Villa	A	W	4–2
27 Dec	Manchester C	H	W	5–2
28 Dec	Sunderland	A	D	0–0
1 Jan	Notts County	H	W	5–1
3 Jan	Arsenal	H	W	3–1
15 Jan	West Bromich	A	W	1–0
22 Jan	Birmingham C	H	W	1–0
5 Feb	Luton T	A	W	3–1
12 Feb	Ipswich T	H	W	1–0
26 Feb	Manchester U	A	D	1–1
5 Mar	Stoke C	H	W	5–1
12 Mar	West Ham U	H	W	3–0
19 Mar	Everton	H	D	0–0
22 Mar	Brighton & HA	A	D	2–2
2 Apr	Sunderland	H	W	1–0
4 Apr	Manchester C	A	W	4–0
9 Apr	Swansea C	H	W	3–0
12 Apr	Coventry C	A	D	0–0
16 Apr	Southampton	A	L	2–3
23 Apr	Norwich C	H	L	0–2
30 Apr	Tottenham H	A	L	0–2
2 May	Nottingham F	A	L	0–1
7 May	Aston Villa	H	D	1–1
14 May	Watford	A	L	1–2

Final League Position

	P	W	D	L	F	A	Pts	
Liverpool	42	24	10	8	87	37	82	1st

League Appearances (goals)
Grobbelaar 42 · Neal 42 (8) · Kennedy A 42 (3)
Lawrenson 40 (5) · Hansen 34 · Thompson 24
Souness 41 (9) · Lee 40 (3) · Whelan 28 (2)
Johnston 32 (7) · Nicol 4 · McDermott 2
Dalglish 42 (18) · Rush 34 (24) · Hodgson 23 (4)
Fairclough 8 (3)

FA CUP

8 Jan	Blackburn R (3)	A	W	2–1
29 Jan	Stoke C (4)	H	W	2–0
20 Feb	Brighton & HA (5)	H	L	1–2

FA Cup Appearances (goals)
Grobbelaar 3 · Neal 3 · Kennedy A 3 · Hansen 3
Lawrenson 3 · Souness 3 · Lee 3 · Johnston 3 (1)
Whelan 1 · Rush 3 (2) · Dalglish 3 (1) · Hodgson 3 (1)

MILK CUP

5 Oct	Ipswich T (2)	A	W	2–1
26 Oct	Ipswich T (2)	H	W	2–0
10 Nov	Rotherham U (3)	H	W	1–0
30 Nov	Norwich C (4)	H	W	2–0
18 Jan	West Ham U (5)	H	W	2–1
8 Feb	Burnley (SF)	H	W	3–0
15 Feb	Burnley (SF)	A	L	0–1
26 Mar	Manchester U (F)	N	W	2–1

(Wembley)

Milk Cup Appearances (goals)
Grobbelaar 8 · Neal 8 (1) · Lawrenson 8 (2)
Kennedy A 8 (1) · Hansen 8 · Thompson 4
Souness 8 (2) · Lee 8 · Whelan 6 (2) · Johnston 6 (1)
Rush 8 (2) · Dalglish 7 · Hodgson 5 (2)
Fairclough 2 (1)

EUROPEAN CUP

14 Sep	Dundalk (1)	A	W	4–1
28 Sep	Dundalk (1)	H	W	1–0
19 Oct	JK Helsinki (2)	A	L	0–1
2 Nov	JK Helsinki (2)	H	W	5–0
2 Mar	Widzew Lodz (3)	A	L	0–2
16 Mar	Widzew Lodz (3)	H	W	3–2

European Cup Appearances (goals)
Grobbelaar 6 · Neal 6 (2) · Kennedy A 6 (2)
Hansen 6 · Thompson 5 · Lawrenson 3 · Souness 6
Lee 6 · Whelan 5 (3) · Johnston 4 (1) · McDermott 1
Rush 5 (2) · Dalglish 5 (1) · Hodgson 5 (2)
Fairclough 1

SEASON 1983-84

FOOTBALL LEAGUE (DIVISION 1)

27 Aug	Wolverhampton W	A	D	1–1
31 Aug	Norwich C	A	W	1–0
3 Sep	Nottingham F	H	W	1–0
6 Sep	Southampton	H	D	1–1
10 Sep	Arsenal	H	W	2–0
17 Sep	Aston Villa	H	W	2–1
24 Sep	Manchester U	A	L	0–1
1 Oct	Sunderland	H	L	0–1
15 Oct	West Ham U	A	W	3–1
22 Oct	QPR	A	W	1–0
29 Oct	Luton T	H	W	6–0
6 Nov	Everton	H	W	3–0
12 Nov	Tottenham H	A	D	2–2
19 Nov	Stoke C	H	W	1–0
26 Nov	Ipswich T	A	D	1–1
3 Dec	Birmingham C	H	W	1–0
10 Dec	Coventry C	A	L	0–4
17 Dec	Notts County	H	W	5–0
26 Dec	West Brom	A	W	2–1
27 Dec	Leicester C	H	D	2–2
31 Dec	Nottingham F	A	W	1–0
2 Jan	Manchester U	H	D	1–1
14 Jan	Wolverhampton W	H	L	0–1
20 Jan	Aston Villa	A	W	3–1
1 Feb	Watford	H	W	3–0
4 Feb	Sunderland	A	D	0–0
11 Feb	Arsenal	H	W	2–1
18 Feb	Luton Town	A	D	0–0
25 Feb	QPR	H	W	2–0
3 Mar	Everton	A	D	1–1
10 Mar	Tottenham H	H	W	3–1
16 Mar	Southampton	A	L	0–2
31 Mar	Watford	A	W	2–0
7 Apr	West Ham U	H	W	6–0
14 Apr	Stoke C	A	L	0–2
18 Apr	Leicester C	A	D	3–3
21 Apr	West Brom	H	W	3–0
28 Apr	Ipswich T	H	D	2–2
5 May	Birmingham C	A	D	0–0
7 May	Coventry C	H	W	5–0
12 May	Notts County	A	D	0–0
15 May	Norwich C	H	D	1–1

Final League Position

	P	W	D	L	F	A	Pts	
Liverpool	42	22	14	6	73	32	80	1st

League Appearances (goals)
Grobbelaar 42 · Kennedy 42 (2) · Neal 41 (1)
Hansen 42 (1) · Lawrenson 42 · Nicol 23 (5)
Lee 42 (2) · Souness 37 (7) · Johnston 29 (2)
Whelan 23 (4) · Wark 9 (2) · Rush 41 (32)
Dalglish 33 (7) · Robinson 24 (6) · Hodgson 5

FA CUP

6 Jan	Newcastle U (3)	H	W	4–0
29 Jan	Brighton & HA (4)	A	L	0–2

FA Cup Appearances (goals)
Grobbelaar 2 · Neal 2 · Kennedy 2 · Lawrenson 2
Hansen 2 · Nicol 2 · Johnston 2 (1) · Souness 2
Lee 2 · Whelan 1 · Rush 2 (2) · Robinson 2 (1)

MILK CUP

5 Oct	Brentford (2)	A	W	4–1
25 Oct	Brentford (2)	H	W	4–0
8 Nov	Fulham (3)	A	D	1–1
22 Nov	Fulham (3R)	H	D	1–1*
29 Nov	Fulham (3R)	A	W	1–0
20 Dec	Birmingham C (4)	A	D	1–1
22 Dec	Birmingham (4R)	H	W	3–0
17 Jan	Sheffield W (5)	A	D	2–2
25 Jan	Sheffield W (5R)	H	W	3–0
7 Feb	Walsall (SF)	H	D	2–2
14 Feb	Walsall (SF)	A	W	2–0
25 Mar	Everton (F)	N	D	0–0*

(Wembley)

28 Mar	Everton (FR)	N	W	1–0

(Maine Road)
*after extra time

Milk Cup Appearances (goals)
Grobbelaar 13 · Hansen 13 · Kennedy 13
Lawrenson 12 · Neal 12 (1) · Nicol 9 (2) · Gillespie 1
Souness 12 (5) · Lee 13 · Johnston 12 · Whelan 5 (3)
Rush 12 (8) · Robinson 9 (3) · Dalglish 8 (2)
Hodgson 4 (1)

EUROPEAN CUP

14 Sep	BK Odense (1)	A	W	1–0
28 Sep	BK Odense (1)	H	W	5–0
19 Oct	Athletic Bilbao (2)	H	D	0–0
2 Nov	Athletic Bilbao (2)	A	W	1–0
7 Mar	Benfica (3)	H	W	1–0
21 Mar	Benfica (3)	A	W	4–1
11 Apr	Dinamo Bucharest (SF)	H	W	1–0
25 Apr	Dinamo Bucharest (SF)	A	W	2–1
30 May	AS Roma (F)	N	D	1–1*

(Rome)
*Liverpool won 4–2 on penalties. Scorers: Neal, Rush, Souness, Kennedy

European Cup Appearances (goals)
Grobbelaar 9 · Hansen 9 · Kennedy 9 · Lawrenson 9
Neal 8 (1) · Nicol 4 · Souness 9 · Johnston 8 (1)
Lee 9 (1) · Whelan 5 (2) · Rush 9 (5) · Dalglish 9 (3)
Robinson 6 (2) · Hodgson 2

SEASON 1984-85

FOOTBALL LEAGUE (DIVISION 1)

25 Aug	Norwich C	A	D	3–3
27 Aug	West Ham U	H	W	3–0
1 Sep	QPR	H	D	1–1
4 Sep	Luton T	A	W	2–1
8 Sep	Arsenal	A	L	1–3
15 Sep	Sunderland	H	D	1–1
22 Sep	Manchester U	A	D	1–1
29 Sep	Sheffield W	H	L	0–2
6 Oct	West Brom	H	D	0–0
12 Oct	Tottenham H	A	L	0–1
20 Oct	Everton	H	L	0–1
28 Oct	Nottingham F	A	W	2–0
3 Nov	Stoke C	A	W	1–0
10 Nov	Southampton	H	D	1–1
18 Nov	Newcastle U	A	W	2–0
24 Nov	Ipswich T	H	W	2–0
1 Dec	Chelsea	A	L	1–3
4 Dec	Coventry C	H	W	3–1
15 Dec	Aston Villa	A	D	0–0
21 Dec	QPR	A	W	2–0
26 Dec	Leicester C	H	L	1–2
29 Dec	Luton T	H	W	1–0
1 Jan	Watford	A	D	1–1
19 Jan	Norwich C	H	W	4–0
2 Feb	Sheffield W	A	D	1–1
12 Feb	Arsenal	H	W	3–0
23 Feb	Stoke C	H	W	2–0
2 Mar	Nottingham F	H	W	1–0
16 Mar	Tottenham H	H	L	0–1
23 Mar	West Brom	A	W	5–0
31 Mar	Manchester U	H	L	0–1
3 Apr	Sunderland	A	W	3–0
6 Apr	Leicester C	A	W	1–0
20 Apr	Newcastle U	H	W	3–1
27 Apr	Ipswich T	A	D	0–0
4 May	Chelsea	H	W	4–3
6 May	Coventry C	A	W	2–0
11 May	Aston Villa	H	W	2–1
14 May	Southampton	A	D	1–1
17 May	Watford	H	W	4–3
20 May	West Ham U	A	W	3–0
23 May	Everton	A	L	0–1

Final League Position

	P	W	D	L	F	A	Pts	
Everton	42	28	6	8	88	43	90	1st
Liverpool	42	22	11	9	68	35	77	2nd

League Appearances (goals)
Grobbelaar 42 · Neal 42 (4) · Hansen 41
Nicol 31 (5) · Kennedy 32 (1) · Lawrenson 33 (1)
Gillespie 12 (1) · Beglin 10 (1) · Whelan 37 (7)
Wark 40 (18) · Molby 22 (1) · Lee 17 · MacDonald 13
Johnston 11 · Dalglish 36 (6) · Walsh 26 (8)
Rush 29 (14) · Robinson 6

FA CUP

5 Jan	Aston Villa (3)	H	W	3–0
27 Jan	Tottenham H (4)	H	W	1–0
16 Feb	York C (5)	A	D	1–1
20 Feb	York C (5R)	H	W	7–0
10 Mar	Barnsley (6)	A	W	4–0
13 Apr	Manchester U (SF)	N	D	2–2

(Goodison Park)

17 Apr	Manchester U (SFR)	N	L	1–2

(Maine Road)

FA Cup Appearances (goals)
Grobbelaar 7 · Neal 7 (1) · Hansen 7 · MacDonald 7
Kennedy 5 · Lawrenson 4 · Nicol 6 · Gillespie 4
Wark 7 (4) · Whelan 7 (4) · Beglin 2 · Lee 1
Rush 6 (7) · Dalglish 7 · Walsh 3 (2)

MILK CUP

24 Sep	Stockport County (2)	A	D	0–0
9 Oct	Stockport County (2)	H	W	2–0
31 Oct	Tottenham H (3)	A	L	0–1

Milk Cup Appearances (goals)
Grobbelaar 3 · Neal 3 · Kennedy 3 · Lawrenson 2
Hansen 2 · Gillespie 3 · Lee 2 · Nicol 2 · Whelan 3 (1)
Wark 3 · Johnston 1 · Molby 1 · Robinson 3 (1)
Walsh 2 · Dalglish 1 · Rush 1

EUROPEAN CUP

19 Sep	Lech Poznan (1)	A	W	1–0
3 Oct	Lech Poznan (1)	H	W	4–0
24 Oct	Benfica (2)	H	W	3–1
7 Nov	Benfica (2)	A	L	0–1
6 Mar	FK Austria Memphis (3)	A	D	1–1
20 Mar	FK Austria Memphis (3)	H	W	4–1
10 Apr	Panathinaikos (SF)	H	W	4–0
24 Apr	Panathinaikos (SF)	A	W	1–0
29 May	Juventus (F)	N	L	0–1

(Brussels)

European Cup Appearances (goals)
Grobbelaar 9 · Neal 9 · Hansen 9 · Lawrenson 9 (1)
Kennedy 6 · Nicol 6 (2) · Beglin 3 (1) · Gillespie 3
Wark 9 (5) · Whelan 9 · Johnston 4 · Lee 4
Rush 6 (5) · Walsh 6 (3) · Dalglish 7 · Robinson 1
MacDonald 3

WORLD CLUB CHAMPIONSHIP

9 Dec	Independiente	N	L	0–1

(Tokyo)

World Club Championship Appearances (goals)
Grobbelaar 1 · Neal 1 · Kennedy 1 · Gillespie 1
Nicol 1 · Hansen 1 · Dalglish 1 · Molby 1 · Rush 1
Johnston 1 · Wark 1

EUROPEAN SUPER CUP

16 Jan	Juventus	A	L	0–2

European Super Cup Appearances (goals)
Grobbelaar 1 · Neal 1 · Kennedy 1 · Lawrenson 1
Nicol 1 · Hansen 1 · Walsh 1 · Whelan 1 · Rush 1
MacDonald 1 · Wark 1 · Gillespie 1

SEASON 1985-86

FOOTBALL LEAGUE (DIVISION 1)

17 Aug	Arsenal	H	W	2–0
21 Aug	Aston Villa	A	D	2–2
24 Aug	Newcastle U	A	L	0–1
26 Aug	Ipswich T	H	W	5–0
31 Aug	West Ham U	A	D	2–2
3 Sep	Nottingham F	H	W	2–0
7 Sep	Watford	H	W	3–1
14 Sep	Oxford U	A	D	2–2
21 Sep	Everton	A	W	3–2
28 Sep	Tottenham H	H	W	4–1
5 Oct	QPR	A	L	1–2
12 Oct	Southampton	H	W	1–0
19 Oct	Manchester U	A	D	1–1
26 Oct	Luton T	H	W	3–2
2 Nov	Leicester C	H	W	1–0
9 Nov	Coventry C	A	W	3–0
16 Nov	West Brom	H	W	4–1
23 Nov	Birmingham C	A	W	2–0
30 Nov	Chelsea	H	D	1–1
7 Dec	Aston Villa	H	W	3–0
14 Dec	Arsenal	A	L	0–2
21 Dec	Newcastle U	H	D	1–1
26 Dec	Manchester C	A	L	0–1
28 Dec	Nottingham F	A	D	1–1
1 Jan	Sheffield W	H	D	2–2
12 Jan	Watford	A	W	3–2
18 Jan	West Ham U	H	W	3–1
1 Feb	Ipswich T	A	L	1–2
9 Feb	Manchester U	H	D	1–1
22 Feb	Everton	H	L	0–2
2 Mar	Tottenham H	A	W	2–1

8 Mar	QPR	H	W	4–1
15 Mar	Southampton	A	W	2–1
22 Mar	Oxford U	H	W	6–0
29 Mar	Sheffield W	A	D	0–0
31 Mar	Manchester C	H	W	2–0
12 Apr	Coventry C	H	W	5–0
16 Apr	Luton T	A	W	1–0
19 Apr	West Brom	A	W	2–1
26 Apr	Birmingham C	H	W	5–0
30 Apr	Leicester C	A	W	2–0
3 May	Chelsea	A	W	1–0

Final League Position

	P	W	D	L	F	A	Pts	
Liverpool	42	26	10	6	89	37	88	1st

League Appearances (goals)

Grobbelaar 42 · Hansen 41 · Lawrenson 37 (3)
Beglin 34 (1) · Nicol 34 (4) · Gillespie 14 (3)
Neal 13 (1) · MacDonald 17 (1) · Kennedy 8
Whelan 39 (10) · McMahon 23 (6) · Johnston 41 (7)
Molby 39 (14) · Lee 15 · Wark 9 (3) · Rush 40 (22)
Walsh 20 (11) · Dalglish 21 (3)

FA CUP

4 Jan	Norwich C (3)	H	W	5–0
26 Jan	Chelsea (4)	A	W	2–1
15 Feb	York C (5)	A	D	1–1
18 Feb	York C (5R)	H	W	3–1
11 Mar	Watford (6)	H	D	0–0
17 Mar	Watford (6R)	A	W	2–1
5 Apr	Southampton (SF)	N	W	2–0
	(White Hart Lane)			
10 May	Everton (F)	N	W	3–1
	(Wembley)			

FA Cup Appearances (goals)

Grobbelaar 8 · Hansen 8 · Lawrenson 7 (1) · Beglin 7
Gillespie 5 · Nicol 4 · Seagreaves 1 · Molby 8 (3)
Whelan 7 (1) · McMahon 4 (1) · Johnston 8 (1)
Wark 4 (2) · MacDonald 2 (1) · Lee 3 · Rush 8 (6)
Dalglish 6 (1) · Walsh 2 (1)

MILK CUP

| 24 Sep | Oldham A (2) | H | W | 3–0 |
| 9 Oct | Oldham A (2) | A | W | 5–2 |

---

29 Oct	Brighton & HA (3)	H	W	4–0
26 Nov	Manchester U (4)	H	W	2–1
21 Jan	Ipswich T (5)	H	W	3–0
12 Feb	QPR (SF)	A	L	0–1
5 Mar	QPR (SF)	H	D	2–2

Milk Cup Appearances (goals)

Grobbelaar 7 · Hansen 7 · Lawrenson 7 · Beglin 7
Nicol 3 · Gillespie 2 · Neal 2 · Seagraves 1
Whelan 7 (3) · Johnston 7 (1) · McMahon 5 (3)
Molby 5 · Wark 3 (1) · Lee 3 · MacDonald 2 (1)
Rush 6 (3) · Walsh 4 (4) · Dalglish 2 (1)

SCREEN SPORT SUPER CUP

17 Sep	Southampton (1)	H	W	2–1
22 Oct	Southampton (1)	A	D	1–1
3 Dec	Tottenham H (2)	H	W	2–0
14 Jan	Tottenham H (2)	A	W	3–0
5 Feb	Norwich C (SF)	A	D	1–1
6 May	Norwich C (SF)	H	W	3–1

(Final versus Everton postponed to following season)

Screen Sport Super Cup Appearances (goals)

Grobbelaar 6 · Lawrenson 6 (1) · Beglin 5 · Nicol 6
Hansen 4 · Neal 1 · Gillespie 3 · Molby 6 (2)
Johnston 5 (1) · MacDonald 4 (2) · Whelan 4
McMahon 4 · Lee 5 · Wark 2 · Walsh 6 (2)
Rush 2 (2) · Dalglish 2 (2)

SEASON 1986-87

FOOTBALL LEAGUE (DIVISION 1)

23 Aug	Newcastle U	A	W	2–0
25 Aug	Manchester C	H	D	0–0
30 Aug	Arsenal	H	W	2–1
3 Sep	Leicester C	A	L	1–2
6 Sep	West Ham U	A	W	5–2
13 Sep	Charlton A	H	W	2–0
20 Sep	Southampton	A	L	1–2
27 Sep	Aston Villa	H	D	3–3
4 Oct	Wimbledon	A	W	3–1
11 Oct	Tottenham H	H	L	0–1
18 Oct	Oxford U	H	W	4–0

---

25 Oct	Luton T	A	L	1–4
1 Nov	Norwich C	H	W	6–2
8 Nov	QPR	A	W	3–1
16 Nov	Sheffield W	H	D	1–1
23 Nov	Everton	A	D	0–0
29 Nov	Coventry C	H	W	2–0
6 Dec	Watford	A	L	0–2
14 Dec	Chelsea	H	W	3–0
20 Dec	Charlton A	A	D	0–0
26 Dec	Manchester U	H	L	0–1
27 Dec	Sheffield W	A	W	1–0
1 Jan	Nottingham F	A	D	1–1
3 Jan	West Ham U	H	W	1–0
17 Jan	Manchester C	A	W	1–0
24 Jan	Newcastle U	H	W	2–0
14 Feb	Leicester C	H	W	4–3
21 Feb	Aston Villa	A	D	2–2
28 Feb	Southampton	H	W	1–0
7 Mar	Luton T	H	W	2–0
10 Mar	Arsenal	A	W	1–0
14 Mar	Oxford U	A	W	3–1
18 Mar	QPR	H	W	2–1
22 Mar	Tottenham H	A	L	0–1
28 Mar	Wimbledon	H	L	1–2
11 Apr	Norwich C	A	L	1–2
18 Apr	Nottingham F	H	W	3–0
20 Apr	Manchester U	A	L	0–1
25 Apr	Everton	H	W	3–1
2 May	Coventry C	A	L	0–1
4 May	Watford	H	W	1–0
9 May	Chelsea	A	D	3–3

Final League Position

	P	W	D	L	F	A	Pts	
Everton	42	26	8	8	76	31	86	1st
Liverpool	42	23	8	11	72	42	77	2nd

League Appearances (goals)

Grobbelaar 31 · Hooper 11 · Hansen 39 · Gillespie 37
Lawrenson 35 · Venison 33 · Beglin 20
Nicol 14 (3) · Spackman 12 · Ablett 5 (1)
Whelan 39 (3) · McMahon 37 (5) · Johnston 28 (3)
Molby 34 (7) · Wark 11 (5) · MacDonald 6
Rush 42 (30) · Dalglish 18 (6) · Walsh 23 (6)
Aldridge 9 (2) · Irvine 2

FA CUP

11 Jan	Luton T (3)	A	D	0–0
26 Jan	Luton T (3R)	H	D	0–0*
28 Jan	Luton T (3R)	A	L	0–3

*after extra time

FA Cup Appearances (goals)

Grobbelaar 3 · Hansen 3 · Gillespie 3 · Lawrenson 3
Venison 2 · Beglin 1 · Ablett 1 · Whelan 3 · Molby 3
Johnston 3 · McMahon 1 · Wark 2 · Rush 3 · Walsh 3
Irvine 1

LITTLEWOODS CUP

23 Sep	Fulham (2)	H	W	10–0
7 Oct	Fulham (2)	A	W	3–2
29 Oct	Leicester C (3)	H	W	4–1
19 Nov	Coventry C (4)	A	D	0–0
26 Nov	Coventry C (4R)	H	W	3–1
21 Jan	Everton (5)	A	W	1–0
11 Feb	Southampton (SF)	A	D	0–0
25 Feb	Southampton (SF)	H	W	3–0
5 Apr	Arsenal (F)	N	L	1–2
	(Wembley)			

Littlewoods Cup Appearances (goals)

Grobbelaar 9 · Hansen 9 · Gillespie 9 · Lawrenson 8
Venison 6 · Nicol 5 (1) · Beglin 6 · McMahon 9 (8)
Whelan 8 (2) · Molby 7 (5) · Johnston 5 · Wark 2 (2)
Spackman 2 · Rush 9 (4) · Dalglish 4 (2) · Walsh 5
Irvine 1 · Mooney 1 · Durnin 1

....

■ In the spring of 1988, Wimbledon won the FA Cup by beating red-hot favourites Liverpool . . . but when the teams met in the Charity Shield the following August, that result was reversed, so Liverpool carried home the trophy.

SCREEN SPORT SUPER CUP

16 Sep	Everton	H	W	3–1
30 Sep	Everton	A	W	4–1

Screen Sport Super Cup Appearances (goals)
Grobbelaar 1 · Hooper 1 · Gillespie 2 · Lawrenson 2
Beglin 2 · Nicol 2 (1) · Venison 2 · Hansen 1
Whelan 2 · Molby 2 · McMahon 2 (1) · Wark 1
MacDonald 1 · Rush 2 (5) · Dalglish 1 · Walsh 1

SEASON 1987-88

FOOTBALL LEAGUE (DIVISION 1)

15 Aug	Arsenal	A	W	2–1
29 Aug	Coventry C	A	W	4–1
5 Sep	West Ham U	A	D	1–1
12 Sep	Oxford U	H	W	2–0
15 Sep	Charlton A	H	W	3–2
20 Sep	Newcastle U	A	W	4–1
29 Sep	Derby County	H	W	4–0
3 Oct	Portsmouth	H	W	4–0
17 Oct	QPR	H	W	4–0
24 Oct	Luton	A	W	1–0
1 Nov	Everton	H	W	2–0
4 Nov	Wimbledon	A	D	1–1
15 Nov	Manchester U	A	D	1–1
21 Nov	Norwich C	H	D	0–0
24 Nov	Watford	H	W	4–0
28 Nov	Tottenham H	A	W	2–0
6 Dec	Chelsea	H	W	2–1
12 Dec	Southampton	A	D	2–2
19 Dec	Sheffield W	H	W	1–0
26 Dec	Oxford U	A	W	3–0
28 Dec	Newcastle U	H	W	4–0
1 Jan	Coventry C	H	W	4–0
16 Jan	Arsenal	H	W	2–0
23 Jan	Charlton A	A	W	2–0
6 Feb	West Ham U	H	D	0–0
13 Feb	Watford	A	W	4–1
27 Feb	Portsmouth	A	W	2–0
5 Mar	QPR	A	W	1–0
16 Mar	Derby County	A	D	1–1
20 Mar	Everton	A	L	0–1
26 Mar	Wimbledon	H	W	2–1
2 Apr	Nottingham F	A	L	1–2
4 Apr	Manchester U	H	D	3–3
13 Apr	Nottingham F	H	W	5–0
20 Apr	Norwich C	A	D	0–0
23 Apr	Tottenham H	H	W	1–0
30 Apr	Chelsea	A	D	1–1
2 May	Southampton	H	D	1–1
7 May	Sheffield W	A	W	5–1
9 May	Luton T	H	D	1–1

Final League Position

	P	W	D	L	F	A	Pts	
Liverpool	40	26	12	2	87	24	90	1st

League Appearances (goals)
Grobbelaar 38 · Hooper 2 · Gillespie 35 (4) · Ablett 17
Venison 18 · Lawrenson 14 · Nicol 40 (6)
Whelan 28 (1) · Spackman 27 · Hansen 39 (1)
Beardsley 38 (15) · Aldridge 36 (26)
Houghton 28 (5) · Barnes 38 (15) · McMahon 40 (9)
Johnston 30 (5) · Molby 7 · Walsh 8 · Dalglish 2
Watson 1 · Wark 1 · MacDonald 1

FA CUP

9 Jan	Stoke C (3)	A	D	0–0
12 Jan	Stoke C (3R)	H	W	1–0
31 Jan	Aston Villa (4)	A	W	2–0
21 Feb	Everton (5)	A	W	1–0
13 Mar	Manchester C (6)	A	W	4–0
9 Apr	Nottingham F (SF)	N	W	2–1
(Hillsborough)				
14 May	Wimbledon (F)	N	L	0–1
(Wembley)				

FA Cup Appearances (goals)
Grobbelaar 5 · Hooper 2 · Gillespie 5 · Ablett 5
Nicol 7 · Whelan 2 · Hansen 7 · Spackman 5
Lawrenson 2 · Venison 2 · Beardsley 7 (3)
Aldridge 6 (2) · Johnston 3 (1) · Houghton 7 (2)
Barnes 7 (2) · McMahon 7 · Molby 1

LITTLEWOODS CUP

23 Sep	Blackburn R (2)	A	D	1–1
6 Oct	Blackburn R (2)	H	W	1–0
28 Oct	Everton (3)	A	L	0–1

Littlewoods Cup Appearances (goals)
Grobbelaar 3 · Gillespie 2 · Spackman 1 · Venison 2
Lawrenson 3 · Nicol 3 (1) · Whelan 3 · Hansen 3
Beardsley 3 · Aldridge 3 (1) · Johnston 2 · Walsh 1
Barnes 3 · McMahon 2 · Wark 1

SEASON 1988-89

FOOTBALL LEAGUE (DIVISION 1)

27 Aug	Charlton A	A	W	3–0
3 Sep	Manchester U	H	W	1–0
10 Sep	Aston Villa	A	D	1–1
17 Sep	Tottenham H	H	D	1–1
24 Sep	Southampton	A	W	3–1
1 Oct	Newcastle U	H	L	1–2
8 Oct	Luton T	A	L	0–1
22 Oct	Coventry C	H	D	0–0
26 Oct	Nottingham F	A	L	1–2
29 Oct	West Ham U	A	W	2–0
5 Nov	Middlesbrough	H	W	3–0
12 Nov	Millwall	H	D	1–1
19 Nov	QPR	A	W	1–0
26 Nov	Wimbledon	H	D	1–1
4 Dec	Arsenal	A	D	1–1
11 Dec	Everton	H	D	1–1
17 Dec	Norwich C	H	L	0–1
26 Dec	Derby C	A	W	1–0
1 Jan	Manchester U	A	L	1–3
3 Jan	Aston Villa	H	W	1–0
14 Jan	Sheffield W	A	D	2–2
21 Jan	Southampton	H	W	2–0
4 Feb	Newcastle U	A	D	2–2
1 Mar	Charlton A	H	W	2–0
11 Mar	Middlesbrough	A	W	4–0
14 Mar	Luton T	H	W	5–0
22 Mar	Coventry C	A	W	3–1
26 Mar	Tottenham H	A	W	2–1
29 Mar	Derby County	H	W	1–0
1 Apr	Norwich C	A	W	1–0
8 Apr	Sheffield W	H	W	5–1
11 Apr	Millwall	A	W	2–1
3 May	Everton	A	D	0–0
10 May	Nottingham F	H	W	1–0
13 May	Wimbledon	A	W	2–1
16 May	QPR	H	W	2–0
23 May	West Ham U	H	W	5–1
26 May	Arsenal	H	L	0–2

Final League Position

	P	W	D	L	F	A	Pts	
Arsenal	38	22	10	6	73	36	76	1st
Liverpool	38	22	10	6	65	28	76	2nd

League Appearances (goals)
Grobbelaar 21 · Hooper 17 · Ablett 35 · Gillespie 15
Venison 15 · Staunton 21 · Burrows 21 · Nicol 38 (2)
Whelan 37 (4) · Molby 13 (2) · Beardsley 37 (10)
Aldridge 35 (21) · Houghton 38 (7) · Rush 24 (7)
Barnes 33 (8) · McMahon 29 (3) · Spackman 12
Marsh 1 · Hansen 6 · MacDonald 3 · Watson 2

FA CUP

7 Jan	Carlisle U (3)	A	W	3–0
29 Jan	Millwall (4)	A	W	2–0
18 Feb	Hull C (5)	A	W	3–2
18 Mar	Brentford (6)	H	W	4–0
15 Apr	Nottingham F (SF)	N	A	0–0
(Hillsborough: abandoned after six minutes)				
7 May	Nottingham F (SF)	N	W	3–1
(Old Trafford)				
20 May	Everton (F)	N	W	3–2*
(Wembley)				

*after extra time

FA Cup Appearances (goals)
Grobbelaar 6* · Hooper 1 · Ablett 7* · Gillespie 2
Venison 1 · Burrows 3 · Staunton 4* · Nicol 7*
Whelan 6* · Molby 3 · Hansen 3* · Beardsley 6 (2)*
Aldridge 7 (6)* · Rush 2 (3) · Barnes 7 (3)*
McMahon 7 (3)* · Houghton 6* · Watson 2
*including the abandoned Hillsborough semi-final

LITTLEWOODS CUP

28 Sep	Walsall (2)	H	W	1–0
12 Oct	Walsall (2)	A	W	3–1
2 Nov	Arsenal (3)	H	D	1–1
9 Nov	Arsenal (3)	A	D	0–0
23 Nov	Arsenal (3R)	N	W	2–1
(Villa Park)				
30 Nov	West Ham U (4)	A	L	1–4

Littlewoods Cup Appearances (goals)
Hooper 6 · Gillespie 1 (1) · Ablett 6 · Venison 4
Staunton 4 · Spackman 4 · Nicol 6 · Whelan 6
Molby 2 (1) · MacDonald 2 · Beardsley 6
Aldridge 5 (2) · Houghton 6 · Rush 4 (1)
Barnes 3 (2) · McMahon 3 (1) · Dalglish 1 · Durnin 1
Watson 1

LEAGUE CENTENARY TOURNAMENT

29 Aug	Nottingham F	H	W	4–1
20 Sep	Arsenal (SF)	A	L	1–2

League Centenary Tournament Appearances (goals)
Grobbelaar 1 · Hooper 1 · Gillespie 2 · Nicol 2
Venison 1 (1) · Ablett 1 · Whelan 2 · Molby 1 (1)
MacDonald 1 · Beardsley 2 · Houghton 2 (1) · Rush 2
Barnes 1 (1) · Staunton 1 (1) · McMahon 1
Dalglish 1 · Durnin 1

SEASON 1989-90

FOOTBALL LEAGUE (DIVISION 1)

19 Aug	Manchester C	H	W	3–1
23 Aug	Aston Villa	A	D	1–1
26 Aug	Luton T	A	D	0–0
9 Sep	Derby County	A	W	3–0
12 Sep	Crystal Palace	H	W	9–0
16 Sep	Norwich C	H	D	0–0
23 Sep	Everton	A	W	3–1
14 Oct	Wimbledon	A	W	2–1
21 Oct	Southampton	A	L	1–4
29 Oct	Tottenham H	H	W	1–0
4 Nov	Coventry C	H	L	0–1
11 Nov	QPR	A	L	2–3
19 Nov	Millwall	A	W	2–1
26 Nov	Arsenal	H	W	2–1
29 Nov	Sheffield W	A	L	0–2
2 Dec	Manchester C	A	W	4–1
9 Dec	Aston Villa	H	D	1–1
16 Dec	Chelsea	A	W	5–2
23 Dec	Manchester U	H	D	0–0
26 Dec	Sheffield W	H	W	2–1
30 Dec	Charlton A	H	W	1–0
1 Jan	Nottingham F	A	D	2–2
13 Jan	Luton T	H	D	2–2
20 Jan	Crystal Palace	A	W	2–0
3 Feb	Everton	H	W	2–1
10 Feb	Norwich C	A	D	0–0
3 Mar	Millwall	H	W	1–0
18 Mar	Manchester U	A	W	2–1
21 Mar	Tottenham H	A	L	0–1
31 Mar	Southampton	H	W	3–2
3 Apr	Wimbledon	H	W	2–1
11 Apr	Charlton A	A	W	4–0
14 Apr	Nottingham F	H	D	2–2
18 Apr	Arsenal	A	D	1–1
21 Apr	Chelsea	H	W	4–1
28 Apr	QPR	H	W	2–1
1 May	Derby County	H	W	1–0
5 May	Coventry C	A	W	6–1

Final League Position

	P	W	D	L	F	A	Pts	
Liverpool	38	23	10	5	78	37	79	1st

League Appearances (goals)
Grobbelaar 38 · Hysen 35 (1) · Burrows 26
Staunton 20 · Nicol 23 (6) · Venison 25 · Hansen 31
Ablett 15 · Gillespie 13 (4) · Whelan 34 (1)
Molby 17 (1) · Beardsley 29 (10) · Houghton 19 (1)
Rush 36 (18) · Barnes 34 (22) · McMahon 38 (5)
Rosenthal 8 (7) · Tanner 4 · Dalglish 1
Aldridge 2 (1) · Marsh 2

FA CUP

6 Jan	Swansea C (3)	A	D	0–0
9 Jan	Swansea C (3R)	H	W	8–0
28 Jan	Norwich C (4)	A	D	0–0
31 Jan	Norwich C (4R)	H	W	3–1
17 Feb	Southampton (5)	H	W	3–0
11 Mar	QPR (6)	A	D	2–2
14 Mar	QPR (6R)	H	W	1–0
8 Apr	Crystal Palace (SF)	N	L	3–4*
(Villa Park)				

*after extra time

FA Cup Appearances (goals)
Grobbelaar 8 · Hysen 8 · Hansen 8 · Nicol 7 (3)
Venison 8 · Burrows 3 · Whelan 8 (1) · Houghton 4
McMahon 8 (1) · Gillespie 2 · Staunton 6
Beardsley 8 (4) · Barnes 8 (5) · Rush 8 (6)

LITTLEWOODS CUP

19 Sep	Wigan Athletic (2)	H	W	5–2
4 Oct	Wigan Athletic (2)	A	W	3–0
(Tie switched from Wigan to Anfield)				
25 Oct	Arsenal (3)	A	L	0–1

Littlewoods Cup Appearances (goals)
Grobbelaar 3 · Hysen 2 (1) · Venison 3 · Nicol 2
Hansen 2 · Burrows 3 · Gillespie 1 · Staunton 3 (3)
Whelan 3 · Houghton 2 · McMahon 2
Beardsley 3 (1) · Barnes 2 (1) · Rush 3 (2) · Molby 3
Ablett 1 · Watson 1

SEASON 1990-91

FOOTBALL LEAGUE (DIVISION 1)

25 Aug	Sheffield U	A	W	3–1
28 Aug	Nottingham F	H	W	2–0
1 Sep	Aston Villa	H	W	2–1
8 Sep	Wimbledon	A	W	2–1
16 Sep	Manchester U	H	W	4–0
22 Sep	Everton	A	W	3–2
29 Sep	Sunderland	A	W	1–0
6 Oct	Derby County	H	W	2–0
20 Oct	Norwich C	A	D	1–1
27 Oct	Chelsea	H	W	2–0
4 Nov	Tottenham H	A	W	3–1
10 Nov	Luton T	H	W	4–0
17 Nov	Coventry C	A	W	1–0
24 Nov	Manchester C	H	D	2–2
2 Dec	Arsenal	A	L	0–3
15 Dec	Sheffield U	H	W	2–0
22 Dec	Southampton	H	W	3–2
26 Dec	QPR	A	D	1–1
30 Dec	Crystal Palace	A	L	0–1
1 Jan	Leeds U	H	W	3–0
12 Jan	Aston Villa	A	D	0–0
19 Jan	Wimbledon	H	D	1–1
3 Feb	Manchester U	A	D	1–1
9 Feb	Everton	H	W	3–1
23 Feb	Luton T	A	L	1–3
3 Mar	Arsenal	H	L	0–1
9 Mar	Manchester C	A	W	3–0
16 Mar	Sunderland	H	W	2–1
23 Mar	Derby County	A	W	7–1
30 Mar	QPR	H	L	1–3
1 Apr	Southampton	A	L	0–1
9 Apr	Coventry C	H	D	1–1
13 Apr	Leeds U	A	W	5–4
20 Apr	Norwich C	H	W	3–0
23 Apr	Crystal Palace	H	W	3–0
4 May	Chelsea	A	L	2–4
6 May	Nottingham F	A	L	1–2
11 May	Tottenham H	H	W	2–0

Final League Position

	P	W	D	L	F	A	Pts	
Arsenal	38	24	13	1	74	18	83	1st
Liverpool	38	23	7	8	77	40	76	2nd

League Appearances (goals)
Grobbelaar 31 · Hooper 7 · Hysen 32 · Burrows 35
Staunton 24 · Nicol 35 (3) · Gillespie 30 (1)
Ablett 23 · Venison 6 · Molby 25 (9) · McMahon 22
Whelan 14 (1) · Houghton 32 (7) · Barnes 35 (16)
Beardsley 27 (11) · Rush 35 (16) · Speedie 12 (6)
Rosenthal 16 (5) · Carter 5 · McManaman 2 · Marsh 2

FA CUP

5 Jan	Blackburn Rovers	A	D	1–1
8 Jan	Blackburn Rovers	H	W	3–0
26 Jan	Brighton & HA	H	D	2–2
30 Jan	Brighton & HA	A	W	3–2
17 Feb	Everton	H	D	0–0
20 Feb	Everton	A	D	4–4
27 Feb	Everton	A	L	0–1

FA Cup Appearances (goals)
Grobbelaar 7 · Hysen 5 · Burrows 5 · Staunton 7 (1)
Nicol 7 · Gillespie 2 · Ablett 6 · Venison 5 · Molby 7
McMahon 4 (2) · Whelan 1 · Houghton 3 (1)
Barnes 7 (1) · Beardsley 5 (2) · Rush 7 (5)
Speedie 2 · Rosenthal 3 · Carter 2 · McManaman 1

LEAGUE CUP

25 Sep	Crewe Alexandra	H	W	5–1
9 Oct	Crewe Alexandra	A	W	4–1
31 Oct	Manchester U	A	L	1–3

League Cup Appearances (goals)
Grobbelaar 3 · Hysen 2 · Burrows 3 · Staunton 2 (1)
Nicol 2 · Gillespie 3 (1) · Ablett 1 · Venison 2
Molby 2 · McMahon 2 (1) · Whelan 1 · Houghton 3 (2)
Barnes 2 · Beardsley 2 · Rush 3 (5) · Rosenthal 3
Marsh 1

Index

221

PHOTOGRAPHIC ACKNOWLEDGEMENTS

Allsport 76, 78-9, 93, 119, 131 bottom, 147, 154, 190 bottom, 196-7, 200, 217, (Howard Boylan) 102, (Simon Bruty) 58-9, 90, 95, 101 bottom, 123 top, 156, 168, 169, (David Cannon) 56, 81, 83, 84, 87 top, 89, 101 top, 120, 122 bottom, 125, 142, 143, 149 top, 149 bottom, 160 top, 166, 194-5, (Chris Cole) 88, (Tony Duffy) 85, (Trevor Jones) 86, (Don Morley) 155, (Jon Nicholson) 167, (D Raban) 71 bottom, (Ben Radford) 133, 150, (Dan Smith) 87 bottom, 103, 105 top, 113 bottom; *Colorsport* end-papers, 2, 3, 4-5 top, 42, 67, 80, 82-3, 100, 121, 128, 140 bottom, 163, 180, 182, 185; *Steve Hale* 13 left, 30, 59, 124, 131; *Hulton Deutsch Collection* 17, 19, 22, 38 top, 129, 134-5, 138, 145 bottom, 171, 183 top; *Billy Liddell* 203, (AB Text & Bilder) 207, (Provincial Press Agency) 32; *Liverpool Daily Post & Echo Ltd* 13 right, 14, 23, 24, 71 top, 145 top, 151, 159 top, 159 bottom, 160 bottom, 173, 178, 186; *Liverpool Football Club/John Cocks* 4 top left, 8, 11, 12, 20, 29 left, 34, 112 bottom, 113 top, 115; *Stan Liversedge* 36, 38 bottom, 40, 43 bottom, 53, 54, 68, 70, 82, 96, 97 top, 97 bottom, 98-9, 98 bottom, 99 top right, 99 bottom, 104, 105 bottom, 106, 107, 108, 110, 112 top, 115 top, 123 bottom, 130, 140 top, 152, 201, 219, (Daily Mirror) 136 right, (L.E. Marsh & Sons) 18 bottom, (Harry Ormesher) 4-5 bottom, 6, 49, 51, 52, 114, 116-17, 122 top, 153, 176, 188, 190 top, 191, 192-3, 194, (Planar Press Agency) 214, (Provincial Press Agency) 7, 74-5, (Sunday People) 43 top, 48, 74; *Bob Paisley* 26, 64, (Evening Express) 46 top, 47 top (Liverpool Daily Post & Echo) 21, 24-5, 211 (Manchester Daily Mail) 47 bottom, (Provincial Press Agency) 46 bottom, 206, 209; *Peter Robinson* 9; *Syndication International* 127, 131 top; *Topham* 212; *Weidenfeld & Nicolson Ltd* 45, (Daily Express) 136 left, (Hulton Deutsch) 15 bottom, 16 bottom, 18 top, 111, (Liverpool Daily Post & Echo) 15 top, 16 top, 28, 29 right, 31, 39 top, 57, 66, 69 top, 75, 77, 109, 148, (London Express Pictures) 35, 61 top, 61 bottom, 63, 69 bottom, 72, 73, 117, 137, 146, 187, (Harry Ormesher) 37, 39 bottom, 141, 161, 164-5, 176-7, (Syndication International) 183 bottom.